ESSAYS

ON

KACMIRI GRAMMAR

ESSAYS

ON

KACMIRI GRAMMAR

BY

GEORGE A.GRIERSON

GYAN

Published by

GYAN

Gyan Publishing House
5, Ansari Road
Daryaganj, New Delhi-110002
Phone: 011-47034999, 9811692060
E-mail: books@gyanbooks.com

Distribution Network
gyanbooks.com
India, USA, Canada, UK, Australia

ISBN: 978-93-6433-726-7 (PB)
First Published, 1899

2nd Impression 2024

Printed at: Gyan Press, Delhi.

ESSAYS ON KACMIRI GRAMMAR
Translator: GEORGE A.GRIERSON

ESSAYS

ON

KĀÇMĪRĪ GRAMMAR

BY

GEORGE A. GRIERSON, C.I.E., PH.D.,
of Her Majesty's Indian Civil Service.

London:
LUZAC & CO.

Calcutta:
THACKER, SPINK & CO.

1899.

DEDICATED

WITH MUCH AFFECTION

TO

THE MEMORY OF

GEORG BÜHLER

BY

One whose privilege it was to know him as a Guide,
as a Counsellor, and as a Friend.

केन रत्नमिदं सृष्टं मित्रमित्यक्षरद्वयम् ।

ADDENDA ET CORRIGENDA.

Page.	Line.	For	Read.
5	14	[illegible]	[illegible]
"	19	Sirinagar	Çrinagar.
8	31	*khạt*	*khạt*^{i}.
11	27	*ū-mātrā*	*ū-mātrā*.
20	26	[illegible] *p?tsuh*	[illegible] *pentsᵘh*.
"	31	[illegible] *ṭhạk*^{a}, *ṭhạk*	[illegible] *ṭhạ̈k*^{a}, *ṭhạ̈k*.
"	32	[illegible] *ṭhạk*^{u}	[illegible] *ṭhāk*^{u}.
27	7	*toh*^{i}	*tǫ̆h*^{i}.
29	23	before [illegible] *i*, [illegible] *y*	in the feminine before a final [illegible] *i* or [illegible] *ya* (*ĕ*).
30	13	*hŏkh*^{u}	*hǫ̆kh*^{u}.
"	14	thread	thread or the like.
"	16	little	thin.
"	17	littleness	thinness.
"	18	*srog*^{u}	*srǫ̆g*^{u}.
"	27	*tsok*^{u}	*tsǫ̆k*^{u}.
31	11	*tsạg*^{u}	*tsạ̈g*^{a}.
"	13	pound	grind.
36	Last	*tsok*^{a}	*tsǫ̆k*^{u}.
"	"	*tswạk*^{a}	*tsǫ̆k*^{a}.
37	"	a snake	a snake, a fountain.
38	16	*dob*^{u}	*dǫ̆b*^{u}.
"	"	*dwabiñ*	*dŏbiñ*.
39	6	39	38.
44	8	Instrumental	Agent.
24	11	*pōth*^{u}	*pōth*^{i}.

Page.	Lines.		
51	11–14	Substitute the following :—	

If the final consonant of a noun in this declension is preceded by उ *u*, that उ *u* is changed to अ *a* in all cases except the Nominative Singular. Thus वाँदुर् *wă̄dur*, a monkey; nom. pl. वाँदर् *wă̄dar*; instr. pl. वाँदरौ सुँतिन् *wă̄darau sạtin*: करुन् *karun*, the act of doing; acc. sg. करनस् *karanas*: पोसतुख् *pŏstukh*, a book; nom. pl. पोसतख् *pŏstakh*.

Page.	Lines.		
56	13	*for* 'tree-trunk'	*read* 'beam of wood.'
58	3–12	*add* कपुर् *kapurᵘ* cloth.	
79	4	*for* '*kunasatdăth*'	*read* '*kunasatath*,' (and so throughout the seventies up to 78).
"	24	*kunanamdăth*	*kunanamath* (and so throughout the nineties).
95	8	*w* or *v*	*w* or *v*, or
106	4	ग्राकँन् *grākạṅ*	ग्राकन् *grākaṅ*.
137	3 from bottom	चड्	चड्
142	19	substances	substantives.
148	16	*kᵘṭᵘ*	*kūṭᵘ*.
202	5	करन्	करन्
237	5 from bottom	वुफोवप	वुफोव
v	2 from bottom	*bŏzen*	*bŏsan*.
ix	2 from bottom	वुफियेव *wuphiyĕwᵘ*	वुफियेयव *wuphiyĕyawᵘ*.

Besides the above, see the special list of *corrigenda* to the list of Kāçmīrī verbs, which is on pp. xci. and ff.

PREFACE.

The following essays on Kāçmīrī originally appeared in the Journal of the Asiatic Society of Bengal for 1896-1899. It is hoped that, as now completed, they will be found to give a much fuller account of that interesting language than has hitherto been available.

Besides those who wish to study Kāçmīrī for its own sake, it is also of considerable interest to comparative philologists. I know of no Indo-Aryan language which in her grammatical construction is so naked and unashamed. With but the thinnest veil of mystery, she freely displays to the ardent eyes of the student, not only the general contour of her graceful form, but each joint, each articulation. Devoid of every feeling of false modesty, she discloses many a secret which is jealously hidden by her more prudish sisters of the south. This fact has been prosaically dwelt upon by me on former occasions,[1] and I need not discuss it further here. It is sufficient to point out that a study of Kāçmīrī is an essential preliminary to any enquiry which deals comparatively with the mutual relations of the modern Aryan vernaculars of India.

Although I believe that I may claim that this work is more full and more accurate than its predecessors, I trust that it will not be taken as intended to supersede the useful little grammar of Mr. Wade. To begin with, I hardly touch upon syntax, a branch of Kāçmīrī grammar which is treated of by that scholar with considerable fulness. Then, the following pages are scarcely meant for the beginner who only wishes to acquire a slight colloquial knowledge of the language. Such students cannot do better than commence with Mr. Wade's book, and, when they have mastered it, they will find it to their advantage, if they wish to proceed further in their studies, to peruse those essays also. I lay stress upon this point, because I have had occasion more than once to differ from Mr. Wade, and to state the fact clearly; and I should be sorry to think that my having done so would lead the reader to suppose that I generally condemned a grammar from which I have myself drawn no little profit and instruction.

[1] See *On Pronominal Suffixes in the Kāçmīrī Language*, J. A. S. B., Vol. lxiv, Part I, pp. 336 and ff., and *On the Radical and Participial Tenses of the Modern Indo-Aryan Languages*, ib. pp. 352 and ff.

One other word of warning is necessary. The language illustrated in this book is that used by the Hindūs of Kashmir, and not that of the Musalmāns. The difference between these two dialects is mainly one of vocabulary, the Musalmāns freely using Persian and Arabic words which are avoided by the Hindūs. For this reason the dialect of the latter is much more purely Kāçmīrī than that of the former, but it should be borne in mind that while the followers of Islām number about 95 per cent. of the population of Kashmir, the Hindūs number less than five. On the other hand, nearly all the old written literature of the country is Hindū, and is in the language illustrated in the present grammar.

There is no fixed system of spelling Kāçmīrī, either in the Persian character used by Musalmāns, or in the Çāradā and Dēva-nāgarī characters used by Hindūs. In such a matter, every writer is a law unto himself, and the student is warned that in reading manuscripts he will find numerous divergencies from the system here adopted. This system is that invented by Īçvara-kaula for recording the grammar of his native language in his excellent Sanskrit work the *Kaçmīra-çabdāmrta*,[1] of which the present book is hardly more than an adaptation to English needs. The true alphabet of the Kāçmīrī language is the Çāradā, but I have abandoned it and used the Dēva-nāgarī for two sufficient reasons. One is that the Çāradā is familiar to very few Europeans, and it is not advisable to add to the difficulties which must be experienced in acquiring a by no means easy language. The other is that no Çāradā types are available.

Surprise may be evinced that so large a space is devoted to the phonology of the language. No less than thirty-two pages are given up to the vowels and the consonants. But epenthetic changes of the former and palatalisations of the latter are so important a feature of Kāçmīrī that too great attention cannot be paid to them. They form the whole groundwork of the somewhat complicated grammar, and once their principles are mastered, the superstructure will be found comparatively easy. The student is advised to read the first two chapters attentively before attacking the more attractive nouns and verbs.

I should be ungrateful if I did not here record my thanks to the kind friends who, possessed of a greater knowledge of the language than I have myself, have given me their assistance on various points. I must specially state my obligations to the Rev. J. Hinton Knowles of Çrīnagar, who with the most liberal generosity has frequently helped me from the stores of his unequalled knowledge of Kāçmīrī.

[1] Edited by the present writer, and published by the Asiatic Society of Bengal.

In conclusion, I may be permitted to express the lively regret which I experience when I call to mind that these pages will never be looked upon by the Friend and Counsellor to whose memory they are dedicated. It was Bühler who first directed my attention to the study of Kāçmīrī, and it was through his help that I was enabled to trace the materials on which these pages are founded. They owe all their inspiration to him; and, during their preparation, hours of what was often monotonous work were cheered by the hope of his kindly appreciation of the final result,—a hope, alas, destined never to be realised.

SYSTEM OF TRANSLITERATION ADOPTED IN THE FOLLOWING PAGES:—

(medial) ᵃ; अ (medial) a, (final) ᵃ, (ă); आ ā; ि ⁱ; इ i; ई ī; ु ᵘ; उ u; ू ᵘ; ऊ ū; ऋ r; (ए ĕ); ए ē; ऐ ai; (ओ ŏ); ओ ō; औ au; ˙ ˜

क ka	ख kha	ग ga	ङ ṅa.
च ca	छ cha	ज ja	ञ ña.
च tsa	छ tsha	ज za	ञ ña.
ट ṭa	ठ ṭha	ड ḍa	ण ṇa.
त ta	थ tha	द da	न na.
प pa	फ pha	ब b	म ma.
य ya, ĕ	र ra	ल la	व wa, ŏ.
श ça	ष ṣa	स sa	ह ha.

Note.— ि ⁱ ु ᵘ and ू ᵘ, are called *i-mātrā*, *u-mātrā*, and *ū-mātrā*, respectively. See p. 3.

When a vowel is modified (usually by a following *mātrā*-vowel or ᵃ) the mark ˡ is placed over the syllable in the Dēva-nāgarī character, and a dot is placed under the vowel in the Roman character. Thus क kạ, का kạ̄, and so on.

When the half-pronounced *a* occurs in the middle of a word, it is represented by *virāma*. Thus पंद्र *pdᵃr*. When it is modified it is transliterated ᵊ. Thus दनु *dᵊnᵘ*. This modification, it will be seen, is not marked in the Dēva-nāgarī character. In this I have followed the native grammarian. At the end of a word, every *a* is only half pronounced. Thus क्रक *krakᵃ*, (see p. 6). When the vowel *a* is pronounced like the *a* in *hat*, it is transliterated *ă*.

The syllable य *ya* is often pronounced like *ĕ*, and the syllable *wa* like *ŏ*: the first representing the sound of the *e* in *met*, and the second that of the *o* in *hot*. In these cases, the syllables are transliterated and *ŏ* respectively. See pp. 26 and 16.

When these *ĕ* and *ŏ* are modified I have not always been consistent in transliteration. In the earlier pages I have represented a modified *ĕ*, by simply *ĕ*, as in लॆलि *lĕl*^{i}, and a modified *ŏ*, by *ŏ*, as in गॊनु *gŏn*^{u} (both on p. 26). Sometimes also I have transliterated the latter by *wọ*, as in *twọh*^{i}, on p. 87. In the later pages, as types became available, I have throughout represented them by *ĕ̤* and *ŏ̤* respectively.

CONTENTS.

Note.— All the above references are to the figures on the outside TOP corner on each page. On the other hand, all references in the text itself are to the figures on the outside BOTTOM corner on each page.

From the Journal, Asiatic Society of Bengal, Vol, LXV. Part, I, No. 3, 1896, p. 280.

On the Kāçmīrī Vowel-System.—*By* G. A. Grierson, C.I.E., I.C.S.

[Read November, 1896.]

The only serious attempt to grapple with the intricacies of Kāçmīrī pronunciation is that contained in Major Leech's grammar of the language contained in pp. 397 and ff. of the *J. A. S. B.*, Vol. XIII, for 1844.

For its time Leech's grammar was a wonderful production, but it has the disadvantage of being entirely written in the Roman character, without any definite system of transcription. He gives lists of words classified according to their vowel sounds, and extending over eight pages. These lists (and I have tested every word in them, in the mouth of a Kāçmīrī Paṇḍit) are in the main accurate, but it is generally difficult and sometimes impossible to identify the words he writes, or to reproduce them in either the Persian or the Nāgarī character.

Kāçmīrī is written both in the Persian and in the Çāradā alphabets. The latter belongs to the family of which Dēvanāgarī is the best known member, and will be represented (for convenience sake) by Dēvanāgarī in this paper. The Persian character is used by the Muḥammadans (who form about 93 per cent.), and the Çāradā (Dēvanāgarī) by the Hindūs (who form, say, 6 per cent.) of the population. Carey in his Serampur translation of the New Testament (1821) used the Çāradā character, but since then Missionaries have used either the Persian or the Roman character. The Persian character, with its facile omission of vowel-marks is not suited for representing the intricate vowel-system of Kāçmīrī. And, indeed, to one who is not familiar with the pronunciation of the language from practical experience, it would be impossible to gain merely a faint idea of the correct pronunciation of most Kāçmīrī words, even from a fully vocalized Persian transcription. This is forcibly illustrated by the late Dr. Burkhard's Essays on Kāçmīrī. He transliterated rigidly from the Persian character, and hence, as a means for giving a practical colloquial acquaintance with the language, his papers are of little value, though of great value in other respects.

The various systems of transliteration into the Roman character with the help of diacritical marks added to the vowels, are based on the Persian method of transcription, and have most of its faults. For instance Wade in his grammar represents three distinct *a* sounds *viz.*, *ä*, a^i and ^{a} by one sign *ạ*. Another *a* sound, *viz.*, a^u, he represents by *ọ*: and at the same time uses the same sign to represent the *ŏ* in *cob*, an altogether different sound.

The Çāradā (Dēvanāgarī) system of writing Kāçmīrī has the advantage of using fixed definite signs for fixed definite sounds. To those accustomed to the simpler, if less perfect systems hitherto in vogue, it, no doubt, looks clumsy, but, after considerable hesitation, I have come to the conclusion that, whether for the purposes of science or for the benefit of learners, the only satisfactory way of transcribing Kāçmīrī in the Roman character is to follow the Çāradā system with a few minor modifications.

The Çāradā system is based upon actual facts of the language. Kāçmīrī differs from other Indian languages in using vowels at the end of a word which are either silent or nearly so, but which modify the pronunciation of the vowel of the preceding syllable. To an Englishman or Russian this is a commonplace of spelling. An Englishman pronounces the *a* in the word *mar*, in a certain way. By adding an *e*, he gets the word *mare*, in which the final *e* is silent, but modifies the pronunciation of the preceding *a*. In Kāçmīrī these silent (or nearly silent) vowels are called by Hindū Grammarians, *mātrās*, and there are three of them, *viz.*, *i-mātrā*, *u-mātrā*, and *ū-mātrā* which are represented in the Çāradā character by the ordinary signs for *i*, *u*, and *ū* respectively with the sign for *virāma* appended. The mark ˡ is also placed over the preceding vowel to show that it is modified. In the Roman character they are conveniently represented by a small ^{i}, ^{u} or ^{ū}, above the line, a dot being placed under the preceding vowel to indicate modification. Examples are कॅरि *kạr*^{i}, they (masc.) were made; कॅरु *kạr*^{u}, he was made; and कॅरू *kạr*^{ū}, she was made. Speaking very roughly, the first may be said to be pronounced something like the English pronunciation of *Kyrie* (in *Kyrie eleison*), the second something like *core* (English mute *e*), and the third something like *kür* (German *ü*). In the Persian character, the first is written کَرِ *kar*^{i}, the second کُرٗ *kur*^{u}, and the third indifferently کَر *kar* or کِر *kir*. Mr. Wade transcribes the first *kạr*^{i}, the second *kọr*, and the third *kạr*.

Of these *mātrās* it may be said that *u* and *ū* are as a rule absolutely silent, while *i* is just heard.

The history of these modified sounds is evident enough. It will suffice to take *u-mātrā* as an example. The Skr. कृतः *kṛtaḥ*, done, became in Apabhramça Prākrit करिउ *kariu*, from which was derived the old Kāçmīrī करु *karu*. By epenthesis, of which the Kāçmīrī is extremely fond, this became pronounced कउर् *kaur* whence we get the modern pronunciation '*core*.' The old spelling was, however, retained, but the mark of *virāma* was added to show that the final *u* was silent. So also क॑रि् *kạr*ⁱ, represents an Apabhramça *करिइ *karii* and क॑रू् *kạr*ᵘ represents an Apabhramça, *करिआ *kariā* or करी *karī*. It can easily be shown that *ū-mātrā* represents an older *ī*, not an older *ū*. Words in *ū-mātrā* are nearly all feminine forms of masculines in *u-mātrā*, a fact which explains the adoption of the long *ū* sign as a substitute for the long *ī*.

Sometimes by the addition of suffixes these *mātrā*-vowels cease to be at the end of a word. If the suffix consists of a single consonant, they are then fully pronounced (still, however, modifying the preceding vowel) and the sign of virāma is omitted. In this case, *ū-mātrā* takes the sound of a short German *ü*. Thus, if we add the suffix *n*, meaning 'by him,' to the above words, we get from क॑रि् *kạr*ⁱ, क॑रिन् *kạrin* (pronounced something like *kyrin*); from क॑रु् *kạr*ᵘ, क॑रुन् *kạrun* (pronounced something like *korun*); and from क॑रू् *kạr*ᵘ, क॑रून् *karūn*, (pronounced something like *kürün*).[1] If, however, the suffix consists of a consonant and a vowel, or more, the *mātrā* vowels remain unpronounced. Thus, take the suffix *w*ᵃ, by you. Adding this to क॑रि् *kạr*ⁱ we get क॑रिव *kạr*ⁱ*w*ᵃ, (pr. *kyrw*ᵃ); to क॑रु् *kạr*ᵘ, we get क॑रुव *kạr*ᵘ*w*ᵃ (*korw*ᵃ); and to क॑रू् *kạr*ᵘ, we get क॑रूव (*kürw*ᵃ). Again, adding the suffix *tha-s*, by thee I (was made), we get क॑रुथस् *kạr*ᵘ*thas* (*korthas*), masc. and क॑रूथस् *kürthas*, fem.

The effect of these mute or *mātrâ* vowels upon pronunciation of preceding vowels, forms the main subject of this paper.

Before dealing with them, it will be convenient to glance at the Kaçmīrī consonantal system. This is, in the main, the same as that which we meet in the Dēvanāgarī Alphabets. It must be observed. however, that Kāçmīrī, has no soft aspirates (*gh*, *jh*, *ḍh*, *dh*, and *bh*), The letter *jh* becomes *z*. Thus from Apabhramça बुज्झइ, *bujjhai*, we have the Kāçmīrī बोज़ि् *bōzi*, he will hear. The other letters simply lose their aspiration, *e.g.*, Hindi √ *ghēr*, surround, but Kāçmīrī *gēr*, and so on.

Kāçmīrī has developed a new set of palatals, *viz.*, च़ छ़ and ज़,

[1] It must be clearly understood that these spellings do not do more than approximately indicate the pronunciation of these words. The exact pronunciation will be dealt with later on.

pronounced (and transliterated) *ts*, *tsh*, and *s* respectively. The nasal ञ *ña* is pronounced *ñyŏ*, and is treated as if it was spelled ञ्य. With Virāma (ञ्) it is pronounced *ñy*, and is treated as if it was ञ्य् *ny*[a].'

As regards transliteration; it seems to me that the only satisfactory way, so far as this article is concerned, is to follow the Çāradā spelling throughout. The mātrā-vowels should be represented by a small letter above the line, and modified vowels should have a dot under them to warn the reader that they *are* modified. *How* they are modified is to be gathered from the particular *mātrā* which follows, and from the following rules. The only exception I make to this system of transcription is the representative of the *ŏ*-sound in *oob*, and the *ĕ*-sound in *ebb*. These, in Çāradā are represented by *wa* (or *ų*) and *ya* respectively, following a consonant. Thus त्वह्य (or तुह्य) *twahya* (or *tųhya*) (pr. *tŏhĕ*). As this *wa* and *ya* do not convey to the reader the sounds they represent, I transliterate them (when they represent these sounds) by *ŏ* and *ĕ* respectively.

I now proceed to deal with the vowels in due order. The lists of words given by Leech, in his paper above referred to, have been carefully read over with me by Paṇḍit Mukund Rām of Sirinagar,[1] and every word which we have been able to identify has been written down in the Dēvanāgarī character, and its pronunciation discussed. Many new words, illustrating new rules, have also been added.

अ *a* is usually pronounced as the short *e* in America.

The following are examples.

शलख् *çalakh*, a beating.
वनख् *wanakh*, thou wilt say.
खटख् *khaṭakh*, thou wilt conceal.
फटख् *phaṭakh*, thou wilt be drowned.
गनख् *ganakh*, thou wilt congeal.
मानख् *mānakh*, thou wilt obey.
रटख् *raṭakh*, thou wilt take.
बरख् *barakh*, thou wilt regret.
सृरख् *sarakh*, thou wilt endure.
अलख् *alakh*, thou wilt be shaken.
वलख् *valakh*, thou wilt throw over a person.
गलख् *galakh*, thou wilt melt.
मरख् *marakh*, thou wilt die.
चटख् *tsaṭakh*, thou wilt tear.
चलख् *tsalakh*, thou wilt flee.
वटख् *vaṭakh*, thou wilt roll up.
पकख् *pakakh*, thou wilt go.
रछख् *rachak*, thou wilt protect.
रनख् *ranakh*, thou wilt cook.
खनख् *khanakh*, thou wilt dig.
मेनख् *mēnakh*, thou wilt measure.
असख् *asakh*, thou wilt laugh.
दज़ख् *dazakh*, thou wilt be burnt.
सरख् *sarakh*, thou wilt experience.
मलख् *malakh*, thou wilt rub.
खलख् *khalakh*, thou wilt be opened.
बलख् *balakh*, thou wilt recover.
डलख् *ḍalakh*, thou wilt slip.
गर *gar*[a], a house.
अचुन् *atsun*, to enter.
अल्यौव् *alyauv*, he shook.

[1] I must express my obligations to Dr. Stein for obtaining for me so excellent an assistant and teacher.

In monosyllabic words ending in an aspirated consonant, *a* takes nearly the sound of the *ă* in *hat*, thus क्रख् *krăkh*, a noise, but क्रख *krak*[a], noises. कठ् *kăṭh*, a ram, gen. sg. कठ संद् *kaṭ*[a] *sand*[a]. This difference is not marked in writing. I shall represent it by *ă*.

A final *a* is very lightly pronounced, and is therefore written above the line, as in *krak*[a], above. With regard to final *ya*, vide post (page 304).

This lightly pronounced [a] also occurs between consonants. In such cases, in the Çāradā character, the two consonants are compounded, and the vowel neglected. We thus get seemingly impossible combinations, such as the word त्स्ह् or literatim *tsh*, which cannot be possibly pronounced as written. The word is really pronounced *ts*[a]*h*, and means 'thou.' So also in many other words, *e.g.*, ह्नु (which I prefer to write हन्ु) pronounced *h*[ə]*n*[u], he has swollen; ड्नु (डन्ु) *d*[ə]*n*[u], he shook out; क्तु (कत्ु) *k*[ə]*t*[u], he was wet; र्श् (रश्) *r*[a]*ç*, spite; ग्हु (गह्ु) *g*[ə]*h*[u], he ground: दद्र् *dad*[ə]*r*[a], the edible part of a cucumber; बब्र् *bab*[ə]*r*[a], a flower; गाट्य् *gāṭ*[a]*j*, clever (fem.); फट्र् *phŏl*[a]*r*,[1] a basket. The sound of this letter is very obscure and closely resembles that of the obscure vowel in the English termination *ble*, usually called the neutral vowel. It is liable to modification by a following *i*-, *u*-, or *ū*-*mātrā*, but its sound is so short, that only an acute ear can distinguish its various shades. Wade illustrates this [a] as well as the *a* modified by *ū*-*mātrā*, by *ạ*. a system which lends to endless confusion, unless some clue is given to the modifying vowel.

Içwara-kaula in his Kāçmīrī *Dhātu-pāṭha*, also notes a modified *ạ*, which is not followed by a mātrā-vowel. It is pronounced slightly more labially than an ordinary *a*: i.e., a tinge of *o* is given to it; and it is, apparently, the short form of *ạ̄* (*ö*). It closely resembles the ordinary sound of *a* in Eastern Bihārī, which is not nearly so broad as the corresponding sound in Bengali, but is still somewhat broader than the usual *a* of Benares-Hindī. The difference between *ạ* is however, so very slight that it would pass unheeded by an ordinary ear. The sound occurs in the following verbal roots (including their causals, which I omit). It will be seen that with the exception of the root प्रखट *prạkh*[a]*ṭ*, which is hardly an exception, in every single instance the *ạ* is followed by a compound consonant the last member of which is *r*.

[1] Içwara-kaula spells all these with compound consonants. I prefer, deliberately, to write them with *virāma*, and shall do so in future. Mr. Hinton Knowles, whose authority is undoubted, would transcribe these words *hun*[u], *dun*[u], *kuṭ*[u] (there is a difference of opinion as to the correct form of the part of the root *kṭ*. I. K. makes it *kt*[u]), *riç* and *guh*[u]. This well illustrates the indefinite nature of the sound which, in the Çāradā character, is represented by *virāma*, or absence of any vowel whatever.

The examples moreover include every case of an *a* followed by such a conjunct given in the *Dhātupāṭha*, and we are entitled to lay down the rule, that when *a* is followed by a compound consonant, the last member of which is *r* (or *ṭ*), it is modified to *ạ*.

अ॑दुर *ạd^{a}r*, be moist.

अ॑न्सुर *ạns^{a}r*, finish.

अ॑बुर *ạb^{a}r*, cloud up.

क॑न्सुर *kạns^{a}r*, be impoverished.

ग॑न्सुर *gạns^{a}r*, count.

छ॑कुर *chạk^{a}r*, scatter.

छ॑ट्सुराव *chạts^{a}rāv*, make white.

छ्व॑पुर *chwạp^{a}r* (pr. almost *chup^{a}r*), spend.

त्स्व॑कुर *tswạk^{a}r* (pr. almost *tsuk^{a}r*), make angry. [defile.

छ्य॑टुर *tshyạṭ^{a}r* (pr. almost *tshiṭ^{a}r*),

छ्य॑वुर *tshyạv^{a}r* (pr. almost *tshiv^{a}r*), put out (fire).

छ्व॑टुर *tshwạṭ^{a}r* (pr. almost *tshuṭ^{a}r*), make short.

ड॑खुर *ḍạkh^{a}r*, depend upon.

त॑त्सुर *tạts^{a}r*, make hot.

त॑न्युर *tạñ^{a}r*, make thin.

त्र॑त्सुराव *trạts^{a}rāv*, cause to fear.

त्र॑सुराव *trạs^{a}rāv*, cause to fear.

त्रुव॑गुराव *trwạg^{a}rāv*, (pr. almost *trug^{a}rāv*), make hard.

थ॑सुर *thạs^{a}r*, make high.

द॑दुराव *dạd^{a}rāv*, make wasted.

द्रुव॑गुराव *drwạg^{a}rāv* (pr. almost *drug^{a}-rāv*), price highly.

द्व॑बुर *dwạb^{a}r* (pr. almost *dub^{a}r*), bury.

न॑न्युराव *nạñ^{a}rāv*, make naked.

न॑टुराव *nạṭ^{a}rāv*, cause to shake.

न्व॑मुर *nwạm^{a}r* (pr. almost *num^{a}r*), cause to bow.

न्व॑वुर *nwạv^{a}r* (pr. almost *nuv^{a}r*), make excessive.

प॑जुर *pạj^{a}r*, fell a hem (in sewing).

प॑सुर *pạs^{a}r*, decide the truth.

प॑ठुर *pạṭh^{a}r* (Mr. Knowles would write *pạṭh^{a}r*), clean (fish).

प्र॑कुट *prạk^{a}ṭ*, be manifest.

फ॑सुर *phạs^{a}r*, entangle.

ब॑चुराव *bạc^{a}rāv*, protect.

ब॑डुर *bạḍ^{a}r*, cause to be great.

ब॑दुराव *bạd^{a}rāv*, bake bread.

ब॑न्सुर *bạns^{a}r*, divide.

ब॑लुर *bạl^{a}r*, cure.

ब्य॑न्युर *byạñ^{a}r* (pr. almost *biñ^{a}r*), make separate.

ब्र॑मुर *brạm^{a}r*, mislead.

म॑त्सुराव *mạts^{a}rāv*, madden.

म॑न्सुर *mạns^{a}r*, make imperfect.

म॑शुर *mạṣ^{a}r*, cause to forget.

म्व॑टुर *mwạṭ^{a}r*, (pr. almost *muṭ^{a}r*), make fat.

म्व॑ण्डुर *mwạṇḍ^{a}r* (pr. almost *muṇḍ^{a}r*), make blunt.

म्व॑दुर *mwạd^{a}r* (pr. almost *mud^{a}r*), be sweet.

र॑छुर *rạtsh^{a}r*, put in order.

ल्य॑दुर *lyạd^{a}r* (pr. almost *lid^{a}r*), be yellow.

व॑डुर *wạḍ^{a}r*, bury.

व्य॑सुर *vyạs^{a}r* (pr. almost *vis^{a}r*), decide.

व्य॑न्युर *vyạñ^{a}r* (pr. almost *viñ^{a}r*), separate.

व्यथर *vyạth^{a}r* (pr. almost *vith^{a}r*), make fat.

व्यदर *vyạd^{a}r* (pr. almost *vid^{a}r*), be slack.

व्यपर *vyạp^{a}r* (pr. almost *vip^{a}r*), cause to pervade.

व्यवर *vyạv^{a}r* (pr. almost *viv^{a}r*), scatter.

स्यञर *sạñ^{a}r*, make deep.

सञ्चर *sạnc^{a}r*, be ready.

स्यसर *syạs^{a}r* (pr. almost *sis^{a}r*), make straight.

स्यञराव *syạñ^{a}rāv* (pr. almost *siñ^{a}rāv*), make soft.

स्यन्दर *syạnd^{a}r* (pr. almost *sind^{a}r*) become red.

स्वचराव *swạts^{a}rāv* (pr. almost *suts^{a}rāv* appease.

स्वम्बर *swamb^{a}r* (pr. almost *sumb^{a}r*) make level.

हटर *hạṭ^{a}r*, make thin.

हन्दर *hạnd^{a}r*, be cold.

ह्वखर *hwạkh^{a}r* (pr. almost *hukh^{a}r*), make dry.

ह्वचराव *hwạts^{a}rāv* (pr. almost *huts^{a}rāv*), cause to become decayed.

ह्वबर *hwạb^{a}r* (pr. almost *hub^{a}r*), conquer.

ह्वमर *hwạm^{a}r* (pr. almost *hum^{a}r*), appease.

When the vowel *a* is modified by *i-mātrā*, it is pronounced nearly as the *ă* in *hat*. The *i-matra* is also very lightly pronounced, both in the same syllable as the *ă*, with the *ă*, as well as in its own syllable. This has led to various methods of transcription. For instance, some transcribe असि by *ais*, and others by *as^i*. The true pronunciation is something like *a^{i}s^i*. I prefer to transcribe it by *ạs^i*, which follows the native system. The *i-mātrā* is shown in its proper place, and a dot (corresponding to the Çāradā ꠱) is placed under the *ạ* to show that it is modified. The following are examples of *a* modified by *i-mātrā*.

असि *ạs^i*, pronounced *a^{i}s^i*, we.

करि *kạr^i*, pr. *ka^{i}r^i*, bracelets.

पपि *pạp^i*, pr. *pa^{i}p^i*, ripe (masc. pl.)

दरि *dạr^i* (*da^{i}r^i*), strong (masc. pl.)

खरि *khạr^i* (*kha^{i}r^i*), having a scald-head (m. pl.)

चरि *tsar^i* (*tsa^{i}r^i*), many (masc. pl.)

ज़रि *zạr^i* (*za^{i}r^i*), deaf (masc. pl.)

खखि *khạkh^i* (*kha^{i}kh^i*), name of caste (masc. pl.)

बडि *bạḍ^i* (*ba^{i}ḍ^i*), great (masc. pl.)

गटि *gạṭ^i* (*ga^{i}ṭ^i*), thin, weak (masc. pl.)

खटि *khạṭ* (*kha^{i}ṭ^i*), cupboards (masc. pl.)

When *a* is followed by *u-mātrā* it takes a sound which it is easy to describe, but which it is difficult to express in writing. It is the short sound corresponding to the long *ō* in the English word *home*. It may be represented by *o*, *i.e.*, the short sound of *ō*. It has nothing to do with the short *ŏ* in the English word *cŏb*, which also occurs in Kāçmīrī but is represented differently (see pages 294 and 304). The *u-mātrā* itself is hardly pronounced at all. Paṇḍits say it can be heard, but when they say they pronounce it, its sound altogether fails to reach my ear. That is probably the fault of my ear, but it is not an exceptionally dull one. All that I hear is the final consonant immediately preceding the *u-mātrā*, pronounced with exceptional clearness. In English, we have a habit of clipping our final consonants. Thus, in the English word *bad*, the *d* is only half pronounced. If we added an *u-mātrā* in Kāçmīrī we should to an English ear, only fully complete the pronunciation of the final *d*, or in other words double it. I would therefore, represent the pronunciation of such a Kāçmīrī word as *bạḍᵘ*, great, by *boḍḍ*, in which the doubled *d* means that the tongue must not only touch the palate to get the sound of *ḍ*, but must also be mostly drawn back, after a perceptible interval, so as to complete the explosion.

The dot under the *ạ* corresponds to the ˌ of the Çāradā character, and warns the reader that the *a* is modified by the following *u-mātrā*.

Wade transcribes this *a* modified by *u-mātrā*, by *ọ*. As he also transcribes the *ŏ* sound of *cob*, by the same sign, great confusion is caused to the learner.

The following are examples of *a* modified by *u-mātrā*.

[Note that every word ending in *u-mātrā* is masculine, and that all nouns ending in *u-mātrā* belong to Wade's 2nd declension].

bạḍᵘ, pronounced *bodd*; great (m. sg.)

khạlᵘ (*kholl*), open, loose.

mạrᵘ (*morr*), a hut, a fowl-house.

dạdᵘ (*dodd*), burnt.

khạtᵘ, (*khott*), a place of concealment, a wall-cupboard.

lạdᵘ (*lodd*), made.

khạḍᵘ (*khoḍḍ*), pudendum muliebre.

kạlᵘ (*koll*), dumb.

phạṭᵘ (*phoṭṭ*), drowned.

rạṭᵘ (*roṭṭ*), taken.

mạtᵘ (*mott*), mad.

lạtᵘ (*lott*), light, gentle (of speaking.)

nạlᵘ (*noll*), an entire cowrie.

bạlᵘ (*boll*), recovered in health.

bạrᵘ (*borr*), a hole in a wall, for entrance.

gạrᵘ (*gorr*), made.

thạdᵘ (*thodd*), tall.

tsạdᵘ (*tsodd*), a round basin for milk.

gạḍᵘ (*godd*), a hole.

tsạṭᵘ (*tsoṭṭ*), cut.

dạlᵘ (*doll*), the skirt of a garment.

nạrᵘ (*norr*), sleeve.

tsạrᵘ (*tsorr*), more.

gạtᵘ (*gott*), thin, weak.

chạtᵘ (*chott*), white.

When *a* is followed by *ū-mātrā* it takes a sound closely corresponding to that of the German *ü*. As in the case of *u-mātrā*, paṇḍits say that the *ŭ-mātrā* is pronounced (be it ever so lightly), but to me, all that I can hear is the full pronunciation of the final consonant, which, under the head of *u-mātrā*, I attempted to illustrate by doubling it. The pronunciation of the word कर् *kạrᵘ*, would therefore be illustrated by *kürr*. Wade represents the *ü* sound by *ạ*, which as before explained, gives rise to confusion. As explained before, I transliterate the Çāradā characters as they stand, the dot under the *ạ*, showing that it is modified by the following *ŭ-mātrā*, and corresponding to the Çāradā [1].

The following are examples of *a* modified by a following *ŭ-mātrā*.

[Most words ending in *ŭ-mātrā* are feminine, and belong to the third declension. There are, however, some masculines, *e.g.*, दान् *dạnᵘ*, a pomegranate, which belong to the first declension.]

कर् *kạrᵘ* (pronounced *kürr*) a beam, she was made by us.

ज़र् *zạrᵘ* (*zürr*), a deaf woman.

बर् *bạrᵘ* (bürr), a crack in wood.

नर् *nạrᵘ* (*nürr*), the lower part of the arm.

अर् *ạrᵘ* (*ürr*) well, strong.

बठ् *bạṭhᵘ* (*büṭṭḥ*), a hob.

दर् *dạrᵘ* (*dürr*), a strong woman.

च़ट् *tsạṭᵘ* (*tsüṭṭ*), she was cut.

ज़ट् *zạṭᵘ* (*züṭṭ*) torn, tattered (fem.)

रट् *rạṭᵘ* (*rüṭṭ*), she was taken.

वट् *wạṭᵘ* (*wüṭṭ*), rolled up.

बड् *bạḍᵘ* (*büḍḍ*), a great woman.

गर् *gạrᵘ* (*gürr*), a pitcher.

छर् *tshạrᵘ* (*tshürr*), empty, a basket.

खर् *khạrᵘ* (*khürr*), a she ass.

वर् *wạrᵘ* (*würr*), dried pease pudding.

पट् *pạṭᵘ* (*püṭṭ*), a small plank.

खट् *khạṭᵘ* (*khüṭṭ*), concealed (fem.)

फट् *phạṭᵘ* (*phüṭṭ*), drowned.

यड् *yạḍᵘ* (*yüḍḍ*), bellies.

The following are examples of *ā*, which is pronounced as in Sanskrit or Hindī.

काठ् *kāṭh*, wood (masc.)

काछ् *kātsh*, glass, pottery (masc.)

काड् *kāḍ*. width (especially of a river) (masc.)

काद् *kād*, a representative (masc.)

गाल् *gāl*, shame (fem.)

टाख् *ṭākh*, name of a caste (masc.)

डाख् *ḍākh*, ashes (masc.)

पाफ् *pāph*, a sin (masc.)

ताख् *tākh*, opening in a wall (masc.)

नाद् *nād*, a sound (masc.)

लॉज् *lāz*, a stake (masc.)

डॉग् *ḍāg*, a club (masc.)

बाड् *bāḍ*, a dancing boy (masc.)

शाद् *çād*, a pillow (masc.)

चाल् *cāl*, centre of a shawl or handkerchief (fem.)

माड् *māḍ*, working of dough (fem.)

बाग् *bāg*, a call to prayers (fem.)

दाद् *dād*, a bullock (masc.)

ब्राद् *brād*, a verandah (masc.)

माछ् *māch*, honey (masc.)

दान् *dān*, a cooking place (masc.)

प्रान् *prān*, an onion (masc.)

वान् *wān*, a shop (masc.)

रान् *rān*, a thigh (fem.)

The letter *ā* is often modified to *ạ̄*, the sound of which may be represented by the German *ö*. It is, however, a prolonged sound, drawled out, so to speak, and there is a touch of the sound of *ā* in the English word *hall* in it, so that *ö* is not a perfectly correct representation, though the nearest available. Another way of considering the sound is to say that it is something between that of the *ea* of *earl*, and the *aw* of *awl*. The sound is a very peculiar one, and can really only be learned by the ear.

The following are examples of this letter, which is evidently derived from a long *ā* followed by an original *i* or *y*. *E. g.* आस् *ạ̄s* is derived from the Skr. *āsyam*, through **āis*.

पांछ् *pạ̄ts*, five.	वाख् *wạ̄kh*, (*wŏkh*) a ringlet (fem.)
लाख् *lạ̄kh*, (pr. *lŏkh*) a stride (fem.)	आस् *ạ̄s*, (*ŏs*) a mouth (masc.)
वाछ्‌ *wạ̄tsh*, (pr. *wŏtsh*) deceiving (fem.)	आर् *ạ̄r*, (*ŏr*) a kind of fruit (masc.) pl. आर् *ạ̄r*).
लाछ्‌ *lạ̄tsh*, (pr. *lŏtsh*) a eunuch (masc.)	क्राज् *krạ̄j*, (*kröj*) a potter's wife, (fem. of क्राल् *krāl*).

When *ā* is followed by *i-mātrā* or by *ū-mātrā* it always becomes modified to *ạ̄*. As usual the *i-mātrā* is very slightly heard both before and after the succeeding consonant. The *ū-mātrā* is, to my ears, not audible, though the preceding consonant is somewhat more strongly pronounced, which I represent by doubling it.

When *ā* is followed by *u-mātrā* it is pronounced *ŏ*, and is so written. Thus take the verb छारुन् *tsārun*, to sort, arrange. The root is छार् *tsār*. The past tense masculine singular is formed by adding *u-mātrā* to the root, and is therefore छोर् *tsŏrᵘ*. The feminine singular past is however, formed by adding *ū-mātrā*, and the original *ā* is therefore not changed to *ŏ*, but is modified to *ạ̄*, thus छार् *tsạ̄rᵘ*. So the masculine plural is छारि् *tsạ̄rⁱ*. The feminine plural, however, is formed by adding *yᵉ* which does not modify the preceding *ā*, and we have छारे *tsāryᵉ* (*i.e.*, *tsārĕ*, see page 304). So also the base क्रान् *krān-*, a relation, has its nom. sg. क्रोनु *krŏnᵘ*, and its nom. pl. क्रानि *krạ̄nⁱ*. Its dative plural is however, क्रानयन् *krānyan* in which the original base क्रान् *krān-* is retained, without modifying the *ā* to *ạ̄* or changing it to *ŏ*, because it is followed by *ya*, and not by *i-mātrā*, *u-mātrā*, or *ū-mātrā*. This point is important. It explains many difficulties in Kāçmīrī declension and conjugation, and, so far as I know, attention has not previously been drawn to it. In dictionaries, the nom. form क्रोनु *krŏnᵘ* is given, but it would be better to give the declensional base क्रान् *krān-*, which is the original word. Note, however, that *a* is the only vowel which is modified not only by *i-mātrā*, but even by a fully pronounced *i* when following it. Thus the dat.

sg. of *krān-* is क्रांनिस् *krạnis*, not क्रानिस *krānis*. This is not the case with other vowels: *e.g.*, the dat. sg. of पोथ् *pōth-* (feminine) is पोथि *pōthi* (fully pronounced *i*), not पूथि *pūthi*, while the nom. sg. (with *i-mātrā*) is पूथि *pūth*^{i}, with the *ō* changed to *ū* (see page 302).

The following are examples of *ạ* followed by *i-mātrā*.

क्रांनि *krạn*^{i}, pr. *krö*^{i}*n*^{i}, relations, (pl. of क्रोनु *krōn*^{u}).

ब्यांलि *byạl*^{i} (*byö*^{i}*l*^{i}), seeds (pl. of ब्योलु *byōl*^{u}).

दांनि *dạn*^{i} (*dö*^{i}*n*^{i}), churn-sticks, (pl. of दोनु *dōn*^{u}).

The following are examples of *ō* followed by *u-mātrā*. As just explained, they are really instances of *ā* being followed by *u-mātrā*, and therefore changed to *ō*. They are all masculine nouns in *u-mātrā*. The nom. masc. plurals all end in *i-mātrā* preceded by *ạ*. Thus *cyōn*$_{u}$, nom. plur. *cyạn*^{i}. The pronunciation of the *ō* is nearly like that of Sanskrit and Hindi, but is slightly drawled till it approaches that of *au* in *cause*, as befits its derivation from *ā* and *u*.

म्योनु	*myōn*^{u} (for *myān-*^{u}) pronounced	*myōnn*, my (masc.)
च्योनु	*cyōn*^{u} (*cyān-*^{u})	*cyōnn*, thine (masc.)
प्रोनु	*prōn*^{u} (*prāṇ-*^{u})	*prōnn*, ancient (masc.)
दोनु	*dōn*^{u} (*dān-*^{u})	*dōnn*, a churn-stick (masc.)
क्रोरु	*krōr*^{u} (*krār-*^{u}).	*krōrr*, a scab
ब्रोरु	*brōr*^{u} (*brār-*^{u})	*brōrr*, a cat (masc.)
चोरु	*cōr*^{u} (*cār-*^{u})	*cōrr*, an idiot (masc.)
क्रोनु	*krōn*^{u} (*krān-*^{u})	*krōnn*, a relation.
शोलु	*çōl*^{u} (*çāl-*^{u})	*çōll*, a kind of grain.
चोनु	*tsōn*^{u} (*tsān-*^{u})	*tsōnn*, he entered.
द्योरु	*dyōr*^{u} (*dyār-*^{u})	*dyōrr*, rich (masc.)
च़ोरु	*tsōr*^{u} (*tsār-*^{u})	*tsōrr*, he was collected, four.
प्योरु	*pyōr*^{u} (*pyār-*^{u})	*pyōrr*, dear (masc.)
ब्योलु	*byōl*^{u} (*byāl-*^{u})	*byōll*, a seed.
द्योनु	*dyōn*^{u} (*dyān-*^{u})	*dyōnn*, a foundation.

The following are examples *ạ* followed by *ū-mātrā*, (including the letter ञ् *ñ*, which is treated as if it was न्यू *ny*^{ū}).

चांरू *cạr*^{ū} (pr. *cörr*), an idiot (fem. of चोरु *cōr*^{u}).

द्यांरू *dyạr*^{ū} (*dyörr*), a rich woman (fem. of *dyōr*^{u}) (rare).

ब्रांरू *brạr*^{ū} (*brörr*), a cat (fem. of ब्रोरु *brōr*^{u}).

आंरू *ạr*^{ū} (*örr*), a shoe-maker's awl (pl. आर्य *ary*^{a}, *i.e.*, *ārĕ*).

कार् *kạr*^{u} (*körr*), a neck.

प्यार् *pyạr*^{u} (*pyörr*), dear, beloved (fem. of प्योर् *pyōr*^{u}). (fem.)

वार् *wạr*^{u} (*wörr*), a small garden

पार् *pạr*^{u} (*pörr*), (fem.)

माज् *mạj*^{u} (*möjj*), a mother.

गार् *gạr*^{u} (*görr*), kernel of Singārā (fem.)

लार् *lạr*^{u} (*lörr*), a cucumber, also she followed, (masc. लोर् *lōr*^{u} he followed).

प्रार् *prạr*^{u} (*prörr*), she was waited for (fem. of प्रोर् *prōr*^{u}, he was waited for).

त्सार् *tsạr*^{u} (*tsörr*), she was collected (masc. त्सोर् *tsōr*^{u}).

रात्स् *rạts*^{u} (*rötsts*), nights (fem.)

दान् *dạn*^{u} (*dönn*), a pomegranate (masc.)

त्सान् *tsạñ* (*tsöny*), she entered (masc. त्सोन् *tsōn*^{u}).

म्यान् *myạñ* (*myöny*), mine (fem. of म्योन् *myōn*^{u}).

च्यान् *cyạñ* (*cyöny*), thine (fem. of च्योन् *cyōn*^{u}).

प्रान् *prạñ* (*pröny*), ancient (fem. of प्रोन् *prōn*^{u}).

The vowel *i* is usually pronounced as in Sanskrit or Hindi. The following are examples:—

निश *nish*^{a}, near.

सिल *sil*^{a}, the disease of consumption (masc.)

फिस् *phis*, a child's penis (fem.)

थिस् *this*, noise of a crack (masc.)

निस् *nis*, take away from him.

निन् *nin*, they will take away.

यिस् *yis*, come to him.

यिन् *yin*, they will come.

यिख् *yikh*, thou wilt come.

दिस् *dis*, give to him.

दिन् *din*, they will give.

विल् *vil*, a short space of time (fem.)

गिल् *gil*, a kind of bird (fem.)

त्सिथ् *tsith*, loss of use of limbs (fem.)

बिठ् *biṭh*, an assembly (fem.)

सिठ् *siṭh*, a whisper (masc.)

छिर् *chir*, the stream of milk that comes out at one pull of the udder (fem.)

जिन् *jin*, a demon (masc.)

हिश् *hiç*, the driving away of fowls, &c. (masc.)

मिश् *miç*, a splinter (fem.)

फिस् फिस् *phis phis*, whispering (masc.)

किस् *kis*, little finger (fem.)

पिलुन् *pilun*, to reach.

किल् *kil*, a thrust (fem.)

चिल् *cil*, a stake (masc.)

सिर् *sir*, a secret.

सिद् *sid*, revenge, spite (masc.)

When the vowel *i* commences a word, it is pronounced *yi*: thus—

इह् *ih*, pronounced *yih*, this (nom.)

इमिस् *imis*, *yimis*, this (acc.)

इथै *ithai*, *yithai*, gratis.

इमाम् *imām*, *yimām*, a Musalmān priest.

इन्दर् *ind*^{a}*r*, *yind*^{a}*r*, a spinning-wheel

इमिकनि *imikani*, *yimikani*, thus.

इछुन् *itshun*, *yitshun*, to wish.

इपट् *ipat*^{a}, *yipüṭṭ*, the yoke of a plough.

When *i* is followed by *i-mātrā* its pronunciation is not affected. The *i-mātrā* is pronounced only *after* the preceding consonant.

इति *it*^{i} (*yit*^{i}), here.

लिवि *liv*^{i}, they were plastered by us.

मिलि *mil*^{i}, reconciliations.

किलि *kil*^{i}, pegs.

निनि *nin*^{i}, about to be taken (masc. plur.)

हिंसि *hiñ*^{i}, the neighing of a horse (fem.)

When *i* is followed by *u-mātrā*, it is pronounced *yu*, and the final consonant is fully pronounced, as usual. In such cases the *i* is often *written yu*, and the *u*-matra omitted: thus;

मिलु *mil*^{u} or म्युल् *myul*, both pronounced *myull*, reconciliation.

कितु *kit*^{u} or क्युत् *kyut*, *kyutt*, on account of.

किलु *kil*^{u} or क्युल् *kyul*, *kyull*, a peg.

लिवु *liv*^{u} or ल्युव् *lyuv*, *lyuvv*, he was plastered by us.

नेचिवु *nĕciv*^{u} or नेच्युव् *nĕcyuv* *nĕcyuvv*, a son.

In the case of three verbs, the different spellings, mean different things; thus

निनु *nin*^{u}, to take, न्युन् *nyun*, the act of taking, both pronounced *nyunn*.

दिनु *din*^{u}, to give, द्युन् *dyun*, the act of giving, *dyunn*.

यिनु *yin*^{u}, to come, य्युन् *yyun*, the act of coming, *yyunn*.

When *i* is followed by *ū-mātrā*, it is pronounced something like *yü*, in which *ü* represents a short German *ü*. Thus

लिव *liv*^{ū}, pronounced *lyüvv*, she was plastered by us.

फिर *phir*^{ū} *phyürr*, she was turned over by us.

Instances of this are rare.

The vowel *ī* is pronounced as in Sanskrit and Hindi, thus,—

शीन् *çīn*, snow (masc.)

When the vowel commences a word, it is pronounced *yī*; thus,

ईरन् *īran*, pronounced *yīran*, an anvil (fem.)

ईरुन् *īrun*, *yīrun*, to float.

ईद् *īd*, *yīd*, the Musalman festival.

ईच् *īts*^{a}, *yīts*^{a}, so much (fem.)

When *ī* is followed by *u-mātrā* it becomes *yū*, and is so written. Thus the word नीलु *nīl*^{u}, blue, becomes, and is written, न्यूलु *nyūl*^{u} (न्यूल् *nyūl* would be better). This accounts for numerous verbal forms of the Past Participle Masculine.

When *ī* is followed by *ū-mātrā* its pronunciation is not affected. The final consonant is merely strengthened slightly by the *ū-mātrā*. The following are examples :

फीर् *phīr*^{u} (pr. *phīrr*), she rambled.
चीर् *cīr*^{u} (pr. *cīrr*), we squeezed her.
शीर् *çīr*^{u} (pr. *çīrr*) we arranged her.
यीर् *yīr*^{u}, (pr. *yīrr*), we arranged her (fem.), used of the warp, in weaving: the object must be fem.
नीर् *nīr*^{u} (pr. *nīrr*), she came out.
गीर् *gīr*^{u} (pr. *gīrr*), we surrounded her.
वीर् *vīr*^{u} (pr. *vīrr*), a willow.
सीर् *sīr*^{u} (pr. *sīrr*), a poke in the ribs.
हीर् *hīr*^{u} (pr. *hīrr*), a head.
सीर् *sīr*^{u} (pr. *sīrr*), a brick.

The Vowel *u* is usually pronounced as in Sanskrit and Hindī. Thus

युन् *yun*, to come.
नुन् *nun*, saltish.
कुस् *kus*, who ?
युस् *yus*, who.
हुम् *hum*, they.
कुस् *kus*, a kind of sweet-meat (masc.)
वुठ् *wuth*, drizzling (masc.)
स्रुठ् *sruth*, a sip (masc.)

When the vowel *u* commences a word it is pronounced *wu*, and is often written वु. Thus

उडर् *uḍar* or वुडर् *wuḍar*, both pronounced *wuḍar*, a plateau (fem.)
उह *uh* or वुह् *wuh* — *wuh*, twenty.
उलर् *ular* or वुलर् *wular* — *wular*, name of a pargana.
उनर् *unar* or वुनर् *wunar* — *wunar*, mist (fem.)
उफुन् *uphun* or वुफुन् *wuphun* — *wuphun*, to fly.
उश *uçk*^{a} or वुश *wuçk*^{a} — *wuçk*^{a}, oats, barley. (fem.)
उठ् *uṭh* or वुठ् *wuṭh* — *wuṭh*, a lip (m.)
उठुन् *uṭhun* or वुठुन् *wuṭhun* — *wuṭhun*, to twist.
उजमल् *uzamal* or वुजमल् *wuzamal* — *wuzamal*, lightning.

There is also a modified *u* which is sounded like the *ŏ* in *cob*, or nearly so. This I represent by *ŏ*. It is very commonly written *wa*. In both cases there is a slight *w* sound preceding the *ŏ*, and, moreover when the vowel is initial the *w* is fully pronounced.

उज़ुल् *ŏzul*^{u} or वज़ुल् *wŏzul*^{u}, both pronounced *wŏzull*, red.

उड्, *ŏḍ* or वड् *wŏḍ*	*wŏḍ*, the crown of the head (fem.)
उडुर् *ŏdur* or वडुर् *wŏdur*	*wŏdur*, the belly.
उखुल् *ŏkhul* or वखुल् *wŏkhul*	*wŏkhul*, a mortar.
उथुन् *ŏthun* or वथुन् *wŏthun*	*wŏthun*, to rise.

When the sound is medial, only *wa* is written not *u*: Thus,—

दवद् *dŏd*, milk (masc.)
खवड् *khŏḍ*, a pit (masc.)
चवल् *tsŏl*, a fireplace (fem.)
मवल् *mŏl*, price (masc.)
पवठ् *pŏṭh*, piles (fem.)
दवख् *dŏkh*, pain (masc.)
छवख् *chŏkh*, a wound (masc.)
नवश् *nŏç*, a daughter-in-law (fem.)
खरवख् *khrŏkh*, a snore (masc.)
सवन् *sŏn*, gold (masc.), a co-wife (fem.)

बवन् *bŏn*, below.
ववल् *wŏl*, dregs of *ghī* (fem.)
ववड् *wŏḍ*, scalp (fem.)
सवल् *sŏl*, drowsiness (fem.)
चवठ् *tsŏṭh*, breaking wind (fem.)
मवख् *mŏkh*, a cut branch (masc.)
दवस् *dŏs*, wall (fem.)
खवठ् *khŏṭh*, false, (used as a nominal verb.)
चवन् *tsŏn*, to the four.
खवन् *khŏn*, elbow (fem.)

In most of these, a faint *w*-sound is heard before the *o*, but it is hardly necessary to represent it, and it need not be considered for practical purposes. If strict rigour of transliteration is required, then we should write *d*^{w}*ŏd*, *kh*^{w}*ŏḍ*, &c. In some words, such as *d*^{w}*ŏd* it is more distinct than others, but it depends partly on individual speakers, and partly on whether the speaker is speaking carefully or not.

When *u* is followed by *i-mātrā* its sound is not changed. As usual the *i* is pronounced both before and after the consonant which precedes it; thus,

गुरि	*gur*^{i},	pronounced *gu*^{i}*r*^{i}, horses.
शुरि	*çur*^{i},	(*çu*^{i}*r*^{i}), children (of either sex).
मुजि	*muj*^{i},	(*mu*^{i}*j*^{i}), a radish.
तुजि	*tuj*^{i},	(*tu*^{i}*j*^{i}), a little piece of reed or thin wood.
बुथि	*buth*^{i},	(*bu*^{i}*th*^{i}) faces (nom. pl.)

When the vowel *u* is followed by *u-mātrā* its pronunciation is very slightly altered. The change is so slight that it is unnecessary, to reproduce it in transliteration, but, in order to show the extreme niceness of Kāçmīrī pronunciation I make the following attempt to teach the reader how to pronounce these two sounds.

When in English we pronounce the *oo* in the word *good*, we pout out the lips, and *keep them pouted* till we have pronounced the *d*. In

Kāçmīrī this word would be written गुडु *guḍ*^{u}, with *u-mātrā*. This *u* we may call *u*^{2}. If, however, after pouting out the lips, we allow them quickly to resume their original position before commencing to sound the *d* of *good*, it will be noticed that a slightly different tone-colour is given to the *oo*. This sound we may call *u*^{1}. In Kāçmīrī, an ordinary *u* is pronounced as *u*^{1}, but when followed by *u-mātrā* it is pronounced as *u*^{2}, the final consonant, as usual being also pronounced more fully than in English. We thus get the following examples

गुरु *gur*^{u}, pronounced *gu*^{2}*rr*, a horse (masc.)
सुरु *sur*^{u}, *su*^{2}*rr*, a daughter's son (masc.)
शुरु *çur*^{u}, *çu*^{2}*rr*, a child (of either sex) (masc.)
हुरु *hur*^{u}, *hu*^{2}*rr*, surplus (masc.)
तुलु *tul*^{u}, *tu*^{2}*ll*, we have lifted him.
कुलु *kul*^{u}, *ku*^{2}*ll*, a tree (masc.)
शुपु *çup*^{u}, *çu*^{2}*pp* a sieve (masc.)
टुकु *ṭuk*^{u}, *ṭu*^{2}*kk*, we have torn him with the teeth.
रुतु *rut*^{u}, *ru*^{2}*tt*, right (not wrong).
बुसु *bus*^{u}, *bu*^{2}*ss*, we have parched him.
वुसु *wus*^{u}, *wu*^{2}*ss*, he bubbled up.
कुनु *kun*^{u}, *ku*^{2}*nn*, sold.
छुनु *tshun*^{u}, *tshu*^{2}*nn*, he put in.
चुकु *tsuk*^{u}, *tsu*^{2}*kk*, sour.
वुरु *wur*^{u}, *wu*^{2}*rr*, rice boiled dry (masc.)
वुलु *wul*^{u}, *wu*^{2}*ll*, a small hole in a wall for ventilation or light (masc.)
दुबु *dub*^{u}, *du*^{2}*bb*, a sound (masc.)
थ्युपु *thyup*^{u}, *thyu*^{2}*pp*, a basket for fruit or animals (masc.)
मुसु *mus*^{u}, *mu*^{2}*ss*, fatigue, a small turnip (masc.)
फुहुरु *phuhur*^{u}, *phuhu*^{2}*rr*, burnt rice at the bottom of a pot.

When the vowel *u* is followed by *ū-mātrā* the pronunciation is hardly affected at all. Merely the final consonant is strengthened: Thus,

गुरू *gur*^{ū}, pronounced *gurr*, a mare.
सुरू *sur*^{ū}, *surr*, a daughter's daughter.
बुसू *bus*^{ū}, *buss*, we have parched her.
मुरू *mur*^{ū}, *murr*, the width of sleeve or trousers at wrist or ankle (fem.)

The vowel *ū* is usually pronounced as in Sanskrit or Hindī, but in some people's mouths it almost becomes *ō*. Examples are

लूठ् *lūṭh*, plunder (masc.)
बूथ् *būth*, a demon (masc.)
कून् *kūn*, a corner (masc.)
रूग् *rūg*, or रोग *rōg*, a disease (pronunciation fluctuating) (masc.)
रूद् *rūd*, rain (masc.)
नून् *nūn*, salt (masc.)
सूठ् *sūṭh*, the puff of smoke from a pipe (masc.)
चूर् *tsūr*, a thief (masc.)
पू *pū*, onomatopœic sound of derision (masc.)
न्यूख् *nyūkh*, he was carried away by them.

When *ū* commences a word it is pronounced, and usually written *wū*: thus

ऊँठ् *ūṭh*, or वूठ् *wūṭh*, both pronounced *wūṭh*, a camel (masc.)

These words are rare, and the above is the only example I know commencing with an original *ū*.

When *ū* is followed by *i-mātrā*, its pronunciation is not affected, but, the *i-matrā* is as usual pronounced both before and after the consonant which precedes it. The following are examples.

पूरि *pūr*^{i}, pronounced *pū*^{i}*r*^{i}, filled (masc. pl.)
टूरि *ṭūr*^{i}, *ṭū*^{i}*r*^{i}, small metal saucers (masc. pl.)
गूरि *gūr*^{i}, *gū*^{i}*r*^{i}, cowherds (masc. pl.)
क्रूरि *krūr*^{i}, *krū*^{i}*r*^{i}, wells (masc. pl.)
द्रूरि *drūr*^{i}, *drū*^{i}*r*^{i}, skins (masc. pl.)
बूलि *būl*^{i}, *bū*^{i}*l*^{i}, language (fem. sg.)
लूलि *lūl*^{i}, *lū*^{i}*l*^{i}, affectionately.
गूलि *gūl*^{i}, *gū*^{i}*l*^{i}, kernels (masc. pl.)
डूलि *ḍūl*^{i}, *ḍu*^{i}*l*^{i}, deserted, as an orphan (masc. pl.)
जूलि *jūl*^{i}, *jū*^{i}*l*^{i}, collected, as alms, in a cloth (fem. sg.)
तूलि *tūl*^{i}, *tū*^{i}*l*^{i}, I have weighed them.
डूनि *ḍūn*^{i}, *ḍū*^{i}*n*^{i}, walnuts (masc. pl.)
तूनि *tūn*^{i}, *tū*^{i}*n*^{i} navels (masc. pl.)

When *ū* is followed by *u-matra* its pronunciation is practically unchanged. Really the lips are moved as described under the head of *u* with *u-mātrā*. This shade of sound I may distinguish by calling it *ū*^{3}.

Thus मूर् *mūr* is pronounced *mū^{1}r*, and मूर *mūr^{u}* is pronounced as *mū^{2}rr*.

The following are examples.

मूर *mūr^{u}*, pronounced *mū^{2}rr*, we rubbed grain between the hands to remove the husk (masc.)

चूर *cūr^{u}*, *cū^{2}rr*, we have rinsed out, or squeezed out (masc.)

खूर *khūr^{u}*, *khū^{2}rr*, a razor (masc.)

सूर *sūr^{u}*, *sū^{2}rr*, finished (masc.)

हूर *hūr^{u}*, *hū^{2}rr*, we have discharged a debt (masc.)

पूर *pūr^{u}*, *pū^{2}rr*, filled (masc.)

शूर *çūr^{u}*, *çū^{2}rr*, we have arranged him (masc.)

टूर *ṭūr^{u}*, *ṭū^{2}rr*, a small metal saucer (masc.)

ग्रूस्त *grūst^{u}*, *grū^{2}st*, a cultivator (masc.)

गूर *gūr^{u}*, *gū^{2}rr*, a cowherd (masc.)

म्यूठ *myūṭh^{u}*, *myū^{2}ṭṭh*, sweet (masc.)

च्यूट *tsyūṭ^{u}*, *tsyū^{2}ṭṭ*, a relish with food (masc.)

न्यूल *nyūl^{u}*, *nyū^{2}ll* green, not ripe (masc.)

ग्यूल *gyūl^{u}*, *gyū^{2}ll*, we ridiculed him (masc.)

न्यूर *nyūr^{u}*, *nyū^{2}rr*, pasturage (masc.), near.

प्यूर *pyūr^{u}*, *pyū^{2}rr*, greasy (masc.)

ल्यूख *lyūkh^{u}*, *lyū^{2}kkh*, we wrote him (masc.)

फ्रूस्त *phrūst^{u}*, *phrū^{2}st*, excellent (masc.)

स्यूठ *syūṭh^{u}*, *syū^{2}ṭṭh*, long, tall (masc.)

ब्यूठ *byūṭh^{u}*, *byū^{2}ṭṭh*, he sat (masc.)

म्यूल *myūl^{u}*, *myū^{2}ll*, we met him (masc.)

च्यून *tsyūn^{u}*, *tsyū^{2}nn*, we have guessed at (masc.)

त्यूर *tyūr^{u}*, *tyū^{2}rr*, sheep (masc.)

क्रूर *krūr^{u}*, *krū^{2}rr*, a well (masc.)

द्रूर *drūr^{u}*, *drū^{2}rr*, skin (masc.)

ग्यूर *gyūr^{u}*, *gyū^{2}rr*, we have encompassed him (masc.)

व्यूग *vyūg^{u}*, *vyū^{2}gg*, a trap door (masc.)

ड्यूठ *ḍyūṭh^{u}*, *ḍyū^{2}ṭṭh*, we have seen him (masc.)

हून *hūn^{u}*, *hū^{2}nn*, a dog (masc.)

मूद *mūd^{u}*, *mū^{2}dd*, dead (masc.)

गूद *gūd^{u}*, *gū^{2}dd*, pudendum (masc.)

बूस *būs^{u}*, *bū^{2}ss*, we have heard (masc.)

टून्	*tün*^{u},	pronounced	*tü*^{a}*nn*, navel (masc.)
मून्	*mün*^{u},		*mü*^{a}*nn*, wall of a house (masc.)
पूर्	*pür*^{u},		*pü*^{a}*rr*, a step (masc.)
दून्	*dün*^{u},		*dü*^{a}*nn*, a cotton cleaner (masc.)
रून्	*rün*^{u},		*rü*^{a}*nn*, a husband (masc.)
रूद्	*rüd*^{u},		*rü*^{a}*dd*, remained (masc.)
लूस्	*lüs*^{u},		*lü*^{a}*ss*, tired.
वून्	*wün*^{u},		*wü*^{a}*nn*, we have woven.
लून्	*lün*^{u},		*lü*^{a}*nn*, we have reaped him.

When *ü* is followed by *ü-mātrā*, its pronunciation is hardly affected: thus

लूर्	*lür*^{ü},	pronounced	*lürr*, a stick (fem.)
खूर्	*khür*^{ü},		*khürr*, a heel (fem.)
गूर्	*gür*^{ü},		*gürr*, a milk-maid (fem.)
डूर्	*dür*^{ü},		*dürr*, a breeches' string (fem.)
ज़ूव्र्	*züv*^{a}*r*^{ü},		*züv*^{a}*rr*, a wooden candlestick (fem.)
कूर्	*kür*^{ü},		*kürr*, a girl (fem.)
डूर्	*dür*^{ü},		*dürr*, an alley (fem.)
मूर्	*mür*^{ü},		*mürr*, a withe (fem.)
मून्	*mün*^{ü},		*münn*, wool of sheep (fem.)
ज़ून्	*zün*^{ü},		*zünn*, moon light (fem.)

There is also a very peculiar *ü*, something like a *long* German *ü*, pronounced through the teeth. It is represented in transliteration by *ų*. The following are examples of its use.

टुर् *tųr*^{ü}, pronounced *tųr*, cold.

पुंछूह् *pųtsüh*, twenty-five.

कुर्	*kųr*^{ü},	pronounced	*kųr*, cruel (fem.) (masc. कूर् *kür*^{u}.)
गुड्	*gųḍ*^{ü},		*gųḍd*, foolish (fem.) (masc. गूड् *güḍ*^{u}.)
कुत्	*kųts*^{ü},		*kųts*, how much? (fem. sg., fem. pl. कुत् *kųts*^{a}.)
चुन्	*tsųn*,		powdered.
ठुक्	*thųk*^{ü},		*thųk*, attacked by the horns of any animal (fem.) (masc. ठूक् *thųk*^{u}).

सुतिन् *sųtin*, by means of.

When the vowel *ṛ* commences a word, it is pronounced *ryĕ*, and the mark ᐩ is placed over it to show modification. Thus ऋतु, a season pronounced *ryāth*. Similarly a medial *ṛ* is modified and is pronounced *rŏ*, e.g., कृन्यौव् *kṛhanyauv*, he became black, pronounced *krăhanyauv*. With ū-*mātrā* following, it is pronounced *rü*, as in कृम् *krm*$^{\bar{u}}$, pr. *krüm*, a tortoise (*kūrmaḥ*). The usual pronunciation of *ṛ* is *ru*, as in कृप्यौन *kṛpyaun*, he cut (with scissors), pr. *krupyaun*.

The vowel *ĕ*, is pronounced as in Sanskrit or Hindī: thus

शेरुन् *çĕrun*, to arrange.
गेरुन् *gĕrun*, to laugh at (also गेलुन् *gĕlun*).
चेर् *tsĕr*, delay, a yellow apricot (fem.)
बेर् *bĕr*, a low wall or border (fem.)
फेल् *phĕl*, a crime, a trick (masc.)
हेर् *hĕr*, a ladder (fem.)
मेन् *mĕn*, measure thou.
सेन् *sĕn*, earn thou.
चेठ् *tsĕṭh*, pound thou.
सेथ् *sĕth*, a fit, epilepsy (fem.)
सेर् *sĕr*, a seer (masc.)
नेर् *nĕr*, go thou out, come thou out.
फेर् *phĕr*, turn thou.
मेल् *mĕl*, unite thou.
देर् *dĕr*, a heap.
गेन् *gĕn*, verses (obsolete).
चेन् *tsĕn*, take thou care.
सेठ् *sĕṭh*, be thou long.
मेठ् *mĕṭh*, be thou sweet.
शेंख् *çĕkh*, suspicion (masc.)

When the vowel *ĕ* commences a word it is pronounced, and may be written, *yĕ*: thus

एल् *ĕl* or येल् *yĕl*,	pronounced	*yĕl*, subjection (masc.)
एर् *ĕr* or येर् *yĕr*,		*yĕr*, wool (masc.)
एरुन् *ĕrun* or येरुन् *yĕrun*,		*yĕrun*, to sort (the warp.)

When *ĕ* is followed by *i*-, *u*-, or *ū*-*mātrā*, it becomes *ī*, *yŭ*, or *ī* respectively, and is so written. This occurs principally in the formation of the past tense of verbs. Thus, from the root फेर् *phĕr*, 'turn,' we get the masc. sg. past by adding *u*-*mātrā*. This gives us फ्यूर् *phyūr*^{u} (for * फेर् *phĕr*-^{u}). The fem. sg. is formed by adding *ū*-*mātrā*. Thus फीर् *phīr*$^{\bar{u}}$ (for *phĕr*-$^{\bar{u}}$). The masc. pl. is formed by adding *i*-*mātrā*; and we get फीरि *phīr*^{i} (for फेरि *phĕr*-^{i}). Finally the fem. pl. is formed by adding *y*^{a}, which does not affect the *ĕ*, and we get फेरे *phĕry*^{a} (*phĕrĕ*, see page 304). Again take feminine bases. The base सेर् *sĕr*-, a brick; its nom. sg. is सीर् *sīr*$^{\bar{u}}$ (for *sĕr*-$^{\bar{u}}$), but its nom. pl. सेरे *sĕry*^{a} (*sĕrĕ*). So खेत् *khĕt*-, a field, nom. sg. खीति *khīt*^{i} (for *khĕt*-^{i}), but nom. pl. खेत्य *khĕty*^{a} (*khĕtĕ*). Again take the masculine base चेन् *tsĕn*- a wall, before *u*-*mātrā* we have the nom. sg. च्यूनु *tsyŭn*^{u}. Before *i*-*mātrā* we have the nom. pl. चीनि *tsīn*^{i}, but the acc. sg. is चेनिस् *tsĕnis*, because the *ĕ* is not followed by any *mātrā*-vowel.

The vowel *ai* is pronounced as in Sanskrit and Hindī. When at the end of a word, it is indifferently written *ai* or *ay*. Thus रुपै or रुपय्. The following are examples.

रुपै *rupai*, a rupee (fem.)
सुरै *surai*, a goglet (fem.)
कोलै *kŏlai*, a wife (fem.)
मूलै *mūlai*, absolutely, root and branch.
खोनै *khŏnai*, elbows even (*niçcayārthē*) (fem.)
सुबहै *subahai*, very early in the morning.
छोपै *tshŏpai*, even silent (H. *cuphī*.)

फुलै *phulai*, a blossom (fem.)
बोनै *bŏnai*, from below, not I.
बुमै *bumai*, even eyebrows (fem.)
रुवै *ruwai*, I shall plant for thee.
वोनै *wŏnai*, I shall weave for thee.
सुवै *suwai*, I shall live for thee.
बोवै *bŏwai*, I shall be for thee.
वलै *walai*, I shall fold for thee.
सुवै *suwai*, I shall sew for thee.
कै *kai*, vomiting.

When *ai* is at the commencement or in the middle of a word it may optionally be pronounced as if it were the modified *ạ̄* (= *ŏ*). This is easily explained when it is remembered that *ạ̄* is derived from *ā* + *i*.

The following are examples.

ऐठ् *aiṭh*, eight, also आठ् *ạ̄ṭh* (*öṭh*.)
वैस् *wais*, age, also वाँस् *wạ̄s* (*wŏs*) (fem.)
मैल् *mail*, desire, also माल् *mạ̄l* (*mŏl*) (masc.)
गैल् *gail*, name of place, also गाल् *gạ̄l* (*göl*) (masc.)
सैद् *said*, a *saiyad*, also साद् *sạ̄d* (*söd*) (masc.)
मैन् *main*, a frog (word seldom used) (masc.)
ज़ैन् *zain*, a wooden bucket, also ज़ान् *zạ̄n* (*zön*) (fem.)
ऐब् *aib*, a defect, also आब् *ạ̄b* (*öb*) (masc.)
वैद् *waid*, name of caste, also वाद् *wạ̄d* (*wöd*), masc.
पैंथ् *paĭth*, a road, also पाँथ् *pạ̄th* (*pŏth*) or पान्थ् *pānth* (masc.)
ऐश् *aiç*, enjoyment, also आश् *ạ̄ç* (*öç*) (masc.)
वैर् *wair*, enmity, also वार् *wạ̄r* (*wör*) (masc.)
सैल् *sail*, a stroll, also साल् *sạ̄l* (*söl*) (masc.)
रैन् *rain*, name of caste, also रान् *rạ̄n* (*rön*) (masc.)
मैथ् *maith*, a corpse, also माथ् *mạ̄th* (*möth*) (masc.)

The vowel *ŏ* is usually pronounced as in Sanskrit or Hindī. The following are examples.

खोर् *khŏr*, a foot (masc.)
ज़ोर् *zŏr*, force (masc.)
मोर् *mŏr*, a peacock (masc.)
पोन् *pŏn*, a frost-crack in hand or foot, the anus (masc.)

पोश् *pŏç*, a flower (masc.)
बोश् *bŏç*, dearness (in price.) (masc.)
रोठ् *rŏṭh*, a kind of bread (masc.)
बोर् *bŏr*, burden (masc.)
सोर् *sŏr*, a hog (masc.)

चोर् *tsōr*, four.
तोल् *tōl*, weight (masc.)
लोल् *lōl*, desire (masc.)
बोल् *bōl*, fickleness (masc.)
मोठ् *mōṭh*, a kind of grain (masc.)
चोठ् *cōṭh*, a bruise (fem.) (rare).
गोस् *gōs*, I went.
प्योस् *pyōs*, I fell.
नियोव् *niyōv*, it was taken by us.
प्रोव् *prōv*, it was obtained by us.
लेख्योव् *lēkhyōv*, it was written by us.
ख्योस् *khyōs*, it was eaten of him by us.
च्योस् *cyōs*, it was drunk of him by us.
लिव्योव् *livyōv*, it was plastered by us.
मिल्योव् *milyōv*, it has been reconciled by us.

In the following trisyllabic words the sound of *ō* is broadened or drawled till it is nearly equivalent to the *au* in *cause*, owing to the *u* in the next syllable.

मोज़ूर् *mōzūrᵘ*, (*mōzūrr*) a cripple.
चोडुर् *tsōḍurᵘ*, (*tsōḍurr*) name of a village.
खोवुर् *khōwurᵘ*, (*khōwurr*) left, not right.
वोवुर् *wōwurᵘ*, (*wōᵤurr*) a weaver.
मोरुख् *mōrukh*, they have killed him.
चोरुख् *cōrukh*, they have tightened him.
वोलुख् *wōlukh*, they have brought down him.
पोवुख् *pōwukh*, they have thrown down him.
बोवुख् *bōwukh*, they have disclosed their wishes.
रोवुख् *rōwukh*, they have lost.
सोवुख् *sōwukh*, they have put to sleep.
चोवुख् *cōwukh*, they have given to drink.
सोरुख् *sōrukh*, they have collected.

Thse are all instances of an original *ā*, changed to *ō* by a following *u*, and the pronunciation is hence the same as that described on page 290.

When non-original *ō* is followed by *i-mātrā* it is pronounced like *ꜵ* (*ō*). It is also so written. The real fact is, however, that this *i-mātrā* only occurs in masc. plurals, in the singular of which the *ō* was followed by *u-mātrā*. Thus क्रोनु *krōnᵘ*, a relation, nom pl. क्रांनि *krānⁱ*. But this *ō* in *krōnᵤ* itself is not original. The base is क्रान् *krān-*, and owing to the following *u-mātrā*, the *ā* in the nominative becomes, and is written *ō*. See under *ā*, page 289. To say that *ō* followed by *i-mātrā* becomes *ꜵ*, is merely to repeat, less accurately, the statement that *ā* followed by *i-mātrā* becomes *ꜵ*. Further examples are therefore unnecessary. A number can be made from the list given on page 290. For the same reason, every *ō* followed by *u-mātrā* represents an original *ā*, for examples of which see page 290.

As regards *ō* followed by *ū-mātrā*, exactly the same remarks apply. Every instance is really one of *ā*, not *ō*, followed by *ū-mātrā*.

Thus take the base ब्रार् *brār-*, cat. Its masc. nom. is formed by adding *u-mātrā*, and is therefore ब्रोर् *brōr*^{u}. Its masc. pl. is formed by adding *i-mātrā* and is therefore ब्रारि *brār*^{i}. So also by adding *ū-mātrā*, to form the feminine, we have ब्रार् *brār*$^{\bar{u}}$, pronounced *brörr*, and so many others. It is unnecessary to give further examples, as sufficient will be found on page 290.

On the other hand, an original *ō* followed by *any* mātrā-vowel becomes *ū*. Thus—

Followed by *i-mātrā.*

The base पोथ्- *pōth-* (fem.), makes its Nom Sg. पुथि *pūth*^{i} (for *pōth*^{u}) (pr. *pu*^{i}*th*^{i}), a book. But the Nom. Pl. is पोथ्य *pōthy*^{a} (*pōthĕ*). So also Dat. Sg. पोथि *pōthi* (pr. *pō*^{i}*thi*), in which the final *i* is fully-pronounced.

Base बोल् *bōl-*, speech ; nom. sg. बुलि *būl*^{i} (for *bōl-*^{i}) (pr. *bū*^{i}*l*^{i})

The √ बोज् *bōz*, hear, makes the Pl. Masc. of its Past tense बुज़ि *būz*^{i} (for *bōz-*^{i}) (pr. *bū*^{i}*z*^{i}), but Pl. Fem. बोज् *bōz*^{a}. The vowel ^{a} is not a *mātrā*-vowel.

√ रोज् *rōz*, remain, Past tense, Pl. Masc. रुदि *rūd*^{i} (for *rōz-*^{i}) (pr. *rū*^{i}*d*^{i}).

Followed by *u-mātrā*

This only occurs in the case of verbs, *e.g.*

√ बोज् *bōz*, hear, Past tense, Sg. Masc. बुज़ु *būz*^{u} (for *bōz-*^{u}) (pr. *būzz*)
√ रोज् *rōz*, remain „ „ रुदु *rūd*^{u} (for *rōz-*^{u})(pl. *rūdd*)
√ दोन *dōn*, card wool, „ दुनु *dūn*^{u} (for *dōn-*^{u})(pr. *dūnn*)

Followed by *ū-mātrā.*

Base कोर् *kōr*—, a girl. Nom. sg. (formed by adding *ū-mātrā*) कुर् *kūr*$^{\bar{u}}$ (for *kōr-*$^{\bar{u}}$) ; but nom. pl. कोर्य *kōry*^{a} (*kōrĕ*).

Base लोर् *lōr-*, a stick. Nom. sg. लुर् *lūr*$^{\bar{u}}$ (for *lōr-*$^{\bar{u}}$)

√ बोज् *bōz*, hear, Past tense, Fem. sg. (formed by adding *ū-mātrā*) बुज् *būz*$^{\bar{u}}$ (for *bōz-*$^{\bar{u}}$) (pr. *būzz*).

√ रोज् *rōz* remain, Past tense, Fem. sg., रुज् *rūz*$^{\bar{u}}$ (for *rōz-*$^{\bar{u}}$), (pr. *rūzz*).

√ दोन् *dōn*, card, Past tense, fem. sg. दुन् *dūn*$^{\bar{u}}$ (for *dōn-*$^{\bar{u}}$), (pr. *dūnn*).

It will thus be seen, that *ō* never appears followed by *i-mātrā*, or by *ū-mātrā*, and that when it appears followed by *u-mātrā* it is not original, but represents an original *ā*.

The pronunciation of *au* is the same as in Skr. and Hindī.

गौव् *gauv*, he went.	ख्यौव् *khyauv*, we ate.
प्यौव् *pyauv*, he fell.	म्यौव् *myauv*, mew of a cat.
च्यौव् *cyauv*, we drank.	

And many other past tenses.

When the syllable *ya* follows a consonant, the *y* is as a rule fully pronounced, as in the following examples. Elmslie, in his dictionary, and Wade represent *ya* by *ĕ* (short), but my paṇḍit assures me that the *y* in the following words is quite fully pronounced. Mr. Hinton Knowles' Musalmān Munshī pronounces all these words with *ĕ*. The difference is probably one of religion: and, as 90 per cent. of Kāçmīrīs are Musalmāns, it would be more generally correct to spell *all* there words with *ĕ*. As, however, this article is written with more special reference to the Hindū grammar of Īçwara Kaula, and the words are written in the Nāgarī character. I write them as follows:—

प्यख् *pyăkh*, thou wilt fall.	ख्यस् *khyas*, eat for him.
द्यद् *dyad*, mother.	व्यथ् *vyăth*, name of the river Jhelum.
म्यस् *myas*, a water-root.	ख्यथ् *khyăth*, having eaten.
च्यस् *cyas*, drink for him.	र्यख् *ryăkh*, a fowl's dung.
च्यथ् *cyăth*, thought.	छ्यख् *chyăkh*, thou art (fem.)
द्यख् *dyăkh*, angry.	ख्यख् *khyăkh*, thou wilt eat.
च्यद् *tsyad*, patience.	द्यल् *dyal*, skin, peel.
च्यल् *tsyal*, squeezing, shampooing.	स्यल् *syal*, cream of tyre.
ह्यल् *hyal*, dirt used as manure.	ड्यक *ḍyak*^{a}, forehead.
ल्यद् *lyad*, horse-dung.	
व्यस् *vyas*, a woman's confidante.	

In the following, the *ya* is pronounced *yu*, owing to the influence of the following *u-mātrā*.

ल्योलु	*lyọl*^{u}, pronounced	*lyull*, a vessel for cooking rice.
ब्योनु	*byọnn*^{u},	*byunn*, separate.
प्योलु	*pyọl*^{u},	*pyull*, a testicle.
द्योलु	*dyọl*^{u},	*dyull*, a soft grass used for packing and matting
च्योलु	*tsyọl*^{u},	*tsyull*, squeezed.
ट्योठु	*ṭyọṭh*^{u},	*ṭyuṭṭh*, bitter.
ह्योलु	*hyọl*^{u},	*hyull*, a lake weed.
छ्योटु	*tshyọṭ*^{u},	*tshyuṭṭ*, leavings.
प्योनु	*pyọn*^{u},	*pyunn*, to fall, or the act of falling.
ख्योनु	*khyọn*^{u},	*khyunn*, to eat, or the act of eating.

ज़्युन् *zyąn*^{u}, pronounced *zyunn*, to be born, the act of being born.

च्युन् *cyąn*^{u}, *cyunn*, to drink, the act of drinking.

So,—

थ्यून् *tsyūn*^{u}, *tsyūnn*, a pillar.

म्यून् *myūn*^{u}, *myūnn*, measured.

When, however, *ya* is followed by *i* or *y* in the next syllable, it is pronounced as a short *ĕ*, (as in *ebb*), and as such I write it in transliteration. So also a final *ya* (y^{a}) is pronounced *ĕ*. In each case a very faint *y* sound is audible before the *ĕ* when the speaker speaks slowly. Thus, it would be more absolutely accurate to represent ल्यलिस् by *lyĕlis*, than by *lĕlis*, but the *y* may be omitted for practical purposes. A final ञ *ña* is treated as if it was *ny*^{a}, and is pronounced *ñĕ* or *nyĕ*. The following are examples:—

ल्यलिस् *lĕlis*, a vessel for cooking rice (acc. sg.) (masc.)

ल्यलि *lĕl*^{i}, do. nom. pl. Cf. *lyąl*^{u} in the preceding list.

ब्यनि *bĕnn*^{i}, separate (masc. pl.)

प्यलिस् *pĕlis*, a testicle (acc. sg.) (masc.)

प्यलि *pĕl*^{i}, do. nom. pl.

द्यलि *dĕl*^{i}, pl. of *dyąl*^{u} (*dyoll*) in the last list.

छ्यलि *tsĕl*^{i}, squeezed (masc. pl.)

ट्यठि *ṭĕṭh*^{i}, bitter (masc. pl.)

ह्यलि *hĕl*^{i}, lake-weeds (masc. pl.)

छ्यति *tshĕti*, leavings.

पच्य *pacĕ*, tablets (fem. pl.)

पोथ्य *pōthĕ*, books (fem. pl.)

करे *karĕ*, they (fem.) were made by us.

तुह्य *tŏhĕ*, you (obl. pl.)

So also ब्यञ *byañ*^{a}, pr. *bĕñyĕ*, a sister.

When the *ya* in this case commences a word, it is pronounced *yĕ*. Thus यमिस *yĕmis*, whom.

As regards *wa*. I have already pointed out, under the head of *u* page 294, that it is often pronounced as *ŏ* (short). This is however, complicated when *u-mātrā* follows, in which case *wa* is pronounced like *a* before *u-mātrā*, the sound of which I transliterate by *o*. It is almost identical with the vowel in the Irish pronunciation of "gun." If, however, the *wa* is followed by *i-mātrā*, the *wa* is pronounced *ŏ* as usual.

ग्वंन् *gŏn*^{u}, pronounced *gonn*, a stack (masc.)

ग्वंनि *gŏn*^{i}, *gŏ*^{i}*n*^{i}, stacks.

द्वंब् *dŏb*^{u}, *dobb*, a washerman (masc.)

द्वंबि *dŏb*^{i}, *dŏ*^{i}*b*^{i}, washermen.

व्वंथ् *wŏth*^{u}, *wotth*, arisen (masc. sg.)

व्वंथि *wŏth*^{i}, *wŏ*^{i}*th*^{i}, arisen (masc. pl.)

हुख *hokh*^{u}, *hokkh*, dry (masc.)

कुब *kob*^{u}, *kobb*, a hunchback (masc.)

छुप *tshop*^{u}, *tshopp*, silent.

हुत *hot*^{u}, *hott*, spoiled (masc.)

लुत *lot*^{u}, *lott*, light, not heavy (masc.)

हुद *hod*^{u}, *hodd*, plain boiled rice (masc.)

तुहि *toh*^{i}, *tö̆h*^{i}, ye (nom. pl.)

फुत *phot*^{u}, *phott*, a basket (masc.)

The fem. of छुप *tshop*^{u} is छुप *tshöp*^{ü}, and is pronounced *tshüpp*, and so for the others.

From the Journal, Asiatic Society of Bengal, Vol. LXVI, Part I, No. 3,
1897, p. 180.

On the Kāçmīrī Consonantal System.— *By* G. A. Grierson, C.I.E., Ph.D., I.C.S.

[Read May, 1897.]

The Kāçmīrī consonantal system is based on that in use in most Aryan languages in India. It can be well represented by the Çāradā Alphabet or by its congener the Dēvanāgarī.

Kāçmīrī has discarded the aspirated soft consonants, *gh*, *jh*, *ḍh*, *dh*, *bh*. When such sounds originally occurred the corresponding unaspirated sounds are substituted. Thus we have Kāçmīrī गेरुन् *gērun* to surround, but Hindi घेरना *ghēr'nā*; Kç. बुवि *bŏvi*, he will be, corresponding to the Sanskrit भवति *bhavati*.

Kāçmīrī has developed a new class of modified palatal consonants, *viz.*, च़ *tsa*, छ़ *tsha*, ज़ *za*, and ञ़ *ña*. These are mostly direct modifications of original palatals. Thus—

Skr.	Kç.
चोरः *cōraḥ*, a thief.	च़ूर् *tsūr*, a thief.
चलति *calati*, he goes.	च़लि *tsali*, he will go.
छलयति *chalayati*, he deceives.	छ़लि *tshali*, he will deceive.
जलम् *jalam*, water.	ज़ल् *zal*, water.

So also we have the Skr. उत्पद्यते *utpadyatē*; Pr. उप्पज्जइ *uppajjai*; from which is derived the Kç. 3rd pers. fut. व्वपज़ि *wŏpazi*, he will be born.

These modified palatals are also developed as secondary formations from dentals, followed by *ū-mātrā*, or by the semi-vowel *y*. Both these sounds are palatal, for *ū-mātrā* represents an original long *ī*.

Thus, take the base रात् *rāt-*, night. Its nominative plural is formed by adding *ū-mātrā*, and is therefore राच़् *rāts*ᵘ.

Again take the root कत् *kat-*, spin. The feminine singular of its Past Participle is formed by adding *ū-mātrā*, and is कच़् *kats*ᵘ. Its

Aorist Participle is formed by adding योव् *yöv*, and is कच़ोव् *katsöv*, the *y* first changing the *t* to *ts*, and then being elided under a subsequent rule.

Again take the adjective तत़ु *tat^{u}*, hot. Its abstract noun is formed by substituting इ + अर् *i* + *ar*, *i.e.*, यर् *yar*, for the final उ ^{u}. We thus get तच़र् *tatsar*, heat, the *y* being elided as in the last case.

Similarly we have the base कथ् *köth-*, a hank, Nom. Pl. क्वछ़ *kwatsh^{a}*; the root वथ *wöth*, arise, Past Part., Fem. Sg., व्वछ़ *wwatsh^{a}*, Aorist Participle वछ़ोव् *wötshöv*; the adj. वथु *wath^{u}*, open, वछ़र् *watshar*, openness.

So, गन्ड् *grand-*, a counting: Nom. Pl. ग्रज़ *grans^{a}*; √ लड् *lad-*, build, Past Part., Fem. Sg., लज़ *las^{a}*, Aorist Part. लज़ोव् *lasöv*; थदु *thad^{u}*, high, थज़र् *thasar*, height.

Again ईरन् *yīran-*, an anvil: Nom. Pl. ईरञ *yīrañ^{a}* (usually written ईरञ् *yīrañ*); √ रन् *ran-*, cook, Past Part., Fem. Sg., रञ *rañ^{a}* (usually written रञ् *rañ*); तनु *tan^{u}*, thin, तञर् *tañar*, thinness.

Note that as in the last instances, a final ञ *ñ^{a}*, is usually *written* ञ् *ñ*, but this does not affect the pronunciation.

Note, also, that the letter य् *y* is elided whenever it immediately follows one of these modified palatals. It is, however, retained in a few verbs. These are given in my List of Kāçmīrī verbs (*J. A. S. B.*, for 1896, p. 308).

Besides the above, other instances of Palatalization occur. Thus,—

(1) Cerebrals become Palatals before इ *i*, य् *y*, but not before *i-mātrā*, or *ū-mātrā*. Thus—

Base पट् *paṭ-*, a tablet: Nom. Sg. Fem., formed by adding *ū-mātrā*, पट़ *paṭ^{a}*, Ag. Sg. formed by adding इ *i* पचि *paci*; Nom. Pl. formed by adding य *y^{a}*, पच्य *pacĕ*.

Base काठ् *kāṭh-*, a stalk: Nom. Sg. Fem., काठ़ *kāṭh^{a}*; Ag. Sg. काछि *kāchi*; Nom. Pl. काछ्य *kāchĕ*.

Base बड् *baḍ-*, great: Nom. Pl., formed by adding *i-mātrā*, बडि *baḍ^{i}* Nom. Sg. Fem. बड़ *baḍ^{a}*; Ag. Sg. Fem. बजि *baji*; Nom. Pl. Fem. बज्य *bajĕ*.

Again मोटु *möṭ^{u}*, fat: Nom. Pl. Masc. म्वटि *mwaṭ^{i}*; मोच्यर् *möcyar* fatness: द्रौठु *drŏthᵘ*, hard; द्राच्यर् *drāchyar*, hardness: मोंडु *moṇḍᵘ*, blunt; मञ्ज्यार् *mŏñjyar*, bluntness.

Again, √ फट *phaṭ*, split: Aorist Participle, फच्योव् *phacyŏv*, but Past Part., Fem. Sg., फटॖ *phọṭᵃ*; Nom. Pl. Masc. फटि *phọṭⁱ*.

मठ् *maṭh-*, forgotten: Aorist Participle, मञ्च्योव् *manchyŏv*; but Past Part., Fem. Sg., मठॖ *mọṭhᵃ*; Nom. Pl. Masc. मठि *mọṭhⁱ*.

√ गंड *gaṇḍ*, bind: Aorist Participle, गञ्ज्योव् *gañjyŏv*; but Past Part., Fem. Sg., गंडॖ *gọṇḍᵃ*; Nom. Pl. Masc. गंडि *gọṇḍⁱ*.

(2) Gutturals become Palatals before *ü-mātrā*, and य *y*, but not before इ *i* or *i-mātrā*.

Thus, बटुकु *baṭukᵘ*, a duck: Fem. Sg., formed by changing *u-mātrā* to *ü-mātrā*, बटॖचॖ *baṭᵘcᵃ*.

होखु *hŏkhᵘ*, dry: Fem. होछॖ *hwọchᵃ*; but Ag. Sg. Masc. होखि *hwọkhⁱ*:

ड्यूगु *ḍyūgᵘ*, a ball of thread: Fem. डीजॖ *ḍījᵃ*; Ag. Sg. Masc. डीगि *ḍīgⁱ*.

Again न्युकु *nyukᵘ*, little: Abstract Noun, formed by adding यर् *yar*, निच्यर् *nicyar*, littleness. त्रुखु *tryukhᵘ*, clever; त्रिछ्यर् *trichyar* cleverness:

स्रोगु *srogᵘ*, cheap, स्रोज्यर् *srŏjyar*, cheapness.

Again, √ थक *thak*, be weary: Past Part., Fem. Sg., थचॖ *thọcᵃ*; Aorist Part. थच्योव् *thọcyŏv*; but Past Part., Masc. Pl., formed by adding इ *ⁱ*, थकि *thọkⁱ*.

√ लेख *lĕkh*, write: Past Part., Fem. Sg. लीछॖ *lichᵃ*; Aorist Part. लेछ्योव् *lĕchyŏv*; Past Part., Masc. Pl. लीखि *likhⁱ*.

√ दग *dag*, pound: Past Part., Fem. Sg. दजॖ *dọjᵃ*; Aorist Part. दज्योव् *dajyŏv*; Past Part., Masc. Pl. दगि *dọgⁱ*.

Exceptions are

च़ोकु *tsokᵘ*, sour: Fem. च़ोकॖ *tswọkᵃ* (vi, 10); च़ोक्यर् *tsŏkyar*, sourness (iv, 48).[1]

खूंखु *khūkhᵘ*, speaking through the nose, fem. खूंखॖ *khūkhᵃ* (vi, 10) Abstr. Noun खूंख्यर् *khūkhyar* (iv, 48).

(3) ल *l* becomes ज *j*, when followed by *ü-mātrā*, or य *y*. Thus,

[1] These and similar references are to the Kāçmīraçabdāmṛta of Īçvara-kaula.

वाल् *wāl*, a serpent's hole: Nom. Pl. वाज् *wāj*ᵃ.

वोलु *wōl*ᵘ, a large ring: Fem. वाजु *wāj*ᵃ, a small ring.

कुमुलु *kumul*ᵘ, delicate: कुमुज्यार् *kumujyār*, delicateness.

वुलु *wūl*ᵘ, fickle: वोज्यर् *wōjyar*, fickleness.

√ पाल *pāl*, protect: Past Part., Fem. Sg. पाज *pāj*ᵃ. But Masc. Pl. पालि *pāl*.

(4) ह् *h*, becomes श *ç* before ü-mātrā, or य् *y*. Thus,—

बाह् *bāh*, the twelfth lunar day: Nom. Pl. बाश् *bāç*ᵃ; पाह् *pāh*, ordure: Nom. Pl. पाश् *pāç*ᵃ.

ह्युहु *hyuh*ᵘ, like: Fem. Sg. हिशु *hiç*ᵃ; Abstr. Noun हिश्यर् *hiçyar*, similarity. च्होहु *tsōh*ᵘ, acrid; Fem. Sg. च्हाश् *tsāç*ᵘ; Abstr. Noun च्हाश्यर् *tsāçyar*.

√ पिह *pih*, pound: Past Part., Fem. Sg. पिशु *piç*ᵃ; Aorist Part. पिश्योव् *piçyōv*; but Past Part., Masc. Pl. पिहि *pihi*.

(5) स् *s* shows a tendency to become छ् *tsh* before ü-mātrā or य् *y*. In such a case, also, the य *y* is as usual elided. Thus,—

कुसु *kūs*ᵘ, youngest: Fem. Sg. कुसु *kūs*ᵃ, or कुछु *kūtsh*ᵃ; Abstr. Noun. कैसर् *kaīsar*, or कैछर् *kaītshar*.

√ बस *bas*, dwell: Past Part., Fem. Sg. बसु *bąs*ᵃ, or (sometimes) बछु *bątsh*ᵃ; Fem. Pl. बस *bas*ᵉ (for बस्य *basē*) or (rarely) बछु *batsh*ᵉ.

√ लोस *lōs*, be weary: Past Part., Fem. Sg. लुसु *lūs*ᵃ or लुछु *lūtsh*ᵃ. Fem. Pl. लोस *lōs*ᵉ or लोछ् *lotsh*ᵉ.

Note that य् *y* is usually elided after स् *s*. This is specially the case in transitive verbs. A list of verbs in which य् *y* is not elided is given in my article on Kāçmīrī verbs already alluded to, J. A. S. B. for 1896, p. 308.

Finally, in Kāçmīrī, no word can end in an unaspirated hard consonant. If an unaspirated hard consonant falls at the end of a word, it is aspirated. Thus,—

Base	त्रक् *trak*, a certain grain measure,	Nom. Sg.	त्रख् *trākh*.
„	अक् *ak*, one,	„	अख् *ākh*.
„	काच् *kāts*, glass,	„	काछ् *kātsh*.
„	कट् *kaṭ*, a ram,	„	कठ् *kāṭh*.
„	हत् *hat*, a hundred,	„	हथ् *hāth*.

Base रात् *rāt*, night, Nom. Sg. राथ् *rāth*.

" कर् + त् *kąr*ᵘ+*t*, done by thee, करथ् *kąruth*.

" ताप् *tāp*, heat, Nom. Sg. ताफ् *tāph*.

This aspiration does not occur if a final त् *t*, or च़् *ts* forms part of a conjunct consonant. Thus,—

Base सच़् *s*ᵃ*ts*, a tailor, Nom. Sg. सच़् *s*ᵃ*ts*.

" मस्त् *mast*, hair, " मस्त् *mast*.

This rule is commonly neglected when writing in the Persian character, in which, for instance करथ् *kąruth* is represented by کرت.

From the Journal, Asiatic Society of Bengal, Vol. LXVII, Part I, No. 1, 1898, p. 29.

On the Kāçmīrī Noun.—*By* G. A. Grierson, C.I.E., Ph.D., I.C.S.

[Read December, 1897.]

A. Gender.

Kāçmīrī nouns are either masculine or feminine. There is no neuter gender in the language. In the case of pronouns, however, there is a relic of a neuter gender, each pronoun having three forms, one, for male living beings, another, for female living beings, and a third for things without life, whether their grammatical gender is masculine or feminine.

The sixth part of Īçvara-kaula's *Kaçmīraçabdāmṛta* deals with gender. The following rules are abstracted from it.

The feminine gender is used for the following purposes (vi. 18.) :—

(*a.*) To denote the female sex, *e.g.*

Masc.	*Fem.*
मंगुर् *mŏṅgur*^{u}, a male kid	मंगॖर् *mŏṅg*^{e}*r*^{e} a female kid.
वछु *wọtsh*^{u}, a male calf	वछॖर् *watsh*^{e}*r*, a female calf.

(*b.*) To denote smallness, *e.g.*

कटुर् *katur*^{u}, a large potsherd	कटॖर् *kat*^{e}*r*^{e}, a small potsherd.

(*d.*) To denote artificiality, *e.g.*

टास् *tās*^{e}, a cough	टाख्यर् *tākh*^{e}*r*, an artificial cough, a "hem."

(*e.*) To denote similarity, *e.g.*

कोथ *koth*^{u}, a load	कॖछ *kwọtsh*^{e}, a bag.
तटुर् *tatur*^{u}, smarting (of a wound)	तटॖर् *tat*^{e}*r*^{e}, the pain felt by an angry person.

(*f.*) To denote special meanings, *e.g.*

नर् *nọr*^{u}, a sleeve	नॖर् *nọr*^{e}, an arm.
खर् *khọr*^{u}, having a scald-head	खॖर् *khọr*^{e}, the disease of scald-head.

1. Words signifying human castes or professions, form their feminines by adding बाय् *bāy* (vi. 2) [to the oblique form used in the case of compound words. *Vide post,* under that head]. [The word then means 'wife of so and so'].

Thus :—

बट *baṭᵉ*, a Brāhmaṇ — बटबाय् *baṭabāy*, a wife of a Brāhmaṇ.

दर् *dar*, name of a Brāhmaṇ caste — दरबाय् *darabāy*, wife of a *Dar*.

कोल् *kaul*, name of a Brāhmaṇ caste — कोलबाय् *kaulabāy*, wife of a *Kaul*.

सोनर् *sönᵃr*, a goldsmith — सोनर्बाय् *sönᵃrbāy*, the wife of a goldsmith.

खार् *khār*, a blacksmith — खारबाय् *khārabāy*, a blacksmith's wife.

We can only use this for human beings. Thus, कोतर्बाय् *kötarbāy* means the wife of a man of the *kötar* caste, and not the wife of a pigeon (कोतुर् *kötur*), the feminine of which is कोतृर् *kötᵉrᵃ*.

Cf. No. 9.

2. When respect is not intended कोलय् *kölay* is substituted for बाय् *bāy* in the meaning of wife (vi. 3). Thus :—

बटकोलय् *baṭakölay ;*

So from

छान् *chān*, a carpenter — छानकोलय् *chānakölay*, the wife of a carpenter.

Cf. No. 9.

(3) All words ending in *u-mātrā*, change it to *ū-mātrā* in the feminine (vi. 4), thus :—

पट *pɑṭᵘ*, a board — पट *pɑṭᵘ*, a tablet.

मोट *moṭᵘ*, fat — मोट *mwɑṭᵘ*.

गर् *gɑrᵘ*, hard — गर् *gɑrᵘ*.

गुर् *gurᵘ*, a horse — गुर् *gurᵘ* a mare.

दुब् *dobᵘ*, a washerman — दुब् *dwɑbᵘ*, a woman who does washing. [Thus जान दुब् *Jānᵃ dwɑbᵘ*, Jāna the washerwoman. A washerman's wife would be दुबिबाय् *dwɑbⁱbāy*.]

खर् *khąrᵘ*, having a scald head	खर् *khąrᶟ*, the disease of scald-head.
गूर् *gūrᵘ*, a cowherd	गूर् *gūrᶟ*, as in ज़ून गूर् *Zūnᵃ gūrᶟ*, Zūna the cowherdess. A cowherd's wife is गूरिबाय् *gūrⁱbāy*.

Note also words like—

कटुर् *katurᵘ*, a large potsherd	कत्र् *katᵊrᶟ*, a small ditto.
मोंगुर् *moŋgurᵘ*, a male kid	मोंग्र् *mȫŋgᵊrᶟ* a female kid.
टटुर् *taturᵘ*, smarting of a wound	टत्र् *tatᵊrᶟ* the pain of anger.
वोवुर् *wöwurᵘ*, a weaver	वोव्र् *wöwᵊrᶟ*, a woman weaver. [A weaver's wife is वोवुरिबाय् *wöwᵊrⁱbāy*.]
गगुर् *gagurᵘ*, a rat	गग्र् *gagᵊrᶟ*.

As in the five last examples, all words of three or more syllables omit a penultimate उ *u*, when forming the feminine (vi. 8). Cf. No. 4*a*.

The word छोट *tshoṭᵘ*, small, makes its feminine छ्वट *tshwąṭᶟ*, or छ्वटिञ् *tshwaṭiñ* (Cf. No. 8.) The latter is only used with reference to human beings. The former is universally used (vi. 5), thus:—छ्वट (or छ्वटिञ्) कूर् *tshwąṭᶟ* (or *tshwaṭiñ*) *kūrᶟ*, a small girl.

So also we have खर् *khar*, an ass, feminine खर् *khąrᶟ* or खरिञ् *khariñ* (see No. 8).

(4). Words ending in ल् *lᵘ*, are subject to the following rules (vi. 7, 8, 29).

(*a*) Words of three syllables and over, ending in *ulᵘ* change *ulᵘ* to *ᵊjᶟ*, thus:—

	Feminine.
गाटुल् *gāṭulᵘ*, clever	गाटज् *gāṭᵊjᶟ*.
फुटुल् *phuṭulᵘ*, a bundle of things tied up in a shawl, &c.	फुटज् *phuṭᵊjᶟ* a small bundle.
चकुल् *tsakulᵘ*, circular	चकज् *tsakᵊjᶟ*.
पटुल् *paṭulᵘ*, a raft	पटज् *paṭᵊjᶟ*, a mat.
ग्वगुल् *gögulᵘ*, a big turnip	ग्वगज् *gögᵊjᶟ*, an ordinary turnip.
चोटुल् *tsöṭulᵘ*, a sodomite	चोटज् *tsöṭᵊjᶟ*.

वाटुलु *wātul*^{u}, a low-caste man	वातृज *wāt*^{y}*j*^{a}.
ठठुलु *ṭaṭhul*^{u}, a wooden vessel	ठठृज *ṭaṭh*^{y}*j*^{a}, a small ditto.

(*b*) Words ending in the suffix वोलु *wōl*^{u}, form the feminine in वाज्यन् *wājĕñ*, thus:—

गर्वोलु *gar*^{a}*wōl*^{u}, a house-holder	गर्वाज्यन् *gar*^{a}*wājĕñ*.

The word वोलु *wōl*^{u}, 'a ring' is not formed with this suffix.

(*c*) Other words in *l*^{u} form their feminines in ज *j*^{a}, thus:—

गूलु *gūl*^{u}, a kernel	गूज *gūj*^{a}, a small ditto.

Words in ओलु *ōl*^{u} change ओ *ō* to आ *ạ̄*, thus:—

वोलु *wōl*^{u}, a small ring	वाज *wạ̄j*^{a}, a small ditto.
मोलु *mōl*^{u}, a father	माज *mạ̄j*^{a}, a mother.
त्रोलु *tsrōl*^{u}, watchman	त्राज *tsrạ̄j*^{a}.

Irregular is—

डुलु *ḍul*^{u}, a large bowl	डुलिजि *ḍulij*^{i}, a small ditto.

(5) Words ending in कु *k*^{u}, खु *kh*^{u}, गु *g*^{u} (and also in क् *k*, ख् *kh*, ग् *g*; but no examples are given) change क् *k* to च् *c*, ख् *kh* to छ् *ch*, and ग् *g* to ज् *j* (vi. 9), thus:—

	Feminine.
बटुकु *batuk*^{u}, a drake	बटृच *bat*^{y}*c*^{a}, a duck.
हॊखु *hokh*^{u}, dry	हॊछ *hwạch*^{a}.
ड्यूंगु *dyūg*^{u}, a ball of string	डींज *dīj*^{a}, a small ditto.

The vowel changes are those prescribed in the declension of nouns. Içvara-kaula occasionally spells बटृच *bat*^{y}*c*^{a} बटृच् *bat*^{y}*c*.

Exceptions are (vi. 10.)

खूंखु *khūkh*^{u}, one who speaks through his nose.	खूंछ *khūkh*^{a}.
च़ॊकु *tsok*^{u}, sour	च़ॊक *tswạk*^{a}.

(6) Words in त *t*, थ *th*, द *d*, or न *n*, with or without *u-mātrā*, change त् *t* to च़् *ts*, थ् *th* to छ़् *tsh*, द् *d* to ज़् *z*, and न् *n* to ञ् *ñ*. As usual, *ū-mātrā* is omitted, in writing, after ञ् *ñ*, (vi. 11.)

मतु *mąt*ᵘ, mad	मचू *mąts*ᵘ.
कथु *koth*ᵘ, a load	कछू *kwǫtsh*ᵘ, a bag.
अवदु *wŏrud*ᵘ, a second husband of one woman.	अवरज़ू *wŏr*ᵊ*z*ᵘ, a woman who has married twice.
वन् *wan*, a forest	वञ् *wąñ*, a grove.
गान् *gān*, a brothel-keeper	गाञ् *gąñ*, a prostitute.
छान् *chān*, a carpenter	छाञ् *chąñ*, as in ज़ून छाञ् *Zūn*ᵉ *chąñ*, Zūna the carpentress.
हूनु *hūn*ᵘ, a dog	हूञ् *hūñ*, a bitch.

(7) Certain words form their feminines by adding र् *r* with various other changes, thus :—

	Feminine.
कंग् *kang*, a brazier	कांगर् *kāg*ᵉ*r*, a small ditto (vi. 12.)
च़ास् *tsās*, a cough	च़ाखर् *tsākh*ᵉ*r*, an artificial cough, (vi. 13.)
त्रख् *trākh*, a certain grain weight	त्रकर् *trak*ᵉ*r*, a scale, (vi. 14.)
मंडु *mond*ᵘ, a log	मंडर् *mŏnd*ᵉ*r*, a small log (vi. 15.)
फतु *phot*ᵘ, a basket	फतुर् *phŏt*ᵘ*r*, a small basket (vi. 16.)
लटु *laṭ*ᵘ, a tail	लटर् *laṭ*ᵉ*r*, a small tail, कुटि लटर् *kūṭ*ⁱ *laṭ*ᵉ*r*, a piece of wood cut off the end of a beam.
वछु *wątsh*ᵘ, a male calf	वछर् *watsh*ᵉ*r*, a female calf.

(8) Certain words form their feminines in इञ् *iñ* (vi. 16–27), thus :—

	Feminine.
हस्तु *hąst*ᵘ, an elephant	हस्तिञ् *hastiñ*.
काव् *kāv*, a crow	काविञ् *kąviñ*.
नाग् *nāg*, a snake.	नागिञ् *nągiñ*.

वूँड् *wūṭh*, a camel	वूँडिञ् *wūṭiñ*.
खर् *khar*, an ass	खरिञ् *khariñ*, (see No. 3) or खर् *khar*ᵃ.

And so other words signifying animals.

व्यठ *vyaṭh*ᵘ, stout	व्यठ *vyaṭh*ᵉ, stout, but वठिञ् *rĕṭhiñ* (in a bad sense) stout, fat.
गूठ *gūṭh*ᵘ, stupid	गूठिञ् *gūṭhiñ*.
बट *bŏṭ*ᵘ, a Tibetan	बटिञ् *bŏṭiñ*, (बुटिञ् *buṭiñ*), or बटबाय् *bŏṭabāy*, a Tibetan woman.
बुगिय् *bugiy*, a master	बुगिञ् *bugiñ*, a mistress.
ज़ल् *zal*, water	ज़लिञ् *zaliñ*, sweat of the feet.
गर *gar*ᵘ, a house	गरिञ् *gariñ*, a good mistress of a house; distinct from गरवाजञ् *gar*ᵘ*wājĕñ*, a female householder (see No. 9.)
दुब *dob*ᵘ, a washerman	द्वबिञ् *dwabiñ*, a washerman's club, but द्वबिबाय् *dwab*ⁱ*bāy*, a washerman's wife.

(9) Certain nouns take अञ् *añ* in the feminine (vi. 28.)

(*a*) Names of castes.

Note that बाय् *bāy* (No. 1) is used as a feminine of respect; कोकय् *kŏkay* (No. 2) is only used of a married woman, when spoken of in connexion with her husband, and without respect; while अञ् *añ* is a general feminine, without signifying respect, thus:—

बट *baṭ*ᵘ, a Brāhman,	बटञ् *baṭañ*, a woman of that caste.
मुसल्मान् *musalmān*, a Musalmān	मुसल्मानञ् *musalmānañ*, a Muhammadan woman.
हाकग्राख् *hākagrākh*, a vegetable seller.	हाकग्राकञ् *hākagrākañ*.
वोञ *wōñ*ᵘ, a shopkeeper	वाञ्यञ् *wāñyañ*, a female shopkeeper.

So also all nouns with the suffix वोलु *wōl*^{u}, (vi. 29) as given in No. 4 (*b*). Thus:—

गर्वोलु *gar*^{a}*wōl*^{u}, a householder गर्वाज्यन् *gar*^{a}*wājĕñ*.

See also No. 8.

(10) If the masculine word ends in र् then the suffix is यन् *ĕñ* (vi. 30), thus (see Secondary Suffixes No. 39.)

Feminine.

सालुर् *sāl*^{a}*r*, a member of bridegroom's party. सालुर्यन् *sāl*^{a}*rĕñ*.

पहर् *pŏhar*, an invited guest पहर्यन् *pŏharĕñ*.

रंगुर् *rang*^{a}*r*, a dyer रंगुर्यन् *rang*^{a}*rĕñ*.

सनुर् *sŏn*^{a}*r*, a goldsmith सनुर्यन् *sŏn*^{a}*rĕñ*.

दांदुर् *dānd*^{a}*r*, a vegetable seller दांदुर्यन् *dānd*^{a}*rĕñ*.

कांदुर् *kānd*^{a}*r*, a baker कांदुर्यन् *kānd*^{a}*rĕñ*.

So also we have—

सोंमु *soñ*^{u}, a co-father-in-law सञ्यन् *sŏñĕñ*.

महाराजु *mahārāz*^{a}, a great king महार्यन् *mahārĕñ*, the wife of a great king, a bride.

राजु *rāz*^{a}, a king राज्यर्यन् *rājyarĕñ*, a queen.

(11) Finally we have डञ् *ḍñ* in the following (vi. 31):—

पंडित् *panḍith*, a pandit पंडित्डञ् *panḍ*^{i}*tḍñ*.

गुजुरु *gujur*^{u}, a forester गुजर्डञ् *gujarḍñ*.

(12) Irregular is (vi. 18)—

मख् *mākh*, an axe मकुच् *mak*^{a}*ts*, a small axe.

B. Number.

Kāçmīrī, has two numbers, a Singular and a Plural. There is no Dual number. The method of forming the plural will appear from the Declensional Paradigms.

C. Case.

Kāçmīrī nouns have, besides the Nominative, two inflected cases the Accusative, and the Agent. Other so-called cases are formed by the addition of postpositions to one of these two. The following are the cases given by Īçvara-kaula.

Formed from the Accusative :—

Genitive,
Locative 1,
Dative 1,
Concomitant.

Formed from the Agent :—

Instrumental,
Locative 2,
Dative 2,
Ablative.

There is no Vocative, but, in case of address, a noun assumes a variety of forms which will be dealt with later on.

There are thus, excluding the Nominative, ten cases.

I now proceed to deal with each case separately.

Accusative.

The Accusative has two forms, a longer and a shorter. The shorter is always the same as the nominative (ii. i. 39.)

In the masculine singular, the longer form always ends in *s*. In the feminine it ends in *a*, *ĕ*, *i*, or *ū-mātrā* (36–40). When the longer form of the accusative singular ends in *i*, that *i* is always fully pronounced. Thus मालि *māli*, not मालि *mạl^i*. In the plural it always ends in *n* (12, 38).

Genitive.

The Genitive is formed by various affixes, added to the long form of the accusative.

In the case of masculine nouns, the *s* of the accusative singular is dropped before the termination, and the final vowel so left is pronounced short, as a *mātrā* vowel. Thus from दय् *day*, God: acc. sg. दयस् *dayas*; gen. sing. दय संदु *day^a sąnd^u*; acc. pl. दयन् *dayan*; gen. plur. दयन् हंदु *dayan hąnd^u*.

So from गुर् *gur^u*, a horse: acc. sg. गुरिस् *guris*; gen. sg., गुरि संदु *gur^i sąnd^u*: acc. pl. गुर्यन् *guryan*; gen. pl. गुर्यन् हंदु *guryan hąnd^u*.

The word with its genitive affix is treated as an adjective agreeing with the object possessed in gender and number.

Thus मालि संदु न्यचिवु *mạl^i sąnd^u necyuv*, the son of the father.

मालि संदि न्यचिवि *mạl^i sąnd^i neciv^i*, the sons of the father.

मालि संज़् कूर् *mǫl*^{i} *sǫnz*^{a} *kūr*^{a}, the daughter of the father.

मालि सन्ज़् कोरे *mǫl*^{i} *sanz*^{a} *kōrĕ*, the daughters of the father.

Moreover this genitive may even be treated as an independent base, and be regularly declined, with case affixes added to it.

Thus from मोलु *mōl*^{u}, a father, the genitive masculine is मालि संदु *mǫl*^{i} *sǫnd*^{u}, which may be declined like a masculine noun in *u-mātrā*, with a dative मालि सन्दि पुछ़् *mǫl*^{i} *sandi putshy*, which can be used instead of the simple dative मालि पुछ़् *māli putshy*. Indeed the dative formed from the genitive is in the case of this word the usual one, and the simple dative is scarcely used (ii. i. 61, 62, 63, 64).

The following are the affixes used to form the genitive :—

A. Masculine nouns with life which are not proper names take

(*a*) in the singular, संदु *sǫnd*^{u}, *E.g.*, दय संदु *day*^{a} *sǫnd*^{u}, of God (46).

(*b*) in the plural, हंदु *hǫnd*^{u}, *E.g.*, दयन् हंदु *dayan hǫnd*^{u}, of Gods (42).

B. All feminine nouns without exception take हंदु *hǫnd*^{u}, both in the singular, and in the plural. *E.g.*, बेन्यि हंदु *bĕñĕ hǫnd*^{u}, of the sister; बेन्यन् हंदु *bĕñan hǫnd*^{u}, of the sisters; पोथ हंदु *pōthĕ hǫnd*^{u}, of the book; पोथ्यन् हंदु *pōthyan hǫnd*^{u}, of the books (42).

C. Masculine nouns without life take.

(*a*) In the singular उकु *uk*^{u}, (48) before which *a* is elided (i. 4), and *i* becomes *y* (i. 10). While when it follows *ū-mātrā*, the *u* of *uk*^{u} is elided (i. 5). *E.g.*, द्यकुकु *dyakuk*^{u}, of a forehead; कुल्युकु *kulyuk*^{u}, of a tree; दानकु *dǫn*^{a}*k*^{u}, of a pomegranate.

(*b*) In the plural, the termination is हंदु *hǫnd*^{u}, as above; *e.g.*, द्यकन् हंदु *dyakan hǫnd*^{u}, of foreheads.

Exception.—The words सोन् *sŏn*, gold, and रोप् *rŏp*, silver, take the termination संदु *sǫnd*^{u} in the singular, when the genitive is used in the sense of 'composed of.' *E.g.*, सोन संदु छतर् *sŏn*^{a} *sǫnd*^{u} *chath*^{a}*r*, an umbrella of gold, a golden umbrella. सोनुकु छतर् *sŏnuk*^{u} *chath*^{a}*r*, would mean an umbrella belonging to gold,—a possessive genitive in fact (ii. i. 47).

NOTE.—When a genitive in उकु *uk*^{u} is treated as a declensional base, the उ *u* becomes अ *a* in the oblique cases (64). Thus पटु *paṭ*^{u}, a woollen cloth. Gen. sg. पट्युकु *paṭyuk*^{u}: Dative, पटि पुछ्य *paṭi putshy* or पट्यकि पुछ्य *paṭeki* (spelled *paṭyaki*) *putshy*.

D. Masculine nouns which are proper names form their genitive singular in उनु *un*^{u}, which is treated exactly like उकु *uk*^{u}, (50). *E.g.*, राधाकृष्णुनु *Rādhākṛṣṇun*^{u} of Rādhākṛṣṇa: राधाकृष्णनि पुछ्य *Rādhākriṣṇani putshy*, for Rādhākṛṣṇa.

The plural is formed regularly with हंदु *hənd*^{u}, e.g. रामन् हंदु *Rāman hənd*^{u}, of (many) Rāmas.

It will thus be seen that the suffix of the genitive of all plural nouns, and of all feminine nouns is हंदु *hənd*^{u}.

When the thing possessed is feminine singular, or masculine or feminine plural, the following changes in the genitive affixes occur:—

THING POSSESSED IN THE

SINGULAR.		PLURAL.	
Masculine.	*Feminine.*	*Masculine.*	*Feminine.*
संदु *sənd*^{u}	संज़ *sənz*^{a} (46, 44)	संदि *sənd*^{i} (46, 43)	सञ्ज़ *sanz*^{a} (46, 45)
हंदु *hənd*^{u}	हंज़ *hənz*^{a} (44)	हंदि *hənd*^{i} (43)	हञ्ज़ *hanz*^{a} (45)
उकु *uk*^{u}	चु *c*^{a} (49)	कि *k*^{i} (48)	च *c*^{a}[1] (49)
उनु *un*^{u}	ञु *ñ* (51)	नि *n*^{i} (50)	ञ *ñă* (51)

Examples in order as:—

मालि संदु न्यचिवु *māl*^{i} *sənd*^{u} *nĕcyuv*, the son of the father.

मालि संज़ कूरु *māl*^{i} *sənz*^{a} *kūr*^{a}, the daughter of the father.

1 So written by Içvara-kaula. च्य *cə* would be more correct, but, च *c* being a palatal letter, there is practically no difference in the pronunciation.

मालि संदि न्यचिवि *māl*^{i} *sąnd*^{i} *nĕciv*^{i}, the sons of the father.

मालि सञ्ज़ कोरे *māl*^{i} *sanz*^{a} *kōrĕ*, the daughters of the father.

मालयन् हंदु गुरु *mālyan hąnd*^{u} *gur*^{u}, the horse of the fathers.

मालयन् हंज़ गुर *mālyan hąnz*^{a} *gur*^{a}, the mare of the fathers.

मालयन् हंदि गुरि *mālyan hąnd*^{i} *gur*^{i}, the horses of the fathers.

मालयन् हञ्ज़ गुरे *mālyan hanz*^{a} *gurĕ*, the mares of the fathers.

कुल्युकु लंग् *kulyuk*^{u} *laṅg*, a bough of a tree.

कुलिच् लंड् *kulic*^{a} *ląṇḍ*^{a}, a twig of a tree.

कुलिकि लंग् *kulik*^{i} *laṅg*, the boughs of the tree.

कुलिच लंजे *kulic*^{a} *ląnjĕ*, the twigs of the tree.

रामुनु न्यचिवु *Rāmun*^{u} *nĕchyuv*, Rāma's son.

रामंज़ कूर *Rāmąñ kūr*^{a}, Rāma's daughter.

रामंनि न्यचिवि *Rāmąn*^{i} *nĕcivi*, Rāma's sons.

रामञ्ज़ कोरे *Rāmaññĕ kōrĕ*, Rāma's daughters.

Locative, 1.

There are two forms of the Locative. The first I shall call Loc. 1. It has the meaning indicated by its postpositions.

This Locative is formed by adding the postpositions अन्दर् *andar* (ii. i. 52), in; मञ्ज़् *mans* (52), in; प्यठ् *pyăṭh* (52), upon; क्यथ् *kyăth* (53), in; to the longer form of the Accusative. In Poetry, वेस् *vęs*^{a} is also used in the sense of 'upon' (52). Thus मूल् *mūl*, a root; Acc. sg. मूलस् *mūlas*; Loc. sg. मूलस् अन्दर् *mūlas andar*; मूलस् मञ्ज़् *mūlas mans*, in a root; मूलस् प्यठ् *mūlas pyăṭh*, on a root; Acc. pl. मूलन् *mūlan*; मूलन् अन्दर् *mulan andar*, in roots.

The postposition क्यथ् *kyăth* can only be used with words which mean a receptacle. Thus we can say थालस् क्यथ् *thālas kyăth*, in a dish; or even नावि क्यथ् *nāvi kyăth*, in a boat; but we cannot say गरस् क्यथ् *garas kyăth*, in a house or मूलस् क्यथ् *mūlas kyăth*, in a root, because a house, or a root, are not used as receptacles for putting things into.

क्यथ् *kyăth* can also be used with any word signifying a means of conveyance, and it must then sometimes be translated by 'on.' Thus गुरिस् क्यथ् *guris kyăth*, or गुरिस् प्यठ् *guris pyăṭh*, on horseback.

Loc. 2 will be dealt with subsequently.

Dative, 1.

There are two forms of the Dative, one formed by adding postpositions to the Accusative, the other by adding postpositions to the Instrumental. The first I shall call Dat. 1, the second, Dat. 2. The Dat. 2, will be subsequently dealt with.

Dat. 1 is formed by adding the postposition क्युतु *kyutᵘ*, for, to the longer form of the Accusative (ii. i. 54, 55). The compound thus formed, agrees in number and gender with the thing given, the word 'given' being taken in its widest sense to agree with the original meaning of the name of the case. The following are the forms which क्युतु *kyutᵘ* takes:—

Sing. Masc. कितु *kitᵘ* (*kyutᵘ*)

Fem. कित्सु *kitsᵘ*

Pl. Masc. किति *kitⁱ*

Fem. कित्स *kitsᵃ*

Thus मालिस् क्युतु अंनुन् पोञु *mạlis kyutᵘ ạnun pōñᵘ*, he brought water (masc. sg.) for the father.

मालिस् कित्सु अंनुन् गाव् *mạlis kitsᵘ ạñᵘn gāv*, he brought a cow (fem. sg.) for the father.

गुरिस् किति अंनिन् रव *guris kitⁱ ạnin ravᵃ*, he brought blankets (masc. pl.) for the horse.

ग्वरस् कित्स अन्यन् पोथ्य *gŏras kitsᵃ añyan pōthĕ*, he brought books (fem. pl.) for the teacher.

Concomitant.

This case is used in the sense of 'with,' or 'accompanying.' It is formed by adding the postpositions सतिन् *sạtin* or सत्य् *sạty* to the longer form of the Accusative (ii. i. 60). Thus मालिस् सतिन् आव्

mǭlis sǫtin āv, he came with his father; बॉयिस् सॅत्य् म्यूलु *bǭyis sǫty myūlᵘ*, he met with his brother; मालयन् सॅतिन् *mālyan sǫtin*, with the fathers.

In this case it is always implied that the person who is accompanied is the principal and he who accompanies, is the appendage (iv. 185).

Thus 'he came with his father' means here that he came in a subordinate character (iv. 185).

If it is wished to reverse the superiority of the parties we must use the word सान् *sān*. Thus मॉलिस् सान् आव् *mǭlis sān āv*, he came with his father, means 'he brought his father along with him.' If सॅतिन् *sǫtin* had been used, it would have meant that the father brought the son along with him (iv. 185).

Agent.

The case of the Agent is formed in the Singular as follows:—

(1) In the case of Masc. nouns ending in consonants by adding अन् *an*; thus दय् *day*, God; Ag. sg. दयन् *dayan*. In the older forms of the language the suffix was इ *i*: e.g., दॅयि दॅपु *dǫyᶦ dǫpᵘ*, by God it was said, God said. The modern phrase would be दयन् दॅपु *dayan dǫpᵘ* (ii. i. 58).

(2) In the case of Masculine nouns (except pronouns) ending in *a*, the same suffixes appear. Thus from ड्यक *ḍyakᵉ*, a forehead; Ag. sg. ड्यकन् *ḍyakan*, or (old) डॅकि *ḍǭkᶦ* (58). Pronouns take *i-mātrā* in the masc. sg., *e.g.*, तॅमि *tǫmᶦ*, by him, (58).

(3) In the case of Masculine nouns ending in *u-mātrā*, *i-mātrā* is substituted for *u-mātrā*. Thus, कॅरु *kǫrᵘ*, a bracelet; Ag. sg. कॅरि *kǫrᶦ* (56).

(4) In the case of Masculine nouns ending in *ū-mātrā*, by adding न् *n*; e.g., from दानू *dǭnᵘ*, a pomegranate; Ag. sg. दानून् *dǭnᵘn*. [Içvara-kaula gives no rule for forming the agent of these nouns, but the above is the correct form.]

(5) In the case of Feminine nouns ending in *a*, by substituting *i* (which is fully pronounced, and not *i-mātrā*) for *a*: e.g.,

from ब्यञ् *bĕñĕ* (spelled *byañ*[a]), a sister; Ag. sg. ब्यञि *bĕñi* (56).

(6) In the case of Feminine nouns ending in *i-mātrā* or *ū-mātrā*, a fully pronounced *i* is substituted for the *i-mātrā* or *ū-mātrā*: e.g., from पूथि *pūth*[i], a book; Ag. sg. पोथि *pōthi*. So from कूर् *kūr*[a], a girl; Ag. sg. कोरि *kōri* (56).

(7) In the case of Feminine nouns ending in consonants, by adding a fully pronounced *i*: e.g., from माल् *māl* a garland, मालि *māli* (56). The irregular nouns, however, which end in *t*, *th*, *d*, *n*, *h*, and *l*, add *ū-mātrā*: e.g., from रात् *rāt*, night; Ag. sg. रात्सू *rāts*[ū]. [This last rule is not expressly stated by Īçvara-kaula, but may be inferred from *sūtra* 7, read with *sūtra* 17.]

The Agent plural is formed by adding *au* (56). Before this, *a* is elided, and *i-mātrā* and *u-mātrā* become *y*. After *ū-mātrā* (except in the case of Feminine nouns in *ū-mātrā*, in which *y* is substituted) *au* becomes *v* (20). Examples are:—

From	Ag. Plural.
दय् *day*, God	दयौ *dayau*
द्यक *dyak*[a], the forehead	द्यकौ *dyakau*
कंरु *kar*[u], a bracelet	करयौ *karyau*
दांनू *dān*[ū], a pomegranate	दांनूव् *dān*[ū]*v*
ब्यञ् *bĕñĕ* (*byañ*[a]), a sister	ब्यञौ *bĕñau*
पूथि *pūth*[i], a book	पोथ्यौ *pōthyau*
कूर् *kūr*[a], a girl	कोर्यौ *kōryau*
माल् *māl*, a garland	मालौ *mālau*
रात् *rāt*, night	रात्सूव् *rāts*[ū]*v*

When postpositions are added to the agent of masculine nouns ending in consonants or *a*, the *n* of the Agent singular is dropped. Thus, from मूल् *mūl*, Ag. sg. मूलन् *mūlan*; Instr. मूल सूतिन् *mūl*[a] *sotin*, not मूलन् सूतिन् *mūlan sotin* (4). [The same rule applies to masculines in *ū-mātrā*, though not stated by Īçvara-kaula.]

Instrumental.

The Instrumental is formed by adding सुँतिन् *s̤ętin* or सुँत्य् *s̤ęty* to the Agent, the final *n* of Masculine nouns in consonants, *a*, or *ū-mātrā* being elided, (ii. i. 4, 59.). Thus—

मूल् *mūl*, a root; Ag. sg. मूलन् *mūlan*; Instr. sg. मूल सुँतिन् *mūl*^{a} *s̤ętin*, by means of a root; Ag. pl. मूलौ *mūlau*; Instr. pl. मूलौ सुँतिन् *mūlau s̤ętin*.

When सुँतिन् *s̤ętin* follows *i-mātrā*, the *i* is fully pronounced (6). Thus कँर् *kər*^{u}, a bracelet; Ag. sg. कँरि *kər*^{i}; Instr. sg. करि सुँतिन् *kari s̤ętin*.

This case can also be formed by adding the same postposition to the agent case of the masculine genitive treated as an independent base, as explained above (61). Thus ड्यक *ḍyak*^{a}, a forehead; masc. gen. sg. ड्यकुक् *ḍyakuk*^{u}; Agent of ditto, ड्यकँकि *ḍyakək*^{i}; Instr. ड्यक सुँतिन् *ḍyak*^{a} *s̤ętin* or ड्यककि सुँतिन् *ḍyakaki s̤ętin*.

So from गुर् *gur*^{u}, a horse. Ag. sg. गुरि *gur*^{i}; Gen. Sg. गुरि सँन्द् *gur*^{i} *sənd*^{u}; Instr. गुरि सुँतिन् *guri s̤ętin*, or गुरि सन्दि सुँतिन् *gur*^{i} *sandi s̤ętin*.

Locative 2.

The Locative 2 has the meaning of 'from in,' and is formed by adding the postposition अन्द्र *andr*^{a} to the Agent, (*n* being dropped in the case of masculines in consonants, and *a*, and *ū-mātrā*.) Thus, from गर् *gar*^{a}, a house; Ag. sg. गरन् *garan*; Loc. 2, sg. गर अन्द्र *gar*^{a} *andr*^{a}, from in the house; ag. pl. गरौ *garau*; Loc. 2, pl. गरौ अन्द्र *garau andr*^{a}, (ii. i. 57).

Examples of the use of this case are गर अन्द्र अन् *gar*^{a} *andr*^{a} *an* bring out from the house, lit. bring from in the house.

गर अन्द्र छुह् जान् लुँक *gar*^{a} *andar*^{a} *chuh jān lək*^{a}, among the people in (lit. from in) the house, (only) so and so is good.

गरौ अन्द्र छुह् जान् आँगुन् *garau andr*^{a} *chuh jān āgun*, the only good thing in the houses is the court-yard.

This form can only be used in the meaning called in Skr. *nirdhāraṇa*, *i.e.*, in words meaning जाति *jāti*, a species (including all plurals); गुण *guṇa*, a quality; क्रिया *kriyā*, an act; संज्ञा *saṁjñā*, an appellation; and means that one of several is taken.

जात्या गुणेन क्रियया संज्ञया वा पृथक्कृतिः ।
समुदायादेकदेशस्य निर्धारणमिति स्मृतम् ॥

Examples:—

Species. A Brāhmaṇa is the best amongst men.

Quality. Amongst cows a black one gives most milk.

Action. Amongst men who go, he who runs is the swiftest.

Appellation. Amongst the pupils Maitra is the cleverest. See Siddhānta Kaumudi (Bibl. Ind. Ed.) I, 311. In all the above "amongst" means "from among."

It is evident that the form can hardly ever be used except in the plural. In the paradigms, singular forms are given for the sake of completeness, but it is doubtful if they can be used in that number.

Dative 2.

According to Īçvara-kaula, this form is only used to a moderate extent (*sāmānya*) (ii. i. 63). It is in fact rarely used. It has the same meaning as the Dat. 1. It is formed by adding पुछ् *putshy* to the Agent, or (as has been explained under the head of the Instrumental) to the Agent case of the Genitive. Before पुछ् *putshy*, as in the case of सतिन् *sʊtin*, *i-mātrā* is fully pronounced. Thus,—पुत्र पुछ् *putrᵃ putshy*, or पुत्र सन्दि पुछ् *putrᵃ sandi putshy*.

Ablative.

The Ablative is formed from the Agent by adding the postpositions प्यठ *pyathᵃ*, literally from on, hence, from near; निश *niçᵃ*, from near; अन्द्र *andrᵃ*, from among, from in (ii. i. 65).

Thus, गाम प्यठ *gāmᵃ pyathᵃ*, from the village; गामौ प्यठ *gāmau pyathᵃ* from the villages; सर्पौ निश *sarpau niçᵃ*, from the serpents; गर अन्द्र द्राव् *garᵃ andrᵃ drāv*, he came out from the house; नावि अन्द्र द्राव् *nāvi andrᵃ drāv*, he came out from the boat, (65).

[Masculine living beings can also add these postpositions, in the singular only, to the longer form of the Accusative. Thus चूरस् निश *tsūras niç*ᵃ, from the thief; गुरिस् निश *guris niç*ᵃ, from the horse.]

The ablative of comparison is formed with the postpositions खोत *khöt*ᵃ or खोतन् *khötan*, निश *niç*ᵃ or निशिन् *niçin*, which are added either to the agent direct, or to the Agent case of the Genitive treated as a base. In the case of some words, *e.g.*, ग्वर् *gör*, a teacher, only the latter idiom is used.

E.g., ग्वर सन्दि खोत छुह् गाटुल् *gör*ᵃ *sandi khöt*ᵃ *chuh gāṭul*ᵘ, he is more clever than the teacher. We cannot say ग्वर खोत *gör*ᵃ *khöt*ᵃ. कन हन्दि (or कन) खोत छुह् त्रकुर् *kañ*ᵃ *handi* (or *kuñ*ᵃ) *khöt*ᵃ *chuh trakur*ᵘ, he is harder than a stone; र्वप निश छुह् स्वन् जान् *röp*ᵃ *niç*ᵃ *chuh sön jān*, gold is better than silver (ii. i. 62).

D. Declension.

Kāçmīrī nouns have four declensions.

The first declension consists of masculine nouns ending in a consonant, in अ *a*, or in अु *ū-mātrā*. The base in this declension ends in *a*.

The second declension consists of masculine nouns ending in उ *u-mātrā*. The base in this declension ends in *i*.

The third declension consists of feminine nouns ending in इ *i-mātrā*, अु *ū-mātrā*, or अॖ *ñ*. The last is only another way of writing अॖ *ñ*ᵃ. It may be considered as the feminine form of the 2nd declension. The base in this declension also ends in *i*, and this declension is closely connected with the second, as feminine and masculine.

The fourth declension consists of feminine nouns ending in a consonant or in अ *a*. Certain feminine nouns of this declension ending in a consonant, are irregular, and form a class by themselves.

There are thus two masculine, and two feminine declensions.

First Declension.

Masculine nouns ending in अ *a*, or in उ *ŭ-mātrā*.

(*a*). Noun ending in a consonant.

चूर् *tsūr*, a thief.

	Singular.	Plural.
Nom.	चूर् **tsūr** (ii. i. 3).	चूर् **tsūr** (3).
Acc.	चूरस् **tsūras** (36, 38).	चूरन् **tsūran** (13, 38).
	चूर् *tsūr* (39).	चूर् *tsūr* (39).
Gen.	चूर संदु *tsūr*ᵃ *sąnd*ᵘ (41, 42, 45).	चूरन् हंदु *tsūran hąnd*ᵘ (42).
Loc. 1.	चूरस् पठ् *tsūras pyăṭh* (52), &c.	चूरन् पठ् *tsūran pyăṭh* (52), &c.
Dat. 1.	चूरस् कितु *tsūras kyut*ᵘ (54, 55).	चूरन् कितु *tsūran kyut*ᵘ (54, 55).
Concom.	चूरस् सुतिन् *tsūras sątin* (60).	चूरन् सुतिन् *tsūran sątin* (60).
Agent.	चूरन् **tsūran** (58).	चूरौ **tsūrau** (56).
	चूरि *tsūr*ⁱ (58) (obsolete).	
Instr.	चूर सुतिन् *tsūr*ᵃ *sątin* (6, 59).	चूरौ सुतिन् *tsūrau sątin* (59).
	चूर सन्दि सुतिन् *tsūr*ᵃ *sandi sątin* (61).	चूरन् हन्दि सुतिन् *tsūran handi sątin* (61).
Loc. 2.	(चूर अन्द्र *tsūr*ᵃ *andr*ᵃ) (4, 57).	चूरौ अन्द्र *tsūrau andr*ᵃ (57).
Dat. 2.	चूर पुछ् *tsūr*ᵃ *putshy* (63).	चूरौ पुछ् *tsūrau putshy* (63).
	चूर सन्दि पुछ् *tsūr*ᵃ *sandi putshy* (63).	चूरन् हन्दि पुछ् *tsūran handi putshy* (63).
Abl.	चूर निश *tsūr*ᵃ *niç*ᵃ (65). [or चूरस् निश *tsūras niç*ᵃ].	चूरौ निश *tsūrau niç*ᵃ (65).

Similarly are declined दय् *day*, God; काव् *kāv*, a crow; स्वन् *sŏn*, gold; र्वप् *rŏp*, silver; पुत्र् *putr*, a son; वथुर् *wathᵃr*, a leaf; तॊमुल् *tŏmul*, husked rice; हार् *hār*, name of a month, Āṣāḍha; मॊंग् *mŏṅg*, name of a grain, *phaseolus mungi;* माग् *māg*, name of a month, Māgha; द्वह् *dŏh*, a day; नाग् *nāg*, a spring; कट् *kaṭ* [nom. sg. and pl. कठ् *kaṭh* (66)], a ram; रत् *rat* [nom. sg. and pl. रथ् *rath*, (66)], blood; पोश् *pŏś*, a flower; वाल् *wāl*, hair; गल् *gal*, the cheek; ग्वर् *gŏr*, a preceptor, a Brāhman.

Numerals take *i* instead of *a* in the Agent and connected cases, *e.g.*, सति सतिन् *sati sạtin*, by sevens (ii. i. 5).

If a noun ends in उर् *ur* [or उन् *un*], the *u* is changed to *a* in all cases except the nominative singular, *e.g.*, वाँदुर् *wãdur*, a monkey; nom. pl. वाँदर् *wãdar;* instr. वाँदरौ सतिन् *wãdarau sạtin* (32). [So infinitives like करुन् *karun*; acc. करनस् *karanas*].

If in the case of masculine nouns of the first declension the final consonant is preceded by the vowel ū, that ū becomes ō, in all cases of the plural except the nominative, but remains unchanged in the singular and in the nominative plural. The following masculine words ending in consonants do not, however, change this ū (35).

मूल् *mūl*, a root.

छूल् *chūl*, a cascade.

डूस् *ḍūs*, a stout club.

भूत् *būt* (nom. sg. भूथ् *būth*, 66), a ghost.

रूद् *rūd*, rain.

लूदर् *lūdᵃr*, eagerly desirous.

लूबर् *lūbᵃr*, eagerly desirous.

ऊँट् *wū̃ṭ* (nom. sg. ऊँठ् *wū̃ṭh*, 66), a camel.

सूर् *sūr*, ashes.

हूश् *hūs*, an uproar.

[चूर् *tsūr*, a thief], and others.

लूक् *lūk* (nom. sg. लूख् *lūkh*, 66), people.

Thus from मूल् *mūl*, acc. pl. मूलन् *mūlan*, not मोलन् *mōlan*.

If a masculine noun ends in क् *k*, च् *ch*, च़् *ts*, ट् *ṭ*, त् *t*, or प् *p*, this final consonant is aspirated in the nom. sg. and pl. (66); thus:—

	Nom. sg. and pl.
त्रक् *trak*, a certain grain measure.	त्रख् *trăkh*.
काच़् *kāts*, glass, a disease of the chest.	काछ़् *kātsh*.
कट् *kaṭ*, a ram.	कठ् *kăṭh*.
रत् *rat*, blood.	रथ् *răth*.
हत् *hat*, a hundred.	हथ् *hăth*.
ताप् *tāp*, sunshine.	ताफ् *tāph*.

The aspiration is very faintly heard, being a final letter, but it affects the preceding vowel. The aspiration does not occur in the other cases; *e.g.*, त्रक सॖतिन् *trakᵃ sătin* (instr.); काच़ सॖतिन् *kātsᵃ sătin*; कट पुछ़् *kaṭᵃ putshy* (dat. 2); तापस् प्यठ् *tāpas pyăṭh* (loc.).

This aspiration does not occur if a final त् *t* or च़् *ts* forms part of a compound consonant (even when a short ᵃ is introduced between them to aid pronunciation) (68); thus:—

सॖच़् *sᵃts*, a tailor (Elmslie, *süts*); nom. sg. and pl. सॖच़् *sᵃts*, not सॖछ़् *sᵃtsh*.

मस्त् *mast*, hair; nom. sg. and pl. मस्त् *mast*, not मस्थ् *măsth*.

The word ब्याख् *byākh*, another (2, 3, 24), becomes बिय् *biy* in all cases except the nom. sg., and is partially declined like a noun ending in *u-mātrā* (2nd declension); thus—

	SINGULAR.	PLURAL.
Nom.	ब्याख् *byākh*	बिय् *biy*.
Acc.	बियिस् *biyis*.	बियन् *biyan*.
Ag.	बियि *biyⁱ*.	बियौ *biyau*.

The Fem. Ag. is बियि *biyi*. In other forms it is the same as the Masc. This is really a compound word: made up of बि *bi*, other, and अख् *ăkh*, one. The oblique forms are made up of the base बि *bi*, together with the emphatic particle य् *y*, which accounts for the apparent irregularities. बि *bi* is of the 2nd declension.

Noun ending in अ *a*.

द्यक *dyak*^{a} a forehead.

	SINGULAR.	PLURAL.
Nom.	द्यक dyak^{a} (ii. i. 1).	द्यक dyak^{a} (1).
Acc.	द्यकस् dyakas (38).	द्यकन् dyakan (38).
	द्यक *dyak*^{a} (39).	द्यक *dyak*^{a} (39).
Gen.	द्यकुक् *dyakuk*^{a} (41, 48).	द्यकन् हन्द् *dyakan hand*^{a} (42).
Loc. 1.	द्यकस् पाठ् *dyakas pyāṭh*, &c., (52, 53).	द्यकन् पाठ् *dyakan pyāṭh*, &c. (52, 53).
Dat. 1.	द्यकस् क्युत् *dyakas kyut*^{a} (54, 55).	द्यकन् क्युत् *dyakan kyut*^{a} (54, 55).
Concom.	द्यकस् सँतिन् *dyakas sątin* (60).	द्यकन् सँतिन् *dyakan sątin* (60).
Agent.	द्यकन् dyakan (i. 5*a*) or द्यकि *dĕk*^{i} (obsolete) (58; i. 4).	द्यकौ dyakau (56; i. 4).
Instr.	द्यक सँतिन् *dyak*^{a} *sątin* (6, 59).	द्यकौ सँतिन् *dyakau sątin* (59).
	द्यककि सँतिन् *dyakaki sątin* (61).	द्यकन् हन्दि सँतिन् *dyakan handi sątin* (61).
Loc. 2.	द्यक अन्द्र *dyak*^{a} *andr*^{a} (4, 57).	द्यकौ अन्द्र *dyakau andr*^{a} (57).
Dat. 2.	द्यक पुछ् *dyak*^{a} *putshy* (63).	द्यकौ पुछ् *dyakau putshy* (63).
	द्यककि पुछ् *dyakaki putshy* (67).	द्यकन् हन्दि पुछ् *dyakan handi putshy* (63).
Abl.	द्यक निश *dyak*^{a} *niç*^{a} (65).	द्यकौ निश *dyakau niç*^{a} (65).

Similarly are declined गर *gar*^{a}, a house; अथ *ath*^{a}, a hand; दान्यं *dānĕ*, rice; बत *bat*^{a}, boiled rice.

(*c*). Noun ending in ॖ *ū-mātrā.*

दानॖ *dạ̄n^{u}*, a pomegranate.

Nom.	दानॖ dạ̄n^{u} (ii. i. 2).	दानॖ dạ̄n^{u} (2).
Acc.	दानुस् dạ̄n^{u}s (38).	दानन् dạ̄n^{u}n (31, 13, 33).
	दानॖ *dạ̄n^{u}* (39).	दानॖ *dạ̄n^{u}* (39).
Gen.	दानुकॖ *dạ̄n^{u}k^{u}* (41, 48).	दानन् हंदॖ *dạ̄n^{u}n hand^{u}* (42).
Loc. 1.	दानस् प्यठ् *dạ̄n^{u}s pyăṭh*, &c. (52, 53).	दानन् प्यठ् *dạ̄n^{u}n pyăṭh*, &c. (52, 53).
Dat. 1.	दानस् क्युतॖ *dạ̄n^{u}s kyut^{u}* (54, 55).	दानन् क्युत् *dạ̄n^{u}n kyut* (54, 55)
Concom.	दानस् सुतिन् *dạ̄n^{u}s sạtin* (60).	दानन् सुतिन् *dạ̄n^{u}n sạtin* (60).
Agent.	दानन् dạ̄n^{u}n.	दानव् dạ̄n^{u}v (20, 31, 56).
Instr.	दानॖ सुतिन् *dạ̄n^{u} sạtin* (59).	दानव् सुतिन् *dạ̄n^{u}v sạtin* (59).
	दानुकि सुतिन् *dạ̄n^{u}ki sạtin* (61).	दानन् हंदि सुतिन् *dạ̄n^{u}n handi sạtin* (61).
Loc. 2.	दानॖ अन्दर *dạ̄n^{u} andr^{u}* (57).	दानव् अन्दर *dạ̄n^{u}v andr^{u}* (57).
Dat. 2.	दानॖ पुछ्य् *dạ̄n^{u} putshy* (63).	दानव् पुछ्य् *dān^{u}v putshy* (63).
	दानुकि पुछ्य् *dạ̄n^{u}ki putshy* (63).	दानन् हंदि पुछ्य् *dạ̄n^{u}n handi putshy* (63).
Abl.	दानॖ निश *dạ̄n^{u} niç^{u}* (65).	दानव् निश *dạ̄n^{u}v niç^{u}* (65).

Içvara-kaula gives no rule for forming the agent singular of these nouns. but दानन् *dạ̄n^{u}n* is the correct form.

The following words are optionally declined as if ending in consonants, गंज़ॖ *gạnz^{u}*, a leather-worker; गासॖ *gạ̄s^{u}*, a grass-seller; बाछॖ *bạ̄ts^{u}*, people of a house; हांज़ *hānz*^{a}, a boatman. Thus, acc. plur. गंज़न् *gąnz*^{a}*n* or गनज़न् *ganzan* (15).

It must be remembered that *ŭ-mātrā* at the end of a word is not pronounced. Before a consonant (as in *dąn*^{a}*v*) it is pronounced like a short German *ü*. It is, also, slightly pronounced in the Instr. Loc. 2, Dat. 2, and Abl. Sing. Before *ŭ-mātrā*, a preceding *a* or *ā* must be modified to *ą* or *ą̄* respectively (70); *e.g.*, as in दांन् *dą̄n*^{a}.

Second Declension.

Masculine Nouns in ु *u-mātrā*.

कंर् *kąr*^{u}, a bracelet.

Nom.	कंरु **kąr**^{u} (ii. i. 8).	कंरि **kąr**^{i} (30).
Acc.	करिस् **karis** (30, 38). कंरु *kąr*^{u} (39).	कर्यन् **karyan** (12, 30, 38). कंरि *kąr*^{i} (39).
Gen.	कर्युकु *karyuk*^{u} (41, 48).	कर्यन् हंदु *karyan hąnd*^{u} (42).
Loc. 1.	करिस् पाठ् *karis pyǟth*, &c. (52, 53).	कर्यन् पाठ् *karyan pyǟth*, &c. (52, 53).
Dat. 1.	करिस् क्युतु *karis kyut*^{u} (54, 55).	कर्यन् क्युतु *karyan kyut*^{u} (54, 55).
Concom.	करिस् संतिन् *karis sątin* (60).	कर्यन् संतिन् *karyan sątin* (60).
Agent.	कंरि **kąr**^{i} (6, 56).	कर्यौ **karyau** (56, 80; i. 10).
Instr.	करि संतिन् *kari sątin* (59). कर्यंकि संतिन् *karĕki sątin* (61).	कर्यौ संतिन् *karyau sątin* (59). कर्यन् हंदि संतिन् *karyan handi sątin* (61).
Loc. 2.	करि अन्दरु *kari andr*^{e} (57).	कर्यौ अन्दरु *karyau andr*^{e} (57).
Dat. 2.	करि पुठ्य् *kari putshy* (63). कर्यंकि पुठ्य् *karĕki putshy* (63).	कर्यौ पुठ्य् *karyau putshy* (63). कर्यन् हंदि पुठ्य् *karyan handi putshy* (63).
Abl.	करि निशु *kari niç*^{e} (65).	कर्यौ निशु *karyau niç*^{e}.

[also गुरिस् निशु *guris niç*^{e} (in the case of masculine nouns with life).]

Similarly are declined गुर् *gur*^{u}, a horse; गूर् *gūr*^{u}, a cow-herd; गूल् *gūl*^{u}, a kernel, especially of the singārā; कुल् *kul*^{u}, a tree.

The final *u* becomes *i* (or *y*) throughout, except in the Nominative Singular, (30).

If the penultimate of a masculine noun contains the vowel *ū*, that *ū* becomes *ō* in all cases of the Plural except the nominative. It does not change in the singular, or in the nominative plural, (34).

Thus गूर् *gūr*^{u}, a cowherd; acc. sg. गूरिस् *gūris*; nom. pl. गूरि *gūr*^{i}, but acc. pl. गोर्यन् *gōryan*.

The following words in *u-mātrā* are exceptions, and do not change the *ū* (35).

कस्तूर् *kastūr*^{u}, the nightingale.

कूट् *kūṭ*^{u}, a tree-trunk.

टूँठ् *ṭsūṭ*^{u}, an apple.

टूर् *ṭūr*^{u}, a woman's eating platter.

डूर् *ḍūr*^{u}, a flower-bed.

नस्तूर् *nastūr*^{u}, having a deformed nose.

Thus from कस्तूर् *kastūr*^{u}, acc. pl. कस्तूर्यन् *kastūryan*.

If a masculine noun ends in *u-mātrā*, and has ओ *ō* in the penultimate, this *ō* becomes *ā* in all cases of the singular except the nominative, and throughout the plural. Moreover, this *ā* is modified to *ạ̄* before *i-mātrā*, and in the accusative singular (69, 70). Thus, वोल् *wōl*^{u}, an earring; acc. sg. वालिस् *wạ̄lis*; gen. sg., वाल्युक् *wālyuk*^{u} (from मोल् *mōl*^{u}, a father, मालि सन्द् *mạ̄l*^{i} *sạnd*^{u}); ag. sg. वालि *wạ̄l*^{i}; instr. sg. वालि सतिन् *wāli sạtin* (here the *i* is not *i-mātrā*, but is fully pronounced); nom. pl. वालि *wạ̄l*^{i}; acc. pl. वाल्यन् *wālyan*; ag. pl. वाल्यौ *wālyau*. Similarly are declined मोल् *mōl*^{u}, a father, and बोय् *bōy*^{u}, a brother; also masculine possessive pronouns, such as म्योन् *myōn*^{u}, mine; च्योन् *cyōn*^{u} thine; सोन् *sōn*^{u}, our.

Thus nom. sg. म्योनु *myōn*^{u}; acc. sg. म्यानिस् *myạ̄nis*; gen. sg. म्यानि संदु *myạ̄n*^{i} *sạnd*^{u}; ag. sg. म्यानि *myạ̄n*^{i}; nom. pl. म्यानि *myạ̄n*^{i}; acc. pl. म्यान्यन् *myānyan*; ag. pl. म्यान्यौ *myānyau*; Instr. sg. म्यानि सुतिन् *myāni sụtin*, or म्यानि सन्दि सुतिन् *myạ̄n*^{i} *sandi sụtin*. So also the others (ii. iii. 11 and ff.)

Moreover, whenever, in this declension, the letter *a* or *ā* is followed by *i-mātrā*, or *u-mātrā*, the *a* or *ā* become *ạ* or *ạ̄* respectively. (ii. i. 70); thus,—

Base पट् *paṭ*, a woollen cloth; nom. sg. पटु *pạṭ*^{u}; ag. sg. पटि *pạṭ*^{i}; nom. pl. पटि *pạṭ*^{i}; but, acc. sg. पटिस् *paṭis* (not पटिस् *pạṭis*, as in the case of वोलु *wōl*^{u}); Instr. sg. पटि सुतिन् *paṭi sụtin* (fully pronounced *i*); acc. pl. पट्यन् *paṭyan*; ag. pl. पट्यौ *paṭyau*. So also हटु *hạṭ*^{u}, the neck; तनु *tạn*^{u}, the body; संदु *sạnd*^{u}, suffix of genitive (acc. sg. सन्दिस् *sandis*; ag. sg. संदि *sạnd*^{i}; instr. sg. सन्दि सुतिन् *sandi sụtin*; nom. pl. संदि *sạnd*^{i}; acc. pl. सन्द्यन् *sandyan*; ag. pl. सन्द्यौ *sandyau*): similarly पट्युकु *paṭyuk*^{u} of a woollen cloth; acc. sg. पट्यकिस् *paṭĕkis*; ag. sg. पट्यकि *paṭyạk*^{i}; instr. sg. पट्यकि सुतिन् *paṭĕki sụtin*; nom. pl. पट्यकि *paṭyạk*^{i}; acc. pl. पट्यक्यन् *paṭĕkyan*; ag. pl. पट्यक्यौ *paṭĕkyau*.

Nouns in *u-mātrā*, of three or more syllables, if they have *u* in the penultimate, omit the *u* before *i-mātrā*, and change it to *a* in all other cases except the nominative singular (73, 75); thus:—

गाटुलु *gāṭul*^{u}, clever; acc. sg. गाटलिस् *gāṭalis*; ag. sg. गाट्लि *gāṭl*^{i} (pronounced *gāṭel*^{i}); instr. sg. गाटलि सुतिन् *gāṭali sụtin*; gen. sg. गाट्लि संदु *gāṭl*^{i} *sạnd*^{u}; nom. pl. गाट्लि *gāṭl*^{i}; acc. pl. गाटल्यन् *gāṭalyan*; ag. pl. गाटल्यौ *gāṭalyau*.

This does not occur in the case of dissyllables; *e.g.*, from कुलु *kul*^{u}, a tree; acc. sg. कुलिस् *kulis*, and not कलिस् *kalis*.

The following words in *u-mātrā*, with *u* in the penultimate, change the penultimate *u* to *a* in all cases except the nominative, and are then declined like nouns of the first declension ending in consonants (74.)

कचुलु *kötshul*^{u}, a porter.

चुटुलु *tsötul*^{u}, a sodomite.

चक्रुलु *tsakul*^{u}, circular.

ग्वगुलु *gögul*^{u}, globular.

वातुलु *wātul*^{u}, a low-caste man.

बतुकु *batuk*^{u}, a drake.

गगुर् *gagur*^{u}, a rat.

म्वङ्गुर् *möngur*^{u}, a kid.

कुकुर् *kökur*^{u}, a cock (iv. 1).

कोतुर् *kötur*^{u}, a pigeon (iv. 1).

So also words in ुर् *r*^{u} signifying professions, &c. (iv. 6, 99 and ff.), *e.g.*, सनुर् *sönur*^{u}, a goldsmith, मनुर् *manur*^{u}, a shell worker.

See secondary suffixes No. 39.

Thus,—

Nom. sg. कचुलु *kötshul*^{u}; acc. sg. कचलस् *kötshalas*; gen. sg. कचल संन्दु *kötshal*^{a} *sąnd*^{u}; ag. sg. कचलन् *kötshalan*; instr. sg. कचल सुतिन् *kötshal*^{a} *sątin*; nom. pl. कचल *kötshal*; acc. pl. कचलन् *kötshalan*; ag. pl. कचलौ *kötshalau*.

If a word ending in *u-mātrā* has *yu* or *i* in the penultimate of the nom. sg., it has *i* in the penultimate in all the other cases (ii. i. 76). [These words are spelt indifferently with *yu* or *i* in the nominative, but are always pronounced as if *yu* was written. Thus मह्न्युवु *mahanyuv*^{u}, or महनिवु *mahaniv*^{u}, a man, both pronounced *mahanyuv*; ज्युठु *zyuth*^{u}, or ज़िठु *zith*^{u}, old, but both pronounced *zyuth*. On the other hand, in other cases, except the nominative, we have only *i*, pronounced as *i*]: thus; ज्युठु *zyuth*^{u}, old; acc. sg. ज़िठिस् *zithis*; ag. sg. ज़िठि *zith*^{i}; nom. pl. ज़िठि *zith*^{i}; acc. pl. ज़िठ्यन् *zithyan*; ag. pl. ज़िठ्यौ *zithyau*.

Similarly, when the penultimate is *yü*, it becomes *ī* before *i-mātrā* or *is*, and *ē* in other cases, except the nom. sg. (77, 78); thus,—

Nom. sg. च्यूनु *tsyünᵃ*, a wall; acc. sg. चीनिस् *tsīnis*; gen. sg. चेन्युकु *tsēnyukᵘ*; ag. sg. चीनि *tsīnⁱ*; instr. sg. चेनि सीतिन् *tsēni sŏtin* (not *i-mātrā*); nom. pl. चीनि *tsīnⁱ*; acc. pl. चेन्यन् *tsēnyan*; ag. pl. चेन्यौ *tsēnyau*.

[The word न्यूलु *nyūlᵘ*, blue, however, has *ī* throughout. Thus, gen. sg. नील्युकु *nīlyukᵘ*; instr. sg. नीलि सीतिन् *nīli sŏtin*; acc. pl. नील्यन् *nīlyan*; ag. pl. नील्यौ *nīlyau*.

So also in य्यूतु *yyūtᵘ*, how much; त्यूतु *tyūtᵘ*, so much; यूतु *yūtᵘ*, this much; change the यू *yü* to *ī* throughout (ii. iii. 27). Thus, यीति *yītⁱ*, how many (nom. pl.); तीति *tītⁱ*; ईति *ītⁱ*, pr. *yītⁱ*.]

The अ *ă* in कतु *kătᵘ*, how many? (ii. iii. 25, 26) becomes ॳ *ạ*, in all cases except the nominative singular. In the obl. cases of the plural, it may optionally become ऐ *ai*. Thus—

	Singular.	Plural.
Nom.	कतु *kătᵘ*.	कति *kạtⁱ*.
Acc.	कतिस् *kạtis*.	कत्यन् *kạtyan* or कैत्यन् *kaityan*.
Ag.	कति *kạtⁱ*.	कत्यौ *kạtyau* or कैत्यौ *kaityau*.

Its fem. is कच़ *kạtsᵃ*.

The word कॊह् *kŏh*, or काह् *kāh*, a certain person, is declined as a feminine ending in a consonant (ii. iii. 29).

Third Declension.

Feminine nouns ending in ि *i-mātrā*, ु *ŭ-mātrā*, or ू *ū*.

पूथि *pūthⁱ*, a book.

(*a*). Nouns ending in ि *i-mātrā*.

Case	Singular	Plural
Nom.	**पूथि pūthⁱ** (ii. i. 9).	**पोथ्य pōthĕ** (11, 33).
Acc.	**पोथ्य pōthĕ** (21, 33, 38, 40).	**पोथ्यन् pōthyan** (12, 38).
	पूथि *pūthⁱ* (39).	पोथ्य *pōthĕ* (39).
Gen.	पोथ्य हंदु *pōthĕ hand^u* (42).	पोथ्यन् हंदु *pōthyan hand^u* (42).
Loc. 1.	पोथ्य प्यठ् *pōthĕ pyăṭh*, &c. (52, 53).	पोथ्यन् प्यठ् *pōthyan pyăṭh* (52, 53).
Dat. 1.	पोथ्य कितु *pōthĕ kyut^u* (54, 55).	पोथ्यन् कितु *pōthyan kyut^u* (54, 55).
Concom.	पोथ्य सतिन् *pōthĕ sạtin* (60).	पोथ्यन् सतिन् *pōthyan sạtin* (60).
Agent.	**पोथि pōthi** (6, 56).	**पोथ्यौ pōthyau** (56; i. 4).
Instr.	पोथि सतिन् *pōthi sạtin* (33, 59).	पोथ्यौ सतिन् *pōthyau sạtin* (59).
	पोथ्य हन्दि सतिन् *pōthĕ handi sạtin* (61).	पोथ्यन् हन्दि सतिन् *pōthyan handi sạtin* (61).
Loc. 2.	पोथि अन्द्र *pōthi andr^a* (57).	पोथ्यौ अन्द्र *pōthyau andr^a* (57).
Dat. 2.	पोथि पुछ् *pōthi putshy* (63).	पोथ्यौं पुछ् *pōthyau putshy* (33, 63).
	पोथ्य हन्दि पुछ् *pōthĕ handi putshy* (63).	पोथ्यन् हन्दि पुछ् *pōthyan handi putshy* (63).
Abl.	पोथि निश *pōthi niç^a* (65).	पोथ्यौ निश *pōthyau niç^a* (65).

Similarly are declined, ङूरि *ṅūrⁱ*, a hoof; खीति *khītⁱ*, a field; चीरि *cīrⁱ*, a lottery ticket.

If the penultimate of a feminine word contains the vowel *ū*, that *ū* becomes *ō* in all cases except the nominative singular. Thus पूथि *pūthⁱ* a book; nom. pl. पोथ्य *pōthĕ* (33).

So also a penultimate ī becomes a ĕ in the same circumstance Thus खीति *khītⁱ*, a field; nom. pl. खेते *khĕtĕ*. The word चीरि *cīrⁱ*, a lottery-ticket or slip, does not, however, change its long ī, and its nom. pl. is चीरे *cīrĕ* (33).

(*b*). Nouns ending in ॖ *ū-mātrā*.

कूर् *kūrᵘ*, a girl.

	Singular	Plural
Nom.	कूर् **kūrᵘ** (ii. 1. 9).	कोरे **kōrĕ** (11, 30, 33).
Acc.	कोरे **kōrĕ** (21, 33, 38, 40).	कोरेन् **kōryan** (12, 30, 33, 38).
	कूर् *kūrᵘ* (39).	कोरे *kōrĕ* (39).
Gen.	कोरे हुन्द् *kōrĕ hạndᵘ* (42).	कोरेन् हुन्द् *kōryan hạndᵘ*.
Loc. 1.	कोरे पठ् *kōrĕ pyạṭh*, &c. (52, 53).	कोरेन् पठ् *kōryan pyạṭh*, &c. (52, 53).
Dat. 1.	कोरे किशु *kōrĕ kyutᵘ* (54, 55).	कोरेन् किशु *kōryan kyutᵘ* (54, 55).
Concom.	कोरे सुतिन् *kōrĕ sạtin* (60).	कोरेन् सुतिन् *kōryan sạtin* (60).
Agent.	कोरि **kōri** (6, 56).	कोरौ **kōryau** (56, 30; i. 4).
Instr.	कोरि सुतिन् *kōri sạtin* (6, 30, 59).	कोरौ सुतिन् *kōryau sạtin* (33, 59).
	कोरे हन्दि सुतिन् *kōrĕ handi sạtin* (61).	कोरेन् हन्दि सुतिन् *kōryan handi sạtin* (61).
Loc. 2.	कोरि अन्द्र् *kōri andrᵘ* (57).	कोरौ अन्द्र् *kōryau andrᵘ* (57).
Dat. 2.	कोरि पुछ् *kōri putshy* (63).	कोरौ पुछ् *kōryau putshy* (63).
	कोरे हन्दि पुछ् *kōrĕ handi putshy* (63).	कोरेन् हन्दि पुछ् *kōryan handi putshy* (63).
Abl.	कोरि निश *kōri niçᵘ* (65).	कोरौ निश *kōryau niçᵘ* (65).

Similarly are declined पटु *pạṭ^{u}*, a tablet; हटु *hạṭ^{u}*, wood; काठु *kāṭh^{u}*, a stalk, especially the non-edible part of asparagus, sugarcane, &c.; बडु *bạḍ^{u}*, a great woman; तञु *tạñ^{u}* (or तञ् *tañ*) a slender woman; लञडु *lạṇḍ^{u}*, a branch.

The final *ū* becomes *i* (or *y*) throughout, except in the nom. sg. (30).

All nouns of this declension ending in टु *ṭ^{u}*, ठु *ṭh^{u}*, or डु *ḍ^{u}*, change the consonant to the corresponding palatal, in all cases except the nominative singular. Thus—

Nom. sing.	Nom. pl.
पटु *pạṭ^{u}*.	पच *pacĕ*.
काठु *kāṭh^{u}*.	काछ *kāchĕ*.
बडु *bạḍ^{u}*.	बज *bajĕ*.

This change only occurs when the word ends in *ū-mātrā* (22). It does not occur when it ends in a consonant (26).

If the penultimate of a feminine word contains the vowel *ū*, that *ū* becomes *ō* in all cases except the nom. singular, thus कूरु *kūr^{u}*, a girl, nom. pl. कोरे *kōrĕ* (33).

The following are exceptions and do not change the *ū* (35). ठुरु *ṭụr^{u}* cold; दूरु *dūr^{u}*, a lane; मूरु *mūr^{u}*, a twig. Thus from ठुरु *ṭụr^{u}*; nom. pl. ठुरे *ṭụrĕ*.

So also a penultimate *ī* becomes *ē* in the same circumstances. Thus, सीरु *sīr^{u}*, a brick, nom. pl. सेरे *sērĕ*. The following words (33) however, do not change,—

गीरु *gīr^{u}*, red-chalk.	Nom. pl.	गीरे *gīrĕ*.
गीदु *gīd^{u}*, child's excrement.		गीद *gīdĕ*.
टीठु *ṭīṭh^{u}*, pride.		टीछ *ṭīchĕ* (22).
तीरु *tīr^{u}*, cold-boiled-rice-pudding.		तीरे *tīrĕ*.
पीरु *pīr^{u}*, a table.		पीरे *pīrĕ*.

Whenever in this declension *ŭ-mātrā* is preceded by *a* or *ā*, the *a* or *ā* become modified to *ạ* or *ạ̄* respectively (70). Thus,

Base पट् *paṭ*, a tablet; nom. sg. पॅटु *pạṭ*ᵘ, but acc. sg. पच्य *pacyŏ*; ag. sg. पचि *paci* (*i* fully pronounced,—not *ĭ-mātrā*); nom. pl. पच *pacĕ*; acc. pl. पच्यन् *pacyan*; ag. pl. पच्यौ *pacyau*.

So,—Base माज् *māj*, a mother; nom. sg. मॉजु *mạ̄j*ᵘ; but acc. sg. माज्य *mājŏ*.

Again; Base, काठ् *kāṭh*, wood; nom. sg. कॉठु *kạ̄ṭh*ᵘ; acc. sg. काछ *kāchŏ*.

(*c*). Nouns ending in ञ् *ñ*.

Similarly are declined all feminine nouns in ञ् *ñ*, thus म्यॉञ् *myạ̄ñ*, mine (fem.).

	SINGULAR.	PLURAL.
Nom.	म्यॉञ् *myạ̄ñ*.	म्याञे *myāñĕ*.
Acc.	म्याञ *myāñŏ*.	म्याञन् *myāñan*.
Ag.	म्याञि *myāñi*.	म्याञौ *myāñau*.

The vowel is only modified in the nom. sing. So also च्यॉञ् *cyạ̄ñ* thine (fem.); सॉञ् *sạ̄ñ*, our (fem.) (ii. iii. 11 and ff).

As the semivowel य *ya* cannot, as a rule, immediately follow च़् *ts*, छ़् *tsh*, or स् *s*, when a noun ends in च़ु *ts*ᵘ, छ़ु *tsh*ᵘ, or सु *s*ᵘ, the य *ya* is elided in declension. Thus मॅच़ु *mạts*ᵘ, mad, (feminine): nom. pl. मच़ *mats*ᵉ, not मच्य *matsŏ*. कॊछ़ु *kwạtsh*ᵘ, a small bag: pl. कॊछ़ *kŏts*ᵉ. वॊर्यसु *wŏr*ᵉ*s*ᵘ, a woman who has married twice, pl. वॊर्यस *wŏr*ᵉ*s*ᵉ. (iv. 51). The य *ya* is, however, retained in the singular. Thus the acc. sg. is मच्य *matsŏ*, कॊछ्य *kŏtshŏ*, and वॊर्यस्य *wŏr*ᵉ*sŏ*.

FOURTH DECLENSION.

Nouns ending in अ *a*, or a consonant.

(*a*). Nouns ending in अ *a*

ब्यञ़ *bĕñĕ*, a sister.

Nom.	ब्यञ़ bĕñĕ (ii. i. 1).	ब्यञ़ bĕñĕ (1).
Acc.	ब्यञ़ bĕñe (38, 40, 39).	ब्यञ़न् bĕñan (38). ब्यञ़ *bĕñĕ* (39).
Gen.	ब्यञ़ हंदु *bĕñĕ hand*[a] (42).	ब्यञ़न् हंदु *bĕñan hand*[a] (42).
Loc. 1.	ब्यञ़ प्यठ् *bĕñĕ pyăṭh* (52, 53).	ब्यञ़न् प्यठ् *bĕñan pyăṭh*, &c. (52, 53).
Dat. 1.	ब्यञ़ क्युतु *bĕñĕ kyut*[a] (54, 55).	ब्यञ़न् क्युतु *bĕñan kyut*[a] (54, 55).
Concom.	ब्यञ़ सुंतिन् *bĕñe sŏtin* (60).	ब्यञ़न् सुंतिन् *bĕñan sŏtin* (60).
Agent.	ब्यञ़ि bĕñi (56; i. 4).	ब्यञ़ौ bĕñau (56, i. 4).
Instr.	ब्यञ़ि सुंतिन् *bĕñi sŏtin* (59).	ब्यञ़ौ सुंतिन् *bĕñau sŏtin* (59).
	ब्यञ़ हंदि सुंतिन् *bĕñĕ handi sŏtin* (61).	ब्यञ़न् हंदि सुंतिन् *bĕñan handi sŏtin* (61).
Loc. 2.	ब्यञ़ि अन्द्र *bĕñi andr*[a] (57).	ब्यञ़ौ अन्द्र *bĕñau andr*[a] (57).
Dat. 2.	ब्यञ़ि पुछ् *bĕñi putshy* (63).	ब्यञ़ौ पुछ् *bĕñau putshy* (63).
	ब्यञ़ हंदि पुछ् *bĕñĕ handi putshy*.	ब्यञ़न् हंदि पुछ् *bĕñan handi putshy* (63).
Abl.	ब्यञ़ि निश *bĕñi niç*[a] (65).	ब्यञ़ौ निश *bĕñau niç*[a] (65).

(*b*). Nouns ending in a consonant.

मालु् *mā̆l*, a garland.

	Singular	Plural
Nom.	**मालु् māl** (ii. i. 10).	**माल mālᵃ** (11).
Acc.	**मालि māli** (37; 38, 40).	**मालन् mālan** (12, 38).
	मालु् *mā̆l* (39).	माल *mālᵃ* (39).
Gen.	मालि हंदु *māli hạndᵘ* (42).	मालन् हंदु *mālan hạndᵘ* (42).
Loc. 1.	मालि पच् *māli pyăṭh*, &c., (52, 53).	मालन् पच् *mālan pyăṭh*, &c., (52, 53).
Dat. 1.	मालि किनु *māli kyutᵘ* (54, 55).	मालन् किनु *mālan kyutᵘ*.
Concom.	मालि स्तिन् *māli sạtin* (60).	मालन् स्तिन् *mālan sạtin* (60).
Agent.	**मालि māli** (56).	**मालौ mālau** (56).
Instr.	मालि स्तिन् *māli sạtin* (59).	मालौ स्तिन् *mālau sạtin* (59).
	मालि हन्दि स्तिन् *māli handi sạtin* (61).	मालन् हन्दि स्तिन् *mālan handi sạtin* (61).
Loc. 2	मालि अन्द्र *māli andrᵘ* (57).	मालौ अन्द्र *mālau andrᵘ* (57).
Dat. 2	मालि पुछ् *māli puṭshy* (63).	मालौ पुछ् *mālau puṭshy* (63).
	मालि हन्दि पुछ् *māli handi puṭshy* (63).	मालन् हन्दि पुछ् *mālan handi puṭshy* (63).
Abl.	मालि निश *māli niçᵘ* (65).	मालौ निश *mālau niçᵘ* (65).

Similarly are declined क्रक् *kruk*, a loud noise; नारिज् *nārij*, a conduit; जंग् *zang*, a thigh.

Note that when a noun ends in क् *k*, च् *c*, च़् *ts*, ट् *ṭ*, त् *t* or प् *p*, these letters are aspirated in the nom. sing. (66, 67); thus—

	Nom. sg.	but Nom. pl.
क्रक् *krak*, a loud noise.	क्रक् *krăkh*.	क्रक *krak*^{a}.
रच़् *rats*, abrus precatorius.	रच़् *rătsh*.	रच *rats*^{a}.
ऋच़् *ṛts*, a sub-caste.	ऋच़् *ṛtsh*.	ऋच *ṛts*^{a}.
नट् *naṭ*, trembling.	नट् *năṭh*.	नट *naṭ*^{a}.
वत् *wat*, a road.	वत् *wăth*.	वत *wat*^{a}.
चाप् *tsāp*, food.	चाप् *tsāph*.	चाप *tsāp*^{a}.

The aspiration, being at the end of a word, is barely audible, but it affects the preceding vowel. It only occurs in the nominative singular.

This aspiration does not occur if a final त् *t* or च़् *ts* forms part (either the first or second member) of a compound consonant (even when a short *a* is inserted to aid pronunciation) (68): thus;—

	Nom. sg.
बत्च् *bat*^{a}*c*, a duck.	बत्च् *bat*^{a}*c* (elsewhere spelled बत्च् *bat*^{a}*c*^{a}, see p. 32).
बक्च़् *bŏk*^{a}*ts*, a female puppy.[1]	बक्च़् *bŏk*^{a}*ts*.
मक्च़् *mak*^{a}*ts*, an axe.	मक्च़् *mak*^{a}*ts*.
नस्त् *nast*, nose.	नस्त् *nast*.

Other compounds are, however, aspirated. Thus,—

	Nom. sg.	Nom. pl.
रेम्प् *rĕmp*, a little.	रेम्प् *rĕmph*.	रेम्प *rĕmp*^{a}.
चाम्प् *tsāmp*, consolation.	चाम्प् *tsāmph*.	चाम्प *tsāmp*^{a}.

The word ज़ाम् *zām*, a husband's sister, is irregular (71). In all cases, except the nominative singular, it becomes ज़ोम् *zōm*, and drops every vowel in the terminations. Thus; acc. sg. ज़ोम् *zōm*; ag. sg.

1 So Içvara-kaula. Mr. H. Knowles informs me that this word means the young of any animal.

ज़ोम् *zōm*; nom. pl. ज़ोम् *zūm*; acc. pl. ज़ोमन् *zōm^{e}n*; ag. pl. ज़ोमव् *zōm^{e}v*; instr. sg. ज़ोम् स्तिन् *zōm sętin*; gen. sg. ज़ोम् हंन्दु *zōm hąnd^{u}*, &c.

The word मूँच् *mūç* (ii. iii. 28), a buffalo-cow, changes ऊ *ū* to *ai* in all cases except the nom. sg., thus—

	SINGULAR.	PLURAL.
Nom.	मूँच् *mūç*.	मैँच *maiç^{e}*.
Acc.	मैँचि *maiçi*.	मैँचन् *maiçan*.
Ag.	मैँचि *maiçi*.	मैँचौ *maiçau*.

The word कूँह् *kūh* or काँह् *kāh*, any one, some one, though of both genders, is always declined as a feminine, in the sg. number. It changes ऊ *ū* and आ *ā* to ऐ *ai* and ह् *h* to स् *s* in all cases except the nom. sg. (ii. iii. 29). It becomes कोन्ट्स् *kōnts* in the plural (ii. iii. 30) and is then declined as a masculine.

Thus,—

	SINGULAR.	PLURAL.
Nom.	कूँह् *kūh*, काँह् *kāh*.	कोन्ट्स् *kōnts*.
Acc.	कैँसि *kaisi*.	कोन्ट्सन् *kōntsan*.
Ag.	कैँसि *kaisi*.	कोन्ट्सौ *kōntsau*.

(*c*). Irregular Feminine Nouns, ending in Consonants.

रात् *rāt*, night.

Nom.	**राथ् rāth** (ii. i. 10, 66).	**रा॑चु rāṭsᵘ** (16, 23).
Acc.	**रा॑चु rāṭsᵘ** (16, 23, 38, 40).	**रा॑चन् rāṭsᵘn** (14, 16, 23, 38).
	राथ् *rāth* (39).	रा॑चु *rāṭsᵘ* (39).
Gen.	रा॑चु ह॑न्दु *rāṭsᵘ hand*ᵘ (42).	रा॑चन् ह॑न्दु *rāṭsᵘn hand*ᵘ (42).
Loc. 1.	रा॑चु मंज़ *rāṭsᵘ manz*, &c. (52, 53).	रा॑चन् मंज़ *rāṭsᵘn manz*, &c. (52, 53).
Dat. 1.	रा॑चु किनु *rāṭsᵘ kyut*ᵘ (54, 55).	रा॑चन् किनु *rāṭsᵘn kyut*ᵘ (54, 55)
Concom.	रा॑चु स॑तिन् *rāṭsᵘ sătin* (60).	रा॑चन् स॑तिन् *rāṭsᵘn sătin*.
Agent.	**रा॑चु rāṭsᵘ** (7, 17).	**रा॑चव् rāṭsᵘv** (20, 56).
Instr.	रा॑चु स॑तिन् *rāṭsᵘ sătin* (59).	रा॑चव् स॑तिन् *rāṭsᵘv sătin* (59).
	रा॑चु हन्दि स॑तिन् *rāṭsᵘ handi sătin* (61).	रा॑चन् हन्दि स॑तिन् *rāṭsᵘn handi sătin* (61).
Loc. 2.	रा॑चु अन्द्र *rāṭsᵘ andr*ᵘ (57).	रा॑चव् अन्द्र *rāṭsᵘv andr*ᵘ.
Dat. 2.	रा॑चु पुछ् *rāṭsᵘ putshy* (63).	रा॑चव् पुछ् *rāṭsᵘv putshy* (63).
	रा॑चु हन्दि पुछ् *rāṭsᵘ handi putshy* (63).	रा॑चन् हन्दि पुछ् *rāṭsᵘn handi putshy* (63).
Abl.	रा॑चु निश *rāṭsᵘ niç*ᵘ (65).	रा॑चव् निश *rāṭsᵘv niç*ᵘ (65).

This group of irregular nouns consists of most feminine nouns in त् *t*, थ् *th*, द् *d*, न् *n*, ह् *h*, and certain nouns in ल् *l*. In all these cases the final consonant is changed as follows :—

त् *t*	becomes	च़् *ts*
थ् *th*		छ़् *tsh*
द् *d*		ज़् *z*
न् *n*		ञ् *ñ*
ह् *h*		श् *ç*
ल् *l*		ज् *j*.

e.g., रात् *rāt*, night ;	Nom. pl.	राँच़् *rặtsᵉ* (23, 14, 16).
कोथ् *kŏth*, a hank ;		क्वछ़् *kwạtshᵉ* (23, 14, 16).
ग्रन्द् *grand*, a counting ;		ग्रंज़् *grạnzᵉ* (23, 14, 16).
ईरन् *yīran*, an anvil ;		ईरञ् *īrạñᵉ* (23, 14, 16).
काह् *kāh*, eleventh lunar day ;		कांश् *kạ̄çᵉ* (19, 14, 16).
वाल् *wāl*, a hole ;		वांज् *wạ̄jᵉ* (27, 14, 16).

Other examples are सत् *sat*, hope ; हान् *hān*, loss ; च़ामन् *tsāman*, cheese.

The words in ल् *l* which follow this declension are वाल् *wāl*, a hole (as that of a serpent) ; साल् *sāl*, a wife's sister ; ज़ाल् *zāl*, a net ; कल् *kal*, thought, consideration ; and हाल् *hāl*, a house, a hall (27, 28). The word हाल् *hāl* when it is at the end of a *masculine* compound is, however, declined regularly ; thus च़ाटहालस् अन्दर् *tsāṭahālas andar* (not च़ाटहांज् अन्दर *tsāṭahạ̄jᵉ andar*,) in the school-house, because च़ाटहाल् *tsāṭahāl* is masculine (28). The words कुंडल् *kuṇḍal*, a kind of cup (especially the cup of a portable stove), and करतल् *kartal* a sword, may optionally be regular. Thus कुंडज् सूतिन् *kuṇḍạjᵉ sọtin* or कुंडलि सूतिन् *kuṇḍali sọtin*, by the cup, (29).

EXCEPTIONS. The following nouns are however declined regularly (24, 25):—

वत् *wat*, a road.

लत् *lat*, a kick.

दत् *dat*, a clod.

थॊत् *thŏt*, an impediment.

चॊत् *tsŏt*, the anus.

चित् *tsitt*, a sprain.

चॅत् *tsŏt*, tumbling head over heels.

गत् *g^{a}t*, a rise in a river, a swift flood.

पोत् *pĭt*, a trifle.

टोंत् *tŏt*, a beak.

कथ् *kăth*, a story.

व्यथ् *vyăth*, the river Jhelum.

खॊन् *khŏn*, the elbow.

तन् *tan*, the body.

नान् *nān*, the navel.

सॊन् *sŏn*, a co-wife.

हन् *han*, a little.

बन् *ban*, a heap, pile.

Thus वति सॅतिन् *wati sạtin*, not वतु सॅतिन् *wạts^{u} sạtin*.

It must be remembered that the *ū-mātrā* modifies a preceding *a* to *ạ*, and *ā* to *ạ̄* (71). When final it is not pronounced. When it precedes a consonant it is pronounced like a short German *ü*. Thus रॊचुव् *rạts^{u}v* is pronounced something like, German, *rötsüv*.

It must also be remembered that words ending in *t* form the nominative singular in *th* (66). Thus the nom. sg. of रात् *rāt*, night, is राथ् *rāth*, and of वत् *wat*, a road, is वथ् *wath*.

The words यड् *yaḍ*, belly; गाव् *gāv*, a cow; थर् *thar*, the back; कर

66

kǒṭh, a fragrant root, *Aucklandia Costus;* वड् *waḍ*, discount; are similarly declined, except that they do not change their final consonant. Thus यड् सतिन् *yaḍ*ⁿ *sⁿtin*, by the belly (7). Nom. pl. यड् *yaḍ*ⁿ (17).

The words खार् *khār*, an ass's load, a certain measure; मार् *mār*, the name of a river; सार् *sār*, a cross-beam, for strengthening; राप् *rāp*, stock-in-trade; follow the same rule. *E.g.*, nom. pl. खोर् *khọr*ⁿ (18). [*Sūtra* 18, apparently only refers to the plural. But the singular follows the same rule, *e.g.*, खोर् सतिन् *khọr*ⁿ *sⁿtin*, by the measure].

The word गाव् *gāv*, abovementioned, changes its *ā* to *ō* in all cases except the nom. sg. (72); thus, acc. sg. गोव् *gōv*ⁿ; ag. sg. गोव् *gōv*ⁿ; nom. pl. गोव् *gōv*ⁿ; acc. pl. गोवन् *gōv*ⁿ*n*; ag. pl. गोवव् *gōv*ⁿ*v*.

II. Composition and Concordance.

Içvara-kaula, in his *Kāçmira-çabdāmṛta*, treats of the two subjects forming the title of this section, in the *Samāsa-prakriyā*, the third portion of his grammar. He treats an adjective in concord with a noun as an example of a *karmadhāraya*, or adjectival compound. Really, as will be seen, it is not a compound at all, but an instance of syntactical agreement. Just as *bonus homo*, in Latin means a good man, and *boni hominis*, of a good man, so *baḍ*ⁿ *lar*ⁿ, in Kāçmiri means a large house, and *baji lari pyaṭh*ⁿ, means from a great house.

In the case of all compounds and concordances the postposition denoting the case is omitted after every member of the compound, except the last, but each member is inflected as if to receive the postposition (iii. 2). Thus, चटु गुर् *chaṭ*ⁿ *gur*ⁿ means, a white horse. The instrumental plural of चटु *chaṭ*ⁿ is चत्यौ सतिन् *chatyau sⁿtin*, and of गुर् *gur*ⁿ is गुर्यौ सतिन् *guryau sⁿtin*, but the instrumental plural of चटु गुर् *chaṭ*ⁿ *gur*ⁿ, is चत्यौ गुर्यौ सतिन् *chatyau guryau sⁿtin*, not चत्यौ सतिन् गुर्यौ सतिन् *chatyau sⁿtin guryau sⁿtin*, by white horses. When there is no postposition these remarks, of course, do not apply. Thus the accusative singular is चतिस् गुरिस् *chatis guris*, and the nom. pl. is चटि गुरि *chaṭ*ⁱ *gur*ⁱ.

Karmadhāraya or adjectival compounds are expressed in Kāçmīrī by an adjective agreeing with its substantive in gender, number and case. The above rule about postpositions must be applied. Thus बॊडु् द्यार् *bǫḍ^{a} dyār* (masc.), great wealth; बड्यन् द्यारन् छुह् ज़ेनान् *baḍyan dyāran chuh zĕnān*, he is earning great wealth (acc. pl.); म्वचि च्वचि सॊतिन् *mŏci tsŏci sǫtin*, by a thick (मॊटु् *moṭ^{a}*) cake (च्वटु् *tsuçǫṭ^{a}*, fem.); त्रिछि कोरि पुछ्य् *trichi kōri putshy*, for a clever (त्र्युखु् *tryukh^{a}*, fem. त्रिछु् *trich^{a}*) girl (कूरु् *kūr^{a}*); बजि लरि प्यठ *baji lari pyaṭh^{a}* from the big (बॊडु् *bǫḍ^{a}*) house (लॊरु् *lǫr^{a}*); बज्य ग्रॊन्ज़ु् हॊन्डु् *bajĕ grǫnz^{a} hǫnd^{a}*, of the big counting (ग्रन्द् *grand*); बडिस् गुरिस् प्यठ् *baḍis guris pyăṭh*, on the great horse (गुर् *gur^{a}*). And so on.

In **Copulative** (*dvandva*) compounds each member of the compound is declined separately, the above rule as to post-positions being observed. Thus, base ताप् *tāp*, light (masc.); गट *gaṭ^{a}*, darkness (fem.). The nom. sg. of ताप् *tāp* is ताफ् *tāph* and the instr. sg. is ताप सॊतिन् *tāp^{a} sǫtin*. So from गट *gaṭ^{a}*, the nom. sg. is गट *gaṭ^{a}*, and the instr. sg. गटि सॊतिन् *gaṭi sǫtin*. The compound noun, 'light and darkness' is nom. sg., ताफ् गट *tāph-gaṭ^{a}*; instr. sg. ताप-गटि सॊतिन् *tāp^{a}-gaṭi sǫtin*, and so on. Again वारु् *wār^{a}* (fem.) is a garden; कुलु् *kul^{a}* (masc.) is a tree; फल् *phal* (masc.) is fruit; and ज़ल् *zal* (masc.) is water. Making these into a copulative compound we have in the dative sg. वारि-कुलि-फल-ज़ल पुछ्य् *wāri-kuli-phal^{a}-zal^{a} putshy*, for the garden, the tree, the fruit, and the water. Sometimes each member is put in the plural, the whole collective idea being plural though each member of the compound is properly in the singular. Thus माजु् *māj^{a}*, a mother, nom. pl. माज्य *mājĕ*; कूरु् *kūr^{a}*, a daughter, nom. pl. कोर्यं *kōrĕ*. Hence माज्य-कोर्यं *mājĕ-korĕ*, mother and daughter. So मॊलि पुथ्र् *mǫl^{i}-puth^{a}r*, father and son (मोलु् *mōl^{a}*, a father; पुथ्र् *puth^{a}r*, a son); हश-न्वश *haç^{a}-nŏṣ^{a}*, mother-in-law (हश् *haç*) daughter in-law (न्वश् *nŏṣ*); ज़ोम्-काकन्य *zōm-kākañĕ*, husband's sister (ज़ाम् *zām*) and brother's wife (काकॊन् *kākǫñ*); पच्य-कूच्य *pacĕ-kūcĕ*, board (पॊटु् *pǫṭ^{a}*) and wood (कूटु् *kūṭ^{a}*).

In **Tatpuruṣa** or appositional compounds, the first member usually takes the form which the word adopts in the agent, the न् *n* of the agent of the 1st declension, being dropped. We may also say that the first member of the compound is put in the genitive, the post-position being dropped, and *y* being changed to *i* (iii. 5).

Thus, ग्राकि-खच् *çrāki-khaç*, the cut of a knife (ग्राख् *çrākh*, fem.).

टोपि-फल् *ṭōpi-phal*ᵘ, the border of a cap (टूपि *ṭūp*ⁱ, fem.).

सर्प-बय स्तिन् *sar*ᵃ*p*ᵃ*-bay*ᵃ *stin*, by the fear (बय *bay*ᵃ, masc.) of a snake (सर्प् *sar*ᵃ*ph*, masc.).

राज़-न्यचिवि पुत्स्य् *rāz*ᵃ*-nĕcivi putshy*, for the son (न्यचुव् *nĕcyuv*ᵘ) of the king (राज़् *rāz*ᵃ).

बट-कोरे हन्द् *baṭ*ᵃ*-kōrĕ hand*ᵘ, of the daughter (कूर् *kūr*ᵃ) of the brāhmaṇa (बट *baṭ*ᵃ).

सुन-डब अन् *sŏn*ᵃ*-ḍab*ᵃ *an*, bring the box (डब *ḍab*ᵃ, masc.) of gold (सुन् *sŏn*, masc.), *i.e.*, the gold box.

म्यचि-फुटु थव् *mĕtsi-phoṭ*ᵘ *thav*, put down a basket (फुटु *phoṭ*ᵘ masc.) (full) of earth (म्यचु *myats*ᵘ).

Irregular formations.

1. When the word पोञु *pōñ*ᵘ, water, forms the second member of one of these compounds, it becomes वोञु *wōñ*ᵘ (iii. 6). Thus,—

गंग-वोञु *gaṅg*ᵃ*-wōñ*ᵘ, the water of the Ganges.

व्यथ-वोञु *vyath*ᵃ*-wōñ*ᵘ, the water of the Jhelum.

शीन-वोञु *çīn*ᵃ*-wōñ*ᵘ, snow-water.

वुग-वोञु *wug*ᵃ*-wōñ*ᵘ, flood-water.

मार्-वोञु *mār*ᵃ*-wōñ*ᵘ, the water of the Mār [see p. 67].

क्रीरि-वोञु *krīr*ⁱ*-wōñ*ᵘ, well (क्र्यूर् *kryūr*ᵘ, masc.) water.

रूद-वोञु *rūd*ᵃ*-wōñ*ᵘ, rain-water.

नाग-वोञु *nāg*ᵃ*-wōñ*ᵘ, spring-water.

2. The words पोञ् *pōñᵃ*, water, दाञ् *dāñᵃ* (masc.) rice, वोञ् *wōñᵃ*, a merchant, and others, become पाँ *pā̃*, दाँ *dā̃*, and वाँ *wā̃* respectively, when (iii. 7, 8) they are first members of one of these compounds. Thus,—

पाँ-त्रख् *pā̃-trăkh*, a measure (4½ sērs) of water.

पाँ-नटु *pā̃-nąṭᵘ*, a water-bucket.

दाँ-खार् *dā̃-khār*, a measure (16 *trăkhs*) of rice.

दाँ-फोटु *dā̃-phoṭᵘ*, a basket (full) of rice.

वाँ-द्यलु *wā̃-dyąlᵘ*, the merchant's straw.

वाँ-कूरु *wā̃-kūrᵘ*, the merchant's daughter.

3. The प *p* of the word पथर् *pąthᵃr*, a leaf, becomes व *w* in masculine compounds (iii. 9). Thus,—

बोञि-वथर् *bōñi-wąthᵃr*, plane-tree-leaves.

पोष-वथर् *pōšᵃ-wąthᵃr*, a flower-petal.

ख्यल्ल-वथर् *khyallᵃ-wąthᵃr*, a leaf of the lotus-grass.

हाक-वथर् *hākᵃ-wąthᵃr*, spinach-leaves.

When, however, the compound is feminine, the word पथर् *pąthᵃr*, becomes पतर् *pątᵃr*. Thus

मुजि पतर् *muji-pątᵃr* (fem.), a radish-leaf.

गगजि-पतर् *gŏgᵃji-pątᵃr* (fem.), a turnip-leaf.

4. The word चुटु *tswąṭᵘ*, a cake (fem.), is restricted in composition to cakes made of grain (iii. 12). Thus

तमुल-चुटु *tŏmᵃlᵃ-tswąṭᵘ*, rice-cake.

कनक-चुटु *kanᵃkᵃ-tswąṭᵘ*, wheat-cake.

वुश्कि-चुटु *wuṣki-tswąṭᵘ*, barley-cake.

If not made of grain, the word मंडु *mwąṇḍᵘ*, must be substituted.

70

Thus

थुल-मंड *thŭlᵉ-mwąṇḍᵉ*, egg-cake.

नदुरि-मंड *nądᵉrⁱ-mwąṇḍᵉ*, lotus-stalk-cake.

च्रांमंन्-मंड *tsāmąnᵉ-mwąṇḍᵉ* (also written, च्रांमंन् *tsāmaṅ-*), cheese-cake.

अद्रक्-मंड *adrak-mwąṇḍᵉ*, ginger-cake [apparently irregular].

The masculine form मंड *monḍᵘ*, can, however, be used for grain cakes, thus

तमुल-मंड *tŏmᵉlᵉ-monḍᵘ*, rice-cake, (तमुल् *tŏmul*, rice).

अब-मंड *abᵉ-monḍᵘ*, a cake of parched meal.

Bahu-vrīhi or relative compounds are similarly formed. When formed of an adjective and a substantive, the adjective is usually put last (iii. 13). Examples are

यड-बड *yaḍᵉ-bąḍᵘ* (not बड-यड *bąḍᵉ-yąḍᵘ*, as we might expect), big-bellied, Skr. *bṛhad-udara*, quasi *udara-bṛhat*.

दारि-ह्युठ *dāri-hyŭṭhᵘ*, long (ह्युठ *hyᵉṭhᵘ*) bearded (दारि *dārᵉ*, fem., a beard).

कन-च्रट *kanᵉ-tsaṭᵘ* having the ear (कन् *kan*, masc.) cut (च्रट *tsaṭᵘ*).

हुनि-बुठ *hŭnⁱ-buṭhᵘ*, dog (हुन *hŭnᵘ*, a dog) faced (बुठ *buṭhᵘ*, a face).

When one member of the compound is a numeral, it is put first, thus

दु-वहर् *du-wahąrᵘ*, occurring every two years.

सत-बोच्र *satᵉ-bŏtsᵘ*, having a family of seven.

पांच्र-पतुर् *pātsᵉ-potur*, having five sons.

Alliterative compounds (which are always feminine) are also classed as *bahu-vrīhis* by Īçvara-kaula (iii. 14); thus

ठल-ठल् *ṭhŏlᵉ-ṭhŏl*, mutual pushing with horns.

टप-टप् *ṭapᵉ-ṭăph*, mutual kicking.

ठूख ठूख् *ṭhŭkᵉ-ṭhŭkh*, mutual pushing with horns.

चप-चप् *capᵉ-căph*, tooth against tooth.

When an adjective is used as an adverb, its form is not changed (v. 5). It stands in the masculine singular.

Thus,—

गोबु गोबु छुह् पकान् *gob^{u} gob^{u} chuh pakān*, he is going slowly.

चटुर् (or चटुर् चटुर्) खेवान छुह् *tsaṭur* (or *tsaṭur tsaṭur*) *khyawān chuh*, he is eating quickly.

लोतु करान् छुह् *lot^{u} karān chuh*, he is doing slowly.

F. Numerals.

The following are the Kāçmīrī numerals from one to ten millions, as written down for me by my Paṇḍit. They differ in several respects from those given by Wade.

CARDINALS.	ORDINALS.
1 अख् *ăkh.*	अक्युमु *akyum^{u}* or गोडनिक *gŏḍañuk^{u}.*
2 ज़ह् *z^{a}h.*	द्वयुमु *dŏyum^{u}.*
3 त्रिह् *trih* or त्रेह् *trĕh.*	त्रेयुमु *trĕyum^{u}.*
4 चोर् *tsŏr.*	चूर्युमु *tsūryum^{u}.*
5 पांछ् *pāṇts* or पाञ्छ् *pānts.*	पूंछ्युमु *pūntsyum^{u}.*
6 षह् *ṣah.*	षयुमु *ṣayum^{u}.*
7 सथ् *săth.*	सत्युमु *satyum^{u}.*
8 ऐठ् *aiṭh.*	ऐठ्युमु *aiṭhyum^{u}.*
9 नव् *nav.*	नव्युमु *navyum^{u}.*
10 दह् *dah.*	दह्युमु *dahyum^{u}.*
11 काह् *kāh.*	काह्युमु *kāhyum^{u}.*
12 बाह् *bāh.*	बाह्युमु *bāhyum^{u}.*
13 त्रुवाह् *truwāh.*	त्रुवाह्युमु *truwāhyum^{u}.*
14 चुदाह् *tsŏdāh.*	चुदाह्युमु *tsŏdāhyum^{u}.*
15 पन्दाह् *pandāh.*	पन्दाह्युमु *pandāhyum^{u}.*

16 षुराह् *şurāh.*	षुरांहुम् *şurạ̄hyum^{a}.*
17 सदाह् *sadāh.*	सदांहुम् *sadạ̄hyum^{a}.*
18 अरदाह् *aradāh.*	अरदांहुम् *aradạ̄hyum^{a}.*
19 कुनवुह् *kunawuh.*	कुनवुहुम् *kunawuhyum^{a}.*
20 वुह् *wuh.*	वुहुम् *wuhyum^{a}.*
21 अकवुह् *akawuh.*	अकवुहुम् *akawuhyum^{a}.*
22 स्तोवुह् *s^{a}tŏwuh.*	स्तोवुहुम् *s^{a}tŏwuhyum^{a}.*
23 त्रुवुह् *trŏwuh.*	त्रुवुहुम् *trŏwuhyum^{a}.*
24 त्सुवुह् *t̲s̲ŏwuh.*	त्सुवुहुम् *t̲s̲ŏwuhyum^{a}.*
25 पूंन्छ्ह् *pȫnts^{a}h.*	पूंन्छ्हुम् *pȫnt̲s̲^{a}hyum^{a}.*
26 षवुह् *şawuh.*	षवुहुम् *şawuhyum^{a}.*
27 सतोवुह् *satŏwuh.*	सतोवुहुम् *satŏwuhyum^{a}.*
28 ऐठोवुह् *aiţhŏwuh.*	ऐठोवुहुम् *aiţhŏwuhyum^{a}.*
29 कुनत्रह् *kunatr^{a}h.*	कुनत्रहुम् *kunatr^{a}hyum^{a}.*
30 त्रह् *tr^{a}h.*	त्रहुम् *tr^{a}hyum^{a}.*
31 अकत्रह् *akatr^{a}h.*	अकत्रहुम् *akatr^{a}hyum^{a}.*
32 दयत्रह् *dŏyatr^{a}h.*	दयत्रहुम् *dŏyatr^{a}hyum^{a}.*
33 त्रयत्रह् *tĕyatr^{a}h.*	त्रयत्रहुम् *tĕyatr^{a}hyum^{a}.*
34 त्सयत्रह् *t̲s̲ŏyatr^{a}h.*	त्सयत्रहुम् *t̲s̲ŏyatr^{a}hyum^{a}.*
35 पांन्छत्रह् *pạ̄nt̲s̲atr^{a}h* or पान्छत्रह् *pānt̲s̲atr^{a}h.*	पांन्छत्रहुम् *pạ̄nt̲s̲atr^{a}hyum^{a}.*
36 षयत्रह् *şayatr^{a}h.*	षयत्रहुम् *şayatr^{a}hyum^{a}.*
37 सतत्रह् *satatr^{a}h.*	सतत्रहुम् *satatr^{a}hyum^{a}.*
38 अरत्रह् *aratr^{a}h.*	अरत्रहुम् *aratr^{a}hyum^{a}.*
39 कुनताजिह् *kunatạ̄jih.*	कुनताजिहुम् *kunatạ̄j^{i}hyum^{a}.*
40 त्सलजिह् *t̲s̲alajih.*	त्सलजिहुम् *t̲s̲alajihyum^{a}.*

78

41 अकतांजिह् *akutājih.* — अकतांजिह्युम् *akatāj'hyum**.[1]

42 द्वयतांजिह् *dŏyatājih.* — द्वयतांजिह्युम् *dŏyatāj'hyum**.

43 त्र्यतांजिह् *tĕyatājih.* — त्र्यतांजिह्युम् *teyatāj'hyum**.

44 च्यतांजिह् *tsŏyatājih.* — च्यतांजिह्युम् *tsŏyatāj'hyum**.

45 पांच्यतांजिह् *pāntsatājih.* — पांच्यतांजिह्युम् *pāntsatāj'hyum**.

46 षयतांजिह् *ṣayatājih.* — षयतांजिह्युम् *ṣayatāj'hyum**.

47 सततांजिह् *satatājih.* — सततांजिह्युम् *satatāj'hyum**.

48 अरतांजिह् *aratājih.* — अरतांजिह्युम् *aratāj'hyum**.

49 कुनवज़ाह् *kunawanzāh.* — कुनवज़ाह्युम् *kunawanzāhyum**.

50 पंच्चाह् *pantsāh.* — पंच्चाह्युम् *pantsāhyum**.

51 अकवज़ाह् *akawanzāh.* — अकवज़ाह्युम् *akawanzāhyum**.

52 द्ववज़ाह् *dŏwanzāh.* — द्ववज़ाह्युम् *dŏwanzāhyum**.

53 त्रवज़ाह् *tr^{a}wanzāh.* — त्रवज़ाह्युम् *tr^{a}wanzāhyum**.

54 च्चवज़ाह् *tsŏwanzāh.* — च्चवज़ाह्युम् *tsŏwanzāhyum**.

55 पांच्चवज़ाह् *pāntsawanzāh.* — पांच्चवज़ाह्युम् *pāntsawanzāhyum**.

56 षवज़ाह् *ṣawanzāh.* — षवज़ाह्युम् *ṣawanzāhyum**.

57 सतवज़ाह् *satawanzāh.* — सतवज़ाह्युम् *satawanzāhyum**.

58 अरवज़ाह् *arawanzāh.* — अरवज़ाह्युम् *arawanzāhyum**.

59 कुनहैठ् *kunahaiṭh.* — कुनहैठ्युम् *kunahaiṭhyum**.

60 शैठ् *çaiṭh* or शेठ् *çēṭh.* — शीठ्युम् *çiṭhyum**.

61 अकहैठ् *akahaiṭh.*[2] — अकहैठ्युम् *akahaiṭhyum**.

62 द्वहैठ् *dŏhaiṭh.* — द्वहैठ्युम् *dŏhaiṭhyum**.

63 त्रहैठ् *tr^{a}haiṭh.* — त्रहैठ्युम् *tr^{a}haiṭhyum**.

64 च्चहैठ् *tsŏhaiṭh.* — च्चहैठ्युम् *tsŏhaiṭhyum**.

65 पांच्चहैठ् *pāntsahaiṭh.* — पांच्चहैठ्युम् *pāntsahaiṭhyum**.

1 Sometimes pronounced *akatājyum**, and so throughout the forties; except forty-nine.

2 Also pronounced *akahāṭh, akahāṭhyum**, and so throughout the sixties, except sixty-nine.

No.	Cardinal	Ordinal
66	ष्हैठ् *ṣ°haiṭh.*	ष्हैठ्युमु *ṣ°haiṭhyum°.*
67	सतहैठ् *satahaiṭh.*	सतहैठ्युमु *satahaiṭhyum°.*
68	अरहैठ् *arahaiṭh.*	अरहैठ्युमु *arahaiṭhyum°.*
69	कुनसतथ् *kunasatăth.*	कुनसतत्युमु *kunasatatyum°.*
70	सतथ् *satăth.*	सतत्युमु *satatyum°.*
71	अकसतथ् *akasatăth.*	अकसतत्युमु *akasatatyum°.*
72	दुसतथ् *dusatăth.*[1]	दुसतत्युमु *dusatatyum°.*
73	त्र्सतथ् *tr°satăth.*	त्र्सतत्युमु *tr°satatyum°.*
74	च्सतथ् *tsŏsatăth.*	च्सतत्युमु *tsŏsatatyum°.*
75	पांन्चसतथ् *pą̃ntsasatăth.*	पांन्चसतत्युमु *pą̃ntsasatatyum°.*
76	ष्सतथ् *ṣ°satăth.*	ष्सतत्युमु *ṣ°satatyum°.*
77	सतसतथ् *satasatăth.*	सतसतत्युमु *satasatatyum°.*
78	अरसतथ् *arasatăth.*	अरसतत्युमु *arasatatyum°.*
79	कुनशीथ् *kunaçīth.*	कुनशीत्युमु *kunaçītyum°.*
80	शीथ् *çīth.*	शीत्युमु *çītyum°.*
81	अकशीथ् *akaçīth.*	अकशीत्युमु *akaçītyum°.*
82	दयशीथ् *dŏyaçīth.*	दयशीत्युमु *dŏyaçītyum°.*
83	त्रयशीथ् *trŏyaçīth.*	त्रयशीत्युमु *trĕyaçītyum°.*
84	च्यशीथ् *tsŏyaçīth.*	च्यशीत्युमु *tsŏyaçītyum°.*
85	पांन्चशीथ् *pą̃ntsaçīth.*	पांन्चशीत्युमु *pą̃ntsaçītyum°.*
86	षयशीथ् *ṣayaçīth.*	षयशीत्युमु *ṣayaçītyum°.*
87	सतशीथ् *sataçīth.*	सतशीत्युमु *sataçītyum°.*
88	अरशीथ् *araçīth.*	अरशीत्युमु *araçītyum°.*
89	कुननमथ् *kunanamăth.*	कुननमत्युमु *kunanamatyum°.*
90	नमथ् *namăth.*	नमत्युमु *namatyum°.*
91	अकनमथ् *akanamăth.*	अकनमत्युमु *akanamatyum°.*

[1] Not दोसतथ् *dŏsatăth*, as we might expect.

92	दुनमथ् *dunamăth.*[1]	दुनमत्युम् *dunamatyum*^{e}.
93	त्रनमथ् *tr*^{e}*namăth.*	त्रनमत्युम् *tr*^{e}*namatyum*^{e}.
94	च़नमथ् *tsŏnamăth.*	च़नमत्युम् *tsŏnamatyum*^{e}.
95	पांच़नमथ् *pāntsanamăth.*	पांच़नमत्युम् *pāntsanamatyum*^{e}.
96	षनमथ् *ṣ*^{e}*namăth.*	षनमत्युम् *ṣ*^{e}*namatyum*^{e}.
97	सतनमथ् *satanamăth.*	सतनमत्युम् *satanamatyum*^{e}.
98	अरनमथ् *aranamăth.*	अरनमत्युम् *aranamatyum*^{e}.
99	नमानमथ् *namānamăth.*	नमानमत्युम् *namānamatyum*^{e}.
100	हथ् *hăth.*	हत्युम् *hatyum*^{e}.
101	अख्हथ् त अख् *ăkh hăth t*^{e} *ăkh,* and so on.	अख्हथ् त अक्युम् *ăkh hăth t*^{e} *akyum*^{e} and so on.
110	अख्हथ् त दह् *ăkh hăth t*^{e} *dah,* and so on.	अख् हथ् त दह्युम् *ăkh hăth t*^{e} *dahyum*^{e} and so on.
200	ज़ुह् हथ् *z*^{o}*h hăth.*	दुहत्युम् *duhatyum*^{e}.
300	त्रिहथ् *trihăth.*	त्रहत्युम् *tr*^{e}*hatyum*^{e}.
400	च़ोर् हथ् *tsŏr hăth.*	च़हत्युम् *tsuhatyum*^{e}.
500	पांच़् हथ् *pānts hăth.*	पांच़हत्युम् *pāntsahatyum*^{e}.
600	षहथ् *ṣahăth.*	षहत्युम् *ṣahatyum*^{e}.
700	सथ् हथ् *săth hăth*	सतहत्युम् *satahatyum*^{e}.
800	ऐठ् हथ् *aiṭh hăth.*	ऐठहत्युम् *aiṭhahatyum*^{e}.
900	नव् शथ् *nav çăth.*	नवशत्युम् *navaçatyum*^{e}.
1000	सास् *sās.*	सांस्युम् *sāsyum*^{e}.
10000	अयुथ् *ayŏth.*	अयुत्युम् *ayŏtyum*^{e}.
100000	लछ् *lăch.*	लछ्युम् *lachyum*^{e}.
1,000,000	प्रयुथ् *prayŏth.*	प्रयुत्युम् *prayŏtyum*^{e}.
10,000,000	करोर् *kŏrŏr.*	करोर्युम् *kŏrŏryum*^{e}.

अख् *ăkh* is one: अखाह् *akhāh*, or अखाह् खण्डा *akhāh khaṇḍā* means 'some one,' or 'about one,' (ii, iii. 38, 45).

[1] Not दूनमथ् *dŏnamăth*, as we might expect.

अख् *ăkh* is thus declined.

Nom.	अख् *ăkh*.
Acc.	अकिस् *akis*.
Gen.	अक्युकु *akyuk*^{u}, or ॲकि सॖंदु *ọk*^{i} *sọnd*^{u}.
Ag.	ॲकि *ọk*^{i}.

अखाह् *akhāh* is only used in the nominative (ii. iii. 38).

अकुय् *aku-y*, fem. ॲक्य् *ọk*^{a}*-y*, is 'only one.' So also कुनु *kun*^{u}, fem. कुन् *kuñ*, means 'only one' (iv. 191).

ज़ह् *z*^{a}*h*, two, becomes द्व् *dw* in all cases except the nom. pl., and is thus declined (ii. iii. 32, 33).

	Sg. (a pair).	Pl. (two).
Nom.	(जोर *jōr*^{a}).	ज़ह् *z*^{a}*h*.
Acc.	(जोरस् *jōras*).	द्वन् *dwan*.
Ag.	(जोरन् *jōran*).	द्वयौ *dwayau*.
Instr.	द्वयि सॊतिन् *dwayi sọtin* (जोर सॊतिन् *jōr*^{a} *sọtin*).	द्वयौ सॊतिन् *dwayau sọtin*.

जोराह् *jōrāh*, 'any pair,' 'some pair,' or 'about two,' is declined in the plural. Thus जोराहौ सॊतिन् *jōrāhau sọtin* (ii. iii. 38). जोराह् खण्डा *jōrāh khaṇḍa*, means 'about two, but a little less' (ii. iii. 45). ज़य् *z*^{a}*-y*, means 'only two.'

There are two words signifying 'a pair,' (iv. 192). These are हॊरु *họr*^{u} (pl. हॊरि *họr*^{i}) and जोर *jōr*^{a} or जूरि *jūr*^{i}.

हॊरु *họr*^{u} is generally used of things without life; thus,—

दॆजॆहॊरु *dĕjĕhọr*^{u}, a pair of ear pendants.

दूरहॊरु *dūr*^{a}*họr*^{u}, a pair of ear rings.

वॊलिहॊरु *wọl*^{i}*họr*^{u}, a pair of rings (वोलु *wol*^{u}).

पुलहॊरु *pul*^{a}*họr*^{u}, a pair of grass sandals.

खावंहर् *khrāv[a]hạr[a]*, a pair of wooden sandals.

अखंहर् *ăkhhạr[a]*, one pair; जुहंहरि *z[a]hhạr[i]*, two pairs; त्रहंहरि *trĕhhạr[i]*, three pairs.

In the villages we find the word हुरि *hür[i]*. Thus दांदहुरि *dãdahür[i]* a pair of bullocks. Here the word is used of a thing with life.

जोर *jōr[a]* or जूरि *jür[i]* is used generally of things with life, but not always. Thus,—

मक्तजूरि *mŏktajür[i]*, a pair of pearls.

दांदजूरि *dãdajür[i]*, a pair of bullocks.

कोतरजूरि *kōtarjür[i]*, a pair of pigeons (कोतुर *kōtur*, a pigeon).

गुरिजूरि *gur[i]jür[i]*, a pair of horses (गुर *gur[a]*, a horse).

अखजोर *akhjōr[a]*, one pair; जुहजोर *z[a]hjōr[a]*, two pairs; त्रहजोर *trĕhjōr[a]*, three pairs.

Note that जोर *jōr[a]* and जूरि *jür[i]* are not interchangeable.

त्रिह् *trih*, three, is thus declined (ii. iii. 34).

Nom. त्रिह् *trih*.

Acc. त्रन् *tryan* (*trĕn*).

Ag. त्रयौ *trĕyau*

The word तार *tār[a]* is indefinite, and means 'about three.' त्रिय् *tri-y*, is 'only three' (ii. iii. 39).

'A group of three,' 'a trio,' is त्रिल *tril[a]*, (masc.), or (iv. 192) त्रिच *tric[a]* (fem.).

So also षह् *ṣah*, six (ii. iii. 34).

Nom. षह् *ṣah*.

Acc. षन् *ṣan*.

Ag. षयौ *ṣayau*.

'About six' is षखाह् *ṣakhāh*. 'Only six' is षय् *ṣa-y* (ii. iii. 42).

'A group of six' (iv. 192) षक *ṣak[a]*. It is also षखाह् *ṣakhāh*, and

षखाह् खण्डा *ṣakhāh khaṇḍā* means 'a group of about six' (ii. iii. 42). The latter usually means a group of a little less than six.

च़ोर् *tsōr*, four, is thus declined (ii. iii. 35).

Nom. च़ोर् *tsōr.*

Acc. च़ोरन् *tsōran* or च़ॊन् *tsŏn.*

Ag. च़ोरौ *tsōrau.*

च़ॊमर *tsŏmar*^{a}, (ii. iii. 40), means 'about four,' and च़ोरय् *tsōra-y* is 'only four' (ii. iii. 40).

च़ाख् *tsākh* means 'a group of four,' 'a four' (iv. 192). च़ाखाह् *tsākhāh* means 'a group of about four, and च़ाखाह् खण्डा *tsākhāh khaṇḍā* means 'a group of a little less than four' (ii. iii. 45).

This numeral in composition becomes च़ *tsŏ*. Thus (*vide post*) च़ॊशवय् *tsŏçaway*, even the four; च़ॊदाह् *tsŏdāh*, fourteen: च़ॊवुह् *tsŏwuh*, twenty-four, and so on.

The word for 'five' is पांछ् *pā̃ntṣ* or पाञ्छ् *pāntṣ*

Nom. पांछ् *pā̃ntṣ.*

Acc. पांछन् *pā̃ntṣan.*

Ag. पांछौ *pā̃tṣau.*

'About five' is पैञ्श *paiç*^{a}, and 'only five' is पांछय् *pā̃ntṣa-y* (ii. iii. 41). पंञ्ज *pã̃nz*^{a} means 'a group of five' (iv. 192). पंञ्जवाह् खण्डा *pã̃nzwāh khaṇḍā* means 'about five but a little less.'

For 'six,' see under 'three.'

The word for 'seven' is सथ् *sath*. It is thus declined—

Acc. सतन् *satan.*

Ag. सतौ *satau.*

'About seven' is सतेठ *satĕth*^{a}. 'Only seven' is सतय् *sata-y* (ii. iii. 43).

सतु *sạt*^{u} is a group of seven (iv. 192). सत्वाह् खण्डा *sạtwāh khaṇḍā* is 'about seven, but a little less.'

The declension and formation of the remaining numerals is regular.

'About' is signified by adding अमर *amar*^{a}, and 'only' by adding अय् *ay* (ii. iii. 44).

Thus ऐठ् *aiṭh*, (acc. pl. ऐठन् *aiṭhan*); 'about eight,' ऐठमर *aiṭhamar*^{a}; 'only eight,' ऐठय् *aiṭha-y*. ऐठि *aiṭh*^{i}, is a group of eight (iv. 192).

ऊठि *ūṭh*^{i} (pl.) is groups of eight (*e.g.* four eights = thirty-two, च़ोर् ऊठि द्वयत्रह् *tsōr ūṭh*^{i} *dŏyatr*^{a}*h*).

नव् *nav*, nine; नवमर *navamar*^{a}, about nine; नवय् *nava-y*, only nine.

नंम् *nąm*^{a} is a group of nine (iv. 192). नंमाह् खण्डा *nąmwāh khaṇḍā* is a group of about nine, but a little less.

दह् *dah*, ten; दहमर *dahamar*^{a}, about ten; दहय् *daha-y*, only ten.

दंह् *dąh*^{a} is a group of ten (iv. 192), and दंहाह् खण्डा *dąhwāh khaṇḍā* is a group of about ten, but a little less.

हथ् *hăth* is a hundred; हथाह् खण्डा *hăthāh khaṇḍā* is a group of about a hundred, but a little less.

The word for 'fifty' is पन्च़ाह् *pantsāh*, the प *pa* of which becomes व *wa* in composition (iii. 10). Thus, अक-वञ्ज़ाह् *aka-wanzāh*, fifty-one; दु-वञ्ज़ाह् *dŏ-wanzāh*, fifty-two; कुन-वञ्ज़ाह् *kun*^{a}*-wanzāh*, forty-nine.

The word for 'sixty' is शेठ् *çēṭh* (iv, 176) or शैठ् *çaiṭh*, the श् *ç* of both of which becomes ह् *h* in composition (iii. 11). Thus कुन-हैठ् *kun*^{a}*-haiṭh*, fifty-nine; दु-हैठ् *dŏ-haiṭh*, sixty-two.

हथ् *hăth*; this is the form which a hundred takes in composition up to and including eight hundred (iv. 115); thus

अख्हथ् *ăkhhăth*, one hundred, ज़्हहथ् *z*^{a}*hhăth* two hundred, त्रिहथ् *trihăth* (dropping ह् *h*), three hundred.

शथ् *çăth*; this is the form which a hundred takes in composition after eight hundred (iv. 116); thus

नव्शथ् *navçăth*, nine hundred; काह्शथ् *kāhçăth*, eleven hundred; बाह्शथ् *bāhçăth*, twelve hundred.

The following terms are peculiar to counting (iv. 174–177).

(*a*) टुंक *ṭŭk*^{a} means two pice.

(*b*) हथ् *hăth* means a pice, when more than two are referred to in counting. Thus, त्रिहथ् *trihăth*, three pice; चोर्हथ् *tsŏrhăth*, four pice; पाँत्सहथ् *pãts-hăth*, five pice. As in the case of numerals, हथ् *hăth*, becomes शथ् *çăth* from nine on. Thus;—नवशथ् *navçăth*. Ten pice are also called सास् *sās*, lit. a thousand.

(c) ज़ंनु *zanᵘ*, this is the word used in counting persons. Thus ज़ंनि पंचाहमर *zan*^{i} *pantsāhmara*, about fifty men. शेठ् ज़ंनि *çĕth zan*^{i}, sixty men.

(*d*) लूख् *lūkh*. This word must be used in counting persons by hundreds or thousands. Thus हथ् लूख *hăth lūk*^{a}, a hundred people; ज़्हहथ् लूख *z*^{a}*hhăth lūk*^{a}, two hundred persons; त्रिहथ् लूख *trihăth lūk*^{a} three hundred people. We also sometimes, however, but rarely, have हथ् ज़नि *hăth zani*, a hundred people, सास् ज़नि *sās zani*, a thousand people, in both of which the *i* is fully pronounced.

When the emphatic य् *y* is added to numerals, we get the following forms—

दशवय् *dŏçawa-y*, or दनवय् *dŏnawa-y* even both.

त्रशवय् *trĕçawa-y* or त्रनवय् *tryanawa-y*, even all three.

चशवय् *tsŏçawa-y* or चनवय् *tsŏnawa-y*, even all four.

पाँत्सवय् *pãtsawa-y*, even all five.

षशवय् *ṣaçawa-y* or षनवय् *ṣanawa-y*, even all six.

सतवय् *satawa-y*, even the seven.

ऐठवय् *aiṭhawa-y*, even the eight.

नववय् *navawa-y* even the nine.

And so on.

The acc. is नववनी *navawanī*. The agent is नवव्यँ *navawĕy*^{i}, and so for all, (iv. 186–188).

We may also say द्वशि दशवय् *dwaç*^{i} *doçawa-y*; नवि नववय् *naw*^{i} *nawawa-y*, and so in all, repeating the first element, (iv. 189).

In multiplication, the numerals take special forms, as follows :—

1. ॲकि क्या नाम् *ạk*^{i} *kyā nām*.
2. दॊगनि *dŏgạn*^{i}.
3. त्रान *trān*^{a}.
4. चाख् *tsākh*.
5. पँछि *pạns*^{i}.
6. षक *ṣak*^{a}.
7. सँति *sạt*^{i}.
8. ऑठि *āṭh*^{i}.
9. नँमि *nạm*^{i}.
10. दँहि *dạh*^{i}.
11. काहि *kāh*^{i}.
12. बाहि *bāh*^{i}.
13. त्रुवाहि *truwāh*^{i}.
14. चदाहि *tsŏdāh*^{i}.
15. पन्दाहि *pandāh*^{i}.
16. षुराहि *ṣurāh*^{i}.
17. सदाहि *sadāh*^{i}.
18. अरदाहि *aradāh*^{i}.
19. कुनवुहि *kunawuh*^{i}.
20. वुहि *wuh*^{i}.
21. अकवुहि *akawuh*^{i}.
30. त्रुहि *tr*^{a}*h*^{i}.
31. अकत्रुहि *akatr*^{a}*h*^{i}.
40. चतजिहि *tsatajih*^{i}.
50. पन्चाहि *pantsāh*^{i}.
60. शेठि *çīṭh*^{i}.
70. सँतति *sat*^{a}*t*^{i}.
80. शीति *çīth*^{i}.
90. नमँति *namạt*^{i}.
100. हँति *hạt*^{i}.

They are used as follows :—

अख् ॲकि क्या नाम् अख् *ăkh ạk*^{i} *kyā nām ăkh*, one one (is) one.

ज़ुह् ॲकि क्या नाम् ज़ुह् *z*^{a}*h ạk*^{i} *kyā nām z*^{a}*h*, two ones (are) two.

त्रिह् दॊगनि षह् *trih dŏgạn*^{i} *ṣah*, three twos (are) six.

सथ् षक दॊयतजिह् *sath ṣak*^{a} *dŏyatājih*, seven sixes (are) forty-two.

These special forms may be called multiplicative numerals. Multiplicatives above ten can only be used with numerals above ten. Thus काह् बाहि अख् हथ् त दॊयत्रुह् *kāh bāh*^{i} *ăkh hăth t*^{a} *dŏyatr*^{a}*h*, eleven twelves (are) a hundred and thirty-two. We cannot say चोर् बाहि अरतजिह् *tsŏr bāh*^{i} *aratājih*, four twelves are forty-eight, because four is not greater than ten. We can only say बाह् चाख् अरतजिह् *bāh tsākh aratājih*, twelve fours (are) forty-eight.

G. Pronouns.

These change their bases in Declension. The following paradigms will give sufficient information.

बह् *bŏh*, I.

Nom.	बह् *bŏh* (ii. iii. 8).	असि *ạs*^{i} (15).
Acc.	म्य *mĕ* (8).	असĕ *asĕ* (15).
Ag.	म्य *mĕ* (8, 9).	असĕ *asĕ* (15).
Gen.	म्योनु *myŏn*^{u} (11).	सोनु *sŏn*^{u} (19).

Genitive Forms.

	SINGULAR.	PLURAL.
Masc.	म्योनु *myŏn*^{u}.	म्यानि *myạ̄n*^{i}.
Fem.	म्यान् *myạ̄ñ*.	म्यान्य *myāñĕ*.

Similarly for the Plural.

चह् *ts*^{a}*h*, thou.

Nom.	चह् *ts*^{a}*h* (ii. iii. 8).	त्वहि *twạh*^{i} (15).
Acc.	च *tsĕ* (8).	तोह *tŏhĕ* (15).
Ag.	च *tse* (8, 9).	तोह *tŏhĕ* (15).
Gen.	च्योनु *cyŏn*^{u} (11).	तुहंदु *tuhạnd*^{u} (18).

Genitive Forms.

	SINGULAR.	PLURAL.
Masc.	च्योनु *cyŏn*^{u}.	च्यानि *cyạ̄n*^{i}.
Fem.	च्यान् *cyạ̄ñ*.	च्यान्य *cyāñĕ*.

Similarly for the Plural.

तिह् *tih*, that (out of sight), he, she, it.

Nom.	Masc. सुह् *suh* (ii. iii. 2); fem. सॊह् *sŏh*, or स *sa* (3); neut. तिह् *tih* (1).	तिम् *tim* (16).
Acc.	(Masc. fem.) तमिस् *tamis* (5); तस् *tas* (20); neut. तथ् *tăth* (7).	तिमन् *timan* (16).
Ag.	(M. n.) तॖमि *tąm*^{i} (5); f. तमि *tami*.	तिमौ *timau* (16).
Gen.	(M. f.) तॖमि सॖन्दॖ *tąm*^{i} *sąnd*^{u}; तसॖन्दॖ *tasąnd*^{u}; तस् *tas* (20); (n.) तम्युकॖ *tamyuk*^{u}.	तिहॖन्दॖ *tihąnd*^{u}; तिमन् हॖन्दॖ *timan hąnd*^{u} (16, 20).

This pronoun only refers to things not within sight. For things within sight हुह् *huh* is used.

The neuter form agrees with all things without life, whether their grammatical gender is masculine or feminine. Thus तथ् पॊथ्य परनस् क्यतॖ प्रङ्ग् *tăth pŏthĕ paranas kyut*^{u} *praŋg*, a couch for reading that book. So in the case of the other pronouns. The plural is the same for all three genders. So elsewhere.

यिह् *yih*, who.

Nom.	Masc. युस् *yus* (ii. iii. 2); fem. य्वस्स *yŏs*^{u} (4); neut. यिह् *yih* (1).	यिम् *yim* (16).
Acc.	(Masc. fem.) यमिस् *yĕmis* (5); यस् *yas* (20), neut. यथ् *yăth* (7).	यिमन् *yiman* (16).
Ag.	(M. n.) यॖमि *yąm*^{i} (5); (f.) यमि *yami* (5).	यिमौ *yimau* (16).

Gen. (M. f.) यमि संन्दु *yạmⁱ* यिहंन्दु *yihạndᵘ*; यिमन् हंन्दु *sạndᵘ*; यसंन्दु *yasạndᵘ* *yiman hạndᵘ* (16, 20).
(20); यस् *yas* (20); (n.)
यम्युकु *yĕmyukᵘ*.

क्याह् *kyāh*, who, what?

Nom. Masc. कुस् *kus* (ii. iii. 2); कम् *kam* (16).
fem. कस *kŏssᵘ* (4);
neut. क्याह् *kyāh* (1).

Acc. (Masc. fem.) कमिस् (5); कमन् *kaman* (16).
कस् *kas* (20); (neut.)
कथ् *kăth* (7).

Ag. (M. n.) कमि *kạmⁱ* (5); कमौ *kamau* (16).
(f.) कमि *kami* (5).

Gen. (M. f.) कमि संन्दु *kạmⁱ* कहंन्दु *kahạndᵘ*; कमन् हंन्दु *sạndᵘ*; कसंन्दु *kasạndu*; *kaman hạndᵘ* (16, 20).
कस् *kas* (20); n. कम्युकु
kamyukᵘ.

इह् *yih*, this.

Nom. Masc. इह् *yih* (ii. iii. 2); इम *yim* (16).
fem. इह् *yih* (3); neut.
इह् *yih* (1).

Acc. (Masc. fem.) इमिस् *yimis* इमन् *yiman* (16)
(5); न्यमिस् *nŏmis* (5);
neut. इथ् *yith* (7); न्यथ्
nŏth (7).

	Singular	Plural
Ag.	(M. n.) इमि *yim*^{i} (5); न्वंमि *nwąm*^{i} (5); (f.) इमि *yimi* (5); न्वमि *nomi* (5).	इमौ *yimau* (16).
Gen.	(M. f.) इमि संन्दु *yim*^{i} *sąnd*^{u}; इसंन्दु *yisąnd*^{u} (20); न्वंमि संन्दु *nwąm*^{i} *sąnd*^{u}; (n.) इम्युकु *yim-yuk*^{u}; न्वम्युकु *nŏmyuk*^{u}.	इहंन्दु *yihąnd*^{u}; इमन् हंन्दु *yiman hąnd*^{u} (16, 20).

हुह् *huh*, that (within sight).

	Singular	Plural
Nom.	Masc. हुह् *huh* (ii. iii. 2); fem. हॊह् *hŏh* (3); neut. हुह् *huh* (1).	हुम् *hum* (16).
Acc.	(Masc. fem.) हुमिस् *humis* (5); अमिस् *amis* (6); neut. हुथ् *huth* (7).	हुमन् *human* (16).
Ag.	(M. n.) हुमि *hum*^{i} (5); अंमि *ąm*^{i} (6); (f.) हुमि *humi* (5); अमि *ami* (5).	हुमौ *humau* (16).
Gen.	(M. f.) हुमि संन्दु *hum*^{i} *sąnd*^{u}; अंमि संन्दु *ąm*^{i} *sąnd*^{u}; हुसंन्दु *husąnd*^{u}; असंन्दु *asąnd*^{u} (20); (n.) हुम्युकु *humyuk*^{u}; अम्युकु *amyuk*^{u}.	हुहंन्दु *huhąnd*^{u}; हुमन् हंन्दु *human hąnd*^{u} (16, 20).

This pronoun only refers to things within sight. For things out of sight, तिह् *tih* is used.

The Reflexive Pronoun.

The word पान *pān*^{u}, self, is declined only in the singular (ii. iii. 36). Its genitive is irregular (37). Thus,—

Nom.	पान *pān*^{u}, self or selves.	
Acc.	पानस् *pānas*, self or selves.	
Gen.	पनुनु *panun*^{u} (fem. पनॆञ् *panañ*).	
Ag.	पान *pān*^{u}, by self or selves (NOT पानन् *pānan*).	

[Example म्य पान कॊरुम् *mĕ pān*^{u} *karu-m* by me, myself, it was done].

The word पान् *pān*, meaning the human body is declined regularly in both numbers, like a noun of the first declension. Its genitive is hence पानुकु *pānuk*^{u} (ii. iii. 36, 37).

Pronominal adjectives (ii. iii. 25–27).

यूतु *yūt*^{u}, this much.	Fem.	यॊच़ु *yŏts*^{u}.
त्यूतु *tyūt*^{u}, that much.		त्यॊच़ु *tyŏts*^{u}.
य्यूतु *yyūt*^{u}, how much.		य्यॊच़ु *yyŏts*^{u}.
कूतु *kūt*^{u}, how much.		कॊच़ु *kŏts*^{u}.

The declension of these is given under the head of nouns, see p. 55.

Indefinite Pronouns.

काँह् *kā̃h* or कूँह् *kũh* or काँछाह् *kā̃tshāh* any one, some one, (m. and f.) (ii. iii. 29, 30, 31).

	Singular.	Plural.
Nom.	कूँह् *kũh* काँह् *kā̃h* or काँछाह् *kā̃tshāh*.	कॆंच़् *kĕnts*.
Acc.	कैँसि *kaisi*.	कॆंच़न् *kĕntsan*.
Ag.	कैँसि *kaisi*.	कॆंच़ौ *kentsau*.

In the singular it is always declined like a feminine noun, even in the masculine.

कॆंछाह् *kĕtshāh*, means 'any thing' (ii. iii. 31).

It is not declined.

H. Emphatic and Indefinite Particles.

(ii. iii. 21 : iv. 126).

The particle य् *y* is added to all words to give emphasis. It may be added either to the main word or to the declensional or conjugational suffix. When added to a word ending in a consonant it becomes अय् ^{a}*y*. Thus,—

तसंन्दुय् *tasạnduy*, even his,	from तसंन्द् *tasạnd*^{u}, his.
तमि संन्दुय् *tạm*^{i} *sạnduy*, even his,	तमि संन्द् *tạm*^{i} *sạnd*^{u}, his.
ग्वरसय् अन्दर् *gŏras*^{a}*y andar*, even in the preceptor.	ग्वरस् अन्दर् *gŏras andar*, in the preceptor.
ग्वरनय् अन्दर् *gŏran*^{a}*y andar*, even in the preceptors.	ग्वरन् अन्दर् *gŏran andar* in the preceptors.
ग्वरनय् हन्दि पुछ्य् *gŏran*^{a}*y handi putshy*, even to the preceptors.	ग्वरन् हन्दि पुछ्य् *gŏran handi putshy* to the preceptors.

or

ग्वरन् हन्दिय् पुछ्य् *gŏran handiy putshy*

or

ग्वरन् हन्दि पुछिय् *gŏran handi putshiy.**

गाटुलुय् *gāṭuluy*, certainly clever,	from गाटुल् *gāṭul*^{u}, clever.
करानय् छुह् *karān*^{a}*y chuh*, he is certainly doing.	करान् छुह् *karān chuh*, he is doing.
कर्योनय् *karyōn*^{a}*y*, he certainly did.	कर्योन् *karyōn*, he did.
करिय् *kariy*, he will certainly do.	करि *kari*, he will do.
तिथय् *tithay*, even in that manner.	तिथ *tith*^{a} in that manner.

The word सोर् *sōr*^{u}, all, always takes this suffix (ii. iii. 22).

Thus,—

Nom. sg. सोरुय् *sōruy*; Nom. pl. सारिय् *sạriy*; instead of सोर् *sōr*^{u} सारि *sạr*^{i}, respectively.

* पुछ्य् *putshy* is really another way of writing पुछि *putshi*.

When य् *y* is suffixed to the letter औ *au*, the two together become अव़्य् *av^ay*, (ii. iii. 23).

Thus,—

गुर्यव़्य् सूँतिन् *guryav^ay sụtin*, by the horses certainly, from गुर्यौ सूँतिन् *guryau sụtin*, by the horses.

नमव़्य् सूँतिन् *namav^ay sụtin*, even by the nails, from नमौ सूँतिन् *namau sụtin*.

Indefiniteness is shown by adding आह् *āh* to a noun in the nom. sing. The termination cannot be added to other cases (ii. iii. 38).

कथाह् *kathāh*, any story, from कथ् *kăth*, a story; अखाह् *akhāh*, some one, any one, from अख् *ăkh*, one; जोराह् *jōrāh*, some pair or other, from जोर *jōr^a*, a pair. The last may, however, be declined, thus जोराहौ सूँतिन् *jōrāhau sụtin* by any pair.

When खण्डा *khaṇḍā* is added to these words, it indicates a slight diminution. Thus क्रुह् *kruh*, a *kōs*; क्रुहाह् *kruhāh*, about a *kōs*; क्रुहाह् खण्डा *kruhāh khaṇḍā*, about a *kōs*, but a little less; so दोहाह् खण्डा *dōhāh khaṇḍā*, about a day, but something less; रथाह् खण्डा *ṛathāh khaṇḍā*, about a season but something less; रुपयाह् खण्डा *rupayāh khaṇḍā*, about a rupee, but something less. The syllable आह् *āh* may be omitted, and then खण्ड् *khaṇḍ* not खण्डा *khaṇḍā* is used. Thus, क्रुह् खण्ड् *kruh khaṇḍ*, about a *kōs*, but a little less.

The suffix स् *s^a* added to a word signifies a group, or number. Thus, from कट् *kăṭh*, rams, कट्स् *kăṭs^a*, a number of rams; from गुरि *gur^i*, horses, गुरिस् *guris^a*, a number of horses, a troop of horses; from रुपय *rupayĕ*, rupees, रुपयेस् *rupayĕs^a*, a number of rupees; कने *kanĕ* stones, कनेस् *kanĕs^a*, a heap of stones (ii. iii. 46).

The word पहान् *pahān* qualifies the word which it follows (iv. 193). Thus,—

बड् पहान् *baḍ^a pahān*, somewhat big.

र्‌यठ् पहान् *ryạth^a pahān*, somewhat stout.

वुशुन् पहान् *wuṣuṇ pahān*, somewhat hot.

दूर् पहान् *dūr pahān*, somewhat distant.

न्यूर् पहान् *nyūr pahān*, somewhat near.

ब्रोठ् पहान् *brōṭh pahān*, somewhat in front.

पथ् पहान् *pāth pahān*, somewhat behind.

चीरि पहान् *tsīr^{i} pahān*, after some time (चेर् *tsēr*, delay).

काशुर् पहान् *kāçur^{u} pahān*, somewhat Kashmiri.

बंगालुकु पहान् *baṅgāluk^{u} pahān*, somewhat Bengali.

वुहुर्युंदु पहान् *wuhuryund^{u} pahān*, somewhat in that direction.

यहुर्युंदु पहान् *yahuryund^{u} pahān*, somewhat in this direction.

The following conjunctions are given by Īçvara-kaula.

त *t^{e}*, and (iv. 178). *E.g.*, सुह् त च़्ह् *suh t^{e} ts^{a}h*, he and thou.

ति *ti*, also (iv. 179). It is also used instead of त *t^{e}* with plurals.

Thus,—सुह् ति च़्ह् ति *suh ti ts^{a}h ti*, he also, you also. महनिवि ति गुपन् ति आय् *mahaniv^{i} ti gupan ti āy*, both the men and the cattle came. We cannot say महनिवि त गुपन् त आय् *mahaniv^{i} t^{e} gupan t^{e} āy*.

बिय *biy^{e}*, means, 'again.' It also means 'other,' (iv. 180). Thus, बिय करिज़ि *biy^{e} kar^{i}zi*, you should do it again. बिय वति *biya wati* by another road.

ज़न् *zan*, like (iv. 181). *E.g.*, तोत ज़न् छुह् परान् *tōt^{e} zan chuh parān*, he reads like a parrot. मालिस् ज़न् छुह् रछान् *mālis zan chuh rachān*, he protects him as if he (the object) was his father.

ह्युहु *hyuh^{u}* (also written हिहु *hih^{u}*), fem. हिशु *hiç^{u}*, means 'like,' (iv. 182, 183). *E.g.*, मालिस् ह्युहु *mālis hyuh^{u}*, like his father, (*e.g.*, this child is like his father). मोलु ह्युहु छुस् *mōl^{u} hyuh^{u} chu-s* (*s* is the dative pronominal suffix of the 3rd person), he is like a father to him. सोन् ह्युहु छुह् नॊपान् *sōn hyuh^{u} chuh nŏpān*, it is shining like gold. We also have phrases like बुडु ह्युहु अनिज़्यन् *buḍ^{u} hyuh^{u} an^{i}zyan*, bring whoever (amongst them) is old, —— not, bring him like an old man.

I. On the Rhyming Repetition of words (*anuprāsa*).

Words of any kind are repeated to show indefiniteness or reciprocity. In such a case the letter व *w* or *v* प *p* is usually substituted in the second word, for the first letter of the original word (viii. i. 30). Thus,

करान् वरान् छुह् *karān warān chuh*, he is doing it or nearly doing it.

द्यार् व्यार् अनिन् *dyār vyār anin*, let him bring the wealth, &c.

बत वत ख्यियिन् *bat° wat° khyayin*, let him eat rice, &c.

अन्वार् वन्वार् *anwār wanwār* or अन्वार् पन्वार् *anwār panwār*, turn and turn about.

If the main word begins with प *p* or व *v* or *w*, the second begins with व *v* or *w* or प *p* respectively (viii. i. 31). Thus,—

पर् वर् *par war*, read (imperative), &c.

पैंस वैंस दितिन् *pais° wais° ditin*, let him give pice and the like.

वाँगन् पाँगन् अन् *wāgan pāgan an*, bring brinjals and other like vegetables.

वाज़ पाज़ छिह् *wāz° pāz° chih*, they are cooks, &c.

The word व्युछु (विछु) *vyuts°*, a collection, makes व्युछु पोछु *vyuts° pōts°*, an omnium gatherum.

There are irregular formations, such as (viii. i. 32).

न्युकु (निकु) सुकु *nyuk° suk°*, a collection. न्युकु *nyuk°* means literally 'a little.'

म्यंडु ट्यंडु *myand° tyand°*, mouthfuls, &c.

हलु कलु *hal° kal°*, crooked, &c.; but

हलु वलु *hal° wal°*, girdles and the like.

हांज़ु गांज़ु *hānz° gānz°*, boatmen, &c.

फलु फ्यलु *phal° phyal°*, ornaments, &c.

ओंटु वोंटु *ōnt° wōnt°*, shallow and the like.

These compounds are feminine when they denote reciprocity. For examples, see p. 71.

J. Forms of address.

92 Instead of a formal vocative case, Kāçmīrī uses a number of Interjections, each causing or not causing changes in the base of the noun with which they are used. The following is an abstract table showing the Interjections described by Īçvara-kaula, in the *Sambuddhi-pāda* (ii. 2) of his grammar. As a rule, before interjectional suffixes, ु *u-mātrā* and ू *ū-mātrā* are changed to इ *i* (or य् *y*).

Ref. to No. of Sūtra.	Interjection.	How used.	Word.	Form of address.
2	हे *hĕ*.	Respectful. By man to man.	नारान् *nārān* (N. P.)	हे नारान् *hĕ nārān*.
				हे नारान् जुव् *hĕ nārān juv*.
	हे *hĕ*—जुव् *juv* (or a caste-word instead of *juv*).		गण कौल् *gaṇᵉ-kaul* (N. P.)	हे गण कौल् *hĕ gaṇᵉ-kaul*.
3	सा *sạ* may be added after any of the above.	Ditto.		हे नारान् सा *hĕ nārān sạ*.
				हे नारान् जुव् सा *hĕ nārān juv sạ*.
				हे राम कौल् सा *hĕ rāmᵉ-kaul sạ*.
4	हतसांहे *hatasạ̄hĕ* may be substituted for हे *hĕ*.	Ditto.		हतसांहे नारान् जुव् *hatasạ̄hĕ nārān juv*.
				हतसांहे राम कौल् *hatasạ̄hĕ rāmᵉ-kaul*.
				हतसांहे नारान् जुव् सा *hatasạ̄hĕ nārān juv sạ*.

	Or हसढे *haṣḍhā*.			हतसढे राम कौल् सा *hatasḍhā rām^{e}-kaul sạ*.
	With these, if neither जुव् *juv* nor any caste-word is used, then सा *sạ* must be added.			हसढे नारान् जुव् *haṣḍhā nārān juv*. हतसढे गन सा. *hatasḍhā gan^{e} sạ*.
5	हे *hā*—बा *bā* used without जुव् *juv* or caste-word.	In addressing a priest, a person of the middle class, or a servant.	नारान् *nārān*.	हे नारान् बा *hā nārān bā*.
6	हतसढे *hatasḍhā* or हतबाहे *hatabāhā*.	If the above are old.	सहस् *sahas^{e}* (N. P.) ज़न *zan^{e}* (N. P.)	हतसढे सहस् बा *hastaḍhā sahas bā*. हतबाहे ज़न बा *hatabāhā zan^{e} bā*.
7	—आ *ā* added either to the bare name or to the caste-word.	In addressing male juniors or inferiors.		नाराना *nārānā*. नारान् जुवा *nārān juvā*.
8	Or preceded by हता *hatā*.	Ditto.	मान *mān^{e}* (N. P.) मान कौल *mān^{e}-kaul*. गुल् *gul^{e}* (N. P.)	हता माना *hatā mānā*. हता मान कौला *hatā mān^{e}-kaulā*. हता गुल्या *hatā gulyā* (note the change of ^{e} to *y*).
9	हा *hā*—ओ *ō*.	In addressing a person at a distance, or in sorrow.	काक् *kāk*, a father.	हा नारानो *hā nārānō*. हा काको *hā kākō*.

94 Ref. to No. of Sūtra.	Interjection.	How used.	Word.	Form of address.
10	हतो *hatō* may be substituted for हा *hā*.	In addressing a person at a distance, or in sorrow.	पर् *parᵊ* (N. P.)	हतो पर्यो *hatō paryō* (note vowel change).
11	—माजॖ *mājᵊ* added to the bare name.	When a man addresses an elder woman.	पार्वत् *pārvat* (N. P.)	पार्वत् माजॖ *pārvat mājᵊ*.
12	बिञ् *biñ*.	When she is moderate in age, or of an age equal to that of the speaker.		पार्वत् बिञ् *pārvat biñ*.
13	हतमाजॖ *hatamājᵊ* or हतबिञ् *hatabiñ* may precede.	As in the two last.		हतमाजॖ पार्वत् माजॖ *hatamājᵊ pārvat mājᵊ*.
			सरस्वत् *saraswat* (N. P.)	हतबिञ् सरस्वत् बिञ् *hatabiñ saraswat biñ*.
				हतबिञ् पार्वत् माजॖ *hatabiñ pārvat mājᵊ*.

14, 15	हाय् hāy—य् y. हतय् hatay—य् y. हतांय् hatāy—य् y.	In addressing female juniors or inferiors.	[illegible] wọtshᵒrᵃ, child.	हाय वछरिय् hāy watshariy (note change of vowel). हतय् वछरिय् hatay watshariy. हतांय् वछरिय् hatāy watshariy.
16, 18, 25	हतबा hatabā—बा bā.	When a woman addresses a man or woman respectfully. More especially in addressing a priest.	हिमत् himat (N. P.)	हतबा हिमत् बा hatabā himat bā.
17, 18, 25	हतबा hatabā—औ au. हतौ hatau—औ au.	Ditto, in addressing familiars or juniors (male or female).		हतबा काकौ hatabā kākau. हतौ काकौ hatau kākau. हतौ हिमत् कोलौ hatau himat kōlau.
19, 25	हतबा hatabā—अ a. हतौ hatau—अ a.	Ditto.	काक् kāk, a father. गन gaṇᵉ, (N. P.)	हतबा काक hatabā kākᵉ. हतौ गन hatau gaṇᵉ.
20, 25	हतबा hatabā—अ बाय a bāyᵉ. हतबा hatabā—अ बायौ a bayau. हतौ hatau—अ	Used by women in addressing men or women by their proper names only,	महादेव् mahādēv (N. P.)	हतबा महादेव बाय hatabā mahādēvᵉ bāyᵉ. हतबा महादेव बायौ hatabā mahādēvᵉ bāyau.

Ref. to No. of Sūtra.	Interjection.	How used.	Word.	Form of address.
	बाबौ *a bāyau.*	we cannot say हतबा काक बाय *hatabā kāk° bāy°*, O father.		हतौ महादेव बाबौ *hutau mahādēv° bāyau.*
21 } 25 }	हतोव् *hatōv*—औ *au.*	Used by women in addressing a man or woman at a distance.	मनसा राम् *manasā rām* (N. P.)	हतोव् मनसा रामौ *hatōv manasā rāmau*
22		Also by Musalmān women in addressing their husbands.	कादिर् *kạdir.*	हतोव् कादिरौ *hatōv kạdirau.*
23		Not by Brāhmaṇī women, who only use the following.		
24	हत *hat°.*	Used by a Brāhmaṇī women when addressing her husband, when she is		हत *hat°.*

		alone with him, and she is near by. She does not mention his name. Merely uses the interjection.		
26	आहन् *āhan.*	May be prefixed to any of the foregoing to signify concurrence, 'yes.'		आहन्सा *āhansạ̄.* आहन्बा *āhanbā.* आहनो *āhanō.* आहन् मॉजू *āhan mạ̄jū.* आहन् बिञ् *āhan biñ.* आहनिय् *āhaniy.* आहनू *āhanū.* आहनुव् *āhanuv.*
27	ह *ha.*	Used affirmatively with verbs, with the above.		आहन्सा करान् हसा छुह् *āhansạ̄ karān hasạ̄ chuh*, yes, Sir, he *is* doing.
28				आहन्सा कॊरुन् हसा *āhansạ̄ kạru-n hasạ̄*, yes, Sir, he *did* do.
30				

98

Ref. to No. of Sūtra.	Interjection.	How used.	Word.	Form of address.
				आहन्सा बत हसा छुह् रनान् *āhansā batᵉ hasā chuh ranān*, yes, Sir, he *is* cooking rice.
29	न *na.*	Similarly used as a negative.		नबा करान् नबा छुह् *nabā karān nabā chuh*, no, Sir, he is not doing.
				आहन्सा नारान् हसा छुह् पूथि परान् *āhansā nārān hasā chuh pūth*ⁱ *parān* yes, Sir, Nārāyaṇa *is* reading the book.
				आहन्बा राम हबा छुस् नन्दर् करान् *āhanbā Rāmᵃ habā chu-s nöndᵉr karān*, yes, Sir, Rāma *is* having his sleep.

From the Journal, Asiatic Society of Bengal, Vol. LXVII, Part I, No. 3,
1898, p. 193.

On Primary Suffixes in Kāçmīrī.—*By* G. A. Grierson, C.I.E., Ph.D., I.C.S.

[Read August, 1898.]

These are treated in the *Kṛdanta-prakriyā* of Īçvara-kaula's *Kaçmīra-çabdāmṛta.* They form nouns (including adjectives and participles) by direct accretion to verbal roots. Many of them would be properly classed as verbal forms.

1. आन् *ān.* This is used to make present participles. It does not change for gender or number, and is added direct to the root (ix. i. 2).[1] Thus,—

Root.	Present Participle.
कर् *kar*, do.	करान् *karān*, doing.
बोज़ *bōz*, hear.	बोज़ान् *bōzān*, hearing.

If the root ends in a vowel, the letter व *w* is inserted (3). Thus,—

दि *di*, give.	दिवान् *diwān*, giving.
खि *khi*, eat.	ख्यवान् *khyawān*, eating.
चि *ci*, drink.	च्यवान् *cyawān*, drinking.

Note that all verbs ending in इ *i* change इ *i* to य *ya*, except नि *ni*, take, दि *di*, give, यि *yi*, come.

This form is frequently used adverbially (4). Thus परान् परान् कॊरुन् *parān, parān, kǫrun*, coming, coming, he made it.

This form corresponds to the Sanskrit present participle.

2. इथ् *ith.* Used to form a past participle absolute or conjunctive participle, corresponding to the Sanskrit conjunctive participle in त्वा *tvā*, or य *ya* (त्य *tya*). Thus,—

कर् *kar*, do.	करिथ् *karith*, having made.

[1] References, here, and elsewhere, to Īçvara-kaula's *Kaçmīra-çabdāmṛta.*

A preceding long आ *ā* (not short अ *a*) is modified. Thus,—

दार *dār*, place. दारिथ् *dạrith*.

ओ *ō* and ए *ē* become ऊ *ū* and ई *ī* respectively before this prefix (14,15). Thus,—

बोश् *bōs*, hear. बूशिथ् *būsith*, having heard.

मेन् *mēn*, measure. मीनिथ् *mīnith*, having measured.

If a root ends in इ *i*, the final इ *i*, together with the suffix become यथ् *yăth* (ix. i. 7, 8). Thus,—

हि *hi*, take. ह्यथ् *hyăth*, having taken.

खि *khi*, eat. ख्यथ् *khyăth*, having eaten.

Exceptions are—

नि *ni*, take. निथ् *nith*, having taken.

दि *di*, give. दिथ् *dith*, having given.

यि *yi*, come. यिथ् *yith*, having come.

When the root वुड् *wuḍ*, fly, signifies *mōkṣa*, final release, it becomes वुजिथ् *wujith*, having obtained final release; but वुडिथ् *wuḍith*, having flown (ix. i. 9).

The root मश्राव् *mąṣ[a]rāv*, cause to forget, usually forms मश्राविथ् *mąṣ[a]rạvith*, regularly, but in the phrase 'to cause to forget death,' it becomes मासविथ् *māṣawith*. Thus,—

मरन् मासविथ् *marun māṣawith*, having caused (so and so) to forget death (ix. i. 10).

The suffix क्यथ् *kyăth*, may be added to this form. Thus, करिथ् क्यथ् *karith kyăth*, having done (ix. i. 6).

3. इ *i* (ix. i. 11–15). This is used instead of इथ् *ith*, when the word is repeated to represent frequentative action. In this case both a preceding अ *a* and a preceding आ *ā* are modified. Thus,—

कर् *kar*, do. करि करि *kạr[i] kạr[i]*, having made over and over again.

मार् *mār*, beat. मारि मारि *mạr[i] mạr[i]*, having beaten repeatedly.

कार् *kār*, boil. कारि कारि *kạr[i] kạr[i]*, having boiled repeatedly.

As in the case of इथ *ith*, preceding ॏ *ō* and ॊ *ŏ* become ई *ī* and ऊ *ū* respectively. Thus,—

ट्येट *ṭsēt*, pound. — ट्सीटि ट्सीटि *tsītⁱ tsītⁱ*, having pounded continually.

बोज़ *bōz*, hear. — बूज़ि बूज़ि *būzⁱ būzⁱ*, having heard continually.

So also we have—

ब्यह *bĕh*, sit. — बिहि बिहि *bihⁱ bihⁱ*, having sat continually.

When a root ends in इ *i*, the final vowel together with the suffix become य *ya* (*ĕ*); or the form in थ् *th* may be used (12). Thus,—

खि *khi*, eat. — ख्य ख्य *khĕ khĕ* or ख्याथ् ख्याथ् *khyāth khyāth*, having eaten frequently.

चि *ci*, drink. — च्य च्य *cĕ cĕ* or च्याथ् च्याथ् *cyāth cyāth*, having drunk frequently.

Exceptions are, as usual,—

नि *ni*, take. — नि नि *ni ni* or निथ् निथ् *nith nith*, having taken frequently.

दि *di*, give. — दि दि *di di* or दिथ् दिथ् *dith dith*, having given frequently.

यि *yi*, come. — यि यि *yi yi* or यिथ् यिथ् *yith yith*, having come frequently.

4. वुनु *wunᵘ* (fem. वंञ् *wạñ*; plur. masc. वंनि *wạnⁱ*, fem. वञ् *waññ*) used to form nouns of agency (ix. i. 25–27). Thus,—

कर *kar*, make. — करवुनु *karawunᵘ*, a maker.

If a root ends in इ *i*, अव *aw* is inserted and the इ *i* changed to य *y*. Thus,—

खि *khi*, eat. — ख्यववुनु *khyawawunᵘ*.

चि *ci*, drink. — च्यववुनु *cyawawunᵘ*.

Exceptions are,—

नि *ni*, take. — निववुनु *niwawunᵘ*.

दि *di*, give. — दिववुनु *diwawunᵘ*.

यि *yi*, come. — यिववुनु *yiwawunᵘ*.

5. वोलु *wōl*^{u}, (fem. वाज्यञ् *wājëñ*; plur. masc. वालि *wāl*^{i}, fem. वाज्यञ *wājëñë*) is also used to form nouns of agency. For examples, see below (ix. i. 28–31).

6. ग्राख् *grākh* (fem. ग्राकञ् *grākañ*, *vide ante*, p. 34). Also used to form nouns of agency (ix. i. 28–31).

These two last suffixes are really secondary ones, (see Sec. Suff. No. 9, 10). They are added to abstract verbal nouns, especially to that in उन् *un* (No. 16), the उन् *un* being changed to अन् *an*. Thus,—

कर *kar*, make.	करुन् *karun*, making.	करन्वोलु *karanwōl*^{u}, or करन्ग्राख् *karangrākh*, a maker.
पर *par*, read.	परुन् *parun*, reading.	परन्वोलु *paranwōl*^{u}, or परन्ग्राख् *parangrākh*.

If the abstract noun is feminine (see No. 31*m*) and ends in न् *n*, that न् *n* is changed to ञु *ñ*^{u} or ञ् *ñ*.

ज़ान *zān*, (31*m*) know.	ज़ान् *zān* (fem.) or ज़ानुन् *zānun* (masc.) knowledge.	ज़ाञुवोलु (ज़ाञ्वोलु) *zāñ*^{u}*wōl*^{u} *zāñwōl*^{u}) or ज़ानन्वोलु *zānanwōl*^{u}, or ज़ाञुग्राख् *zāñ*^{u}*grākh*, (ज़ाञ्ग्राख् *zāñgrākh*), or ज़ानन्ग्राख् *zānangrākh*, a knower.

These two suffixes can only be used with feminine abstract nouns when the verb expresses a condition of the body or mind. Thus ज़ान *zān*, know, expresses a condition of the mind, and therefore we can say ज़ाञुवोलु *zāñwōl*^{u}. But the verb ग्रज़् *graz*, roar, which also has a feminine abstract noun (see No. 31*g*.) ग्रज़् *graz*, cannot form ग्रज़्वोलु *grazwōl*^{u}, because the verb does not express a condition of the mind or body. We can only use the masculine abstract noun, thus, ग्रज़न्वोलु *grazanwōl*^{u}.

If a root ends in इ *i*, the इ *i* becomes य् *y* before अन् *an*, and अन् *an* becomes अन *ana*. Thus,—

खि *khi*, eat.	ख्यनवोलु *khyanawōl*^{u}, ख्यनग्राख् *khyanagrākh*, } an eater.
चि *ci*, drink.	च्यनवोलु *cyanawōl*^{u}, a drinker.

Exceptions are,—

नि *ni*, take.	निनवोलु *ninawōl**, or निनग्राखु *ninagrākh*, a taker.
दि *di*, give.	दिनवोलु *dinawōl**, &c., a giver.
यि *yi*, come.	यिनवोलु *yinawōl**, &c., a comer.

7. नलु *nal*.

8. ललु *lal*.

9. अलु *al*, लु *l*.

These three are used as follows with the roots दि *di* and दाव *dāv* in special senses, all obscene. Thus,—

दिनलु *dinal*, an unchaste woman.

माज्यदिनलु *mājĕdinal*, "*mātṛgāmī*;" बेन्यदिनलु *bĕñĕdinal*, "*svasṛgāmi*," कोरिदिनलु *kōridinal*, "*kanyāgāmī*."

माज्यदिललु *mājĕdilal*, "*mātṛgāmī*."

दावलु *dāwal*, an unchaste woman.

माज्यदावलु *mājĕdāwal*, "*mātṛgāmī*;" बेन्यदावलु *bĕñĕdāwal*, "*svasṛgāmī*;" कोरिदावलु *kōridāwal*, &c.

माज्यदिलु *mājĕdil*, "*mātṛgāmi*," &c. (ix. i. 32–35).

10. उ * (fem. इ *; plur. masc. इ *i*, fem. अ *ĕ*). This is the termination of past participles. This form is now, however, always used as a past tense, and the true participle is described later on (No. 12) (ix. i. 36–39). Examples are,—

कर *kar*, make.	कॊरु *kọr**, (it was) made.
पर *par*, read.	पॊरु *pọr**, (it was) read.
खन *khan*, dig.	खॊनु *khọn**, (it was) dug.

This suffix is added to all transitive and impersonal verbs (*i. e.*, verbs of the first conjugation), and, as a verbal form, is used when the logical subject (in the case of the agent) is in the first or third person.

It cannot be used when it is in the second person. Thus, कॊरु *kọr** may mean, 'it was done by me,' or 'it was done by him,' but cannot mean 'it was done by you.' So ऒसु *ọs**, it-was-laughed by me or by him.

In the case of Intransitive Verbs, it follows the conjugation of these verbs, and is only used in the case of those verbs which are known as "Listed Verbs" (*vide* A List of Kāçmīrī Verbs, *ante*, Vol. LXV, Part I, page 306). These I shall in future call verbs of the second conjugation. It is then used only in the 3rd person. Thus,—

चल *tsal*, flee. चलु *tsọl°*, he fled.

Non-listed Intransitive Verbs, which I shall in future call verbs of the third conjugation, do not use this form in उ °, but take the Aorist form in औव् *auv*, or ओव् *ōv*, used in their case for the Past third person sing. Thus,—

व्यथ *vyath*, be fat. व्यथ्यौव् *vyathyauv*, (not व्यथु *vyọth°*), he was fat.

The final व् *v* is dropped before suffixes, and we thus get व्यथ्यौस् *vyathyau-s*, I was fat.

The following verbs are irregular (ix. i. 37, 38),—

चि *ci*, drink, makes च्यौव् *cyauv* (it was) drunk.

खि *khi*, eat, ख्यौव् *khyauv* (it was) eaten.

नि *ni*, take, न्यूव् *nyūv* (it was) taken.

Besides this there are other irregular forms, such as द्युतु *dyut°*, from √ *di*, 'give'; which will be subsequently described under the head of verbs.

This suffix, उ °, is frequently met in other nouns, which are not verbal forms, *e.g.*, व्यथु *vyọth°*, fat.

11. औव् *auv*, or ओव् *ōv* (fem. एय *ey°*; plur. masc. एय् *ey*, fem. एय *ey°*).

This is the termination of the Aorist Participle of verbs of the first and second conjugations, and of the Past Participle of verbs of the third conjugation. As regards its use, see No. 10. The final व् *v* and य् *y* are omitted before suffixes. The form is an old past participle, and can be used with all verbs.

12. मतु *mọt°* (fem. मचु *mọts°*; plur. masc. मति *mọt^i*, fem. मच *mats°*). This is used to form the true Past Participle. It is compounded with No. 11, in the case of verbs of the first and second conjugations

and with No. 12 in the case of verbs of the third conjugation, and both members of the compound change for gender, number and case.

The word is also written and pronounced मुतु *mut^{u}*, (fem. मॅचु *mạts^{u}*; plur. masc. मॅति *mạt^{i}*, fem. मचु *mats^{u}*) (ix. i. 40).

Examples of the use of this participle are,—

A. First Conjugation. (Form 10).

कॅरुमॅतु *kạr^{u}mạt^{u}*, or कॅरुमुतु *kạr^{u}mut^{u}*, made.

Singular.

	Masc.	Fem.
Nom	कॅरुमॅतु *kạr^{u}mạt^{u}*.	कॅरुमॅचु *kạr^{u}mạts^{u}*.
Acc.	कॅरिमतिस् *kạr^{i}matis*.	करेमचि *karĕmatsĕ*.
Ag.	कॅरिमॅति *kạr^{i}mạt^{i}*.	करिमचि *karimatsi*.

Plural.

	Masc.	Fem.
Nom.	करिमॅति *kạr^{i}mạt^{i}*.	करेमचु *karĕmats^{u}*.
Acc.	कॅरिमत्यन् *kạr^{i}matyan*.	करेमचन् *karĕmatsan*.
Ag.	कॅरिमत्यौ *kạr^{i}matyau*.	करेमचौ *karĕmatsau*.

Note,—1. The irregular declension of the first half of the compound.

2. The feminine termination of the singular, मचे *matsĕ*. We should (according to iv. 51) expect मचु *mats^{u}*, but my paṇḍit assures me that मचे *matsĕ* is the correct form. Compare p. 59, *ante*.

The above declension is as given by my paṇḍit, and is not given by Ī-k.

B. Second Conjugation. (Form 10).

चॅलुमॅतु *tsạl^{u}mạt^{u}*, or चॅलुमुतु *tsạl^{u}mut^{u}*, fled.

Sing.	Masc.	चॅलुमॅतु *tsạl^{u}mạt^{u}*.
	Fem.	चॅजुमॅचु *tsạj^{u}mạts^{u}* (*vide ante*, pp. 32, 33).
Plur.	Masc.	चॅलिमॅति *tsạl^{i}mạt^{i}*.
	Fem.	चजेमचु *tsajĕmats^{u}*.

C. Third Conjugation. (Form 11).

Singular.

	Masc.	Fem.
Nom.	व्यथ्योमतु *vyaṭhyōmạṭ^{u}*.	व्यथ्योमचु *vyaṭhyōmạts^{u}*.
Acc.	व्यथ्योमतिस् *vyaṭhyōmaṭis*.	व्यथ्योमच *vyaṭhyōmatsĕ*.
Ag.	व्यथ्योमति *vyaṭhyōmạṭ^{i}*.	व्यथ्योमचि *vyaṭhyōmatsi*.

Plural.

	Masc.	Fem.
Nom.	व्यथ्योमति *vyaṭhyōmạṭ^{i}*.	व्यथ्योमच *vyaṭhyōmats^{a}*.
Acc.	व्यथ्योमत्यन् *vyaṭhyōmaṭyan*.	व्यथ्योमच्यन् *vyaṭhyōmatsan*.
Ag.	व्यथ्योमत्यौ *vyaṭhyōmaṭyau*.	व्यथ्योमच्यौ *vyaṭhyōmatsau*.

The following forms are irregular :—

From	Past Participle.
यि *yi*, come.	आमतु *āmạṭ^{u}*.
अच *ats*, enter.	चामतु *tsāmạṭ^{u}*.
नेर *nēr*, issue.	द्रामतु *drāmạṭ^{u}*.
प्रस *pras*, give birth.	प्यामतु *pyāmạṭ^{u}*.
ज़ि *zi*, be born.	ज़ामतु *zāmạṭ^{u}*.
मर *mar*, die.	मूमतु *mūmạṭ^{u}*, or मूदुमतु *mūd^{u}mạṭ^{u}*.

Of all these, except मूदुमतु *mūd^{u}mạṭ^{u}*, the first number of the compound does not change for number or case. Thus,—

Sing.	Masc.	आमतु *āmạṭ^{u}*.
	Fem.	आमचु *āmạts^{u}*.
Plur.	Masc.	आमति *āmạṭ^{i}*.
	Fem.	आमच *āmats^{a}*.

The forms for मुद्मंतु *mūdᵘmạtᵘ* are.

Sing. Masc. मुद्मंतु *mūdᵘmạtᵘ*.

Fem. मुमंचु *mūmạtsᵘ*.

Plur. Masc. मुदिमंति *mūdⁱmạtⁱ*.

Fem. मुमच *mūmạtsᵃ*.

In other words मुद्मंतु *mūdᵘmạtᵘ* is only used in the Masculine.

13. मुतु *mutᵘ*, see No. 12 मंतु *mạtᵘ*.

14. अनय् *anay*. This gives the force of the past conjunctive participle, negatived (ix. i. 51).

कर *kar*, make.	करनय् *karanay*, not having made.
गर *gar*, make.	गरनय् *garanay*, not having made.
पर *par*, read.	परनय् *paranay*, not having read.
पोठ *pŏṭh*, be fat.	पोठनय् *pŏṭhanay*, not having become fat.
हि *hi*, buy.	ह्यनय् *hĕnay*, not having bought.

Irregular are,—

नि *ni*, take.	निनय् *ninay*, not having taken.
दि *di*, give.	दिनय् *dinay*, not having given.
यि *yi*, come.	यिनय् *yinay*, not having come.

15. अनी *anī*. This is the first of a series of forms, connected with the Sanskrit participle in अनीयः *anīyaḥ*. It is used as an impersonal future passive participle, like the Latin *faciendum* (ix. i. 50). Thus,—

कर *kar*, make.	करनी *karanī*, it is to be made.
पक *pak*, go.	पकनी *pakanī*, it is to be gone.
वुथ *wŏth*, rise.	वुथनी *wŏthanī*, it is to be risen (one must rise).
चि *ci*, drink.	च्यनी *cĕnī*, it is to be drunk.
हि *hi*, buy.	ह्यनी *hĕnī*, it is to be bought.

Irregular, as usual are,—

नि *ni* take.	निनी *ninī*, it is to be taken.
दि *di*, give.	दिनी *dinī*, it is to be given.
यि *yi*, come.	यिनी *yinī*, it is to be come.

16. उन् *un.*

17. अंनु *ạn*^{u}.

18. उनु *un*^{u}.

These three are used indifferently for one another (ix. ii. 2, 3). The first is of the first declension, and the second and third of the second. Their declension is as follows :—

	SINGULAR.	PLURAL.
Nom.	करन् *karun.*	करन् *karan.*
Acc.	करनस् *karunas.*	करनन् *karanan.*
Ag.	करनन् *karanan.*	करनौ *karanau.*
Obl.[1]	करन *karan*^{a}	करनौ *karanau.*
Nom.	करंनु *karạn*^{u} or करनु *karun*^{u}.	करंनि *kar*^{e}*n*^{i}.
Acc.	(not used).	(not used).
Ag.	करंनि *kar*^{e}*n*^{i}.	(not used).
Obl.[1]	करनि *karani.*	(not used).

If the root ends in इ *i*, the first and third forms are not used (ix. i. 21, 24). We only have forms like,—

	NOM. MASC.	ACC. SING.
खि *khi*, eat.	ख्यंनु *khyạn*^{u}.	ख्यनस् *khyanas.*
हि *hi*, buy.	ह्यंनु *hyạn*^{u}.	ह्यनस् *hyanas.*
चि *ci*, drink.	च्यंनु *cyạn*^{u}.	च्यनस् *cyanas.*

Exceptions, as usual, are,—

नि *ni*, take.	निनु or न्युनु *nyun*^{u}.	निनस् *ninas.*
दि *di*, give.	दिनु or द्युनु *dyun*^{u}.	दिनस् *dinas.*
यि *yi*, come.	यिनु or य्युनु *yyun*^{u}.	यिनस् *yinas.*

This is used,—

(*a*) As an adjective.

(*b*) As an abstract verbal noun.

(*a*) As an adjective, it is equivalent to the Sanskrit participle in अनीयः *anīyaḥ*. Thus, करन् *karun* or करंनु *karạn*^{u}, means 'it is to be

[1] The oblique form is that form which the agent case assumes before post-positions.

made' (masc.). Its feminine is करॅञ् *karạñ*. Examples of its use are,—

इह् पाठ् छुह् परुन् (or परॅनु) *yih pāṭh* (masc.) *chuh parun* (or *parạnᵘ*), this lesson is to be read.

इह् पूथि छह् परॅञ् *yih pūthⁱ* (fem.) *chĕh parạñ* this book is to be read.

This adjective is used in a peculiar idiom with the verb गछ् *gatṣh*, go, be proper (Cf. French *ça ira*). The past of this verb, in this sense is गॅछु *gạtṣhᵘ*, not गौव् *gauv*. It is only used in the future and past tenses, not in the present. Examples of the idiom are (ix. i. 42).

चॅह् गछख् मारॅनु (or मारुनु) *tsᵃh gatṣhakh mārạnᵘ* (or *mārunᵘ*) you deserve a beating, literally you will go with propriety to be beaten.

चॆ गछि सुह् मारॅनु *tsĕ gatṣhi suh mārạnᵘ*, you ought to beat him, literally, he will go to be beaten by you.

चॆ गछि स ज़नान मारॅञ् *tsĕ gatṣhi sᵃ zanānᵃ mārạñ*, you should beat that woman, literally, that woman will go to be beaten (fem.) by you.

चॆ गॅछु सुह् नॆचिवु मारॅनु *tsĕ gạtṣhᵘ suh nĕchyuvᵘ mārạnᵘ*, you should have beaten that boy, lit., that boy went to be beaten by you.

चॆ गॅछ़ स ज़नान मारॅञ् *tsĕ gạtṣhᵃ sᵃ zanānᵃ mārạñ*, you should have beaten that woman.

The same form is used with the verb लग *lag*, be proper, in much the same sense. This is only used in the Future and Past Conditional tenses (ix. i. 43). Thus,—

तॅतु लगि चॆ गछॅनु *tạtᵘ lagi tsĕ gatṣhạnᵘ*, you should go there. Here the participle is impersonal, and the phrase is literally, the going there by you will be proper. If the object is feminine, the participle must be feminine. Thus,—

चॆ लगि मारॅञ् स ज़नान *tsĕ lagi mārạñ sᵃ zanānᵃ*, you should beat that woman, literally, that woman will be proper to be beaten by you.

So, also in the Past Conditional तॅतु लगिहे गछुनु *tạtᵘ lagihĕ gatṣhunᵘ* one (I, you, &c.) should have gone there.

The root पज़ *paz*, be proper, is used in exactly the same way (ix. i. 44). Thus, चॆ पज़िहे सुह् मारुनु *tsĕ pazihĕ suh mārunᵘ* you should have beaten him. Lit. He would have been proper to be beaten by you.

Instead of the agent case, the genitive can be used, in all these idioms (ix. i. 45). Thus we may say,—

च्योनु गछि सुह् मारनु *cyōnᵘ* (instead of *tsě*) *gatshi suh mārạnᵘ*.

च्योनु गछि स सनान मारनु *cyọ̄ñ* (fem.) *gatshi sᵘ sanānᵘ mārạñ*.

So also in the plural,—

च्योनि गछन् तिम् मारनि *cyọ̄nⁱ gatshan tim mārᵊnⁱ*, you should beat them.

च्यानु गछन् तिम मारनु *cyāñě gatshan timᵘ māraññě*, you should beat them (fem.).

Pronominal suffixes can also be added to the main verb (not to the participle) (ix. i. 46). The formation of these suffixes will be dealt with in the chapter on verbs.

गछुस् करुनु *gạtshu-s karunᵘ*, it should have been done *to him*.

गछुय् करनु *gạtshu-y karạnᵘ*, it should have been done for thee.

लगयस् करुन् *lagy-as karun*, it should be done for him.

पज़्यम् करुन् *pazy-am karun*, it should be done for me.

(*b*) As a substantive, the form is used as a masculine Abstract Verbal Noun, or Infinitive (ix. ii. 2, 3 and ff). Thus,—

कर् *kar*, make.	करुन् *karun*, करनु *karạnᵘ*, or करुनु *karunᵘ*, the act of making, to make.

The accusative singular is used with the post-position क्युतु or क्युतु *kyutᵘ* (ix. i. 17) to form a dative. *E.g.*, परनस् क्युतु *paranas kyutᵘ*, for reading. Thus,—

परनस् क्युतु प्रङ्ग् *paranas kyutᵘ prang*, a couch for reading. क्युतु *kyutᵘ* is an adjective.

We thus have,—

परनस् क्युतु प्रङ्ग् *paranas kyutᵘ prang*, a couch (masc. sg.) for reading.

परनस् किति गर् *paranas kitⁱ garᵘ*, houses (masc. pl.) for reading.

परनस् कित्सु चूकि *paranas kitsᵘ cūkⁱ*, a chair (fem. sg.) for reading.

परनस् कित्स चोकॆ *paranas kitsᵘ cōkě*, chairs for reading.

In all the above it will be seen that the essential meaning of the verb is active. A couch for reading means a couch for reading something,—*e.g.*, a book,—and the verb is not changed whatever the gender of the object may be. Thus पूथि *pūth*^{i}, a book, is feminine, but we still say

यिह् पूथि (or यिथ् पोथ्य) परनस् क्युत् प्रग् *yih pūth*^{i} (or *yith pōthĕ*) *paranas kyut*^{u} *prang*, a couch for reading this book.

We may also use the dative of other verbal nouns in the same way. Thus, त्सेटनस् क्युत् *tsĕṭanas kyut*^{u} or (No. 30*d*.) त्सेटस् क्युत् *tsĕṭas* (masc.) *kyut*^{u}, for grinding to powder; ग्रज़नस् क्युत् *grazanas kyut*^{u} or (No. 31*g*.) ग्रज़ि क्युत् *grazi* (fem.) *kyut*^{u}, for roaring.

But if the verb is used passively then it agrees with the subject in gender, and the form is no longer substantival but adjectival. Thus, 'a book for reading' means 'a book for being read,' and we must say,—

परॅञ् किज़ु पूथि *parᵃñ kitsᵃ pūth*^{i}.

On the other hand we say परनस् किज़ु चूकि *paranas kitsᵃ cūk*^{i}, because the phrase means a chair for reading, and not a chair for being read.

Note that when the verb is used passively, it is in the form of the *nominative* feminine, not in the accusative, although preceding किज़ु *kitsᵃ*.

We may also use the nominative masculine before क्युत् *kyut*^{u} (ix. i. 22, 23) when the verb is used passively. Thus परुनु (or परुन् or परॅनु) क्युत् पोस्तुक् *parun*^{u} (or *parun* or *parᵃn*^{u}) *kyut*^{u} *pŏstukh* (masc. sg.), a book for reading. We thus get the following adjectival forms when the verb is used passively,—

Masc. Sg. परॅनु क्युत् पोस्तुक् *parᵃn*^{u} *kyut*^{u} *pŏstukh*, a book for reading.

(We cannot say परॅनु क्युत् प्रग् *parᵃn*^{u} *kyut*^{u} *prang*, a couch for reading).

Masc. Pl. रॅनिनि किति हाख् *ranᵃn*^{i} *kit*^{i} *hākh*, vegetables for cooking.

Fem. Sg. परॅञ् किज़ु पूथि *parᵃñ kitsᵃ pūth*^{i}, a book for reading.

Fem. Pl. करञ़ किच़ काम्य *karañĕ kitsa kāmĕ*, businesses (fem. pl.) to be done.

These are all capable of declension. Thus,—(acc.) परनस् कितिस् पुस्तकस् छुह् थवान् *paranas kitis pŏstakas chuh thawān*, he places a book for reading.

The oblique base of the form in अंनु *ạnª* is used to indicate a purpose (ix. i. 18). I note that in poetry the form ends in अने *anĕ*, not in अनि *ani*. Thus,—

परनि (or poetical परने) गछान् छुह् *parani* (or poetical *paranĕ*) *gatshān chuh*, he goes to read. रननि गौव् *ranani gauv*, he went to cook.

When the word समख *samakh*, meet, is used in this form, it means to pay a visit of condolence. Thus, समखनि गौव् *samakhani gauv*, he went to pay a visit of condolence. Otherwise the ordinary dative of the verbal noun in उन् *un* is used. Thus, समखन पुछ़् रूदु *samakhana putshy rūdª*, he stopped to meet him (ix. i. 19).

This verbal form is used to form Inceptive and Desiderative compounds. Thus,—

Inceptive compounds, are made with the infinitive in अंनु *ạnª* or उनु *unª*, and the verb हि *hi*, take (viii. i. 57). Thus, सुह् छुह् खत् लेखुनु ह्यवान् *suh chuh khăth lĕkhunª hyawān*, he begins to write a letter; करुन् ह्यवान् छुह् *karun hyawān chuh*, he begins to do. If the object is feminine, the feminine infinitive is used. Thus, सुह् छुह् ज़नान मारंञ़् ह्यवान् *suh chuh zanānª mārạñ hyawān*, he begins to beat the woman. These forms are however, almost always used in the past tense. Thus, करुन् ह्योतुन् *karun hyọtun*, he began to read, (and is doing it now). तमि छुह् खत् लेखुनु ह्योतुमोतु *tạmⁱ chuh khăth lĕkhunª hyọtªmọtª*, he has begun to write the letter. Literally, by him the letter to-be-written has been taken. So तमि छेह् ज़नान मारंञ़् ह्यचमच़ *tạmⁱ chhĕh zanānª mārạñ hĕtsªmạtsª*, he has begun to beat the woman (ix. i. 41).

Another way of forming inceptive compounds is to use the oblique form of the infinitive with the verb लग *lag* already mentioned. Thus,—

सुह् करनि लगु *suh karani lạgª*, he began to do.

सुह् लॊगु खथ् लेखनि *suh lạg*^{e} *khăth lĕkhani*, he began to write the letter.

सुह् लॊगु ज़नान मारनि *suh lạg*^{e} *zanān*^{e} *mārani*, he began to beat the woman. It will be observed that this form of the verbal noun does not change for gender.

Similarly, **Desiderative compounds** are made with the verb इछ् *yitsh*, wish. Thus,—

सुह् छुह् खथ् लेखुनु इछान् *suh chuh khăth lĕkhun*^{e} *yitshān*, he wishes to write the letter.

सुह् छुह् ज़नान मार्‌ॖन् इछान् *suh chuh zanān*^{e} *mārạñ yitshān*, he wishes to beat the woman.

तॆमि इछ़ ज़नान मार्‌ॖन् *tạm*^{i} *yitsh*^{a} *zanān*^{e} *mārạñ*, he wished to beat the woman.

In the formation of this abstract noun the following **irregularities** appear (ix. ii. 4). Only one form of the infinitive is given, but the others follow the same rule,—

तल *tal*, fry.	तलुन् *talun* or तल्युन् *talyun*.
बस *bas*, fry, serve.	बसुन् *basun* or बस्युन् *basyun*.

Some verbs only use their Abstract Noun in the Feminine, and, moreover, are then sometimes irregular in their formation (ix. ii. 24 and ff.). They are the following:—

	Abstract Nouns.
च़र *tsar*, be inwardly wrathful (impersonally).	च़रिन् *tsariñ*, inward wrath.
च़ुव *tsuv*, quarrel (impersonally).	च़ुविन् *tsuviñ*.

[These two, when used with other verbs, take the *regular* feminines in phrases like,—

अमिस् ह्यॊचुन् च़र्‌ॖन् *amis hȫts*^{a}*n tsarạñ*, he began to be angry. Literally, being angry began to him].

मोरव *mōrav*, bear (of pain, impersonally).	मोरवुन् *mōrav*^{a}*ñ*.
मर्छ़ *marts*, be impatient (used impersonally).	मर्छ़ुन् *marts*^{a}*ñ*.

19. अ॑ण् *ạñ*.

20. इण् *iñ*.

21. अण् *ᵃñ*.

These are all Feminine forms of the masculine verbal adjectives, and of the masculine abstract nouns or infinitives, in उन् *un*, अ॑नु *ạnᵘ*, or उनु *unᵘ* (Nos. 16–18). No. 19 is the regular feminine of all three, and is discussed under the head of those suffixes.

It is also specially used to form a feminine abstract noun in the case of the following verb.

चेन *tsēn*, know by a sign, चेनव॑ण् *tsēnavạñ* the giving of a sign (ix. ii. 43).

In the case of the following verbs it is only used in the fem. pl. (अण् *añᵃ*) (ix. ii. 42),—

कड *kaḍ*, bring out.	कडण् *kadañᵃ*, blaming.
पांडर *pāḍᵃr*, blame.	पांडरण् *pāḍᵃrañᵃ*, blaming.
शुक *çruk*, weep.	शुकण् *çrukañᵃ*, weeping.

A few verbs (mostly connected with female ideas, and mostly used impersonally) have no masculine forms, and are also discussed under the head of Nos. 16–18.

They have only feminine abstract nouns or infinitives in इण् *iñ*, or अण् *ᵃñ*. For easy reference, I repeat them here.

The two following form their abstract or infinitives in इण् *iñ*, and in no other way (ix. ii. 24). That is to say they have no infinitive in उन् *un*.

त्सर *tsar*, be inwardly wrathful, whether referring to a man or a woman, always used impersonally, and always in the feminine. Thus, तस् त्स॑र *tas tsạrᵃ* (fem.), of him or her inward wrath was felt, *i.e.*, he or she was inwardly angry. Abstract noun or infinitive त्सरिण् *tsariñ*, not त्सरुन् *tsarun* or त्सर॑ण् *tsarạñ*, inward wrath. त्सरुन् *tsarun*, does occur, but it is the abstract noun or infinitive of another verb, त्सर *tsar*, increase.

Other examples of the use of this curious verb is तस् त्सरान् छस् *tas tsarān chhēh* (fem.) he or she is inwardly angry. तस् त्सरि *tas tsari*, he or she will be angry.

चुव *tsuv*, (ix. ii. 24) quarrel, also used impersonally, and in the feminine. Abstract noun or infinitive चुविञ् *tsuviñ*, quarrelling.

Examples of use,—

Present tense, सुह् छुह् चुवान् *suh chhuh tsuvān*, he is quarrelling.

Future tense, सुह् चुवि *suh tsuvi*, he will quarrel.

Past tense, only used in the feminine,—

तमि चुव *tąmi tsuv*, by him quarrelling was done.

तमि चुव *tami tsuv*, by her quarrelling was done.

Note, that in the Past, it is always used impersonally, and in the feminine gender though it may refer to males.

We thus see that चर *tsar* is always construed with the genitive (तस् *tas*), but चुव *tsuv*, in the Present and Future as an ordinary Intransitive Verb, and in the Past as an Impersonal Verb.

The two following verbs, form their abstract nouns or infinitives in अञ् *ᵃñ*, and in no other way.

मोरव *mōrav*, (viii. iii. 25) bear pain, used impersonally and in the feminine in the past tenses only. Abstract noun or infinitive मोरवञ् *mōravᵃñ*.

Examples of the use of this verb,—

Present tense, सुह् छुह् मोरवान् *suh chuh mōravān*, he is bearing pain.

Future tense, सुह् मोरवि *suh mōravi*, he will bear pain.

Past tense, तमि मोरव *tąmi mōrąv* (fem. impersonal) (pain) was borne by him, he bore pain.

मर्छ *martsa* (ix. ii. 25), be impatient. Abstract noun, or infinitive, मर्छञ् *martsᵃñ*.

Examples of use,—

Present tense, तस् छस् मर्छान् *tas chhĕh* (fem.) *martsān*, of that man, or of that woman, there is impatience.

Future tense, तस् मर्छि *tas martsi*, of that man, or of that woman, there will be impatience.

Past tense, तस् मर्छ *tas mąrts*, of that man, or of that woman, there was impatience.

It is thus construed exactly like चर *tsar*.

The following verbs optionally form feminine abstract nouns or infinitives in अञ् ^{a}*ñ*, in addition to the ordinary masculine one in उन् *un* (ix. ii. 26).

खस् *kh*^{a}*s*, pluck the hair. In the case of this verb, खसुन् *kh*^{a}*sun* (masc.) is used when men are referred to, and खसञ् *kh*^{a}*s*^{a}*ñ* (fem.) when women are referred to (*sensu obscœno*).

फिच *phits*, forget; फख *phŏç*, be inwardly angry; फुह *phuh*, be inwardly angry. In the last two the fem. abstract noun is used of the wrath of females.

वसव *wasav*, moisten; वुछ *wuts*, be burnt.

The following verbs optionally form the feminine abstract noun in इञ् *iñ*, in addition to the ordinary masculine one in उन् *un* (ix. ii. 27–32).

सार *sār*, feel (see No. 26); खुत *khut*, dig from below; टुव *ṭuv*, close (of a flower); डुव *ḍuv*, sweep; डल *ḍal*, pass over; त्रुक *truk* (see No. 30*a*), bite in pieces; थेक *thĕk*, praise; नच *nats*, dance; नट *naṭ*, tremble; नम *nam*, bend; वुस *wus*, appear (as water from a spring); वुठ *wuṭh*, twist; वुप *wup*, burn inside; लिव *liv*, smear (makes लिविञ् *liviñ*, or लिपिञ् *lipiñ*); ल्यव *lyav*, lick; कर *kar*, do (करिञ् *kariñ*, however, only means a mason's trowel); वट *waṭ*, twist (वटिञ् *waṭiñ* means a collection); फर *phar*, steal (फरिञ् *phariñ* means a female thief). Thus, सारिञ् *sāriñ*, feeling.

If the secondary suffix अल् *al* (sec. suf. No. 6) is ever used with any abstract verbal noun, it cannot be used with the masculine form, but only with the feminine form in इञ् *iñ* (ix. ii. 27). This अल् *al* is only used with a few verbs. Thus, थेकिञल् *thĕkiñal*, a praiser; नटिञल् *naṭiñal*, a trembler, and so on.

22. अन् *an*, (masculine). Used to form masculine abstract nouns in the case of three verbs (ix. ii. 41). Thus,—

चि *ci*, drink.	च्यन् *cyan* (masc.) drinking.
खि *khi*, eat.	ख्यन् *khyan* (masc.) drinking.
हि *hi*, place.	ह्यन् *hyan* (masc.) placing.

20. अन् *an* (fem.). Used to form feminine abstract nouns in the case of the following verbs (ix. ii. 35; 37) कपट *kapaṭ*, cut; दन् *d*^{a}*n*,

shake out dust; नखाव *nakhāv*, obliterate; पिल *pil*, arrive; फिर *phir*, turn over (pages); माश *māś*, be intent upon; मिलव *milav*, unite; मुचर *mutsar*, open; मूर *mūr*, shell (pease, &c.); ल्यव *lyav*, lick; वुठ *wuth*, twist; वुह *wuh*, be not extinguished; आदुर *ād*ᵉ*r*, mix; खंडुर *khaṇḍ*ᵉ*r*, divide; ल्वकुटुर *tsh*ŏ*t*ᵉ*r*, make small; ज़ीठुर *zīth*ᵉ*r*, make long; टोटुर *ṭŏṭ*ᵉ*r*, have insufficient means of livelihood; पीठुर *pīth*ᵉ*r*, blame and instruct; फुटुर *phuṭ*ᵉ*r*, break; बडुर *baḍ*ᵉ*r*, make great; बागुर *bāg*ᵉ*r*, divide; म्वटुर *mŏṭ*ᵉ*r* make thick; वोवुर *wōw*ᵉ*r*, shave metal.

Thus, कपटन् *kapaṭan* (fem.) cutting.

The verb गिलव *gilav*, whirl about, forms गिलन् *gilan*, which means 'an attempt' (ix. ii. 36).

The verb नव *nav*, be new, forms न्वव्रन् *nŏv*ᵉ*ran*, raking up an old story against a person (ix. ii. 38).

The verb लार *lār*, touch, forms लारन् *lāran*, which means 'trembling' (ix. ii. 40).

Some people use this form with the roots त्वनुर *tŏn*ᵉ*r*, dilute; त्वतुर *tŏts*ᵉ*r*, make hot; स्यवुर *syŏs*ᵉ*r*, make straight (ix. ii. 39).

24. रब् *rab*. This is optionally used in the case of the root मश *maś*, to form a masculine verbal abstract noun (ix. ii. 5). Thus, मश्रब् *maśrab*, forgetting.

25. ु *u*, this is optionally used to form masculine verbal abstract nouns from the three following roots (ix. ii. 6).

द्वदर *dŏdar*, rot.	द्वद्रु *dŏdar*ᵘ, rotting.
ज़्वज़र *zŏzar*, wither.	ज़्वज़्रु *zŏzar*ᵘ, withering.
स्वसर *sŏsar*, decay.	स्वस्रु *sŏsaru*, decaying.

26. ु *u* is used optionally to form feminine verbal abstract nouns in the case of the following verbs (viii. ii. 62, 63, 68, 72, 79).

तछ *tach*, pare, त्वछु *tŏch*ᵘ, scratching (also तछ् *tăch*); रछ *rach*, protect, र्वछु *rŏch*ᵘ, protection; छांड *tshāḍ*, search, छ्वडु *tsŏḍ*ᵘ, searching; छांड *tshāṇḍ*, search (with a nasal), makes either छ्वंडु *tshŏṇḍ*ᵘ, or छांड् *tshāṇḍ*; छान *chān*, sift, छ्वनु *chŏn*ᵘ; दोन *dŏn*, card cotton, दूनु *dŭn*ᵘ; चार

thār, be quick, थारु *thạ̄r*^{u} ; बाबर *bā̆bar*, be quick, बाँबरु *bā̆bạr*^{u} ; सार *sạ̄r*, feel, सांरु *sạ̄r*^{u} (*vide* p. 210) ; हंदुर *hạnd*^{a}*r*, be cold, हंदुरु *hạnd*^{a}*r*^{u}.

27. अ *a* (masc.) ; used optionally to form masculine verbal abstract nouns in the case of the following verbs (ix. ii. 7).

छ्वम्ब *chŏmb*, husk ; ज़्वस *zŏs*, cough ; बगार *bagār*, fry in oil ; ब्यह *bĕh*, sit ; लम *lam*, pull ; ल्वस *lŏs*, be weary ; वुन *wun*, be unlucky.

Thus, छ्वम्ब *chŏmb*^{a}, the act of husking, and so on.

28. अ *a* (fem.) used optionally to form a feminine abstract verbal noun in the case of the verb वुंग *wuṅg*, to howl like a dog, in a special meaning (ix. ii. 57).

Thus, वुंग *wuṅg*^{a}, lying awake at night on account of some care.

वुंग् *wuṅg*, means a dog's howl.

29. आव् *āv*. Used optionally in the case of the verb लद् *lad*, send, build, elevate, push, when it means 'build,' to form a masculine abstract noun. लदाव् *ladāv*, also means, the wages of building (ix. ii. 8).

30. ——— (masc.). Several verbs optionally drop all suffixes to form abstract nouns. In such cases roots ending in hard consonants aspirate them in the nominative singular and plural. These roots are classed according to their final letters. In the case of causal roots ending in अव *av*, the अव *av* is dropped.

(*a*) क *k*, certain verbs in क *k* and कव *kav*, make optional verbal abstract nouns by changing the क *k* or कव *kav* to ख् *kh* (ix. ii. 9). These verbs are,—

छ्वकव *chŏkav*, wash.

छ्वक *tshŏk*, become speechless.

टक *ṭak*, bite in two with a noise.

टुक *ṭuk*, bore like a rat.

ट्वकव *ṭŏkav*, cause to disappear.

टुक *ṭhuk*, bury.

त्रुक *truk*, cut to pieces, eat (*vide* p. 210).

थक *thak*, be weary.

पाकव *pākav*, cook.

फुक *phuk*, blow up fire.

ब्रक *brak*, clench with the teeth.

Thus, छुख् *chŏkh*, the act of washing. त्सुख् *tshŏkh*, speechlessness and so on. The root फुक *phuk* becomes फ्वख् *phŏkh*, when it means 'to puff.' Otherwise it is simply फुख् *phukh*, the blowing of a fire.

(*b*) ग *g*. This case is exactly similar to the preceding one. It occurs in the case of three verbs (ix. ii. 10). Thus,—

	OPTIONAL FORM OF ABSTRACT NOUN.
द्वगव *dŏgav*, husk.	द्वग् *dŏg*, husking.
रंग *rańg*, paint.	रंग् *rańg*, painting.
सगव *sagav*, water plants.	सग् *sag*, watering.

(c) त्स *ts* (ix. ii. 11). It occurs only in the case of the verb,—

वांत्स *wą̈ts*, cheat; abstract noun वांत्स् *wą̈tsh*, cheating.

(*d*) ट *ṭ* (ix. ii. 12).

त्सेट *tsĕṭ*, powder; लूट *lūṭ*, rob; वाट *wāṭ*, join. These can form abstract nouns in ठ *ṭh*. Thus, त्सेठ् *tsĕṭh*, pounding to powder.

(*e*) ड *ḍ* (ix. ii. 13).

गंड *gaṇḍ*, tie; optional abstract noun, गंड् *gaṇḍ*, tieing.

(*f*) न *n* (ix. ii. 14).

खन *khan*, dig; त्सुन *tshĕn*, cut; optional abstract nouns, खन् *khan*, digging, त्सुन् *tshĕn*, cutting.

(*g*) प *p*. The following verbs optionally make their abstract nouns in फ् *ph* (ix. ii. 15).

कांप *kąmp*, tremble; क्रप *krp*, cut with scissors; त्साप *tsāp*, chew (Cf. No. 31*n*.); जप *sap*, mutter prayers; टप *ṭap*, kick of a horse, &c.

Thus, कांफ् *kąmph*, trembling, and so on.

(*h*) म *m* (ix. ii. 16).

ब्रम *bram*, be in error; abstract noun, optionally, ब्रम् *bram*.

(*i*) र *r* (ix. ii. 17).

चार *cār*, tie tightly.

चीर *cīr*, wring out.

तार *tār*, cross over (active).

फुकार *phukār*, speak in anger, bubble up (of steam).

फार *phyăr*, strain (liquid).

मार *măr*, beat.

सार *sŏr*, remember.

Thus, optional abstract noun, चार् *căr*, tieing tightly.

(*j*) ल *l* (ix. ii. 18).

चॊल *tsŏl*, force inside (active).

छल *tshal*, cheat.

ज़ुल *z°l*, scrape.

तोल *tōl*, weigh.

दल *dal*, split (active).

मेल *mēl*, meet.

Thus, optional abstract noun, चॊल् *tsŏl*, forcing inside.

(*k*) व *w* (ix. ii. 19).

ज़ुव *zuv*, live.

डुव *ḍuv*, sweep.

ताव *tăr*, heat.

अछव *wŏhav*, curse.

These optionally form their abstract nouns in व् *v*. Thus, ज़ुव् *zuv*, life; अछव् *wŏhav*, cursing.

(*l*) स *s* (ix. ii. 20).

रस *ras*, be juicy.

हुसव *h°sav*, incite.

Thus, रस् *ras*, juiciness; हुस् *h°s*, inciting.

(*m*) ह् *h* (ix. ii. 21, 22).

गह *g°h*, grind.

चह *ts°h*, suck.

गह् *g°h*, grinding; चह् *ts°h*, sucking. The former also makes गस् *gas*, grinding.

31. ——— (fem.). Several verbs optionally drop all suffixes to form feminine abstract nouns. In such cases, roots ending in hard consonants aspirate them in the nominative singular. These roots are classed according to their final letters.

In the case of causal roots ending in अव *av*, the अव *av*, is dropped. The following are the verbs :—

(*a*) क *k* (ix. ii. 56).

छक *chak*, scatter.

छिक *chik*, sprinkle.

चमक *camak*, shine.

त्सक *t*^{e}*k*, run.

फुंक *phŭk*, smell.

शंक *çŏk*, doubt.

Thus, छख् *chăkh*, (fem.) a scattering, a sowing of seed; शंख् *çŏkh* (fem.), doubting.

(*b*) ख *kh* (ix. ii. 75).

There is only one, and it is irregular. लेख् *lĕkh*, write, makes लेफ् *lĕph*, a writing (nom. pl. लेफ *lĕph*^{e}).

(*c*) ग *g* (ix. ii. 57).

ज्राग *zāg*, be watchful.

टोंग *ṭŏg*, emit a loud cry.

दग *dag*, beat.

मंग *mang*, ask.

लग *lag*, be with.

लाग *lāg*, imitate.

वुंग *wung*, bark (of a dog).

शोंग *çŏng*, sleep.

Thus, ज्राग् *zāg*, watchfulness. वुंग् *wung*, is, specially, a dog's howl. वुंग *wung*^{e}, means the lying awake at night owing to some care.

(*d*) च *ch* (ix. ii. 61).

तच *tach*, pare.

मन्दच *mandach*, be ashamed.

Thus, तच् *tăch*, scratching. The first may also form तंच् *tąch*^{e} (62).

(*e*) ट्स *ts* (ix. ii. 58).

पट्स *pats*, trust with a loan.

रोट्स *rōts*, be preferred.

श्रोट्स *çrōts*, be pure.

Thus, पछ् *pǎtsh*, trust (of all kinds), रोछ् *rötsh*, preference.

(*f*) छ् *tsh* (ix. ii. 59).

इछ *yitsh*, wish.

प्रिछ *pritsh*, ask.

Thus, इछ् *yitsh*, wishing. We say प्रिछगारि कर्नस् *pritsh*^{u}*-gạr*^{u} *kạr*^{u}*-n-as*, asking, &c., was done by him for him.

(*g*) स *s* (ix. ii. 64).

ग्रस *gras*, roar.

Thus, ग्रस् *gras*, a roaring; ग्रसि क्युतु *grasi kyut*^{u}, for roaring (ix. i. 17).

(*h*) ट *ṭ* (ix. ii. 65).

छूँट *tsū̃ṭ*, break wind with noise.

छट *tshaṭ*, winnow.

फुट *phuṭ*, be broken.

Thus, छठ् *tshǎṭh*, winnowing.

(*i*) ठ *ṭh* (ix. ii. 66).

ट्यठ् *ṭyǎṭh*, be bitter. The abstract noun, ट्यठ् *ṭyǎṭh*, means necessity, necessariness.

Thus, तमाकि ट्यठ् *tamākⁱ ṭyǎṭh*, the want of tobacco.

(*j*) ड *ḍ* (ix. ii. 67, 68).

मांड *mā̃ḍ*, mix.

छांड *tshā̃ḍ*, search.

The latter makes छांड् *tshā̃ḍ*, or छँडु *tshã̄ḍ*^{u}. [The verb छाड *tsāḍ*, search, without the nasal, always makes छडु *tsạḍ*^{u}].

(*k*) त *t* (ix. ii. 69).

न्यत *nyat*, shear.

लतव *latav*, kick.

Thus, न्यथ *nyǎth*, a shearing; लथ *lǎth*, a kick.

(*l*) द *d* (ix. ii. 70).

पद् *pad*, break wind.

प्यद् *pyad*, be cognisant of.

पंद् *pǒnd*, sneeze.

Thus, पंद् *pǒnd*, a sneeze.

(*m*) न *n* (ix. ii. 71).

आमन *āman*, change for the bad.

ज्ञान *zān*, know.

Thus, आमन् *āman*, a change for bad.

(*n*) प *p* (ix. ii. 73).

चाप *tsāp*, gnaw.

Thus, चाप् *tsāph*, a gnawing (Cf. No. 30*g*.).

(*o*) फ *ph* (ix. ii. 74).

वुफ *wuph*, fly.

Thus, वुफ् *wuph* a flying.

(*p*) ब *b* (ix. ii. 76).

रंब *ramb*, be beautiful.

पूब *pūb*, be beautiful.

Thus, रंब् *ramb*, beauty.

(*q*) य *y* (ix. ii. 77).

प्रय *pray*, be pleased with.

Thus, प्रय् *pray*, love.

(*r*) र *r* (ix. ii. 78).

आवर *āwar*, cover.

डखर *ḍakh*ᵊ*r*, depend upon.

तुर *tur*, be cold.

थथर *thathar*, be quick.

दोर *dōr*, run.

मुर *mūr*, husk.

लार *lār*, touch.

सखर *sakhar*, set forth.

लार् *lār*, means absconding. The verb दूंछर *dūntsh*ᵊ*r*, separate, forms दूछ् *dūntsh*, separating (ix. ii. 60). The verb, वडर *waḍ*ᵊ*r*, bury makes वड् *waḍ* (ix. ii. 67).

(*s*) ल *l* (ix. ii. 80).

गांगल *gãgal*, }
ग्रांगल *grãgal*, } be disturbed in one's work.

टाल *ṭāl*, go away with indifference.

तंबल *tambal*, change one's mind.

म्वकल *mŏkal*, be released.

व्वलल *wŏlal*, adorn.

शहल *çahal*, be cold.

Thus म्वकल् *mŏkal*, release.

(*t*) व *w*, (ix. ii. 81).

दव *dav*, run.

Thus, दव् *dav*, running.

32. इश् *iç* (ix. ii. 33). This is used optionally to form feminine abstract nouns or infinitives, in the case of the following verbs.

त्स्वक *tsŏk*, be angry; तप *tap*, become hot; लंग *lang*, be lame.

Thus, त्स्वकिश् *tsŏkiç*, anger.

The √ मिलव *milav*, unite, irregularly forms मिलमिश् *milamiç* (ix. ii. 34).

33. अक *ak* (nom. sg. अख *akh*) (fem.), used to form a feminine abstract noun in the case of the verb पोठ *pöṭh*, be fat; *e.g.*, पोठख् *pöṭhakh*, fatness (ix. ii. 45).

34. अत् *at* (nom. sg. अथ् *ath*) (fem.), used to form feminine abstract nouns in the case of the following verbs (ix. ii. 44).

अर्स *ars*, earn; बाव *bāv*, declare one's intentions; व्वपस *wŏpas*, become; श्रप *çrap*, decay; स्यद *syad*, succeed; गर *gar*, make; वट *waṭ*, twist; शेहल *çahal*, be cold; ह्यक *hyak*, be able.

Thus, अर्सत् *arsat*; nom. sg. अर्सथ् *arsath*, earning.

35. अय् *ay* (fem.), used to form feminine abstract nouns in the case of the following verbs (ix. ii. 46).

वखन *wakhan*, tell; खार *khār*, ascend; ज़ाग *zāg*, be watchful; वाल *wāl*, take down; नच *nats*, dance; ह्वख *hŏkh*, be dry; आमन *āman*, change for the bad.

Thus, वखनय् *wakhanay*, telling. The verb मंग् *magg*, ask, forms मांगय् *mãgay*, asking (ix. ii. 47).

The verb बांग॒र् *bãg°r*, divide, forms बागय् *bâgay*, division, or बागनय् *bâganay* (ix. ii. 48, 54).

The verb ज़ेन् *zĕn*, conquer, forms ज़िय् *ziy*, victory (ix. ii. 49).

From the verb साव् *sâv*, sleep, comes the derivative, वुदसावय् *udasâvay*, waking, lying awake (ix. ii. 50).

The simple word सावय् *sâvay*, means 'happiness' (ix. ii. 51).

From the verb आमन् *âman*, change for the worse, already mentioned, we also have हामनय् *hâmanay*, a false charge (ix. ii. 52).

From the verb लाग् *lāg*, cultivate, we have लागनय् *lāganay*, cultivation (ix. ii. 53).

From the verb साद् *sād*, accomplish, we have सादनय् *sādanay*, a chief cause (ix. ii. 55).

36. अवञ् *awañ* (fem.) (with unmodified vowel). This is added to a verb to signify wages (ix. ii. 82, 83, 84). Thus,—

करवञ् *karawañ*, (fem.), the wages of doing; परवञ् *parawañ*, the wages of reading; लोनवञ् *lōnawañ*, the wages of reaping; रोज़वञ् *rōzawañ*, the wages of remaining.

If the root ends in a vowel the suffix is ववञ् *wawañ*. Thus,—

(दि *di*) दिववञ् *diwawañ*, the wages of giving; निववञ् *niwawañ*, the wages of taking; ख्यववञ् *khyawawañ*, the wages of eating; च्यववञ् *cyawawañ*, the wages of drinking.

37. अन्हार् *anhār*, used to signify fitness (ix. ii. 91). Thus,—

करन्हार् *karanhār*, fit to be done.

गंडन्हार् *gaṇḍanhār*, fit to be bound.

If the verb ends in a vowel, the suffix becomes अनहार् *anahār*. Thus,—

ख्यनहार् *khyanahār*, fit to be eaten.

च्यनहार् *cyanahār*, fit to be drunk.

ह्यनहार् *hyanahār*, fit to be placed.

But as usual,—

निनहार् *ninahār*, fit to be taken;

दिनहार् *dinahār*, fit to be given;

यिनहार् *yinahār*, fit to come.

The verb लग *lag* makes लगहार् *lagahār*, which simply means 'worthy.'

On Secondary Suffixes in Kāçmīrī.—*By* G. A. Grierson, C.I.E.

[Read August, 1896.]

The following account of Secondary Suffixes in Kāçmīrī is based on the fourth part of Īçvara-kaula's *Kaçmīra-çabdāmṛta.* Some of the so-called suffixes are evidently merely nouns in composition, but I have thought it best to retain them.

The following suffixes express **Relationship.**

1. पुतु *pūt*^{a} (iv. 1).[1] This Suffix (the Skr. पोतः *pōtaḥ*) added to a noun in the form of the instrumental singular case (the न् *n* of the first declension being dropped), signifies son, *e.g.*,—

> दर् *dar*, (instr. दरन् *daran*) a certain caste, दर-पुतु *dar*^{a}*-pūt*^{a}, the son of a man of that caste.
>
> कौल् *kaul*, a certain caste, कौल-पुतु *kaul*^{a}*-pūt*^{a}, the son of a man of that caste.
>
> त्युकु *tyuk*^{a} (instr. टिकि *tik*^{i}), a certain caste, टिकि-पुतु *tik*^{i}*-pūt*^{a}, the son of a man of that caste.
>
> काव् *kāv*, a crow, काव-पुतु *kāv*^{a}*-pūt*^{a}, a young crow.
>
> कट् *kaṭ*, a ram, कट-पुतु *kaṭ*^{a}*-pūt*^{a}, a young ram.

Apparently irregular are,—

> म्यॅ-पुतु *myä-pūt*^{a}, a young ram; कोकर्-पुतु *kŏkar-pūt*^{a} a chicken; कोतर्-पुतु, *kōtar-pūt*^{a} a young pigeon; and पछिन्-पुतु *pachin-pūt*^{a}, a young bird.

This Suffix can only be used with generic terms, such as the above. It cannot be used with proper names (iv. 2).

Note.—The word त्सूर-पुतु *tsūr*^{a}*-pūt*^{a}, either means the son of a thief (त्सूर् *tsūr*), or may be applied to children as a term of endearment (iv. 3).

[1] References here and elsewhere to the *Kaçmīra-çabdāmṛta.*

When the Suffix is added to the word मिञ् *mĭñ*, a kiss, मिञ्-पूतु *mĭñĕ-pūt*^{u}, or मञ्-पूतु *mŏñĕ-pūt*^{u}, means simply a kiss (iv. 4).

2. कठ् *kăṭh.* This word also means son, but is rarely used, except in abuse, or anger (iv. 5), *e.g.*,—

> चूर-कठ् *tsūr*^{a}*-kăṭh*, son of a thief.
>
> गान-कठ् *gān*^{a}*-kăṭh*, son of a pimp.
>
> पोग-कठ् *pōg*^{a}*-kăṭh*, son of destruction.
>
> वाज़-कठ *wāz*^{a}*-kăṭh*, son of a cook.
>
> रास-कठ् *rās*^{a}*-kăṭh*, son of adultery.
>
> कु-कठ् *kŏ-kăṭh*, (कुपुत्र) a bad son.

We also, however, find सु-कठ् *sŏ-kăṭh*, a good son (सुपुत्रः) and सुख-कठ् *sŏkh*^{a}*-kăṭh*, a son of happiness (सुखपुत्रः).

3. कटु *kaṭ*^{u}. This Suffix, on the contrary is used as a term of praise, with words signifying castes or professions (iv. 6), *e.g.*,—

> बट-कटु *baṭ*^{a}*-kaṭ*^{u}, a real son of a brāhman (*i.e.*, a good brāhman).
>
> So दर-कटु *dar*^{a}*-kaṭ*^{u}, कौल-कटु *kaul*^{a}*-kaṭ*^{u}.
>
> छान-कटु *chān*^{a}*-kaṭ*^{u}, a real son of a carpenter, a good carpenter.

Apparently irregular in not having a final ^{a} for the first member, are words like,—

> सोन्‌र-कटु *sŏn*^{a}*r-kaṭ*^{u}, a real son of a gold-smith, a good gold-smith.
>
> मन्‌र-कटु *man*^{a}*r-kaṭ*^{u}, a real son of a shell-worker, a good shell-worker, cf. No. 38.

We find also (from मैंष् *mĕṣ*, a buffalo, *ante*, p. 63), मैंष-कटु *maṣ*^{a}*-kaṭ*^{u}, a buffalo-calf.

4. तुर् *tur*^{u}, fem. तर् *t*^{a}*r.* This Suffix is associated with the relationship of first-cousin (iv. 8, 9, 10). Thus,—

> पफतुर् बोयु *pŏphatur*^{u} *bŏy*^{u}, the son of a paternal aunt (*lit.*, brother by a paternal aunt).
>
> मासतुर् बोयु *māsatur*^{u} *bŏy*^{u}, the son of a maternal aunt.
>
> मामतुर् बोयु *māmatur*^{u} *bŏy*^{u}, the son of a maternal uncle.
>
> पफतर् बेञ *pŏphat*^{a}*r bĕñĕ*, the daughter of a paternal aunt.

मासतॖर् ब्यन *mâsat°r bĕñĕ*, the daughter of a maternal aunt.

मामतॖर् ब्यन *māmat°r bĕñĕ*, the daughter of a maternal uncle.

Irregular is पितुरु बोयु *pitur° bōy°* (fem. पितॖर् ब्यन *pit°r bĕñĕ*), the son (daughter) of a paternal uncle.

So also we have पफतॖर् बॉयि काकॖञ *pŏphat°r bāy' kākạñ*, the wife of the son of a paternal aunt.

Similarly for the other wives, मासतॖर् बॉयि काकॖञ *mâsat°r bāy' kākạñ*; मामतॖर् बॉयि काकॖञ *māmat°r bāy' kākạñ*, and पितॖर् बॉयि काकॖञ *pit°r bāy' kākạñ*.

5. थॖर् *th°r*, fem. ज़ॖ *z°* indicates, with a change in the termination of the root-word, the relationship of nephew (iv. 11, 12, 13). Thus,—

बाबथॖर् *bābath°r*, brother's son (बोयु *bōy°*, a brother).

बावॖज़ *bāw°z°*, brother's daughter.

ब्यनथॖर् *byanath°r*, sister's son (ब्यन *bĕñĕ* a sister).

ब्यनॖज़ *byan°z°*, sister's daughter.

द्यारथॖर् *dyārath°r*, son of a husband's brother, (द्रुयु *dryuy°*, a husband's brother).

द्यारज़ *dyāraz°*, the daughter of a husband's brother.

The following Suffixes form adjectives of possession.

6. अल् *al*, fem. अल् *al*. This Suffix is restricted to natural possessions, *i.e.*, when a thing or quality is spoken of as not only accompanying an object, but as actually forming part of it (iv. 15–19), cf. No. 9. When added to verbal nouns, they must be in the feminine form, see p. 210.

As usual, the noun to which the suffix is added takes the form of the instrumental singular, but before अ *a*, इ *i* becomes य् *y*, and अ *a*, for अन् *an*, is dropped. Thus,—

From.	We have.	
दारॖ *dạr°*, a beard.	दार्यल् *dāryal*,	fem. दार्यल् *dāryal*, bearded.
ग्वॊंछ् *gōṭsh*, a moustache.	ग्वॊंछल् *gōṭshal*,	moustached.
डख् *ḍăkh*, a hair-curl.	डखल् *ḍakhal*,	curly-headed.
बब् *bab*, bosom.	बबल् *babal*,	bosomed.
कोछ् *kōch*, belly.	कोछल् *kōchal*,	bellied.

ह्यग् *hyang*, a horn.	ह्यगल् *hyangal*,	horned.
ठूख् *ṭhūkh*, blow of a horn.	ठूकल् *ṭhūkal*,	striking with the horn.
ठोल् *ṭhŏl*, blow of a horn.	ठोलल् *ṭhŏlal*,	striking with the horn.
चप् *tsăph*, a bite.	चपल् *tsapal*,	biting.
फश् *phaç*, brightness, cleanness.	फशल् *phaçal*,	well-dressed.
गेञ् *gĕñ*, a wrinkle.	गेञल् *gĕñal*,	wrinkled.
स्यस् *syas*, a wart.	स्यसल् *syasal*,	warted.
पोंद् *pŏnd*, a sneeze.	पोंदल् *pŏndal*,	one who sneezes.
मछोच *machŏṭsc*, moles.	मछोचल् *machŏṭscal*,	covered with moles.
चास् *tsās*, a cough.	चासल् *tsāsal*,	one who has a cough.
टुँस् *ṭsŭṭ*, crepitus ventris.	टुँसल् *ṭsŭṭal*,	one who breaks wind.

So also we have,—

हाच् *hāṭsh*, an accusation (fem.).	हाचल् *hāṭsal*,	one who brings an accusation (*not* an accused person).
ज़्यव् *zyav*, a tongue.	ज़्यवल् *zyaval*,	a calumniator. The

word does not mean possessing a tongue, which is ज़्यविसंस् *zĕvisạst*, or ज़्यविवोल् *zĕviwŏl*, (No. 9).

When this suffix is added to the words बेञ *bĕñĕ*, a sister, and कूर् *kūr*, a daughter, the compound implies incestuous sexual connexion, thus, बेञाल् *bĕñăl*, कोर्यल् *kŏryal*. To convey the idea of possessing a sister or a daughter we must say बेञवोल् *bĕñŏwŏl*, कोरेवोल् *kŏrĕwŏl*, (No. 9).

The word दाड् *dạr*, a beard, optionally takes the suffix याल् *yāl* thus दार्यल् *dāryal*, or दाडियाल् *dạryāl*, bearded (iv. 19).

The word यड् *yaḍ*, a belly, becomes यडल् *yaḍal*, having a large belly, pot-bellied (iv. 30). On the other hand यडल् *yaḍ*ᵉ*l*, means 'gluttonous' (iv. 31). So from हर् *har*, a quarrel, we have हरुल् *har*ᵉ*l*, quarrelsome (iv. 32), and from जट् *jaṭ*, hair, जटुल् *jaṭ*^{a}*l*, very hairy (iv. 33).

7. लड् *lad*, fem. लड् *lad*. This suffix is sometimes used instead of अल् *al*, but usually in a bad sense (iv. 20, 21). Thus,—

फक् *phak*, a stink.	फकलड् *phakalad* fem.	फकलड् *phakalad* stinking.
छ्वक् *tshŏk*, slyness.	छ्वकलड् *tshŏkalad*,	sly.
छ्वक् *chŏk*, a sore.	छ्वकलड् *chŏkalad*,	full of sores.
बक् *bak*, a cry.	बकलड् *bakalad*,	prating.
दख् *dŏkh*, pain.	दखलड् *dŏkhalad*,	pained.
द्राग् *drāg*, a famine.	द्रागलड् *drāgalad*,	afflicted with famine.

This termination cannot be substituted for अल् *al* in every case. For instance we cannot say गोछलड् *gŏtshalad*, डखलड् *ḍakhalad*, or बबलड् *babalad*. But with some words both अल् *al* and लड् *lad* can be used. Thus besides ग्यञल् *gĕñal*, we can have ग्यञलड् *gĕñalad*, wrinkled; besides स्यसल् *syasal*, स्यसलड् *syasalad*, warted; and besides छासल् *tsāsal*, छासिलड् *tsāsilad* (*sic*). When the word फस् *phaç* means eccentricity, it takes the termination लड् thus फसलड् *phaçalad*, mad, eccentric. When it means brightness, it takes the termination अल् thus फसल् *phaçal*.

8. योर् *yōr*^{u}, fem. यार् *yạr*^{i}. This suffix occurs in the following words. It is added as usual to the instrumental in the first two cases. In the last it is irregular (iv. 22, 23):—

पज़ु *pạs*^{u}, truth.	पज़िस्योर् *pạs*^{i}*yōr*^{u},	fem. पज़िस्यार् *pạs*^{i}*yạr*^{i}, truthful.
अपज़ु *apạs*^{u}, untruth.	अपज़िस्योर् *apạs*^{i}*yōr*^{u},	fem. अपज़िस्यार् *apạs*^{i}*yạr*^{i}, untruthful.
मंज़्युमु *mạnsyum*^{u},	मंज़्युमुयोर् *mạnsyum*^{u}*yōr*^{u},	a go between, a medium.

The last word is really a compound substantive and its fem. is मंज़िमयारेंञ् *mansim*^{a}*yārĕñ*.

9. वोलु *wōlᵉ*, fem. वाजञ् *wōjĕñ* ; a suffix signifying possession, when the thing possessed accompanies the possessor, but does not actually form part of it (iv. 24). (Cf. No. 6).

As elsewhere, the suffix is added to the instrumental singular. Thus,—

द्यार् *dyār*, (masc.) wealth. द्यारवोलु *dyārawōlᵉ* fem. द्यारवाजञ् *dyārawōjĕñ*, wealthy.

लंर् *lḁrᵉ*, (fem.) a house. लरिवोलु *lariwōlᵉ*, लरिवाजञ् *lariwōjĕñ*, possessing a house.

जाय् *çāy*, (fem.) a place. जायिवोलु *çāyiwōlᵉ*, जायिवाजञ् *çāyiwōjĕñ*, possessing a place.

कूर् *kūrᵉ*, a daughter. कोरिवोलु *kōriwōlᵉ*, कोरिवाजञ् *kōriwōjĕñ*, possessing a daughter.

नेचिवु *nĕcyuvᵉ*, a son. नेचिविवोलु *nĕcivⁱwōlᵉ*, नेचिविवाजञ् *nĕcivⁱwō-jĕñ*, possessing a son.

But,—

गुपुन् *gupun*, a quadruped. गुपनवोलु *gupanwōlᵉ*, possessing herds.

गर् *garᵉ*, a house. { गर्वोलु *garwōlᵉ*, the master of a house. गरवोलु *garawōlᵉ*, possessing a house. }

10. ग्राख् *grākh*, fem. ग्राकञ् *grākañ*. This may be used instead of वोलु *wōlᵉ* in the same sense (iv. 24). Thus,—

लंर् *lḁrᵉ*, a house, लरिग्राख् *larigrākh*, fem. लरिग्राकञ् *larigrākañ*, possessing a house, and so on.

11. हंतु *hḁtᵉ*, fem. हंचु *hḁtsᵉ*. This suffix denotes inconvenience experienced by the mind or feeling, but not by the corporeal body (iv. 25). The usual rule is followed in adding the suffix. Thus,—

न्यंदुर् *nyandᵉr* (fem.), sleep, न्यंदुरिहंतु *nyandᵉrihḁtᵉ*, fem. न्यंदुरिहंचु *nyandᵉrihḁtsᵉ*, afflicted with sleep.

त्रेष् *trĕṣ* (masc.) thirst. त्रेषहंतु *trĕṣahḁtᵉ*, thirsty.

बुछ *bŏchᵉ*, hunger. बछहंतु *bŏchahḁtᵉ*, hungry.

क्रूद् *krūd*, anger. क्रूदहंतु *krūdahḁtᵉ*, angry.

गुम *guma*, sweat. गुमहंतु *gumahḁtᵉ*, sweaty.

टाफ् *tāph*, sunshine. टापहॅटु *tāpahạt*^{u}, feeling the sunshine.

तुर् *tụr*, cold. तुरिहॅटु *tụrihạt*^{u}, feeling cold.

आर् *ār*, pity. आरहॅटु *ārahạt*^{u}, pitiful.

In the two following the adjectives formed do not necessarily refer to mind or feeling,—

लवु *law*^{u}, dew. लवहॅटु *lawahạt*^{u}, dewy.

ताव् *tāw*, warmth. तावहॅटु *tāwahạt*^{u}, warm.

E.g., तावहॅटू बुतराथ् *tāwahạts*^{ü} *butarāth*, warm ground.

12. वॅटु *vyạt*^{u}, fem. वॅटू *vyạts*^{ü}. This suffix is added in the case of the words मंदछु *mandach*^{u}, shame; मोदु *mōd*^{u}, respect; मानु *mān*^{u}, honour, in the same meaning as वोलु *wōl*^{u} (iv. 26). Thus,—

मंदछवॅटु *mandachavyạt*^{u}, fem. मंदछवॅटू *mandachavyạts*^{ü}, ashamed.

मोदवॅटु *mōdavyạt*^{u}, fem. मोदवॅटू *mōdavyạts*^{ü}, respected.

मानवॅटु *mānavyạt*^{u}, fem. मानवॅटू *mānavyạts*^{ü}, honoured.

So also,—

बर्सावॅटु *barsāvyạt*^{u}, fem. बर्सावॅटू *barsāvyats*^{ü}, wealthy.

13. आन् *ān*, fem. आन् *ān*, added to the words दंद् *dand*, a tooth, and नस् *nast*, a nose, in a bad sense (iv. 28).

Thus, दंदान् *dandān*, fem. दंदान् *dandān*, having an ugly tooth.

नस्तान् *nastān*, having an ugly nose.

14. ु ^{u}, fem. ू ^{ü}. This is used with the same words in the same meaning (iv. 29).

नॅस्तु *nạst*^{u}, fem. नॅस्तू *nạst*^{ü}.

दॅंदु *dạnd*^{u}, fem. दॅंदू *dạnd*^{ü}.

15. ऊरु *ūr*^{u}, fem. ऊरू *ūr*^{ü}, a variant of the preceding (iv. 29).

नस्तूरु *nastūr*^{u}, fem. नस्तूरू *nastūr*^{ü}.

दंदूरु *dandūr*^{u}, fem. दंदूरू *dandūr*^{ü}.

16. अट् *at*, fem. अट् *at*, added to वैस् *wais*, age, gives वैसट् *waisat*, meaning 'very old.' Added to रुस् *r*^{u}*s*, malice, we have रुसट् *r*^{u}*sat*, malicious (iv. 34, 35).

17. इट् *iṭ*, fem. इट् *iṭ*, is used as follows (iv. 36–38).

From अछि *ach*^{i}, the eye.	अछीट् *achīṭ*, fem. अछीट् *achīṭ*, having the evil eye.
रूप् *rūp*, beauty.	रूपिट् *rūpiṭ*, very beautiful.
लूब् *lūb*, desire.	लूबिट् *lūbiṭ*, covetous.
स्यव् *syav*, tongue.	स्यविट् *sĕviṭ*, a calumniator.

18. ऊठ् *ūṭh*, fem. ऊठ् *ūṭh*, as in ल्यख् *lyăkh* (fem.) abuse, ल्यकल् *lyakal*, or ल्यकलूठ् *lyakalūṭh*, abusive (iv. 39).

The following suffixes form **Abstract Nouns**.

19. अर् *ar*, (masc.) added to adjectives (iv. 41). This termination is added in the usual way to the form of the case of the agent, *i* becoming *y*. Thus,—

ब्युय् *byuy*^{u}, stale.	बिय्यर् *biyyar*, staleness.
त्सर् *tsar*^{u}, much.	त्सर्यर् *tsaryar*, excess.
फहर् *phahur*^{u}, hard.	फहर्यर् *phaharyar*, hardness.
नव् *nav*^{u}, new.	नव्यर् *navyar*, newness.
पप् *pap*^{u}, ripe.	पप्यर् *papyar*, ripeness.
फफ् *phaph*^{u}, stammering.	फफ्यर् *phaphyar*, stammeringness.
ग्वब् *gŏb*^{u}, heavy.	ग्वब्यर् *gŏbyar*, heaviness.
ओम् *ōm*^{u}, unripe.	आम्यर् *ămyar*, unripeness.
गश् *gaç*^{u}, silent.	गश्यर् *gaçyar*, silence.
त्सोठ् *tsŏṭ*^{u}, acrid.	त्साठ्यर् *tsăṭyar*, acridity.
फरिश् *phariç*^{a}, hard (fem).	फरिश्यर् *phar*^{i}*çyar*, hardness.

The last adjective is only used in the feminine.

The main word is also subject to the following changes,—

(*a*) If the adjective is of three or more syllables, अर् *ar* becomes आर् *ār* (iv. 42). Thus,—

व्वज़ुल् *wŏzul*^{u}, red.	व्वज़्यार् *wŏzajyār*, redness (see *i*. below).
म्वकुल् *mŏkul*^{u}, free.	म्वकज्यार् *mŏkajyār*, free.

(*b*) This rule is, however, not universal (iv. 44). Thus,—

अपॅसॖ *apạs**, untruthful.	अपसर् *apasar*, untruthfulness (see *h.* below).
क्रॅहॖनॖ *krhẹn**, black.	क्रहञर् *krhañar*, blackness (see *h.* below).
काटुर् *kāṭsur**, tawny.	काटर्यर् *kāṭsaryar*, tawniness.
कावुर् *kāwur**, dark-blue.	कावर्यर् *kāwaryar*, dark-blueness.
क्रपुनॖ *krpun**, miserly.	क्रपञर् *krpañar* miserliness (see *h.* below).
कायुर् *kāyur**, pinewood.	कायर्यर् *kāyaryar*, the nature of pinewood.
खोवुर् *khōwur**, left (not right).	खोवर्यर् *khōwaryar*, leftness.
ग्यशोमॖ *gĕçyōm**, light black.	ग्यशाम्यर् *gĕçyāmyar*, light blackness.
चतुर् *tsatur**, skilful.	चतॖर्यर् *tsat*ryar*, skilfulness.
विषॅमॖ *wiṣạm**, uneven.	विषम्यर् *wiṣamyar*, unevenness.

(*c*) The word टोठॖ *ṭōṭh**, dear, beloved, forms टाठञार् *ṭāṭhañār* or टाछ्यर् *ṭāchyar*, belovedness (iv. 43).

(*d*) When the word हश् *haç*, a mother-in-law, takes अर् *ar*, the word हशर् *haçar* is only used in low abuse. The right word for the condition of a mother-in-law is हशतोनॖ *haçatōn** (No. 27) (iv. 45).

(*e*) The suffix is optional in the case of the following (iv. 46).

कॊबॖ *kọ̆b**, hunchbacked.	कॊबॖ *kọ̆b**, or कब्यर् *kŏbyar*, hunchbackedness.
गॊपॖ *gọp**, silent.	गॊपॖ *gọp** or गप्यर् *gapyar*, silence.

(*f*) When the adjective ends in *u-mātrā* preceded by क् *k*, ख् *kh*, or ग् *g*, these letters become च् *c*, छ् *ch*, and ज् *j* respectively (iv. 47). Thus,—

न्युकॖ *nyuk**, little.	निच्यर् *nicyar*, littleness.
टॊकॖ *ṭọk**, sharp.	टच्यर् *ṭacyar*, sharpness.
हॊखॖ *họ̆kh**, dry.	हॊछ्यर् *hŏchyar*, dryness.

त्रिखु *tryukh*ᵘ, clever.	त्रिछ्यर् *trichyar*, cleverness.
द्रुग *drọ̆g*ᵘ, dear.	द्रुज्यर् *drŏjyar*, dearness.
स्रुग *srọ̆g*ᵘ, cheap.	स्रुज्यर् *srŏjyar*, cheapness.

Exceptions are (iv. 48), *vide ante*, pp. 32, 182,—

चुकु *tsọ̆k*ᵘ, sour.	चुक्यर् *tsŏkyar*, sourness.
खूंखु *khūkh*ᵘ, speaking through the nose.	खूंख्यर् *khūkhyar*, nasality of voice.

(*g*) Under similar conditions, ट् *ṭ* becomes च् *c*, ठ् *ṭh* becomes *ch*, ड् *ḍ* becomes ज् *j*, and ण् *ṇ* becomes ञ् *ñ* (iv. 49). Thus,—

मोटु *mọ̆ṭ*ᵘ, fat.	मच्यर् *mŏcyar*, fatness.
गटु *gạṭ*ᵘ, dark.	गच्यर् *gacyar*, darkness.
द्रोठु *drŏṭh*ᵘ, hard.	द्रछ्यर् *drăchyar*, hardness.
मूठु *mūṭh*ᵘ, lazy.	मैछ्यर् *maīchyar*, laziness.
मोंडु *mọ̆ṇḍ*ᵘ, blunt.	मोंज्यर् *mŏñjyar*, bluntness.
बडु *bạḍ*ᵘ, great.	बज्यर् *bajyar*, greatness.
प्रोणु *prŏṇ*ᵘ, old.	प्राञर् *prāñar*, oldness, (see *h*, for elision of *y*).

(*h*) Under similar circumstances, त् *t* becomes च् *ts*, थ् *th* becomes छ् *tsh*, द् *d* becomes ज़्, and न् *n* becomes ञ् *ñ*, after all of which य् *y* is elided (iv. 50, 51). Thus,—

तत *tạt*ᵘ, hot.	तचर् *tatsar*, heat.
मतु *mạt*ᵘ, madness.	मचर् *matsar*, madness.
रतु *rᵘt*ᵘ, good.	रचर् *rᵘtsar*, health of body (iv. 41).
वथु *wạth*ᵘ, open.	वछर् *watshar*, openness.
थदु *thạd*ᵘ, high.	थज़र् *thazar*, height.
मंदु *mạnd*ᵘ, sick.	मंज़र् *manzar*, sickness.
तनु *tạn*ᵘ, thin.	तञर् *tañar*, thinness.
गुमनु *gumạn*ᵘ, slightly dirty.	गुमञार् *gumañār* (see *a*) slight dirtiness.
तमनु *tamạn*ᵘ, black.	तमञार् *tamañār*, blackness.
तुरनु *tụrạn*ᵘ, cold.	तुरञार् *tụrañār*, coldness.

अंनु *an**, blind. — अञर् *aňar*, blindness.

कटमलियुनु *kaṭamalyun**, half-clean. — कटमलिञार् *kaṭamaliňār*, half-cleanness.

From the word पनुनु *panun**, own, we get irregularly पानञार् *pānaňār*, selfness.

Similarly य् *y* is elided in other cases after modified consonants. Thus, in प्राञर् *prāňar* in (*g*) above, so,—

छोटु *tshǭṭs**, empty. — छोत्सर् *tshōtsar*, emptiness.

अछु *aṭsh**, weak. — अछर् *aṭshar*, weakness.

पोसु *pǫs**, true. — पसर् *pasar*, truth.

(*i*) So also, when *u-mātrā* is preceded by ल् *l*, the ल् *l* becomes ज् *j* (iv. 52). Thus,—

खोलु *khǫl**, open. — खज्यर् *khajyar*, openness.

वोलु *wǒl**, fickle. — वोज्यर् *wǒjyar*, fickleness.

कुमुलु *kumul**, delicate (see *a*). — कुमज्यार् *kumajyār*, delicateness.

वोजुलु *wǒzul**, red. — वोजज्यार् *wǒzajyār*, redness.

सायुलु *sāyul**, fine. — सायज्यार् *sāy*jyār*, fineness.

पिशुलु *piçul**, soft. — पिशज्यार् *piçajyār*, softness.

(*j*) Similarly we have (iv. 53),—

त्रकुर् *trakur**, hard. — त्रकज्यार् *trakajyār* or त्रकर्यर् *trakaryar*, hardness (see *b*).

(*k*) Similarly ह् *h* becomes श् *ç* (iv. 54). Thus,—

ह्युहु *hyuh**, like. — हिश्यर् *hiçyar*, similarity.

ट्सोहु *tsōh**, acrid. — ट्साश्यर् *tsāçyar*, acridity.

(*l*) Similarly स् *s* optionally becomes छ् *tsh* (iv. 55). Thus,—

कैसु *kās**, youngest. — कैछर् *kaitshar* or कैसर् *kaisar*, the condition of a youngest son.

20. इमी *imī* (fem.). This is optionally used instead of अर् *ar*, after बोडु *bǫḍ**, great, thus बडीमी *baḍīmī*, or बज्यर् *bajyar* (No. 19, *g*), greatness (iv. 56).

21. यार् *yạr*^{ü} (fem.). This is optionally used instead of अर् *ar*, in the two following words (iv. 57).

शुच् *çrūts*^{u}, pure.	शुचियार् *çrūts*^{i}*yạr*^{ü} or शोचर् *çrōtsar* (20, *h*), purity.
छ्यॊट् *tshyọt*^{u}, impure.	छॆटियार् *tshẹ̆t*^{i}*yạr*^{ü} or छॊचर् *tshŏcyar* (20, *g*), impurity.

22. स् *s* (fem.). This is added to words ending in योर् *yōr*^{u}. Thus from (iv. 58).

मन्स्युम्-योर् *mansyum*^{u}*-yōr*^{u}, a go-between (see No. 8).	मन्सिम्-यार्स् *mansim*^{ü}*-yār*^{ü}*s* (the fem. form of मन्स्युम् *mansyum*^{u} is used), the office of a go-between.
पॊज़ियोर् *pọz*^{i}*yōr*, truthful.	पॊज़ियार्स् *pọz*^{i}*yār*^{ü}*s*, truthfulness.
अपॊज़ियोर् *apọz*^{i}*yōr*^{u}, untruthful.	अपॊज़ियार्स् *apọz*^{i}*yār*^{ü}*s*, untruthfulness.

So (cf. No. 21).

शुचियार्स् *çrūts*^{i}*yạr*^{ü}*s*, purity, and

छॆटियार्स् *tshŏt*^{i}*yạr*^{ü}*s*, impurity.

23. इल् *il* (fem.), used to form abstract nouns from substances, not from adjectives (iv. 59).

Thus, पण्डिथ् *paṇḍith*, a paṇḍit, पॊण्डिल् *pọṇḍ*^{i}*til*, the condition of a paṇḍit.

छान् *chān*, a carpenter.	छॊनिल् *chạnil*, the condition of a carpenter.
गोर् *gōr*, a priest.	गूरिल् *gūril*, the condition of a priest.

This suffix cannot be used with every word. Sometimes No. 24, must be used. We cannot for instance, say, from दॊसिल् *dŏsil*, a plasterer, दॊसिलिल् *dọs*^{i}*lil*, the office of a plasterer. We can only say दॊसिलाज़् *dọs*^{i}*lạz* (iv. 60).

The word लॊच् *lọtsh*, a eunuch, is irregular. It forms लॊचिल् *lọtshil*, or लूचिल् *lūtshil* (iv. 62).

24. आड्स् *ḍs*, (fem.), used optionally instead of the proceeding (iv. 59, 60). Thus,—

पॊण्डिलाड्स् *pọṇḍ'lạs*, the condition of a paṇḍit.

छान्डाड्स् *chānḍs*, the condition of a carpenter.

गोरडाड्स् *gōrḍs*, the condition of a priest.

दॊशिलाड्स् *dọ̄ś'lạs*, the condition of a plasterer.

25. इलाड्स् *ilạs*, (fem.), is a compound of the two preceding which is sometimes used (iv. 61).

मॊतु *mọtᵘ*, a madman. — मतिल् *matil* or मॊतिलाड्स् *mọt'lạs*, the condition of a madman. If मॊतु *mọtᵘ* is used to mean 'mad,' (as an adjective), its abstract noun would be मत्सर् *matsar* (No. 19, *h*).

ब्रेठ् *brēṭh*, ignorant. — ब्रीठिलाड्स् *brīṭh'lạs*, ignorance.

So गुरिलाड्स् *gur'lạs*, छॊनिलाड्स् *chọn'lạs*.

26. वय् *way*, (fem.), used to mean the wages of any act (ix. ii. 85–87). Thus,—

छानवय् *chānaway* (fem.), the wages of a carpenter.

दॊशिलवय् *dọ̄silᵉway* (fem.), the wages of a plasterer.

From नाव् *nāv*, a boat, we have नावय् *nāvay*, the hire of a boat.

From बोरु *bōrᵉ* or बार् *bār*, a burden, we have बॊरवय् *bạrᵉvay*, the wages of a porter.

27. तोनु *tōnᵘ* (masc.). This gives a meaning of relationship. It is added, as usual to the agent form (iv. 63). Thus,—

मोलु *mōlᵘ*, a father. — मॊलितोनु *mọl'tōnᵘ*, fatherhood.

माजु *mạjᵃ*, a mother. — माजितोनु *mājitōnᵘ*, motherhood.

बोयु *bōyᵘ*, a brother. — बॊयितोनु *bạy'tōnᵘ*, brotherhood.

पुथर् *puthᵉr*, a son. — पुत्रतोनु *putᵉratōnᵘ*, sonhood.

हश् *haç*, mother-in-law. — हशतोनु *haçatōnᵘ*, mother-in-law-hood.

28. पोनु *pŏn*^{u}, used instead of No. 27 when the relationship is not intimate (iv. 63). Thus,—

व्यस् *vyas*, a comrade.	व्यसपोनु *vyasapŏn*^{u}, comradeship.
दाय् *dāy*, a nurse.	दायपोनु *dāyapŏn*^{u}, nursehood.
पोजु *pŏj*^{u}, low.	पाजिपोनु *pāj*^{i}*pŏn*^{u}, lowness of position (in a household).

29. उत् *ut* (masc.), used with the following words (iv. 64).

पथर् *path*^{a}*r*, an enemy.	पतरुत् *pat*^{a}*rut*, enemyhood.
म्यथर् *myath*^{a}*r*, a friend.	म्यतरुत् *myat*^{a}*rut*, friendhood.
पितुर् *pitur*, a father.	पितुरुत् *piturut*, fatherhood.
रेशु *rṣ*^{u}, a saint.	रेश्युत् *rṣyut*, sainthood.
बन्द् *band*, a relation.	बन्दुत् *bandut*, relationship.

30. उन् *un* (masc.), used with the following word (iv. 65).

मैथ् *maith*, a corpse.	मैतुन् *maitun*, the condition of a corpse.

31. उस् *us* (masc.), used with the following words (iv. 66, 67).

म्वन्ड् *mŏṇḍ*, a widow.	म्वन्डुस् *mŏṇḍus*, widowhood.
दूबु *dob*^{u}, a washerman (Cf. p. 34).	दुबुस् *dŏbus*, a washerman's club, but दुबिल् *dŏbil*, the condition of a washerman (No. 23).

32. बदु *bạd*^{u} (masc.), used in the following (iv. 68).

सन् *sŏn*, a co-wife.	सन्बदु *sŏnbạd*^{u}, co-wifehood.

[So also पितृरिबदु *pit*^{a}*r*^{i}*bạd*^{u}, fatherhood; बायिबदु *bāy*^{i}*bạd*^{u}] or बाजिबदु *bāj*^{i}*bạd*^{u}, brotherhood, commensality (iv. 69).

The suffix is used with the numerals 100, and above (iv. 70), as follows:—

हथ् *hăth*, a hundred.	हतबदु *hatabạd*^{u}, hundreds.
सास् *sās*, a thousand.	सासबदु *sāsabạd*^{u}, thousands.
लछ् *lăch*, a hundred thousand.	लछ्यबदु *lachyabạd*^{u}, hundreds of thousands.

Applied to vegetables, it means a bundle,—

हाख् *hākh*, spinach.	हाकबॖड् *hākabạdᵘ*, a bundle of spinach.
मुज् *muj*, a radish.	मुजिबॖड् *mujibạdᵘ*, a bundle of radishes.
गगॖज् *gŏgᵃj*, a turnip.	गगॖजिबॖड् *gogᵃjibạdᵘ*, a bundle of turnips.

In all the above, as usual, the suffix is added to the form of the agent. मुज् *muj*, may also be मुजि *muj*ⁱ, and it would then form मुज्यबॖड् *mujĕbạdᵘ*. Cf. No. 82 post.

33. बठ् *băṭh* (fem.), used in the following, बाजिबठ् *bājⁱbăṭh*, commensality (see No. 32), (iv. 69).

34. उलॖ *ulᵘ* fem. ॵज् *ᵃjᵃ*, used to form adjectives as follows (iv. 72–87).

गाट *gāṭᵘ*, wisdom.	गाटुलॖ *gāṭulᵘ*, fem. गाटॵज् *gāṭᵃjᵃ*, skilful.
कण्ड् *kŏṇḍ*, a large spring, also a large round earthen vessel.	कण्डुलॖ *kŏṇḍulᵘ*, fem. कण्डॵज् *kŏṇḍᵃjᵃ* circular.
गण्ड् *gaṇḍ*, a knot.	गण्डुलॖ *gaṇḍulᵘ*, fem. गण्डॵज् *gaṇḍᵃjᵃ*, in quantities, wholesale.
गॖथ् *gᵃth*, current of a river.	गॖतुलॖ *gᵃtulᵘ*, fem. गॖतॵज् *gᵃtᵃjᵃ*, excessive, very much.
गद् *gad*, (not used).	गदुलॖ *gadulᵘ*, fem. गदॵज् *gadᵃjᵃ*, very much.
ठॖठ् *ṭạṭhᵘ*, a weight (usually of grain) weighing twelve seers.	ठठुलॖ *ṭaṭhulᵘ*, fem. ठठॵज् *ṭaṭhᵃjᵃ*, large enough to hold a *ṭạṭhᵘ*.
दॗगु *dọgᵘ*, a fist.	दगुलॖ *dŏgulᵘ* fem. दगॵज् *dŏgᵃjᵃ*, shaped like a fist, lumpish.
पॗतॖ *pọṭᵘ*, a child.	पतुलॖ *pŏtulᵘ*, fem. पतॵज् *pŏtᵃjᵃ*, an image, an idol.

मोल् *mŏl*, price.	मोलुलु *mŏlul*^{u}, fem. मोलजु *mŏl*^{e}*j*^{a}, costly, high-priced.
साद् *sād*, taste.	सादुलु *sādul*^{u}, fem. सादजु *sād*^{e}*j*^{a}, taste, nice to eat.
कोछ् *kŏtsh*, bag.	कोछुलु *kŏtshul*^{u}, fem. कोछजु *kŏtsh*^{e}*j*^{a}, a porter.
छोख् *chŏkh*, cleansing.	छोकुलु *chŏkul*^{u}, fem. छोकजु *chŏk*^{e}*j*^{a}, clear, distinct.
त्सट् *tsăṭh*, cutting.	त्सटुलु *tsaṭul*^{u}, fem. त्सटजु *tsaṭ*^{e}*j*^{a}, a thief.
पथ् *păth*, trust.	पतुलु *patul*^{u}, fem. पतजु *pat*^{e}*j*^{a}, a raft (fem. a mat).
चोथ् *tsŏth*, the anus.	चोतुलु *tsŏtul*^{u}, fem. चोतजु *tsŏt*^{e}*j*^{a}, a sodomite.
राथ् *rāth*, night.	रातुलु *ratul*^{u}, night-time.
दोह् *dŏh*, day.	दुहुलु *duhul*^{u}, day-time.
मून् *mūn*, wool.	मुनुलु *munul*^{u}, fem. मुनजु *mun*^{e}*j*^{a}, woollen (with short antepenult).

35. युलु *yul*^{u}, fem. इजु *ij*^{a}, used to form adjectives as follows (iv. 88–95).

टपु *ṭąp*^{u}, ringlets.	टप्युलु *ṭapyul*^{u}, fem. टपिजु *ṭapij*^{a}, having much hair.
जट *jaṭ*^{a} (pl.), matted hair.	जट्युलु *jaṭyul*^{u}, fem. जटिजु *jaṭij*^{a}, having matted hair.
दाह् *dāh*, burning.	दह्युलु *dahyul*^{u}, fem. दहिजु *dahij*^{a}, piteous (with short antepenult).
रस् *ras* flavour.	रस्युलु *rasyul*^{u}, fem. रसिजु *rasij*^{a}, full of flavour, imparting flavour. *E.g.*, रस्युलु छुह् ग्यवान् *rasyul*^{u} *chuh gyawān*, he is singing sweetly.

मछ् *mătsh*, consolation.	मछ्युलु *matshyulᵘ*, fem. मछिज् *matshijᵃ*, consolatory.
स्रुह् *srĕh*, affection.	सिह्युलु *srihyulᵘ*, fem. सिहिज् *srihijᵃ*, affectionate (with change of antepenult, vowel).
मिष् *miṣ*, a rag-nail, a piece of loose skin at the nail, a dolly-idler.	मिष्युलु *miṣyulᵘ*, the same as *miṣ*; also a splinter or thorn under the nail.
स्यख् *syăkh*, sand.	सेक्युलु *sĕkyulᵘ*, fem. सेकिज् *sĕkijᵃ*, sandy, *e.g.*, सेकिज् बुतराथ् *sĕkijᵃ butarāth*, sandy soil; also sandy-tasty, mealy, of fruit.
माज् *mājᵃ*, a mother.	माज्युलु *mājyulᵘ*, shy, tied to his mother's apron strings.

36. युनु *yunᵘ*, fem. इञ् *iñ*, occurs as follows (iv. 96).

मल् *mal*, dirt.	मल्युनु *malyunᵘ*, fem. मलिञ् *maliñ*, dirty.

The termination also implies measure or weight (iv. 109). Thus,—

त्रख् *trăkh*, a weight or measure of four and three quarter seers.	त्रांक्युनु कठ् *trạ̈kyunᵘ kăṭh*, a ram weighing a *trăkh*; त्रांक्युनु नटु *trạ̈kyunᵘ naṭᵘ*, a jar holding a *trăkh*.
सेर् *sēr*, a seer.	सीर्युनु थाल् *sīryunᵘ thāl*, a dish holding a seer.
खार् *khār*, a measure of sixteen *trăkhs*.	खांर्युनु बोरु *khạ̄ryunᵘ bōrᵘ*, a load weighing a *khār*.
चुत्रोकु *tsŏtrŏkᵘ*, a measure of four *trăkhs*.	चुत्रांक्युनु *tsŏtrạ̈kyunᵘ*, containing that measure.
पल् *pal*, four *tolahs*.	पल्युनु *palyunᵘ*, weighing four tolahs.
पांसुवु *pā̃suvᵘ*, half a *trăkh*.	पांसवुनु *pā̃zaçunᵘ*, measuring half a *trăkh* (iv. 110).

It will be observed that all the above are more or less irregular.

The suffix is also used with the words for sixty and seventy (iv. 111).

शेठ् *çēṭh*, sixty.	शीठ्युनु *çīṭhyun*^{u}, worth sixty.
सतथ् *satath*, seventy.	सतत्युनु *satatyun*^{u}, worth seventy.

We cannot do this with other numbers. Thus we say दहन् हंदु दांद् *dahan hạnd*^{u} (genitive) *dãd*, a bullock worth ten.

It is also used with pronouns (iv. 112). Thus,—

त्यूतु *tyūt*^{u}, so much.	तीत्युनु *tītyun*^{u}, worth so much.
य्यूतु *yyūt*^{u}, how much.	यीत्युनु *yītyun*^{u}, worth how much.
कूतु *kūt*^{u}, how much?	कुत्युनु *kụ̄tyun*^{u}, worth how much?
यूतु *yūt*^{u}, this much.	ईत्युनु *yītyun*^{u}, worth this much.

We also have (iv, 113).

वरिह्य *warihy*, a year.	वार्ष्युनु *wạ̄rṣyun*^{u}, of one year; one year old.

37. उनु *un*^{u}, is used as follows (iv. 97–98).

कुटु *k*^{u}*ṭ*^{u}, a beam.	कुटुनु *kūṭun*^{u}, a small beam, a stick.
दग् *dag*, a blow.	दगुनु *dagun*^{u}, a club, a mace.

38. र् *r*, is used with the following words to signify profession or calling (iv. 99–108).

रंग् *rang*, colour.	रंगर् *rang*^{a}*r*, a dyer.
सोन् *sōn*, gold.	सोनर् *sōn*^{a}*r*, a goldsmith.
मन् *man*, a precious stone.	मनर् *man*^{a}*r*, a lapidary.
चम् *tsam*, skin.	चमर् *tsam*^{a}*r*, a leather worker.
दांद् *dãd*, a bull.	दांदर् *dãd*^{a}*r*, a vegetable seller.
कांद् *kãd* (not used).	कांदर् *kãd*^{a}*r*, a baker.
डास् *ḍās*, destruction.	डासर् *ḍās*^{a}*r*, a destroyer.
फास् *phās*, discord.	फासर् *phās*^{a}*r*, a causer of discord.
बंग *bang*^{a}, Indian hemp.	बंगर् *bang*^{a}*r*, a hemp-smoker.
बम् *bam*, an impediment.	बमर् *bam*^{a}*r*, an impeder.
लम *lam*^{a}, delay.	लमर् *lam*^{a}*r*, a delayer.
लाब् *lāb*, interest.	लाबर् *lāb*^{a}*r*, a money lender.

साल् *sāl*, invitation. — सालर् *sālᵊr*, a member of a bride-groom's party.

लूट् *lūṭh*, plunder. — लूटर् *lūṭᵊr*, a plunderer.

भ्रम् *bram*, delusion. — भ्रमर् *bramᵊr*, a deluder.

Irregular is,—

लूब् *lūb*, covetousness. — लूदर् *lūdᵊr*, a coveter.

[Others write these words रंगुर् *rangurᵊ*, सनुर् *sönurᵊ*, &c. Thus making the termination उर् *urᵊ*, not र् *r*].

39. गर् *gᵊrᵊ*, (masc.), fem. गर् *gᵊrᵊ*, used to signify a profession relating to anything sold (ix. ii. 88, 89). Thus,—

लायगर् *lāĕgᵊrᵊ*, (लाय *lāĕ* is fem. pl.), a seller of parched grain.

गंडनगर् *ganḍangᵊrᵊ*, a book binder.

कंगनगर् *kaŋgañᵊ*-(plur.)-*gᵊrᵊ*, a comb-seller.

मंडनगर् *manḍangᵊrᵊ*, a man who kneads cloth in water (to soften it).

This is not used with words which have other forms, like सनर् *sönᵊr*, in preceding list.

From दान *dānĕ*, paddy, we have, irregularly, दांगर् *dāgᵊrᵊ*, a paddy seller, *vide ante*, p. 70.

40. युम् *yumᵊ*, fem. इम् *imᵊ*, used to form ordinals (iv. 114.)

अख् *ăkh*, one. — अख्युम् *akyumᵊ*, fem. अकिम् *akimᵊ*, first.

दह् *dah*, ten. — दह्युम् *dahyumᵊ*, fem. दहिम् *dahimᵊ*, tenth.

वुह् *wuh*, twenty. — वुह्युम् *wuhyumᵊ*, twentieth.

हथ् *hăth*, a hundred. — हत्युम् *hatyumᵊ*, hundredth.

सास् *sās*, a thousand. — सास्युम् *sāsyumᵊ*, thousandth.

कॊत *kᵊtsᵊ* (masc.), कत *katsᵊ* (fem.), how many? (plur.) — कत्युम् *katsyumᵊ*, fem. कत्सिम् *katsimᵊ*, which out of many?

यीति *yitⁱ* (masc. plur.), how many. — यीत्युम् *yityumᵊ*, fem. यीतिम् *yitimᵊ*, which out of many.

तीति *tit*ⁱ, that many.	तीतुम् *tityum*ᵘ, fem. तीतिम् *titim*ᵃ, that out of many.
ईति *yit*ⁱ, this many.	ईतुम् *yītyum*ᵘ, fem. ईतिम् *yitim*ᵃ, this out of many.

41. र ⁱ, fem. र *i*, denotes place of origin (iv. 117). Thus,—

सोपोर् *sövpōr*, Sopor, name of a town.	सोपूरि नाव् *sövpūr*ⁱ *nāv*, a boat of Sopor; fem. सोपोरि *sövpōri*.
ईरान् *yīrān* Persia.	ईरांनि गुर् *yīrąnⁱ gur*ᵘ, a Persian horse; fem. ईरानि *yīrāni*.
चीन् *cin*, China.	चीनि खोस् *cinⁱ khōs*ᵘ, a China cup; fem. चीनि *cīni*.
हिन्दुस्तान् *hindustān*, India.	हिन्दुस्तांनि कपुर् *hindustąnⁱ kapur*, Indian cloth; fem. हिन्दुस्तानि *hindustāni*.

42. उर् *ur*ᵘ, used as follows (iv. 118).

कशीर् *kaçīr* (fem.), Kashmir.	कांशुर् कंग् *kāçur*ᵘ *köŋg* Kashmiri saffron.

So कांशुर् पश्मीन *kāçur*ᵘ *paçmīn*ᵘ, Kashmiri *pashmeena;* कांशिर् कठ *kāçir*ᵃ *köth* (fem.), aucklandia costus from Kashmir.

43. उक् *uk*ᵘ, fem. च् *c*ᵃ. This is used to signify origin, either in place or time. If उक् *uk*ᵘ is preceded by य् *y*, युक् *yuk*ᵘ becomes *ic*ᵃ in the feminine. It is really one of the genitive particles (p. 37) (iv. 119, 120).

कति *kati*, where?	कत्युक् *katyuk*ᵘ, fem. कतिच् *katic*ᵃ, of where?
तति *tati*, there.	तत्युक् *tatyuk*ᵘ, fem. ततिच् *tatic*ᵃ, of there.
इति *yiti*, here.	इत्युक् *yityuk*ᵘ, fem. इतिच् *yitic*ᵃ, of here.
यति *yati*, where.	यत्युक् *yatyuk*ᵘ, fem. यतिच् *yatic*ᵃ, of where.
हुति *huti*, here.	हुत्युक् *hutyuk*ᵘ, fem. हुतिच् *hutic*ᵃ, of here.

कर् *kar*, when.	करुकु *karuk*^{u}, fem. करंचु *karçc*^{u}, of what time.
गर *gar*^{u}, a house.	गरुकु *garuk*^{u}, fem. गरंचु *garçc*^{u}, domestic.
राथ् *rāth*, yesterday.	रातुकु *rātuk*^{u}, fem. रातंचु *rātçc*^{u}, of yesterday.
परुसु *parus*^{u}, the day before yesterday.	पर्सुकु *par*^{u}*suk*^{u}, fem. पर्संचु *par*^{u}*sçc*^{u}, of the day before yesterday.
दछ्युनु *dachyun*^{u}, south.	दछिन्युकु *dạch*^{i}*nyuk*^{u}, of the south.
ख़ोवुरु *khōwur*^{u}, north.	ख़ोवर्युकु *khōw*^{u}*ryuk*^{u}, of the north.

The word अस् *as*, to-day, makes अस्युकु *asyuk*^{u}, of to-day.

44. युमु *yum*^{u} (or इमु), fem. इमु *im*^{u}. This termination is added to the post-position पारि *pār*^{i}, beyond (cf. No. 70). When phrases like कमि पारि *kami pār*^{i} occur, the मि *mi* of the pronoun is elided when this suffix is added (iv. 120). Thus,—

पारि *pār*^{i}, beyond.	पार्युमु *pāryum*^{u}, fem. पारिमु *pārim*^{u}, born in the country beyond (the hills). May also be written पारिमु and so throughout.
कमिपारि *kamipār*^{i}, in what direction.	कपार्युमु *kapāryum*^{u}, of what direction.
तमिपारि *tamipār*^{i}, in that direction.	तपार्युमु *tapāryum*^{u}, of that direction.
यमिपारि *yamipārī*, in what direction.	यपार्युमु *yapāryum*^{u}, of what direction.
हुमिपारि *humipār*^{i}, beyond that.	हुपार्युमु *hupāryum*^{u}, of over there.
इमिपारि *yimipār*^{i}, in this direction.	इपार्युमु *yipāryum*^{u}, of this direction.
अमिपारि *amipār*^{i}, in that (visible) direction.	अपार्युमु *apāryum*^{u}, of that direction.

So also we have,—

ब्रोठ् *brŏth*, in front.	ब्रुठ्युम् *brŭthyum°*, of the front.
पथ् *păth*, behind.	पत्युम् *patyum°*, of the rear.
ह्यूर् *hyūr°*, above.	हीर्युम् *hīryum°*, of above.
प्यठ् *pyăth*, above.	पेठ्युम् *pĕthyum°*, of above.
तल् *tal*, below.	तल्युम् *talyum°*, of below.
बोन् *bŏn*, below.	बन्युम् *bŏnyum°*, of below.
अन्दर् *and°r*, within.	अन्दर्युम् *and°ryum°*, of within.
न्यबर् *nyab°r*, outside.	न्यबर्युम् *nyab°ryum°*, of outside.
मंज़् *manz*, in.	मंज़्युम् *manzyum°*, internal (Cf. Nos. 8 and 22).

45. ख्यल् *khyal°*, fem. ख्यज् *khĕj°*, signifies multitude (iv. 121).

गाव् *gāv*, a cow.	गोव्ख्यल् *gŏv°khyal°*, a herd of cows. *Vide ante*, p. 67.
गुर् *gur°*, a horse.	गुरिख्यल् *gur¹khyal°*, a troop of horse.
गुपन् *gupan*, cattle.	गुपन्ख्यल् *gupankhyal°*, a herd of cattle.
त्यूर् *tyūr°*, a ram.	तीरिख्यल् *tīr¹khyal°*, a herd of rams.
ज़नान् *zanān°*, a woman.	ज़नानख्यल् *zanān°khyal°*, a group of women.
महन्युव् *mahanyuv°*, a man.	महनिविख्यल् *mahaniv¹khyal°*, a crowd of men.

It will be observed that the termination is added to the Nominative Plural.

46. अय् *ay*, used as follows (iv. 122).

लूख् *lūkh*, people.	लूकय् *lūkay*, a crowd of people.

47. उन् *un°*, fem. न् *ñ*, the genitive termination. It is used to form adjectives also (iv. 123). Thus,—

पान् *pān°*, self.	पनुन् *panun°*, fem. पनंन् *panañ*, own.

Note that in this word the long vowel of the base is shortened.

48. उद् *ud*^{u}, fem. ज़् *s*^{a}. This is used as follows (iv. 124).

पर् *par*, another.	परुद् *parud*^{u}, fem. पर्ज़् *parąs*^{a}, another's.

49. थ *th*^{a}, used to form **adverbs of manner** (iv. 125), with elision of a preceding ह् *h* (iv. 131). So also in other cases. Thus,—

तिह् *tih*, that.	तिथ *tith*^{a}, in that manner.
यिह् *yih*, who.	यिथ *yith*^{a}, how.
क्याह् *kyāh*, what?	क्यथ *kyath*^{a}, how? (vowel shortened, iv. 129).
इह् *yih*, this.	इथ *yith*^{a}, thus.
हुह् *huh*, thus.	हुथ *huth*^{a}, in that manner.

50. थ *th*^{u}, fem. छ् *tsh*^{a}, forming **adjectives of manner** (iv. 126). Thus,—

तिथ् *tyuth*^{u}, fem. तिछ् *titsh*^{a}, of that kind.

यिथ् *yyuth*^{u}, fem. यिछ् *yitsh*^{a}, of what kind.

किथ् *kyuth*^{u}, fem. किछ् *kitsh*^{a}, of what kind?

इथ् *yuth*^{u}, fem. इछ् *yitsh*^{a}, of this kind.

हुथ् *huth*^{u}, fem. हुछ् *hutsh*^{a}, of that kind.

51. पाठि *pāṭh*^{i} or पाठिन् *pāṭhin*, used pleonastically after adverbs of manner, and similarly after other words (iv. 127, 128, 129). Thus,—

तिथपाठि *tith*^{a}*pāṭh*^{i}, in that way.

यिथपाठि *yith*^{a}*pāṭh*^{i}, how.

क्यथपाठि *kyath*^{a}*pāṭh*^{i}, how?

इथपाठि *yith*^{a}*pāṭh*^{i}, thus.

हुथपाठि *huth*^{a}*pāṭh*^{i}, in that way.

So also तिथपाठिन् *tith*^{a}*pāṭhin*, &c.

So also we have,—

बिय *biy*^{a}, other.	बियपाठिन् *biy*^{a}*pāṭhin*, otherwise.
सोरुय् *sōruy*, all.	सारिय्पाठि *sāriypāṭh*^{i}, in every way.
हल् *hąl*^{u}, crooked.	हलिपाठि *hąl*^{i}*pāṭh*^{i}, crookedly.

In the same way the termination can be added to the genitive of any noun.

E.g., तसंन्दि पाठि *tasạnd*^{i} *pāṭh*^{i}, like that.

गुरि संन्दि पाठि *gur*^{i} *sạnd*^{i} *pāṭh*^{i}, like the horse.

So also we have phrases like क्यथतान्पाठि *kyath*^{a}*-tāñ-pāṭh*^{i}, in any manner. तान् *tāñ* = Skr., अपि *api*.

52. रंग *rang*^{a}, used to form **adverbs of manner** as follows (iv. 130).

तमिरंग *tamirang*^{a}, in that manner.

यमिरंग *yamirang*^{a}, how.

कमिरंग *kamirang*^{a}, how ?

इमिरंग *yimirang*^{a}, thus.

ऊमिरंग *humirang*^{a}, in that manner.

अमिरंग *amirang*^{a}, in that manner.

अकिरंग *akirang*^{a}, in one manner (from अख् *ăkh*, one).

द्वयिरंग *dwayirang*^{a}, in two ways (from ज़्ह् *z*^{a}*h*, two).

त्रयरंग *trĕyarang*^{a}, in three ways (from त्रिह् *trih*, three).

सारिरंग *sārirang*^{a}, in every way (from सोर् *sōr*^{u}, all).

यत्सिरंग *yatsirang*^{a}, in many ways (from यत्सु *yạts*^{u}, very).

सिठाहिरंग *siṭhāhirang*^{a}, in many ways (from सिठाह् *siṭhāh*, very).

53. इ ^{i}, to form **adverbs of place** from pronominal bases (iv. 132). Thus,—

तति *tạt*^{i}, there.

यति *yạt*^{i}, where.

कति *kạt*^{i}, where ?

इति *yit*^{i}, here.

ऊति *hut*^{i}, there.

अति *ạt*^{i}, there.

So also we have (iv. 155), formed from words which are not pronominal bases,—

ब्रोठ् *brōṭh*, before.	ब्रूठि *brūṭh*^{i}, in front.
पत् *păth* behind.	पति *pạt*^{i}, in behind.

खोवुर् *khōwur*^{u}, left.	खोवुरि *khōw*^{u}*r*^{i} (p. 53), on the left.
दछुन् *dachyun*^{u}, right.	दछिनि *dachin*^{i} (p. 54), on the right.
तल् *tal*, below.	तलि *tal*^{i}, below.
प्यठ् *pyăṭh*, above.	प्यठि *pyaṭh*^{i}, above.

54. अन *an*, अनी *anī*, अनस् *anas*, अनन् *anan*, added pleonastically to the adverbs of place mentioned in No. 53 (iv. 133, 135). Thus,—

कत्यन् *katyan*, कत्यनी *katyanī*, कत्यनस् *katyanas*, or कत्यनन् *katyanan*, where?

तत्यन् *tatyan*, तत्यनी *tatyanī*, तत्यनस् *tatyanas*, or तत्यनन् *tatyanan*, there.

यत्यन् *yatyan*, यत्यनी *yatyanī*, यत्यनस् *yatyanas*, or यत्यनन् *yatyanan*, where.

अत्यन् *atyan*, अत्यनी *atyanī*, अत्यनस् *atyanas*, or अत्यनन् *atyanan*, there, &c.

55. इ *i*, to form **adverbs of motion from** (iv. 132). Thus,—

तति *tati*, from there, thence.

यति *yati*, from where, whence.

कति *kati*, from where? whence?

इति *yiti*, hence.

हुति *huti*, thence.

अति *ati*, thence.

56. प्यठ *pyaṭh*^{e}, added pleonastically to the adverbs of motion from, mentioned in No. 55 (iv. 134). Thus,—

ततिप्यठ *tatipyaṭh*^{e}, thence.

यतिप्यठ *yatipyaṭh*^{e}, whence.

कतिप्यठ *katipyaṭh*^{e}, whence?

इतिप्यठ *yitipyaṭh*^{e}, hence.

हुतिप्यठ *hutipyaṭh*^{e}, thence.

This is merely the post-position of the ablative. Cf. Hindūstānī कहाँ से *kahā̃ sē*.

57. ओर् *ōr* used to form **adverbs of place** as follows (iv. 136).

तोर् *tōr* there; योर् *yōr*, where; कोर् *kōr*, where? योर् *yōr*, here; होर् *hōr*, there; ओर् *ōr*, there.

When the suffix य् *y*, even, is added, ओ *ō* becomes ऊ *ū*. Thus,—

तूर्य् *tūry*, even there; यूर्य् *yūry*, even where; कूर्य् *kūry*, even where? यूर्य् *yūry*, even here; ऊर्य् *ury*, even there.

58. तु *tᵘ*, or तुथ् *tuth*, used to form **adverbs of place** (iv. 136). Thus,—

तंतु *tạtᵘ* or ततुथ् *tatuth*, there; यंतु *yạtᵘ* or यतुथ् *yatuth*, where; कंतु *kạtᵘ* or कतुथ् *katuth*, where? इतु *yitᵘ* or इतुथ् *yituth*, here; हतु *hutᵘ* or हतुथ् *hututh*, there; अंतु *ạtᵘ*, or अतुथ् *atuth*, there.

With emphatic य् *y*, these become, तंतुय् *tạtuy*, ततुथ्य् *tatuthᵘy*, even here; यंतुय् *yạtuy* or यतुथ्य् *yatuthᵘy*, even where, and so on (p. 88).

59. ओर *ōrᵘ*, used to make **adverbs of motion from** (iv. 137). Thus,—

तोर *tōrᵘ*, thence; योर *yōrᵘ*, whence; कोर *kōrᵘ*, whence? योर *yōrᵘ*, hence; होर *hōrᵘ*, thence; ओर *ōrᵘ*, thence.

60. अलि *ali* or अंलि *ạlⁱ*, used to make **adverbs of time** (iv. 138). Thus,—

त्यलि *tĕli*, or त्यंलि *tẹ̆lⁱ*, then; यलि *yĕli* or यंलि *yẹ̆lⁱ*, when; क्यलि *kĕli* or क्यंलि *kẹ̆lⁱ*, when?

This termination is not used with other pronouns. The word for 'now' is वुन् *wŏñ*. 'Even now' is वुन् *wuñ* (iv. 139). 'When?' is also कर् *kar* (iv. 140).

61. इ *i*, or इ *ⁱ*, used to form **adverbs of time** (iv. 141, 143). It is really the case of the agent, sometimes masc., and sometimes (to agree with विज़ि *wizi* understood) fem. Thus,—

From—

रातुल *rātulᵘ*, night time. रातलि *rātᵘli*, by night.

We also have रात्क्युत *rātkyutᵘ*, with the dative post-position (iv. 142).

दोहुल *dŏhulᵘ*, day time. दोहलि *dŏhᵘli*, by day.

न्यहफोल *nyahaphọlᵘ*, break of dawn. न्यहफोलि *nyahaphŏli*, at daybreak.

सुल *sulᵘ*, earliness. सुलि *suli*, early.

यंचूकालु *yọts*ᵘ*kāl*, delay.	यंचूकालि *yọts*ᵘ*kāl*ⁱ, late.
कालु *kāl*, time.	कालि *kāl*ⁱ, at the (right) time.

We have also कालिक्यथ *kāl*ⁱ*kyăth*, the day after to-morrow. क्यथ *kyăth* is the sign of the Locative. Again ततिकालिक्यथ *totikāl*ⁱ*kyăth*, two days after to-morrow.

विसु *wis*ᵘ, time, takes this suffix, which is in this case, clearly the agent singular, in the following phrases.

कमिविसि *kamiwisi*, when? तमिविसि *tamiwisi*, then; यमिविसि *yamiwisi*, when; &c.

62. स् *s*, used to form **adverbs of time** in the following. It is really the accusative singular (iv. 144).

कोजु *kōj*ᵘ, the forenoon meal.	कोजिस् *kājis*, at the time of the forenoon meal.
मिम्युसु *mimyus*ᵘ, the afternoon meal.	मिमिसिस् *mimisis*, at the time of the afternoon meal.

63. अन् *an*, used to form **adverbs of time**, especially with regard to the divisions of the day (iv. 145).

मंद्युन् *mandyuñ*ᵘ, midday.	मंदिञन् *mandiñan* at midday.
दुपहर् *dupahar*, midday.	दुपहरन् *dupaharan*, at midday.
कालचन् *kālacan*, evening.	कालचनन् *kālacanan*, at evening.
बतन्यंग् *batanyaṅg*, the time of the night meal.	बतन्यंगन् *batanyaṅgan*, at the time of the night meal.
बतदब् *batadab*, the time of going to bed after the night meal.	बतदबन् *batadaban*, at bed time.
अड्राथ् *aḍrāth*, midnight.	अड्रातन् *aḍrātan*, at midnight.
पत्युमुपहर् *patyum*ᵘ*pahar*, the last watch of the night.	पतिम्पहरन् *patimpaharan*, in the last watch of the night.

We even find this with foreign words, as,—

सुब्ह् *sub*ᵃ*h*, morning.	सुब्हन् *sub*ᵃ*han*, at morn.
शाम् *çām*, evening.	शामन् *çāman*, at eve.

64. अ *a*, used to signify **distribution**, with the prefix प्रथ *prăth* (iv. 146). Thus,—

दुह् *dŏh*, a day.	प्रथदुह *prăthdŏh*ᵃ, day by day.

(Also दह *dŏh^{e}*, day by day, iv. 147).

पहर् *pahar*, a watch. — प्रथ्पहर *prăthpahar^{e}*, at each watch.

वरिह्य् *warihy*, a year. — प्रथ्वरिह्य *prăthwarihy^{e}*, yearly.

प्रथ् *prăth*, also simply governs the accusative.

Thus,—

अख् *ăkh*, one. — प्रथ् अकिस् *prăth akis*, one by one.

विस् *wis^{e}*, time. — प्रथ् विसि *prăth wisi*, each time.

महन्युव् *mahanyuv^{u}*, a man. — प्रथ् महनिविस् *prăth mahanivis*, man by man.

ज़नान *zanăn^{e}*, a woman. — प्रथ् ज़नानि *prăth zanăni*, woman by woman.

When य् *y*, even, is added to the phrase प्रथ्दह *prăthdŏh^{e}*, the प्रथ् *prăth* is always dropped. Thus, always, दहय् *dŏhay*, even day by day (iv. 148). प्रथ्दहय् *prăthdŏhay*, is not used.

65. पथ् *păth*, is also used to signify **distribution**, as follows (iv. 149).

दहपथ् दह *dŏhapăth dŏh^{e}*, day by day.

वरिह्यपथ् वरिह्य *warihyapăth warihy^{e}*, year by year.

ज़निपथ् ज़नि *zanipăth zani*, person by person.

66. उस् *us*, used as follows (iv. 150, 151, 152).

यिह् *yih*, this. — यिहुस् *yihus*, this year.

ब्रोंठ् *brŏṭh*, before. — ब्रोंठुस् *brŏṭhus*, next year.

पथ् *păth*, behind. — परुस् *parus*, last year (with change of *t* to *r*).

प्रोर् *prōr^{u}*, belonging to the year before last. — प्रार्युस् *prāryus*, in the year before last.

67. किनि *kin^{i}*, used to form **adverbs of direction from** (iv. 153); added to No. 55. Thus,—

ततिकिनि *tatikin^{i}*, thence; यतिकिनि *yatikin^{i}*, whence; कतिकिनि *katikin^{i}*, whence? यितिकिनि *yitikin^{i}*, hence; हुतिकिनि *hutikin^{i}*, thence.

ब्रोंठ् *brŏṭh*, before. — ब्रुठिकिनि *brŭṭh^{i}kin^{i}*, from before.

पथ् *păth*, behind. — पतिकिनि *pat^{i}kin^{i}*, from behind.

दछुनु *dachyunᵘ*, right.	दछिनिकिनि *dachinⁱkinⁱ*, from the right.
खोवुरु *khŏwurᵘ*, left.	खोवुरिकिनि *khŏwᵘrⁱkinⁱ*, from the left.
तलु *tal*, below.	तलिकिनि *tạlⁱkinⁱ*, from below.
प्यठ *pyăṭh*, above.	प्यठिकिनि *pĕṭhⁱkinⁱ*, from above.

68. कनि *kani*, used to form **adverbs of direction from** (iv. 153), with No. 59. तोरकनि *tŏrakani*, from there; योरकनि *yŏrakani*, from where; कोरकनि *kŏrakani*, whence? होरकनि *hŏrakani* or ओरकनि *ŏrakani*, thence.

So also we have, signifying **cause**,—

तमिकनि *tamikani* or तवकनि *tawakani*, for that reason.

यमिकनि *yamikani* or यवकनि *yawakani*, for what reason.

कमिकनि *kamikani* or कवकनि *kawakani*, for what reason?

इमिकनि *yimikani* or इवकनि *yiwakani*, for this reason.

हुमिकनि *humikani* (not हुवकनि *huwakani*), for that reason.

अमिकनि *amikani* or अवकनि *awakani*, for that reason.

It is also used with words of **time** to signify **uncertainty** (iv. 154). Thus,—

अज़्कनि *azkani*, perhaps to-day; पगाह्कनि *pagāhkani*, perhaps to-morrow; कालिक्याठ्कनि *kạlⁱkyăthkani*, (see No. 61), about the day after to-morrow; ऒत्रकनि *ŏtrakani*, about the day before yesterday; दहुम्कनि *dạhumkani*, about the tenth (lunar) day; हारकनि *hārakani*, about *aṣādha*.

69. पत *patᵉ*, used to form **adverbs of time after** (iv. 153). Thus,—

तमिपत *tamipatᵉ*, after then.

तवपत *tawapatᵉ*, after then, and so on, as in No. 68.

70. पारि *pạrⁱ*, to indicate **direction from** or **in** (iv. 156). Cf. No. 44). Thus,—

कमिपारि *kamipạrⁱ* or कपारि *kapạrⁱ*, in or from what direction?

तमिपारि *tamipạrⁱ*, or तपारि *tapạrⁱ*, in or from that direction.

यमिपारि *yamipạ̄r*^{i}, or यपारि *yapạ̄r*^{i}, in or from what direction.

इमिपारि *yimipạ̄r*^{i} or इपारि *yipạ̄r*^{i}, in or from this direction.

हुमिपारि *humipạ̄r*^{i} or हुपारि *hupạ̄r*^{i}, in or from that direction.

अमिपारि *amipạ̄r*^{i} or अपारि *apạ̄r*^{i}, in or from that direction.

And so on. So also,—

दछिनिपारि *dachin*^{i}*pạ̄r*^{i}, from or on the right; खोवुरिपारि *khōu*^{a}*r*^{i}-*pạ̄r*^{i}, from or on the left; ब्रुठिपारि *brūṭh*^{i}*pạ̄r*^{i}, in or from the front; पतिमिपारि *patim*^{i}*pạ̄r*^{i}, in or from behind.

From च़ोर् *tsōr*, four, we have च़ोपारि *tsōpạ̄r*^{i} or च़ोवापारि *tsōwāpạ̄r*^{i}, in or from all round, *i.e.*, all four directions.

But च़ोरिपारि *tsōripạ̄r*^{i}, in or from four directions only (iv. 157). As usual these nouns take the case of the agent.

71. कुन् *kun*, added to **adverbs of place** to signify **direction** (iv. 158). Thus (No. 57), तोर्कुन् *tōrkun*, in that direction; योर्कुन् *yōrkun*, in what direction; कोर्कुन् *kōrkun*, in what direction? योर्कुन् *yōrkun*, in this direction; होर्कुन् *hōrkun*, in that direction; ओर्कुन् *ōrkun*, in that direction.

तुर्य्कुन् *turykun*, even in that direction; यूर्य्कुन् *yūrykun*, even in what direction.

Again (No. 58), ततुकुन् *tạt*^{u}*kun*, in that direction; यतुकुन् *yạt*^{u}*kun*, and so on.

In these last the final तु *t*^{u} of the first element may be changed to थ् *th*. Thus,—

तथ्कुन् *tathkun*, in that direction; यथ्कुन् *yathkun*, in what direction; कथ्कुन् *kathkun*, in what direction? इथ्कुन् *yithkun*, in this direction; हुथ्कुन् *huthkun*, in that direction; अथ्कुन् *athkun*, in that direction. With emphatic य् *y* we get, तथ्य्कुन् *tathykun*, even in that direction; यथ्य्कुन् *yathykun*, even in what direction, and so on.

Similarly we have,—

गाम् *gām*, a village.	गाम्कुन् *gāmkun*, in the direction of the village.
गर *gar*^{a}, a house.	गरकुन् *garakun*, in the direction of the house.

कॊल् *kŏl*, (fem.), a river. — कॊलिकुन् *kŏlikun*, towards the river.

वॊर् *wạ̄r*^{a}, a garden. — वारिकुन् *wārikun*, towards the garden.

ह्यॊर् *hyọr*^{u}, ह्युर् *hyur*^{u}, or ह्यूर् *hyūr*^{u}, above. — ह्यॊर्कुन् *hyọr*^{u}*kun*, ह्युर्कुन् *hyur*^{u}*kun*, or ह्यूर्कुन् *hyūr*^{u}*kun*, towards above.

बॊन् *bŏn*, below. — बॊन्कुन् *bŏnkun*, towards below.

The suffix can also be used as a post-position added to the accusative. Thus,—

मोलु *mōl*^{u}, a father. — मॊलिस् कुन् *mọ̄lis kun*, towards the father.

मॊजु *mọ̄j*^{a}, a mother. — माज्य कुन् *mājĕ kun*, towards the mother.

So तमिस् कुन् *tamis kun*, towards him; यमिस् कुन् *yamis kun*, towards whom.

72. उवु *uv*^{u}, (fem. ॵवु *ọv*^{a}), signifies **composed of** (iv. 159). Thus,—

सॊन् *sŏn*, gold. — सॊनुवु *sŏnuv*^{u}, fem. सॊनॵवु *sonọv*^{a}, made of gold.

म्यॊतु *mĕts*^{a}, earth. — म्यॊत्स्युवु *mĕtsyuv*^{u}, fem. म्यॊत्स्यॵवु *mĕtsyọv*^{a} made of earth.

काठ् *kāṭh*, wood. — काठुवु *kāṭhuv*^{u}, made of wood.

In all the above, the suffix is added to the form of the agent, but a final *a* is elided.

73. बुस्य् *busy*, fem. the same, signifies **dependent on** (iv. 160). Thus,—

लूख् *lūkh*, people. — लूखबुस्य् *lūkhabusy*, dependent on people; belonging to other people.

खॊड् *khŏḍ*, a hollow. — खॊडबुस्य् *khŏḍabusy*, dependent on a hollow; *i.e.*, buried in the ground.

कॊलय् *kŏlay*, a wife. — कॊलयबुस्य् *kŏlayabusy*, dependent on a wife; having only one relation,—his wife.

74. ल्यक् *lyakᵘ*, fem. ल्यच् *lĕcᵃ*, used with अड् *aḍ*, half, as follows (iv. 161).

अडल्यक् *aḍalyakᵘ*, incomplete : *e.g.*

अडल्यच् कोम् *aḍlĕcᵃ kōm*, an incomplete action.

अडल्यच् लर् *aḍalĕcᵃ larᵃ*, an incomplete house.

75. रिंग् *riṅg*, used as follows (iv. 162) to make **diminutives.**

अब्र् *abᵃr*, a cloud. — अब्ररिंग् *abᵃrariṅg*, a slight cloud.

दुह् *dᵃh*, smoke. — दुहरिंग् *dᵃhariṅg*, a slight cloud of smoke.

वाव् *wāw*, wind. — वावरिंग् *wāwariṅg*, a little wind.

76. लुथ् *lᵃth*, (fem.), used to form **diminutives** of words signifying breath or light (iv. 163). Thus,—

प्राण् *prāṇ*, life. — प्राणलुथ् *prāṇalᵃth*, a spark of life.

शाह् *çāh*, breath. — शाहलुथ् *çāhalᵃth*, a trace of breath.

गाश् *gāç*, light. — गाशलुथ् *gāçalᵃth*, a very little light.

चोंग् *tsōgᵘ*, a lamp. — चोंगिलुथ् *tsōgⁱlᵃth*, a little lamp.

The final थ् *th* becomes त् *t* in declension. Thus, acc. sg. प्राणलुति *prāṇalᵃti* (not प्राणलुथ्य *prāṇalᵃtsᵃ*).

77. तुर् *tᵃr* (fem.), used to form **diminutives** of words meaning cloths (iv. 164).

कपुर् *kapur*, cotton cloth. — कपर्तुर् *kapartᵃr*, a piece of cloth.

पट् *patᵘ*, woollen cloth. — पटितुर् *patⁱtᵃr*.

78. छल् *chal* (fem.), used to form **diminutives**, especially of clothes (iv. 165).

कपुर् *kapur*, cotton cloth. — कपरछल् *kaparchal*, a piece of cotton cloth.

चोट् *tsōtᵃ*, a cake. — चोचछल् *tsōcĕchal*, a piece of cake.

बुर्ज *burjᵉ*, a *bhurja* leaf. — बुर्जछल् *burjachal*, a piece of *bhurja* leaf.

पट् *patᵃ*, a tablet. — पचछल् *pacĕchal*, a piece of board.

क्रहमाज् *krhnamāz*, the liver. — क्रहमाज्छल् *krhnamāz chal*, a piece of liver.

79. तिलिम् *tilim*, also forms similar diminutives (iv. 165).

Thus कपर्तिलिम् *kapartilim*; त्सच्तिलिम् *tsŏčtilim*; बुर्जतिलिम् *burja-tilim*, &c.

It is smaller than a thing formed with No. 78.

80. रेम्फ् *rēmph* (fem.) (*vide ante*, p. 62), used to form diminutives, and in pity (iv. 166). Thus,—

गुर् *gur*^{u}, a boy.	गुरिरेम्फ् *gur*^{i}*rēmph*, a poor little boy.
गुर् *gur*^{u}, a horse.	गुरिरेम्फ् *gur*^{i}*rēmph*, a poor little horse.
महन्युव् *mahanyuv*^{u}, a man.	महनिविरेम्फ् *mahaniv*^{i}*rēmph*, a poor man.
छूँठ् *tsū̃th*^{u}, an apple.	छूँठिरेम्फ् *tsū̃th*^{i}*rēmph*, a little apple.

81. रेछ् *rētsh* (fem.), indicates connexion, including the idea of partition (iv. 167). Thus,—

कपुर् *kapur*, cotton cloth; कपर्रेछ् *kaparrētsh*, a piece of cloth.

मातामाल्रेछ् छह् *mātāmālrētsh chŏh*, there is some slight relationship with his maternal grandfather.

82. संड् *sanḍ* (masc.), added to words signifying vegetables or wood, to signify a little (iv. 168). Thus,—

हाख् *hākh*, spinach.	हाकसंड् *hākasanḍ*, a little spinach.
काठ् *kāṭh*, wood.	काठसंड् *kāṭhasanḍ*, a little wood.
पोश् *pōṣ*, a flower.	पोशसंड् *pōṣasanḍ*, a few flowers.
स्युन् *syun*^{u}, firewood.	सिनिसंड् *sin*^{i}*sanḍ*, a little firewood.
स्युन् *syun*^{u}, vegetables, meat, &c., (eaten with rice).	सिनिसंड् *sin*^{i}*sanḍ*, a few vegetables (not meat. If meat is included in the idea, *sanḍ* cannot be used).
मुजि *muj*^{i}, a radish (Cf. No. 32 *ante*).	मुजेसंड् *mujĕsanḍ*, a few radishes.

83. कांञ् *kāñ* (fem.), used in the same way as No. 82 (iv. 168). Thus,—

हाककांञ् *hākakāñ*, a little spinach; काठकांञ् *kāṭhakāñ*, a little wood; पोशकांञ् *pōṣakāñ*, a few flowers; so सिनिकांञ् *sin*^{i}*kāñ*; सिनिकांञ् *sin*^{i}*kāñ*; मुजेकांञ् *mujĕkāñ*.

84. टुलु *tul^u* (masc.), also used in the same way as No. 82 (iv. 168). Thus;— हाकटुलु *hākatul^u*, a little spinach; काठटुलु *kāṭhatul^u*, a little wood: पोषटुलु *pōṣatul^u*, a few flowers. So शिनिटुलु *sin^itul^u*; सिनिटुलु *sin^itul^u*; मुज्यटुलु *mujĕtul^u*.

We may also add वा *ā* (iv. 170). Thus हाकटुलुवा *hākatulwā*, a little spinach.

85. थोपु *thōp^u* (masc.), also used in the same way as No. 82 (iv. 168). Thus,—

हाकथोपु *hākathōp^u*; काठथोपु *kāṭhathōp^u*; पोषथोपु *pōṣathōp^u*; शिनिथोपु *sin^ithōp^u*; सिनिथोपु *sin^ithōp^u*; मुज्यथोपु *mujĕthōp^u*.

86. फलु *phal^u*, used to signify a little more especially of any kind of grain (iv. 169). Thus,—

दाञ़ *dāñĕ*, paddy.	दांफलु *dāphal^u*, a little paddy. *Vide ante*, p. 70.
तमुल् *tŏmul*, rice.	तमुलफलु *tŏm^alaphal^u*, a little rice.
कर *kar^a*, peas.	करफलु *karaphal^u*, a few peas.
मंग् *mŏṅg*, *mung*.	मंगफलु *mŏṅgaphal^u*, a little *mung*.

So also,—

च़ञ *ts^añ*, charcoal.	च़ञफलु *ts^añĕphal^u*, a little charcoal.
बठु *baṭh^u*, cowdung fuel.	बठिफलु *baṭh^iphal^u*, a little cowdung fuel.
म्यच़ *mĕts^a*, earth.	म्यच़फलु *mĕtsĕphal^u*, a little earth.

फलु *phal^u*, in the plural, means 'grains,' and is not used as a diminutive. Thus,—

दांफलि *dāphal^i*, grains of paddy; तमुलफलि *tŏm^alaphal^i*, grains of rice, &c.

वा *ā* may be added to फलु *phal^u*. Thus (iv. 170) बतफल्वा *bataphalwā*, a little boiled rice.

87. म्यय् *mŏy* or म्यया *mŏyā*, may be used to form diminutives with any of the words mentioned in Nos. 75 to 86, except kinds of wood and grain (Nos. 82 and 86) (iv. 170). Thus;—

अब्रम्यय् *ab^aramŏy* or अब्रम्यया *ab^aramŏyā*, a small cloud; दुहम्यया *d^ahamŏyā*, slight smoke; वावम्यया *wāwamŏyā*, slight wind; हाकम्यया

hākamŏyā, a little spinach (only used of cooked spinach. हाकतुला *hākatulā* (cf. 84) means both cooked and uncooked); पोश्मया *pŏṣamŏyā*, a few flowers; त्सुनमया *ts^añămŏyā*, a little charcoal; मत्समया *mĕtsŏ-mŏyā*, a little earth; बतमया *batamŏyā*, a little boiled grain.

88. हन् *han* or हना *hanā*, used exactly like No. 87 (iv. 170). Thus,—

वंबुरहन् *çb^arahan* or वंबुरहना *çb^arahanā*, and so on.

89. बल् *bal*, is added to any word to indicate the presence of water, or a place for offering sacrifices to minor deities or spirits (iv. 171, 172, 173). Thus we have.

व्यथबल् *vyathabal*, wherever the water of the Jhelam flows. *E.g.*, (to a man going to bathe) त्सह् कंतु गछख्? व्यथबल् *ts^ah kqt^a gatshakh*? *vyathabal*. Where are you going? (Answer) to *vyathabal*, *i.e.*, to bathe in the Jhelam.

So गंगबल् *gaggabal*, name of a well-known bathing place. मांरबल् *mạr^abal*, *vide ante*, p. 67, the water of the river Mār. पोखरिबल् *pŏkharibal*, a tank (with water in it), name of a well-known tank. क्रीरिबल् *krīr^ibal*, a well; आवरिञबल् *āwariñŏbal*, a place where a funeral pyre is set up (always on the bank of a river); शिम्शानबल् *çimçānabal*, a burning ghat, (always on the bank of a river).

सबबल् *sababal*, a place where a wedding dinner party is carried on

वुरबल् *wurabal*, the place where the cooking fires (*wur*) for a bridegroom's party are used; कोंदबल् *kŏdabal*, a brick or potter's kiln; राज़बल् *rāzabal*, a burning *ghāṭ* (*rāz* is the superintendent of a burning ghāṭ. Hence, here used for a ghāṭ). ग्रटबल् *graṭabal*, the site of a Persian wheel. वारबल् *vārabal*, the place where water (Skr. वारि *vāri*,) is offered to ancestors; *i.e.*, according to Kāçmīrī custom, a bathing place.

From the Journal, Asiatic Society of Bengal, Vol. LXVIII, Part I, No. 1, 1899, p. 1.

On the Kāçmīrī Verb.—*By* G. A. Grierson, C.I.E., Ph.D., I.C.S.

[Read January, 1899.]

The Kāçmīrī Verb is treated in the *Ākhyāta-* and *Kṛdanta-prakriyās* of Īçvara-kaula's *Kaçmīraçabdāmṛta*.

Verbal roots may end either in a consonant or in a vowel. When a root ends in a consonant, the vowel अ *a* is added to assist the pronunciation. Thus the root कर् *kar* is written कर *kar*^{a}. It is still, however, considered to be a root ending in a consonant and is referred to as such. The final अ *a* is dropped before adding the conjugational suffixes. For this reason, throughout this series of papers, I shall so far depart from the rule of strict transliteration, that I shall not write the final अ *a* of roots ending in consonants, although that final अ *a* will be written in the Nāgarī character.

When a root ends in a vowel, that vowel is always इ *i*. There are only eight of these roots, of which five belong to the first, and three to the third conjugation, as follows,—

First Conjugation.—खि *khi*, eat; चि *ci*, drink; दि *di*, give; नि *ni*, take; and हि *hi*, take.

Third Conjugation.—ज़ि *zi*, be born; पि *pi*, fall; and यि *yi*, come.

As in the above examples, all verbs will be quoted under their root-forms.

Excepting the verbs नि *ni*, take, दि *di*, give, and यि *yi*, come, all verbs whose roots end in vowels change the final इ *i* to य *ya*(*ĕ*) throughout (viii. ii. 11). Thus, the present participle of all these verbs is made by adding वान् *wān* to the root. But the present participle of खि *khi*, eat, is ख्यवान् *khyawān*, not खिवान् *khiwān*. On the other hand, the present participle of नि *ni*, take, is निवान् *niwān*, not न्यवान् *nyawān*. This rule is a most important one, and will be met over and over again in the following pages.

Conjugation.

There are three conjugations of verbs. They only differ in the formation of the Causal Voice, and of the past participles and of the tenses derived from them. Their consideration is postponed till these tenses come to be dealt with.

Voice.

There are three voices: the Active, the Passive, and the Causal.

The Active Voice.

This is formed by adding the conjugational suffixes to the root direct according to the rules to be hereafter detailed.

The Passive Voice.

This is formed by conjugating the oblique form of the verbal noun in उन् *un*, that is to say, the shortened form of the Instrumental Singular which is used before post-positions, and which ends in अन *an*^{e}, with the verb यि *yi*, come, which may either precede or follow. Thus, from the verb कर *kar*, make, the verbal noun is करुन् *karun*. The oblique form of this is करन *karan*^{e}, and the Passive is करन यि *karan*^{e} *yi*, be made, literally, come into making. Compare the Hindī देखने में आता है *dēkh'nē mẽ ātā hai*, it comes into seeing, it is seen (viii. i. 49).

Examples of the use of the Passive are (viii. i. 50).

> रनन यिवान् छुह् बत *ranan*^{e} *yiwān chuh bat*^{e}, the rice is coming into cooking, *i.e.*, is being cooked.

पानय् छुह् यिवान् करन *pāna-y chuh yiwān karan*^{e}, he, himself, is being made.

Even neuter verbs can take the passive form, without, in this case, changing their meaning (viii. i. 51). Thus,—

सोतान् छुह् *sötān chuh*; or

सोतन यिवान् छुह् *sötan*^{e} *yiwān chuh*, he is shining. The latter example is literally, he is coming into shining.

दसान् छुह् *dasān chuh*, or

दसन यिवान् छुह् *dasan*^{e} *yiwān chuh*, he is burning.

The root बोस़ *bös*, hear, when used in the passive means 'see' (viii. i. 52). Thus,—

बोस़ान् छुह् *bösān chuh*, he hears, but,

बोस़न यिवान् छुह् *bösan*^{e} *yiwān chuh*, he is being seen.

बोस़न आव् *bösan*^{e} *āv* (*āv*, is the irregular past tense of *yi*), he was seen.

बोस़न यियि *bösan*^{e} *yiyi*, he will be seen.

If we want to express the passive of the verb 'to hear,' we must use a periphrasis. Thus,—

बोस़नस् अन्दर् यिवान् छुह् *bösanas andar yiwān chuh*, he is coming into hearing, he is being heard.

The root गर *gar*, work metal, may mean 'to become hard' in the Passive (viii. i. 53). Thus,—

गरन यिवान् छुह् *garan*^{e} *yiwān chuh*, it is being worked, or it is becoming hard.

The root नि *ni*, take, may mean 'to have the attention distracted' in the Passive (viii. i. 55). Thus,—

निन यिवान् छुह् *nin*^{e} *yiwān chuh*, he is being distracted, or he is being taken.

The root हि *hi*, take, may mean 'to be engaged in' in the Passive (viii. i. 56). Thus, ह्यन यिवान् छुह् *hyan*^{e} *yiwān chuh*, he is engaged (in a business), or he is being taken.

The root डेश *ḍēś*, see, is irregular. Its Passive is formed thus, द्रेठ् यिवान् छुह् *drēṭh yiwān chuh*, he is being seen (viii. i. 54).

In adding this termination अन *an*°, we must remember that in the case of the verbs नि *ni*, take, दि *di*, give, यि *yi*, come, the first अ *a* is elided (viii. ii. 11). Thus, निन यिवान् छुह् *nin*° *yiwān chuh*, he is being taken.

दिन यिवान् छुह् *din*° *yiwān chuh*, he is being given.

यिन यिवान् छुह् *yin*° *yiwān chuh*, it is being come by him, *i.e.*, he is coming. In the case of other verbs ending in इ *i*, that vowel becomes य् *y*. Thus,—

खि *khi*, eat, ख्यन यिवान् छुह् *khyan*° *yiwān chuh*, he is being eaten.

हि *hi*, take, ह्यन यिवान् छुह् *hyan*° *yiwān chuh*, he is being taken.

चि *ci*, drink, च्यन यिवान् छुह् *cyan*° *yiwān chuh*, it is being drunk.

The Causal Voice.

A root is made causal by adding अनाव् *anāw* (viii. iv. 2, 3). Thus, कर *kar*, make; करनाव *karanāw*, cause to make. So, in the present tense, करान् छुह् *karān chuh*, he makes; करनावान् छुह् *karanāwān chuh*, he causes to make.

Exceptions—

The root वुफ *wuph*, fly, is regular. Thus, वुफनावान् छुह् *wuphanāwān chuh*, he causes to fly. But when the causal verb means 'to incite,' the *n* is changed to *l* (viii. iv. 4). Thus, वुफलावान् छुह् *wuphalāwān chuh*, he incites.

Intransitive roots containing three *akṣaras* omit the अन् *an* of अनाव् *anāw* in forming causals (viii. iv. 7). Thus,—

From—

ओबर *wŏbar*, be finished.	ओबरावान् छुह् *wŏbarāwān chuh*, he finishes.
काश्र *kātsar*, be tawny.	काश्ररावान् छुह् *kātsarāwān chuh*, he makes tawny.
कुमल *kumal*, be tender.	कुमलावान् छुह् *kumalāwān chuh*, he makes tender.
चोखर *cŏkhar*, be contracted.	चोखरावान् छुह् *cŏkharāwān chuh*, he makes contracted.

छींछन *tshĕ̃tshan*, be light. — छींछनावान् छुह् *tshĕ̃tshanāwān chuh*, he makes light.

मन्दछ *mandach*, be ashamed. — मन्दछावान् छुह् *mandachāwān chuh*, he makes ashamed.

वॊज़ल *wŏzal*, be red. — वॊज़लावान् छुह् *wŏzalāwān chuh*, he makes red.

समख *samakh*, become visible. — समखावान् छुह् *samakhāwān chuh*, he makes visible.

वॊपज़ *wŏpaz*, be born. — वॊपज़ावान् छुह् *wŏpazāwān chuh*, he produces.

This exception does not apply to transitive verbs, which are regular. Thus,—

कमव *kamav*, earn. — कमवनावान् छुह् *kamavanāwān chuh*, he causes to earn.

कतर *katar*, slice. — कतरनावान् छुह् *kataranāwān chuh*, he causes to cut in slices.

कपट *kapaṭ*, cut (clothes). — कपटनावान् छुह् *kapaṭanāwān chuh*, he causes to cut.

The root वुष्ण *wuṣṇ*, be hot, also drops the अन् *an*. Thus, वुष्णावान् छुह् *wuṣṇāwān chuh*, he makes hot (viii. iv. 8).

The verbs वुज़ *wuz*, be awake; बॊड *bŏḍ*, dive; लार *lār*, touch; पिल *pil*, arrive; कांप *kąmp*, tremble, and रंज़ *ranz*, be pleased, add optionally अव् *av*, instead of अनाव् *anāv* (viii. iv. 5, 14). Thus, वुज़वान् छुस् *wuzawān chu-s*, or वुज़नावान् छुस् *wuzanāwān chu-s*, he wakens him. So कांपवान् छुस् *kąmpawān chu-s*, or कांपनावान् छुस् *kąmpanāwān chu-s*, he causes him to tremble. The root प्रस *pras*, be born, has three forms (viii. iv. 5, 15); *viz.* प्रसवान् छुह् *prasawān chuh*; प्रसनावान् छुह् *prasanāwān chuh*, and पीनवान् छुह् *pīnawān chuh*, he causes to bear children.

The verb यि *yi*, come, makes its causal अननाव *ananāw*. [This is really the causal of अन *an*, bring]. Thus, अननावान् छुह् *ananāwān chuh*, he causes to bring.

The root फट *phaṭ*, be split, makes its causal फाटवान् छुह् *phāṭawān chuh*, or फाटनावान् छुह् *phāṭanawān chuh* (viii. iv. 17).

With regard to roots ending in इ *i*, the following are the forms (viii. iv. 9–13).

SIMPLE VERB.	CAUSAL.
पि *pi*, fall.	पावान् छुह् *pāwān chuh*, he causes to fall.
दि *di*, give.	दावान् छुह् *dāwān chuh*, or दिवनावान् छुह् *diwanāwān chuh*, he causes to give.
नि *ni*, take.	न्यावान् छुह् *nyāwān chuh*, or निवनावान् छुह् *niwanāwān chuh*, he causes to take.
चि *ci*, drink.	च्यावान् छुह् *cyāwān chuh*, or च्यवनावान् छुह् *cyāwanāwān chuh*, he gives to drink.
खि *khi*, eat.	ख्यावान् छुह् *khyāwān chuh*, or ख्यवनावान् छुह् *khyāwanāwān chuh*, he gives to eat.
हि *hi*, take.	ह्यावान् छुह् *hyāwān chuh*, or ह्यवनावान् छुह् *hyawanāwān chuh* (sic), he causes to take.

Regarding यि *yi*, come, see *supra*, p. 5.

Regarding सि *si*, be born, see *post*, p. 9.

Other verbs of the third conjugation form their causals by adding °*rāw* (viii. iv. 20). Before this,—

if the root vowel is		it becomes	
अ *a*		अ॑ *ą*.
आ *ā*	„	आ॑ *ą̄*.
ए *ē*	„	ई *i*.
ओ *ō*	„	उ *ŭ* (viii. iv. 27).

Moreover,—

if the final consonant of the root is		it becomes	
त् *t*			च् *ts*.
द् *d*		„	ज् *z*.
न् *n* or न्न् *nn*		„	ञ् *ñ* (viii. iv. 25).

[The only root of the third conjugation which ends in थ् *th* is पाथ *pāth*, become, and, according to my Paṇḍit, its causal is regular, पाथनावान् छुय् *pāthanāwān chuh*. पांथ्‌रावान् छुय् *pạṭah*ᵉ*rāwān chuh*, is possible, but unusual].

कल *kal*, be dumb.	कंल्‌रावान् छुय् *kạl*ᵉ*rāwān chuh*, he makes dumb.
ग्यब *gŏb*, be too heavy.	ग्यंब्‌रावान् छुय् *gọbarāwān chuh*, he makes too heavy.
व्यठ *vyaṭh*, be fat.	व्यंठ्‌रावान् छुय् *vyạṭh*ᵉ*rāwān chuh*, he makes fat.
काण *kāṇ*, be one-eyed.	कांण्‌रावान् छुय् *kạ̄ṇ*ᵉ*rāwān chuh*, he makes one-eyed.
ठीक *ṭhīk*, stand firmly.	ठीक्‌रावान् छुय् *ṭhīk*ᵉ*rāwān chuh*, he makes to stand firmly.
तेश *tēs*, be sharp.	तीश्‌रावान् छुय् *tīs*ᵉ*rāwān chuh*, he makes sharp.
ब्रेठ *brēṭh*, be a fool.	ब्रीठ्‌रावान् छुय् *brīṭh*ᵉ*rāwān chuh*, he makes foolish.
पोठ *pōṭh*, be fat.	पूठ्‌रावान् छुय् *pūṭh*ᵉ*rāwān chuh*, he makes fat.
लोक *lŏk*, be small.	लूक्‌रावान् छुय् *lūk*ᵉ*rāwān chuh*, he makes small.
छत *chat*, be white.	छंत्‌रावान् छुय् *chạts*ᵉ*rāwān chuh*, he makes white.
तत *tat*, be hot.	तंत्‌रावान् छुय् *tạts*ᵉ*rāwān chuh*, he makes hot.
थद *thad*, be high.	थंज्‌रावान् छुय् *thạz*ᵉ*rāwān chuh*, he elevates.
शोद *çŏd*, be pure.	शंज्‌रावान् छुय् *çọz*ᵉ*rāwān chuh*, he purifies.
बन *ban*, be.	बंञ्‌रावान् छुय् *bạñ*ᵉ*rāwān chuh*, he causes to be.
तन *tan*, be thin.	तंञ्‌रावान् छुय् *tạñ*ᵉ*rāwān chuh*, he makes thin.

The verb चुक *tsŏk*, if it means 'be sour,' makes its causal चुक्रावान् छुह् *tsǫkᵃrāwān chuh;* but if it means 'be angry,' its causal is चुक्रावान् छुह् *tsuᵏkᵃrāwān chuh.* The verb खल *khal*, be loose, makes its causal खल्रावान् छुह् *khǫlᵃrāwān chuh*, or खज्रावान् छुह् *khǫjᵃrāwān chuh.*

The following verbs form their causals optionally by adding either *anāw*, or *ᵃrāw*, (viii. iv. 19, 21, 22, 23).

First Conjugation: चक *chak*, scatter; चप *chap*, pass time; चेन *tsĕn*, know by a sign; मान *mān*, confess.

Second Conjugation: चल *tsal*, flee; च्यन *tshyann*, be split; थक *thak*, be weary; फस *phas*, be entangled; फुट *phuṭ*, be broken; फल *phŏll*, expand (of a flower); मश *maṣ*, forget; राव *rāv*, be lost; हॊख *hŏkh*, be dry; हॊच *hŏts*, decay; श्रप *çrap*, be digested.

Third Conjugation: ट्यठ *ṭyaṭh*, be bitter.

Thus, चीञ्रावान् छुह् *tsīñᵃrāwān chuh*, or चेननावान् छुह् *tsĕnanāwān chuh;* चल्रावान् छुह् *tsǫlᵃrāwān chuh*, or चलनावान् छुह् *tsalanāwān chuh;* ट्यठ्रावान् छुह् *ṭyǫṭhᵃrāwān chuh*, or ट्यठनावान् छुह् *ṭyaṭhanāwān chuh.*

The root चक *chak* does not alter its meaning in the causal in *ᵃrāw*. Thus, चकान् छुह् *chakān chuh*, चक्रावान् छुह् *chǫkᵃrāwān chuh*, both mean 'he scatters.' To give a causal meaning it has चकनावान् छुह् *chakanāwān chuh*, or चक्रनावान् छुह् *chǫkᵃranāwān chuh.*

The root चप *chap* has for its causal चप्रावान् छुह् *chǫpᵃrāwān chuh*, चपनावान् छुह् *chapanāwān chuh*, or चूप्रावान् छुह् *chŏpᵃrāwān chuh.*

The following verbs of the third conjugation form their causals in *anāw*, and not in *ᵃrāw* (viii. iv. 17) कच *kᵃts*, be wet; गॊह *gŏh*, shine; ग्रक *grak*, boil over; सोत *sōt*, shine; टक *ṭᵃk*, run; टेल *ṭēl*, smart; तोष *tōṣ*, be satisfied (according to my Paṇḍit, this verb belongs to the 2nd conjugation); दोर *dōr*, run; नाप *nāp*, shine; नील *nīl*, become blue; पिस *pis*, boil over; पेड *pēḍ*, exude; पोर *pōr*, be competent; प्रार *prār*, wait (according to my Paṇḍit, this verb belongs to the 2nd conjugation); फब *phab*, be excellent; फर *phar*, be stolen; फल *phal*, become old (of clothes); फुश *phuç* or फुह *phuh*, be inwardly angry; फेर *phĕr*, go round; फोर *phōr*, quiver (according to my Paṇḍit, this verb belongs

8

to the 2nd conjugation); बाद् *bād*, be powerful; बास *bās*, become clear (according to my Paṇḍit, this verb belongs to the 2nd conjugation); बुड *buḍ*, be old: ब्रस *bras*, shine; याप *yāp*, pervade; रंब *ramb*, be beautiful; रस *ras*, be full of juice; रोंछ *rötś*, be preferred; रोट *rōṭ*, be stopped; र्‍ड *r°ḍ*, persistently follow; र्‍ण *r°ṇ*, be worn out; ल्यड *lyaḍ*, be conquered; लोर *lōr*, become deficient. Thus, क्छनावान् छुह् *k°tsanāwān chuh*, not क्छ्‍रावान् छुह् *k°ts°rāwān chuh*.

All causal verbs in °*rāw*, may optionally drop the syllable *āw* in the termination, and add °*r* instead of °*rāw* (viii. iv. 24). Thus,—

Instead of—	We may have—
कंल्‍रावान् छुह् *kal°rāwān chuh*	कंल्‍रान् छुह् *kal°rān chuh*
गंब्‍रावान् छुह् *gȫb°rāwān chuh*	गंब्‍रान् छुह् *gȫb°rān chuh*
छंक्‍रावान् छुह् *tsȫk°rāwān chuh*	छंक्‍रान् छुह् *tsȫk°rān chuh*

and so on.

The following verbs form their causals by merely lengthening their root vowels (viii. iv. 28).

तर *tar*, be crossed. Causal तारान् छुह् *tārān chuh*, he crosses.

मर *mar*, die. मारान् छुह् *mārān chuh*, he kills.

डल *ḍal*, pass over. डालान् छुह् *ḍālān chuh*, he causes to pass over.

लग *lag*, be with. लागान् छुह् *lāgān chuh*, he unites.

When मर *mar* (18, 28), means 'unite,' and when लग *lag* (28) means 'suffer pain,' or 'fit,' they are regular. Thus, मरनावान् छुह् *maranāwān chuh*, he causes to unite; लगनावान् छुह् *laganāwān chuh*, he causes to suffer pain.

The following are quite irregular,—

सि *si*, be born. Causal स्वो्‍रान् छुह् *sö°rān chuh*, he brings forth (26).

खस *khas*, ascend. खारान् छुह् *khārān chuh*, he causes to ascend (29).

वस *vas*, descend. वारान् छुह् *wārān chuh*, he brings down (29).

शंग *śōng*, go to sleep.	सावान् छुह् *sāwān chuh*, he puts to sleep (30).
दज़ *daz*, burn.	ज़ालान् छुह् *zālān chuh*, he burns (act.) (31).
डेश *ḍēś*, see.	हावान् छुह् *hāwān chuh*, he shows (32).
गछ *gatsh*.	पकनावान् छुह् *pakanāwān chuh*, he drives.
	गछनावान् छुह् *gatshanāwān chuh*, he despatches (33).
	Thus, गोव्न् पकनावान् छुह् *gōvᵃn pakanāwān chuh*, he drives the cows; गंगाय गछनावान् छुस् *gangāyᵉ gatshanāwān chu-s*, he sends him to the Ganges.
व्वथ *wŏth*, rise.	तुलान् छुह् *tulān chuh*, he raises, he lifts up; but व्वथनावान् छुह् *wŏthanāwān chuh*, he causes so and so to rise (34).

Verbal Suffixes.

Before proceeding to the consideration of the conjugation of the verb, it is necessary to describe in detail one remarkable feature of the Kāçmīrī language, which it shares with other languages of the North-Western group of the Indo-Aryan Vernaculars, namely, the facility with which the meaning of the verbal stem can be modified by the addition of suffixes. Indeed, it may be said that, given the form of a tense-stem, there is usually no conjugation, in the proper sense of the word, at all. In most cases, suffixes, which may be added, or detached, at pleasure, and most of which have an independent recognised existence, are added, and give the various modifications of meaning which we designate number and person, or of negation, affirmation, and so on, by forming true compound words, and without becoming merged in the base in the form of terminations. Thus, take the word कर् *karᵘ*. This means 'made,' and may mean, 'made by me,' 'made by us,' 'made by him' and so on. That is to say, it means, 'I made,' 'we made,' 'he made,' &c. If we wish to lay stress on the person who made, we may say तमि कर् *tamⁱ karᵘ*, 'by him made,' *i.e.*, 'he made.' Instead, however of using तमि *tamⁱ*, the instrumental singular of the third personal pronoun, in Kāçmīrī we may optionally add the suffix न् *n*, which means 'by him,' just as much as तमि *tam*' does, and we get करुन् *karu-n*, which also means 'made by him,' or 'he made.' Suppose we want to express who was made by him, and that the person is the speaker, then we can say बुह् करुन् *bŏh karu-n*, 'I was made by him,' *i.e.*, 'he made me.' Instead, however, of बुह् *bŏh*, we may add the suffix अस् *as*, which means 'I.' We thus get करुनस् *kar^{u}-n-as*, 'I was made by him,' *i.e.*, 'he made me.' Again, if we wish to emphasise the fact that I was the person made, we can add the suffix ति *ti*, and we get the form करुनस्ति *kar^{u}-n-as-ti*, which means, 'I also was made by him,' 'he made me also.' Again, if we want to make the verb interrogative, we can add, after all these, the interrogative particle, आ *ā*, thus, करुनस्त्या *kar^{u}-n-as-ty-ā*, 'was I also made by him?' 'did he make me also?'

The above examples will show the freedom with which these suffixes are used in Kāshmīrī. They can be combined almost *ad infinitum*. These suffixes may be divided into two classes, adverbial and pronominal, and in this order, I now proceed to discuss them.

Adverbial Suffixes.

These suffixes are added to all verbs. Before all these the final ह् *h* of a verbal form is elided (iv. 131). The ordinary rules of *sandhi* also occur. Thus *i* and *u* before *ā* become *y* and *w* respectively, *ya* (*ĕ*) + *ā* becomes *yā*, and *a* + *ā* becomes *ā*.

1. न *n^{a}*. This negatives the verb (viii. i. 13). Thus,—

करान् छुह् *karān chuh*, he makes.	करान् छुन *karān chun^{a}*, he does not make.
करान् छिह् *karān chih*, they make.	करान् छिन *karān chin^{a}*, they do not make.
करान् छेह् *karān chĕh*, she makes.	करान् छेन *karān chĕn^{a}*, she does not make.
करान् छेख् *karān chĕkh*, thou (fem.) makest.	करान् छेखन *karān chĕkhn^{a}*, thou dost not make.
करि *kari*, he will make.	करिन *karin^{a}*, he will not make.
गयोव् *gayŏv*, he went.	गयोवन *gayŏvn^{a}*, he did not go.
पकु *pak^{u}*, he went.	पकुन *pak^{u}n^{a}*, he did not go.

2. आ *ā*. This gives an interrogative force to the verb (viii. i. 14). Thus,—

करान् छुह् *karān chuh*, he makes.	करान् छ्वा (for छुह्+आ,छु+आ) *karān chwā*, does he make?
करान् छेह् *karān chĕh* (lit. *chyah*), she makes.	करान् छ्या *karān chyā*, does she make?
करि *kari*, he will make.	कर्या *karyā*, will he make?
परव् *parav*, we shall read.	परवा *parawā*, shall we read?
कर्योन् *karyōn*, he made.	कर्योना *karyōnā*, made he?
करुन् *kạrun*, he made.	करुना *kạr*^{u}*nā*, made he?
गयोव् *gayōv*, he went.	गयोवा *gayōvā*, did he go?
पकु *pạk*^{u}, he went.	पकुा *pạk*^{u}*ā*, did he go?

In the first and third persons Feminine, अय् *ay* is substituted for आ *ā*, when the person addressed is a woman. If a man is addressed, उ ^{u} is used in the first person Singular, and आ *ā* in the first person Plural, and in the third person.

Thus, करान् छेस *karān chĕs*^{u}, am I (fem.) making? here a man is addressed. If a woman is addressed, the speaker would say छेसय् *chĕsay*.

करान् छ्या असि *karān chyā* (*chĕh* + *ā*) *ạs*^{i}, are we (fem.) making? If a woman is addressed, the speaker must say छेय् *chĕy*. See No. 4.

3. उ ^{u}. This may be substituted for आ *ā*, in the following cases.

(*a*) In the first person Singular Masculine (viii. i. 15) Thus,—

करान् छुस् *karān chus*, I make.	करान् छुस *karān chus*^{u} (instead of करान् छुसा *karān chusā*), am I making?

(*b*) Always in the first person Singular Feminine, when a man is addressed (viii. i. 17). Thus,—

करान् छेस् *karān chĕs*, I (fem.) make.	करान् छेस *karān chĕs*^{u}, am I (fem.) making? Here the speaker is addressing a man. If she was addressing a woman she would say करान् छेसय् *karān chĕsay*.

(*c*) Honorifically in the second person Singular and Plural (viii. i. 15).

करान् छुख् *karān chukh*, thou makest. — करान् छुख *karān chukh*^{a}, does Your Honour make?

करान् छिव *karān chiw*^{a}, you make. — करान् छिव *karān chiw*^{a}, do your Honours make? Note here that the vowel remains short.

4. अय् *ay* or, after a vowel, य् *y*. Used as follows, instead of आ *ā* or अ ^{a}.

(*a*) In the first person Singular and Plural Feminine, and in the third person Singular and Plural Feminine (viii, i. 17, 18), when a woman is addressed. Thus,—

करान् छस् *karān chĕs*, I (fem.) make. — करान् छसय् *karān chĕsay* am I (fem.) making? Here the speaker is addressing a woman. If she were addressing a man, she would say करान् छस *karān chĕs*^{a}.

करान् छय् अँसि *kărān chĕh as*^{i}, we (fem.) make. — करान् छय् अँसि *karān chĕy as*^{i}, are we (fem.) making?

करान् छय् स्व *karān chĕh sŏh*, she makes. — करान् छय् स्व *karān chĕy sŏh*, is she (fem.) making?

करान् छय् तिम *karān chĕh tim*^{a}, they (fem.) make. — करान् छय् तिम *karān chĕy tim*^{a}, are they (fem.) making?

In the three last, the speaker is also addressing a woman. If she were addressing a man, she would say छा *chyā*, instead of छय् *chĕy*.

(*b*) In the second person Feminine optionally instead of अ *a*, when a woman is addressed honorifically (viii. i. 16). Thus,—

करान् छख् *karān chĕkh*, thou (fem.) makest. — करान् छखय् *karān chĕkhay*, or करान् छख *karān chĕkh*^{a}, is Your Honour (fem.) making? Here the speaker is necessarily addressing a woman.

करान् छव *karān chĕw*^{a}, you (fem.) make. — करान् छवय् *karān chĕway*, or करान् छव *karān chĕw*^{a}, are Your Honours (fem.) making? The speaker is again addressing women.

5. ति *ti* (iv. 179). This suffix is used to signify 'also,' 'indeed.' Thus,—

करान् छुह् *karān chuh*, he makes.	करान् छुति *karān chuti*, he makes also.
करि *kari*, he will make.	करिति *kariti*, he will indeed make.

6. ना *nā*, नय् *nay* (viii. i. 14, 16). This is a compound of न *nᵉ* (No. 1) and आ *ā* (No. 2) or ॳ *ᵉ* (No. 3), or of न *nᵉ*, and अय् (No. 4). It gives the force of an interrogative negative, and is used like the separate parts. Thus,—

करान् छुह् *karān chuh*, he makes.	करान् छुना *karān chunā*, does he not make?

So करान् छेना *karān chĕnā*, does she not make?

कर्योन् *karyōn*, he made.	कर्योन्ना *karyōnnā*, did he not make?
करि *kari*, he will make.	करिना *karinā*, will he not make?
करान् छख् *karān chĕkh*, thou (fem.) makest.	करान् छखना *karān chĕkhnā*, dost thou (fem.) not make? करान् छखनय् *karān chĕkhnay*, does Your Honour (fem.) not make?
करान् छव *karān chĕwᵉ*, you (fem.) make.	करान् छवना *karān chĕwᵉnā*, do you (fem.) not do? or करान् छवनय् *karān chĕwᵉnay*, do Your Honours (fem.) not make?

7. त्या *tyā* or त्यय् *tyay*. This is a combination of ति *ti*, (No. 5) and आ *ā* (No. 2), or अय् *ay* (No. 4). It implies a question with emphasis (viii. i. 14). Thus,—

करान् छुत्या *karān chutyā*, does he *make* (it)?

कर्योन्त्या *karyōntyā*, did he *make* (it)?

करित्या *karityā*, will he *make* (it)?

करान् छवत्यय् *karān chĕwᵉtyay*, do Your Honours (fem.) *make* (it)?

8. सन *sanᵉ*, सना *sanā*, आसन *āsanᵉ*, used in a question with doubt. If there is an interrogative word also in the sentence, it is added to it. Otherwise it is added to the verb. [सना *sanā* is not used with a verb].

14

The आ *ā* of सना *sanā* and आसन *āsan*°, is suffix No. 2 already described (viii. i. 25, 28). Thus,—

खेवान् छ्वासन *khyawān chwāsan*° (*chuh* + *āsan*°), is he really eating?

क्यासन खेवान् छ्वा *kyāsan*° (*kyāh* + *san*°) *khyawān chwā*, what, is he really eating?

क्यासना खेवान् छुह् *kyāsanā khyawān chuh*, what, is he eating?

बट कैत्यासन आसान् छिह् *baṭ*° *kaityāsan*° (*kait*ⁱ + *āsan*°) *āsān chih* how many brahmans are there really?

कर्सना बाग्नि यिवान् छुह् *karsanā bāgⁱ yiwān chuh*, at what hour is he coming? (*kar* = when? बाग्नि *bāgⁱ* = Skr. *bhāga*, a portion of the day or night).

कर्सना यियि *karsanā yiyi*, when will he come?

कुत्यसना आसहान् *kutⁱsanā āsahān*, how many may there be?

कतिसना ओसु *katisanā ōs*°, where was he?

9. सां *sā̃*. This is the vocative particle (*vide ante*, Vol. lxvii, p. 92). It is used exactly like सन *san*°. Thus,—

कैत्यासां लूख् आसि *kaityāsā̃* (*kait*ⁱ + *ā-sā̃*) *lūkh āsⁱ*, how many people were there?

Pronominal Suffixes.

1. Before these as before all other suffixes, the final ह् *h* of a verb is elided (iv. 131). So also, an initial अ *a* of a suffix is elided when the verb, either after the elision of ह् *h* or not, ends in a vowel (viii. i. 39). Thus, छुह् + अम् *chuh* + *am* becomes first छु + अम् *chu* + *am*, and then छु + म् *chu* + *m* = छुम् *chum*, there is to me.

2. If the final ख् *kh* of a suffix is followed by another pronominal (not an adverbial) suffix commencing with a vowel, the ख् *kh* becomes ह् *h* (viii. i. 38). Thus,—

करान छुहस् *karān chu-h-as* (for *chu-kh* + *as*), thou makest for him.

करान् छुहख् *karān chu-h-akh*, thou makest for them.

3. The termination अव् *av* becomes ओ *ō* before suffixes (viii. ii. 18). Thus,—

करोथ् *karō-th* (*karav* + *ath*), we shall make thee.

4. The termination इव् *iv* becomes यू *yū* before suffixes. Thus,—

कर्यूम् *karyū-m* (for *kariv* + *am*), make ye for me, or make ye me.

When suffixes are added to the root direct, in the second singular imperative, a उ *u* is inserted (viii. i. 16). Thus,—

कर् *kar*, make thou. करुम् *karu-m*, make thou for me, or make me.

When suffixes are added to the 3rd person singular of the Future, indicative, the अ *a* of the suffix is not elided. Thus, करि *kari*, he will make, कर्यस् *kary-as*, not करिस् *kari-s*, he will make for him. This does not hold with the suffixes of the second person. Thus, करिय् *kari-y*, he will make for thee, करिव *kari-w*ᵃ, he will make for you.

[When interrogative and other adverbial suffixes are added to the verb, they follow the pronominal suffix. *E.g.*, छुमा *chu-m-ā*, is there to me? So छुमासन *chu-m-āsan*ᵃ, &c.].

Some verbs are never used without pronominal suffixes of the dative case (viii. i. 45). These are,—

चर् *tsar*, be inwardly wrathful.

फश *phŏç*, be inwardly wrathful.

फुह *phuh*, be inwardly wrathful.

मर्च *marts*, be inwardly wrathful.

वुच *wuts*, be burnt.

फिच *phits*, forget.

त्यंब *tyamb*, look eagerly (viii. iii. 45).

Moreover these verbs are always conjugated in the feminine, whether the subject is masculine or feminine. They are then used as impersonal verbs. Thus,—

चरान् छेस् *tsarān chĕ-s*, lit. there is inward anger to him. *I.e.*, he is inwardly angry.

Similarly, फशान् छेस् *phŏçān chĕ-s*, फुहान् छेस् *phuhān chĕ-s*, मर्चान् छेस् *martsān chĕ-s*. Again चरान् छेम् *tsarān chĕ-m*, there is inward anger to me, I am inwardly angry, and so on. Again, वुचान् छेस् *wutsān chĕ-s*, there is burning to him, *i.e.*, he is burning (inwardly); फिचान् छेस् *phitsān chĕ-s*, there is forgetfulness to him, he forgets: त्यंबान् छेस् *tyambān chĕ-s*, he looks eagerly.

Sometimes full pronouns are used instead of suffixes (viii. i. 46). Thus,—

तमिस् त्सरान् छय् *tamis tsarān chĕh*, there is inward anger to him.

The verb गछ् *gatsh*, be proper, be desirable, is also used with the dative (viii. i. 47). Thus,—

तमिस् गछान् छुह् सि परहाँ *tamis gatshān chuh si parahą̄*, to him it is desirable that I should read. He thinks it proper that I should read. This is only in the third person. For the other persons always, and for the third person optionally, suffixes are used when they exist (viii. i. 48). Thus,—

गछान् छुम् *gatshān chu-m*, it is proper for me.

गछान् छुह् *gatshān chuh* (no suffix), it is proper for us.

गछान् छुय् *gatshān chu-y*, it is proper for thee.

गछान् छुव *gatshān chu-wᵉ*, it is proper for you.

गछान् छुस् *gatshān chu-s*, it is proper for him.

गछान् छुख् *gatshān chu-kh*, it is proper for them.

This applies only to the present tense.

First Person.

The suffix of the *Nominative Singular* is अस् *as*, which is not used with the Future tense (viii. i. 43). Thus,—

करान् छुस् *karān chu-s*, I make.

पंकुस् *pąku-s*, I went.

कर्योनस् *karyō-n-as*, I (*as*) was made (*karyō*) by him (*an*). *I.e.*, he made me.

But कर् *karᵉ*, not करस् *kara-s*, I shall make. करस् *kara-s* means 'I shall make for him' (*vide post*, third person).

For *other cases of the singular*, the suffix is अम् *am* (viii. i. 24). Thus,—

करान् छुम् *karān chu-m*, he makes me, or for me.

करान् छिम् *karān chi-m*, they make me, or for me.

कंरुम् *kąru-m*, made by me, I made.

There are no *Plural Suffixes* of the first person: the full pronouns are used instead (viii. i. 44). Thus,—

करान् छुह् असे *karān chuh asĕ*, he makes us, and so on.

SECOND PERSON.

For the *Nominative Singular* the suffix is अख् *akh*, which is used as follows (viii. i. 36). Thus,—

करान् छुख् *karān chhu-kh*, thou makest.

करख् *kara-kh*, thou wilt make.

करहाख् *karahā-kh*, (if) thou hadst made.

पकुख् *paku-kh*, thou wentest.

कॊर्मख् *kar°-m-akh*, thou wast made by me, *i.e.*, I made thee.

कर्योनख् *karyō-n-akh*, thou wast made by him, *i.e.*, he made thee.

For the *Accusative Singular*, अथ् *ath* is used in the first person singular and plural (viii. i. 37). Thus,—

करथ् *kara-th*, I shall make thee.

करोथ् *karō-th* (*karav + ath*), we shall make thee.

करान् छुसथ् *karān chu-s-ath*, I make thee.

करान् छिथ् *karān chi-th*, we make thee.

We cannot use this suffix with the third person. Thus, we cannot say करिथ् *kari-th*, he will make thee. We must use instead the suffix अय् *ay*, which properly belongs to the Dative. Thus,—

सुह् करिय् *suh kari-y*, he will make thee, or for thee.

तिम् करनय् *tim karan-ay*, they will make thee, or for thee.

सुह् करान् छुय् *suh karān chu-y*, he makes thee, or for thee.

तिम् करान् छिय् *tim karān chi-y*, they make thee, or for thee.

The same suffix (अथ् *ath*) is also used for the *Agent Singular* with the past tenses of transitive verbs. Thus,—

कॊरुथ् *karu-th*, made by thee, *i.e.*, thou madest.

कर्योथ् *karyō-th*, made by thee, *i.e.*, thou madest.

For the *Dative Singular* and also (when the verb is in the third person) for the *Accusative Singular*, the suffix अय् *ay* is used (viii. i. 40). Thus,—

करान् छुय् *karān chu-y*, he makes for thee, or thee.

करान् छुसय् *karān chu-s-ay*, I make for thee.

करान् छिय् *karān chi-y*, we make for thee.

करान् छिय् *karān chi-y*, they make for thee, or thee.

करिय् *kari-y*, he will make for thee, or thee.

This form is liable to certain changes in the Aorist and Pluperfect tenses of verbs. These will be found duly explained in the proper place. With the Past Conditional this suffix may have the force of the Accusative.

For all cases of the *Plural*, the suffix is व *w*ᵒ. Thus,—

Nominative—

करान् छिव *karān chi-w*ᵒ, you make.

Accusative or *Dative*—

करान् छुव *karān chu-w*ᵒ, he makes you, or for you.

करान् छिव *karān chi-w*ᵒ, they make you, or for you.

करान् छुसव *karān chu-s-w*ᵒ, I make you, or for you.

Agent—

कॊऱ्व *kạr*ᵘ*-w*ᵒ, made by you, you made.

THIRD PERSON.

There is no pronominal suffix of the *Nominative Singular or Plural.*

The pronominal suffix of the *Dative Singular* is अस् *as* (viii. i. 33). Thus,—(masculine).

करान् छुसस् *karān chu-s-as*, I make for him.

करान् छुहस् *karān chu-h-as* (*chu-kh+as*, thou makest for him.

करान् छुस् *karān chu-s*, he makes for him.

करान् छिस् *karān chi-s*, we make for him.

करान् छिवस् *karān chi-wa-s*, you make for him.

करान् छिस् *karān chi-s*, they make for him.

करस् *kara-s*, I shall make for him.

So also for the feminine, करान् छेसस् *karān che-s-as.*

[This suffix is also used for the *Accusative*, when the verb is in the third person. Thus, करान् छुस *karān chu-s*, he makes him, करान् छिस् *karān chi-s*, they make him].

For other oblique cases of the singular, अन् *an* is used (viii. i. 34). Thus,—

Accusative—

करान् छुहन *karān chu-h-an* (*chu-kh+an*), you make him.

खेवान् छुहन् *khyawān chu-h-an*, you eat him.

अस् *as* is however, used for अन् *an* with the third person. Thus, करान् छुस् *karān chu-s*, not करान् छुन् *karān chu-n*, he makes him.

Agent—

कॅरुन् *kạru-n* (कॅर् *kạr*^{u} + अन् *an*), made by him, he made.

For all cases of the plural, the suffix is अख् *akh* (viii. i. 35). Thus,—

करान् छुसख् *karān chu-s-akh*, I make for them, or I make them.

करान् छुख् *karān chu-kh*, he makes for them, or makes them.

कॅरुख *kạru-kh*, made by them, they made.

Moods and Tenses.

The Kāçmīrī verb has four Moods, *viz.*, the Indicative, the Imperative, the Benedictive, and the Conditional.

The Indicative Mood is usually credited with eight tenses, *viz.*,—

1. The Present.
2. The Imperfect.
3. The Future.
4. The Past.
5. The Aorist.
6. The Pluperfect.
7. The Perfect.
8. The Periphrastic Pluperfect.

Of these, Nos. 2, 7, and 8, are not discussed by Içvara-kaula in his grammar. I shall, however, give short notices of them for the sake of completeness. Nos. 1, 2, 7, and 8, are all periphrastic tenses, made up of Participles conjugated with auxiliary verbs. In No. 1, the Present participle is conjugated with the Present tense of the auxiliary verb, and in No. 2, it is conjugated with the Past tense of the same. In No. 7, the Past participle is conjugated with the Present tense of the same verb, and in No. 8, with its Past tense.

The Imperative Mood has three tenses, *viz.*,—

1. The Present.
2. The Future.
3. The Past.

The Present Imperative has two forms, a Simple, and a Modified.

The Benedictive Mood has one tense, which may be called the Future.

The Conditional Mood has two tenses, *viz.*,—

1. A Present-Future. This is the same in form as the Future Indicative.
2. A Past.

Other tenses may be manufactured on the analogy of Hindi, but they are not in frequent use. Thus, सुह करान् आसि *suh karān āsi*, equivalent to the Hindi वह करता होगा *wah kar'tā hōga*, he will (probably) be making. It is unnecessary to make a list of these. They can be made up as required.

Some verbs are irregular in the use of their tenses. These are the following.

The root ज़ान *zān*, know, when it means to know how to do a thing, uses the Future in the sense of the Present (viii. i. 58). Thus,—

करुन् ज़ानि *karun zāni*, he knows how to make a thing.

परुन् ज़ानन् *parun zānan*, they know how to read.

So also, स्याठाह् ज़ानि *syaṭhāh zāni*, he knows a great deal.

विद्या ज़ानि *vidyā zāni*, he is a learned man (lit. he knows knowledge).

In the same way, in writing the ceremonial part of a letter, a past tense is sometimes used instead of the imperative. Thus, तमिस् ल्यूखुथ् सोन् नमस्कार् *tamis lyūkhu-th sōn° namaskār*, to him was there written-by-thee our compliment, *i.e.*, write our compliments to him.

The root पाथ *pāth*, be, become, has no regular Present; and uses the Future for that tense (viii. i. 59). Thus,—

पाथ *pāth°*, I am.	पाथव् *pāthaw*, we are.
पाथख् *pāthakh*, thou art.	पाठिव् *pāṭhiv*, you are.
पाथि *pāthi*, he is.	पाथन् *pāthan*, they are.

For the Past tense, the following forms are used.

1	पाथहाँ *pāthahā̤*, I was.	पाथहाव् *pathahā̤v*, we were.
2	पाथहाख् *pāthahā̤kh*, thou wast.	पाठिहीव् *pāṭh'hīv*, you were.
3	पाथिहे *pāthihē*, he was.	पाथहान् *pāthahā̤n*, they were.

These forms are properly those of the Past Conditional. This verb has no verbal nouns.

Gender, Number and Person.

Gender.

The verb has two Genders, Masculine and Feminine. The Future Indicative, and the Imperative, Benedictive, and Conditional Moods, do not however, make any change for Gender. Their Masculine and Feminine forms are identical.

Some verbs are conjugated only in the Feminine. They are all impersonal. They are,—

चर *tsar*, be inwardly wrathful (viii. i. 45).

फश *phŏç*, be inwardly wrathful.

फुह *phuh*, be inwardly wrathful.

मर्च *marts*, be inwardly wrathful.

वुच *wuts*, be burnt.

फिच *phits*, forget.

त्यंब *tyamb*, look eagerly, (viii. iii. 45).

चुव *tsuv*, quarrel (viii. iii. 9).
मोरव *mōrav*, bear pain.
} These two are feminine and impersonal in the past tenses only.

The peculiarities of these verbs will be found described in the proper places. The first six form one group, which is known as the चरादि *tsarādi*, or '*tsar* and the others,' which will be frequently met with in the course of this article.

Number. There are two numbers,—singular and plural (viii. i. 4). There is no dual. तिम् छिह् परान् *tim chih parān*, means .'they two,' or 'they (many) are reading.'

Person. There are three persons,—first, second, and third (viii. i. 3).

The first person is more worthy than the second, and the second than the third (viii. i. 5).

Thus, सुह् त चह् परिव् *suh* t^{a} $ts^{a}h$ *pariv*, do thou and he read (imperative).

चह् त बुह् परव् $ts^{a}h$ t^{a} *bŏh parav*, let thee and me read.

सुह् त बुह् परव् *suh* t^{a} *bŏh parav*, let him and me read.

सुह् त चह् त बुह् परव् *suh* t^{a} $ts^{a}h$ *ta bŏh parav*, let him and thee and me read.

Auxiliary Verbs, and Verbs Substantive.

There are many verbs meaning 'to be' in Kāçmīrī. The following are the two commonest forms, and they are used not only as verbs substantive, but also as auxiliary verbs.

PRESENT. I am (viii. i. 11, 12).

	SINGULAR.		PLURAL.	
Person.	Masculine.	Feminine.	Masculine.	Feminine.
1	छुस् *chu-s.*	छॖस् *chŏ-s.*	छिह् *chih.*	छॖह् *chĕh.*
2	छुख् *chu-kh.*	छॖख् *chŏ-kh.*	छिव *chi-w*^{a}.	छॖव *chŏ-w*^{a}.
3	छुह् *chuh.*	छॖह् *chĕh.*	छिह् *chih.*	छॖह् *chŏh.*

Negative form छुसन *chu-s-n*^{a}, &c., see p. 11.

Interrogative form छुसा *chu-s-ā*, छुस *chu-s*^{a}, &c., see p. 12.

Negative-interrogative form छुसना *chu-s-nā*, see p. 14.

Emphatic form छुस्ति *chu-s-ti*, see p. 14.

Emphatic-interrogative form छुस्त्या *chu-s-ty-ā*, see p. 14.

PAST. It was.

	SINGULAR.		PLURAL.	
Person.	Masculine.	Feminine.	Masculine.	Feminine.
1	ओसुस् *ōsu-s.*	आसॖस् *ạs*^{ŭ}*-s.*	आसि *ạs*^{i}.	आस *ās*^{a}.
2	ओसुख् *ōsu-kh.*	आसॖख् *ạs*^{ŭ}*-kh.*	आसिव *ạs*^{i}*-w*^{a}.	आसव *ās*^{a}*-w*^{a}.
3	ओसु *ōs*^{u}.	आसॖ *ạs*^{ŭ}.	आसि *ạs*^{i}.	आस *ās*^{a}.

Negative form ओसुसन *ōsu-s-n*^{a}, &c., see p. 11.

Interrogative form ओसुसा *ōsu-s-ā*, &c., see p. 12.

Negative-interrogative form ओसुसना *ōsu-s-nā*, &c., see p. 14.

Emphatic form ओसुस्ति *ōsu-s-ti*, &c., see p. 14.

Emphatic-interrogative form ओसुस्त्या *ōsu-s-ty-ā*, &c., see p. 14.

These verbs take the usual pronominal suffixes. The following are examples.

सुह् छुम् *suh chu-m*, he is to me, *est mihi*, I have him.

स छय् *s^a* *chŏ-y*, she is to thee, thou hast her.

तिम् छिस् *tim chi-s*, they are to him, he has them.

सुह् ओसुम *suh ōsu-m*, he was to me, I had him.

स आस्स् *s^a ạ̄s^a-s*, she was to him, he had her.

Any other tenses required of the auxiliary verb are formed (like the past) regularly from the root आस *ās*, be. Thus, Future आसि *āsi*, he will be. It is unnecessary to give these forms.

THE CONJUGATION OF THE ACTIVE VERB.

Verbal Nouns.

THE INFINITIVE. This is formed by adding उन् *un*, उनु *un*^{u}, or अंनु *ạn*^{u} to the root. It is an abstract noun. Its formation is fully described in the chapter on Primary Suffixes. See Nos. 16, 17, 18 (*ante* Vol. lxvii, pp. 202 and ff.) Examples are करुन् *karun*, करुनु *karun*^{u}, and करंनु *karạn*^{u}, to make, making (ix. ii. 2, 3).

करुन् *karun*, belongs to the first declension, and the other two to the second. All are masculine. They are declined as follows.

Singular.	Nom.	करुन् *karun*.	करुनु *karun*^{u} or करंनु *karạn*^{u}.
	Acc.	करनस् *karanas*.	Not used.
	Ag.	करनन् *karanan*.	करॖनि *kar*^{a}*n*^{i}.
	Obl.	करन *karan*^{a}.	करनि *karani*.
Plural.	Nom.	करन् *karan*.	करॖनि *kar*^{a}*n*^{i}.
	Acc.	करनन् *karanan*.	Not used.
	Ag.	करनौ *karanau*.	Not used.
	Obl.	करनौ *karanau*.	Not used.

The various cases are used as gerunds. Thus, Dat. करनस् क्युतु *karanas kyut*^{u}, for making. The oblique form in अनि *ani*, is specially used to indicate intention (ix. i. 18). Thus, परनि गछान् छुह् *parani gatshān chuh*, he is going to read; रननि गौव् *ranani gauv*, he went to cook; खेनि गछि *khĕni gatshi*, he will go to eat.

Roots ending in vowels form the Infinitive only in अंनु *ạn*^{u} (ix. i. 21, 24). Thus, from खि *khi*, eat, ख्यंनु *khyạn*^{u}; from चि *ci*, drink, च्यंनु *cyạn*^{u}. This applies only to the nominative singular. Thus, Acc. Sing., ख्यनस् *khyanas*. As usual, नि *ni*, take; दि *di*, give: and यि *yi*, come, are exceptions. Their Infinitives are निनु (न्युनु) *nyun*^{u}, Acc. Sing., निनस् *ninas*, or निनिस् *ninis*, and so on for the other two.

The following verbs have feminine infinitives. They never use the ordinary masculine forms (ix. ii. 24, 25).

त्सर *tsar*, be inwardly wrathful. Infinitive त्सरिञ् *tsariñ*, to be so.
त्सुव *tsuv*, quarrel. „ त्सुविञ् *tsuviñ*, to quarrel.
मोरव *mōrav*, bear pain. „ मोरवॖञ् *morav*^{a}*ñ*, to bear pain.
मर्त्स *marts*, be impatient. „ मर्त्सॖञ् *marts*^{a}*ñ*, to be impatient.

The verbs खॖस *kh*^{a}*s*, pluck the hair; फित्स *phits*, forget; फॊश *phōç*, be inwardly angry; फुह *phuh*, be inwardly angry; वशव *wazav*, moisten; and वुत्स *wuts*, be burned, may either have a masculine infinitive in उनु *un*, etc., or a feminine one in ॖञ् ^{a}*ñ* (ix. ii. 25, 26). Thus, खॖसुनु *k*^{a}*sun* or खॖसॖञ् *k*^{a}*s*^{a}*ñ*, to pluck the hair (*sensu obscœno*). A great many other verbs also optionally form abstract nouns of the feminine gender. These are all described under the head of primary suffixes.

Nouns of Agency. There are three forms of these. The first is made by adding अवुनु *awun*^{u}, to the root. Thus, करवुनु *karawun*^{u}, a doer (ix. i. 25–27). If the root ends in इ *i*, अव *aw* is inserted, and the इ *i* is changed to य *y*. Thus, खि *khi*, eat, ख्यववुनु *khyawawun*^{u}, a doer. Exceptions, as usual, are नि *ni*, take; दि *di*, give; and यि *yi*, come. These form their nouns of agency as follows, निववुनु *niwawun*^{u}, a taker, and so on for the other two. The feminine of करवुनु *karawun*^{u} is करवॊञ् *karawọñ*, and the noun is thus declined. See article on Primary Suffixes, No. 4, (Vol. lxvii, p. 195).

		Masculine.	Feminine.
Singular.	Nom.	करवुनु *karawun*^{u}.	करवॊञ् *karawọñ*.
	Acc.	करवनिस् *karawanis*.	करवञॆ *karawañĕ*.
	Ag.	करवॖनि *karaw*^{a}*n*^{i}.	करवञि *karawañi*.
Plural.	Nom.	करवॖनि *karaw*^{a}*n*^{i}.	करवञॆ *karawañĕ*.
	Acc.	करवन्यन् *karawunyan*.	करवञन् *karawañan*.
	Ag.	करवन्यौ *karawanyau*.	करवञौ *karawañau*.

The second form of the Noun of Agency is made by adding अन्वोलु *anwōl*^{u}, to the root (ix. i. 28–31). Thus, करन्वोलु *karanwōl*^{u}, a doer. An example of a verb ending in a vowel is ख्यनवोलु *khyanawōl*^{u}, in which अ *a* is inserted before वोलु *wōl*^{u}. As an example of नि *ni*, दि *di*, and यि *yi*, we may give निनवोलु *ninawōl*^{u}. Sometimes वोलु *wōl*^{u} can be added to a feminine abstract noun, thus, ज्ञान्वोलु *säñwōl*^{u}, a knower. Regarding these see the article on Primary Suffixes, Nos. 5 and 6, (Vol. lxvii, p. 196).

The feminine of करन्वोलु *karanwōl*^{u} is करन्वाज्यन् *karanwājĕñ*, and the noun is thus declined.

		MASCULINE.	FEMININE.
Singular.	Nom.	करन्वोलु *karanwōl*^{u}.	करन्वाज्यन् *karanwājĕñ*.
	Acc.	करन्वालिस् *karanwālis*.	करन्वाज्यनि *karanwājĕñĕ*.
	Ag.	करन्वालि *karanwāl*^{i}.	करन्वाज्यनि *karanājĕñi*.
Plural.	Nom.	करन्वालि *karanwāl*^{i}.	करन्वाज्यनि *karanwājĕñĕ*.
	Acc.	करन्वाल्यन् *karanwālyan*.	करन्वाज्यनन् *karanwājĕñan*.
	Ag.	करन्वाल्यौ *karanwālyau*.	करन्वाज्यनौ *karanwājĕñau*.

The third form of the Noun of Agency is made by adding अन्ग्राख् *angrākh* to the root (ix. i. 28–31). Thus, करन्ग्राख् *karangrākh*, a doer. The feminine is करन्ग्राकन् *karangrākañ* (vi. 28). It is declined regularly. Thus, Acc. Sing., masc. करन्ग्राकस् *karangrākas*, fem., करन्ग्राकनि *karangrākañĕ*. Verbs ending in vowels have the same irregularities as in the second form. Thus, ख्यनग्राख् *khyanagrākh*, an eater, निनग्राख् *ninagrākh*, a taker.

Verbal Adjectives, or Participles.

These are Present, Future, or Past. The Past Participles are either Verbal or Adjectival. Verbal Past Participles are the original Past Participles of the verb, but are not now used as participles. Nowadays they are only used as bases for the formation of Past tenses. Adjectival Past Participles are modern formations from the Verbal Past Participles, and are nowadays the only forms used as participles proper. Verbal Past Participles have three forms, *viz.*, the Past, the Aorist, and the Pluperfect.

The Present Participle. This Participle is an active one. It has been fully described under the head of Primary Suffixes, (No. 1; Vol. lxvii, p. 193). The following *resumé* is given for the sake of convenience. It is formed by adding

आन् *ān* to the root (viii. i. 19; ix. i. 2). Thus, कर् *kar*, make, Pres. Part. करान् *karān*. It does not change for gender or number.

The roots नि *ni*, take, दि *di*, give, and यि *yi*, come, take वान् *wān*, thus निवान् *niwān*, दिवान् *diwān*, यिवान् *yiwān*. Other roots ending in इ *i* change the इ *i* to य *ya*, and add वान् *wān*. Thus, खि *khi*, eat, Pres. Part. ख्यवान् *khyawān*, चि *ci*, drink, च्यवान् *cyawān* (viii. i. 19, 20; ix. i. 3).

When a Present Participle is repeated, it means that the thing is done frequently (ix. i. 4). Thus दिवान् दिवान् गौव् *diwān diwān gauv*, he kept giving as he went.

The Future Participle. This is a passive Participle, equivalent to the Latin Future Participle in *-endus*, or the Sanskrit Participle in अनीयः *anīyaḥ*. It is the same in form as the Infinitive in उन् *un*, उनु *un*^{u} or अंनु *ąn*^{u}. Thus, यिह् पाठ् छुह् परुन् *yih pāṭh chuh parun*, this lesson is to be read, *ayaṁ pāṭhaḥ paṭhanīyaḥ*. यिह् पुथि छेह् परंञ् *yih pūth*^{i} *chĕh parąñ*, this book is to be read, *iyaṁ pustikā paṭhanīyā*. In the case of Intransitive Verbs, the participle takes an impersonal passive signification. Thus, चलुन् *tsalun*, it is to be fled, *calanīyam*, तस् छुह् चलुन् *tas chuh tsalun*, it is to be fled by him, he must flee. Note that the Agent is always put in the Accusative (which is an old Dative), and not in the Agent case, as we might expect. For further particulars regarding the use of this Future Participle, see the article on Primary Suffixes, Nos. 16–18, (Vol. lxvii, pp. 204 and ff.)

The Future Impersonal Participle. Another impersonal Future Participle Passive is formed by adding अनी *anī* to the root (ix. i. 50). It is formed with both Transitive and Intransitive verbs. Thus तस् करनी *tas karanī*, it is to be done by him, he must do; तस् पकनी *tas pakanī*, he must go. See Primary Suffix No. 14 (Vol. lxvii, p. 201).

The Verbal Past Participle. These will be fully dealt with when describing the past tenses. Suffice it at present to say that the Past Verbal Past Participle only occurs in the first and second conjugations, and is formed by adding उ *u-mātrā* to the root. Thus, first conjugation, कंरु *kąr*^{u}, done; second conjugation, चंलु *tsąl*^{u}, gone. In the case of verbs of the first conjugation, it is a Passive Participle, and in the case of verbs of the second conjugation, which are all intransitive, it is a Neuter Participle. See also article on Primary Suffixes, (No. 10; Vol. lxvii, p. 197). This Past Participle refers to something which has lately happened.

Aorist Verbal Past Participle. This will also be fully dealt with when describing the Aorist Tense. It is formed by adding योव् *yōv* or यौव् *yauv*, to the root. Thus, कर्योव् *karyōv* or कर्यौव् *karyauv*, done. The Participle occurs for all conjugations, with this difference, that in the first and second conjugations it is an Aorist or Indefinite Past, and contains no idea of proximity or remoteness of time. In the case of verbs of the third conjugation, which have no Verbal Past Participle, it is used instead of that Participle, and refers to something which has lately happened. See, also, Primary Suffix, No. 11, (Vol. lxvii, p. 198).

Pluperfect Verbal Past Participle. This will also be fully dealt with when describing the Pluperfect tense. It is formed by adding याव् *yāv* to the root. Thus, कर्याव् *karyāv*, done. In the case of verbs of the first and second conjugations it implies that the action has taken place a long time ago. In the case of verbs of the third conjugation it takes the place of the Aorist Participle, the proper form of which has been used up for the Past. These verbs have a special form for the true Pluperfect Participle, which need not be described here.

The Adjectival Past Participle. These are formed by adding the termination मतु *mat°* or मुतु *mut°*, to a verbal Past Participle. In the case of verbs of the first and second conjugations, this is added to the Past Participle in ॖ *u-mātrā*, and in the case of verbs of the third conjugation to the Aorist Participle in योव् *yōv* or यौव् *yauv*, the final व् *v* of which is elided. Both members of the compound thus formed are liable to changes of inflexion and gender (ix. i. 40). See also article on Primary Suffixes, (No. 12; Vol. lxvii, p. 198). Examples are,—

First Conjugation.

कॖरमतु *kar°mat°*, or कॖरमुतु *kar°mut°*, made; which is thus declined.

Singular.

	Masc.	Fem.
Nom.	कॖरमतु *kar°mat°* or कॖरमुतु *kar°mut°*.	कॖरमॖचॖ *kar°matsa°*.
Acc.	कॖरिमतिस् *kar'matis*.	करॆमचॆ *karĕmatsĕ*.
Ag.	कॖरिमति *kar'mat'*.	करिमचि *karimatsi*.

PLURAL.

	Masc.	Fem.
Nom.	करिमंति *kạr*^{i}*mạt*^{i}.	करेमच *karĕmaṭs*^{a}.
Acc.	करिमत्यन् *kạr*^{i}*matyan.*	करेमच्रन् *karĕmaṭsan.*
Ag.	करिमत्यौ *kạr*^{i}*matyau.*	करेमच्रौ *karĕmaṭsau.*

SECOND CONJUGATION.

बुवुमंतु *bŏv*^{u}*mạt*^{u}, or बुवुमुतु *bŏv*^{u}*mut*^{u}, become.

Singular.	Masc.	बुवुमंतु *bŏv*^{u}*mạt*^{u}.
	Fem.	बुवुमंचु *bŏv*^{u}*maṭs*^{a}.
Plural.	Masc.	बुविमंति *bŏv*^{i}*mạt*^{i}.
	Fem.	बुवमच *bŏvĕmaṭs*^{a}.

THIRD CONJUGATION.

व्योमंतु *vyaṭhyŏmạt*^{u}, व्यौमंतु *vyaṭhyaumạt*^{u}, व्योमुतु *vyaṭhyŏmut*^{u}, or व्यौमुतु *vyaṭhyaumut*^{u}, become fat, from व्य *vyaṭh*, be fat. It is thus declined,—

SINGULAR.

	Masc.	Fem.
Nom.	व्योमंतु *vyaṭhyŏmạt*^{u}, &c.	व्येमंचु *vyaṭhyĕmaṭs*^{a}.
Acc.	व्येमतिस् *vyaṭhyĕmatis.*	व्येमच् *vyaṭhyĕmaṭsĕ.*
Ag.	व्येमंति *vyaṭhyĕmạt*^{i}.	व्येमचि *vyaṭhyĕmaṭsi.*

PLURAL.

	Masc.	Fem.
Nom.	व्येमंति *vyaṭhyĕmạt*^{i}.	व्येमच *vyaṭhyĕmaṭs*^{a}.
Acc.	व्येमत्यन् *vyaṭhyĕmatyan.*	व्येमच्रन् *vyaṭhyĕmaṭsan.*
Ag.	व्येमत्यौ *vyaṭhyĕmatyau.*	व्येमच्रौ *vyaṭhyĕmaṭsau.*

Verbal Adverbs, or Conjunctive Participles.

There are two of these, a Present and a Past.

The PRESENT CONJUNCTIVE PARTICIPLE. This is formed from the Present Participle by adding ि *i-mātrā*, and modifying the preceding long आ *ā*. Thus, from कर *kar*, make, Present Participle, करान् *karān*,

Present Conjunctive Participle, करॉणि *karạn*^{i}, on making, at the time of making. It is used in sentences like the following सुह् करॉणि गौव् *suh karạn*^{i} *gauv*, he went away as he was doing it. This form is not mentioned by Īçvara-kaula, and, according to my paṇḍit, is only used by rustics. It is more elegant to use the simple Present Participle. Thus, सुह् करान् गौव् *suh karān gauv*.

The Past Conjunctive Participle. This form corresponds to the Sanskrit Conjunctive Participle in त्वा *tvā*, or य *ya* (त्य *tya*), and means 'having done so and so.' It is fully described in the Article on Primary Suffixes, (No. 2; Vol. lxvii, p. 193), and the more important information there given is here repeated for the sake of convenience. It is formed by adding इथ् *ith* or इथ् क्याथ् *ith kyāth*, to the root. Thus, करिथ् *karith*, having made, परिथ् *parith*, having read. So also करिथ् क्याथ् *karith kyāth*, having made, and परिथ् क्याथ् *parith kyāth*, having read (ix. i. 5, 6).

Before this suffix a radical आ *ā* is modified, a radical ए *ē* becomes ई *ī*, and a radical ओ *ō* becomes ऊ *ū* (ix. i. 13–15). Thus,—

From—

कार् *kār*, boil.	कॉरिथ् *kạrith*, having boiled.
मार् *mār*, beat.	मॉरिथ् *mạrith*, having beaten.
तार् *tār*, pass over.	तॉरिथ् *tạrith* having passed over.
छेट् *tsēṭ*, pound to powder.	छीटिथ् *tsīṭith*, having pounded to powder.
लेख् *lēkh*, write.	लीखिथ् *līkhith*, having written.

[So also—

ब्यह् *byah*, sit.	बिहिथ् *bihith*, having sat].
खोछ *khōts*, fear.	खुछिथ् *khutsith*, having feared.
बोज़् *bōs*, hear.	बूज़िथ् *būsith*, having heard.
तोल् *tōl*, weigh.	तूलिथ् *tūlith*, having weighed.

Roots ending in vowels, form their Conjunctive Participle as follows (ix. i. 7, 8).

खि *khi*, eat.	ख्याथ् *khyāth*, having eaten.
चि *ci*, drink.	च्याथ् *cyāth*, having drunk.

हि *hi*, take. ह्यथ् *hyăth*, having taken.

सि *si*, be born. स्यथ् *syăth*, having been born.

पि *pi*, fall. प्यथ् *pyăth*, having fallen.

But—

दि *di*, give. दिथ् *dith*, having given.

नि *ni*, take. निथ् *nith*, having taken.

यि *yi*, come. यिथ् *yith*, having come.

So also, ख्यथ् क्यथ् *khyăth kyăth*, &c.

The following are irregular,—

वुड *wuḍ*, fly, when it means to obtain salvation (*mōkṣa*) makes वुजिथ् *wujith*. Thus, वुजिथ् गौव् *wujith gauv*, having obtained salvation, he went, *i.e.*, he went to heaven, but वुडिथ् गौव् *wuḍith gauv*, having flown, he went, *i.e.*, he flew away (ix. i. 9).

The causal verb मंश्राव *maṣᵃrāw*, cause to forget, makes माशविथ् *māṣawith*, when the object forgotten is death. Thus, मरुन् माशविथ् *marun māṣawith*, having caused to forget death. If anything else is forgotten, it is मंश्राविथ् *maṣᵃrāwith*, regularly (ix. i. 10).

When the Conjunctive Participle is repeated, to imply continuous action, the थ् *th* is dropped, and the final *i* becomes *i-mātrā* (ix. i. 11, 12). Thus,—

करि करि *kọrⁱ kọrⁱ*, having made, having made, *i.e.*, having kept making.

बूसि बूसि *būsⁱ, būsⁱ*, having kept hearing.

कारि कारि *kọ̄rⁱ kọ̄rⁱ*, having kept boiling.

तारि तारि *tārⁱ tārⁱ*, having continued passing people over.

Verbs ending in vowels optionally retain the थ् *th*. Thus, खे खे *khĕ khĕ*, or ख्यथ् ख्यथ् *khyăth khyăth*, having kept eating. दि दि *di di*, or दिथ् दिथ् *dith dith*, having kept giving.

Negative Conjunctive Participle. This is formed by adding अनय् *anay* to the root (ix. i. 51). Thus, करनय् *karanay*, not having done. See Primary Suffix, No. 14, (Vol. lxvii, p. 201).

A. Indicative Mood.

1. Present Tense.

The same form is used both for the Definite, the Habitual, and the Indefinite Present (viii. i. 7–10). Thus, परान् छुह् *parān chuh*, he is reading, or he is in the habit of reading, or he reads. So we have,—

ईश्वर् जगतस् रछान् छुह् *Īçwar sagatas rachān chuh*, God protects the world.

पान पानस् रछान् छुह् *pānᵃ pānas rachān chuh*, by himself (*i.e.*, by his own power) he protects himself. *Ātmanā atmānaṁ pālayati.*

व्याकरन् परान् छुह् लड़कु *myākaraṇ parān chuh lŏkutᵘ*, the boy is reading (*i.e.*, has arrived at that stage of his studies) grammar.

गङ्गाय गछान् छुह् प्रथ् कुंभस् *gaŋgāyᵃ gatshān chuh prăth kumbas.* He visits (is in the habit of visiting) the Ganges at every *kumbha* festival.

क्याह् छुह् मूर्त करान् *kyāh chuh murts karān*, does he make images? (is that his profession?)

क्याह् छुह् जान् लेखान् *kyāh chuh jān lĕkhān*, is the holy man writing (and going on writing)?

क्याह् छुह् रतु ग्यवान् *kyāh chuh rətᵘ gyawān*, is the good man singing?

This tense is found by adding the Present Tense of the auxiliary verb to the Present Participle of the principal verb, which does not change for gender or number. It is therefore thus conjugated.

I make, or *am making*.

	Singular.		Plural.	
Person.	Masculine.	Feminine.	Masculine.	Feminine.
1	करान् छुस् *karān chus.*	करान् छस् *karān chĕs.*	करान् छिह् *karān chih.*	करान् छह् *karān chĕh.*
2	करान् छुख् *karān chukh.*	करान् छख् *karān chĕkh.*	करान् छिव *karān chiwᵉ.*	करान् छव *karān chĕwᵉ.*
3	करान् छुह् *karān chuh.*	करान् छह् *karān chĕh.*	करान् छिह् *karān chih.*	करान् छह् *karān chĕh.*

33

Negative form, करान् छुस्न *karān chusn*^{a}, I do not make, &c., see p. 11.

Interrogative form, करान् छुसा *karān chusā*, करान् छुस *karān chus*^{a}, &c., do I make? see p. 12.

Negative Interrogative form, करान् छुस्ना *karān chusnā*, &c., do I not make? see p. 14.

Emphatic form, करान् छुस्ति *karān chusti*, &c., I do indeed make, see p. 14.

Emphatic Interrogative form, करान् छुस्त्या *karān chustyā*, &c., do I indeed make? see p. 14.

In this, and in other periphrastic tenses, it is elegant to put the auxiliary before the verb (viii. i. 22, 23, 24) when standing in a sentence. Thus,—

> बत छुह् सुह् ख्यवान् *bat*^{a} *chuh suh khyawān*, he is eating rice, is more elegant than बत सुह् ख्यवान् छुह् *bat*^{a} *suh khyawān chuh*, though both are correct.
>
> तव पत छुह् आसनस् प्यठ् बिहिथ् पूज़ा करान् *taw*^{a} *pat*^{a} *chuh āsanas pyăṭh bihith pūzā karān*, after that; he is doing worship having sat down on a seat, is more elegant than तव पत आसनस् प्यठ् बिहिथ् पूज़ा करान् छुह् *taw*^{a} *pat*^{a} *āsanas pyăṭh bihith pūzā karān chuh*, though both are correct.

So the following is the most elegant order,—ईश्वर छुह् आसान् काशिय अंदर *īçwar chuh āsān kāçiy*^{a} *andar*, God exists in Benares. When, however, the verb stands by itself as in the paradigm, the auxiliary always follows.

The following are examples of the use of pronominal suffixes, (pp. 15 and ff)—

> बुह् छुसथ् करान् *bŏh chus-ath karān*, I make thee (viii. i. 37).
>
> असि छिथ् करान् *as*^{i} *chi-th karān*, we make thee.
>
> बुह् छुसन् करान् *bŏh chus-an karān*, I make him.
>
> बुह् छुसस् करान् *bŏh chus-as karān*, I make for him.
>
> बुह् छुसव करान् *bŏh chus-aw*^{a} *karān*, I make you.
>
> बुह् छुसख् करान् *bŏh chus-akh karān*, I make them.

Similarly for the other persons, which are all regular, except सुह् छुस् करान् *suh chu-s karān*, he makes him, or for him (not छुन् *chu-n*) (see p. 19).

2. Imperfect Tense.

This tense is not described by *Īçvara-kaula*. It is formed exactly like the Present, except that the Past tense of the Auxiliary Verb is used instead of the Present. Thus,—

I was making.

	Singular.		Plural.	
Person.	Masculine.	Feminine.	Masculine.	Feminine.
1	करान् ओसुस् *karān ōsus.*	करान् आसूस् *karān ạsᵃs.*	करान् आसि *karān ạsⁱ.*	करान् आस *karān āsᵉ.*
2	करान् ओसुख् *karān ōsukh.*	करान् आसूख् *karān ạsᵃkh.*	करान् आसिव *karān ạsⁱwᵉ.*	करान् आसव *karān āsᵉwᵉ.*
3	करान् ओसु *karān ōsᵘ.*	करान् आसू *karān ạsᵃ.*	करान् आसि *karān ạsⁱ.*	करान् आस *karān āsᵉ.*

The various adverbial suffixes are added as in the case of the Present Tense. They will be found in detail under the paradigm of the auxiliary verb, and need not be repeated here. One example will suffice. करान् ओसुसन *karān ōsusnᵉ*, I was not making. As in the case of the Present, in a formal sentence, it is more elegant to place the auxiliary before the present participle. Thus, बत ओसु सुह् ख्यवान् *batᵉ ōsᵘ suh khyawān*, he was eating rice.

Pronominal suffixes are added as in the Present. Thus,—

बुह् ओसुसथ् करान् *bŏh ōsus-ath karān*, I was making thee.
असि आसिथ् करान् *asⁱ ạsi-th karān*, we were making thee.
बुह् ओसुसय् करान् *bŏh ōsus-ay karān*, I was making for thee.
बुह् ओसुसन् करान् *bŏh ōsus-an karān*, I was making him.
बुह् ओसुसस् करान् *bŏh ōsus-as karān*, I was making for him.
बुह् ओसुसव करान् *bŏh ōsus-awᵉ karān*, I was making you.
बुह् ओसुसख् करान् *bŏh ōsusakh karān*, I was making them.
सुह् ओसुस् करान् *suh ōsu-s karān*, he was making him or for him.
(not ओसुन् *ōsu-n*).

And so others.

3. Future Tense.

This tense is conjugated as follows (viii. ii. 28).

	Singular.	Plural.
1	कर *kar*ᵃ, I shall make.	करव् *karav*, we shall make.
2	करख् *karakh*, thou wilt make.	करिव् *kariv*, you will make.
3	करि *kari*, he will make.	करन् *karan*, they will make.

Roots ending in vowels insert म् *m* in the first person of both numbers. Before इ *i*, they insert य् *y*. As usual, all roots ending in इ *i*, except नि *ni*, take, दि *di*, give, and यि *yi*, come, change the final इ *i* of the root to य *ya* (29). We thus get for the future of खि *khi*, eat,—

	Singular.	Plural.
1	ख्यम *khyam*ᵃ.	ख्यमव् *khyamav*.
2	ख्यख् *khyakh*.	ख्ययिव् *khĕyiv*.
3	ख्ययि *khĕyi*.	ख्यन् *khyan*.

From दि *di*, give, we have,—

	Singular.	Plural.
1	दिम *dim*ᵃ.	दिमव् *dimav*.
2	दिख् *dikh*.	दियिव् *diyiv*.
3	दियि *diyi*.	दिन् *din*.

This tense has a special interrogative form, which is thus conjugated (30, 31).

	Singular.	Plural.
1	करा *karā*, shall I do or make.	करव *karaw*ᵃ.
2	करख *karakh*ᵃ.	करिव *kariw*ᵃ.
3	कर्यो *karyā*.	करन *karan*ᵃ.

Pronominal suffixes are added to this tense as usual, except that the third person singular is slightly irregular, being कर्येम् *karyam* (he will make me), &c., not करिम् *karim*, &c. (viii. ii. 29). So कर्येस् *karyas*, not करिस् *karis*, and all other suffixes added to this person of this tense. When, however, the suffixes of the second person is added there is no irregularity. Thus, करिय् *kariy*, not कर्येय् *karyay*. Remember that final

36

ख् *kh* becomes ह् *h* before a suffix. We thus get the following forms which will do as samples.

Added to first person,—

करस् *kara-s*, I shall make for him.

करन् *kara-n*, I shall make him.

करोस् *karō-s*, we shall make for him.

करोन् *karō-n*, we shall make him.

Added to second person,—

करहस् *karah-as*, thou wilt make for him.

करहन् *karah-an*, thou wilt make him.

कर्यूस् *karyū-s*, you will make for him.

Added to third person,—

कर्यम् *kary-am*, he will make me.

करिय् *kari-y*, he will make thee or for thee. (It should be remembered that the suffix अथ् *ath* is not used with the third person).

करिव *kari-wᵉ*, he will make you or for you.

कर्यस् *kary-as*, he will make him, or for him. (अस् *as* is not used with the third person).

कर्यख् *kary-akh*, he will make them or for them.

करनस् *karan-as*, they will make him or for him.

करनख् *karan-akh*, they will make them or for them.

Interrogative forms would be such as करस *kara-s-ᵉ*, shall I make for him?

The feminine impersonal verbs ज़र *ṭsar*, to be inwardly wrathful, &c. (see pp. 16 and 22), are thus conjugated, this tense making no distinction between masculine and feminine.

ज़र्यम् *ṭsary-am*, there will be inward anger to me. I shall be inwardly angry.

असि ज़रि *asi ṭsari*, we shall be inwardly angry.

ज़रिय् *ṭsari-y*, thou wilt be inwardly angry.

ज़रिव *ṭsari-wᵉ*, you will be inwardly angry.

शर्यस् *tsary-as*, he will be inwardly angry.

शर्यख् *tsary-akh*, they will be inwardly angry.

On the Past Tenses Generally.

Kāçmīrī has three Simple (as distinct from Periphrastic) Past Tenses,—the Past, the Aorist, and the Pluperfect.

There are three conjugations of verbs in these tenses. The first conjugation includes all active and impersonal verbs.

The second conjugation includes the following neuter (viii. iii. 77–97) verbs,—

1. थक *thak*, be weary.
2. पक *pak*, go.
3. समख *samakh*, become visible, be seen, meet a person.
4. ह्वख *hŏkh*, become dry.
5. तग *tag*, be possible, be known how to be done.
6. लग *lag*, be with, suffer pain, fit.
7. शंग *çŏng*, lie down, go to sleep.
8. क्‌श *kᵃts*, be wet.
9. खोश *khots*, fear.
10. पश *pats*, trust with a loan.
11. रोश *rōts*, be preferred.
12. व्यश *vyats*, pervade, fit into.
13. ह्वश *hŏts*, go bad, decay.
14. गछ *gatsh*, be proper (गछ *gatsh*, go, belongs to the third conjugation).
15. व्वपज़ *wŏpas*, be born.
16. दज़ *das*, be burnt.
17. रोज़ *rōs*, stop, stand.
18. फट *phat*, split (of wood), sprout (of a plant), sink into water.
19. फुट *phut*, be broken.
20. रोट *rōt*, be stopped (also third conjugation).
21. बुड *bŏḍ*, dive, sink.
22. वात *wāt*, arrive.
23. व्वथ *wŏth*, stand up.
24. छ्यन *tshyann*, be bored, be torn, be split.
25. सपन *sapan*, सपज़ *sapas*, or सपद् *sapad*, be complete.
26. वुप *wup*, burn inside (see below).
27. श्रप *çrap*, evaporate, be digested be soaked up (see below).
28. प्रय *pray*, be pleased.
29. लय *lay*, be worth.
30. वय *way*, be fit to eat, agree with, suit.
31. खर *khar*, be disliked.
32. तर *tar*, be crossed.
33. फर *phar*, be stolen, be a cause of loss to.
34. फेर *phĕr*, go round, rot, regret, be inverted.
35. मर *mar* die, (मऱ *mar*. unite,

belongs optionally (viii. iii. 91) to the first conjugation).

36. सोर *sōr*, be spent, exhausted (of things).
37. गल *gal*, melt.
38. चल *ṭsal*, flee, escape.
39. डल *ḍal*, pass over.
40 डोल *ḍōl*, be unused.
41. फल *phal*, bear fruit, become old (of clothes), be divided.
42. फ्वल *phȍll*, expand (of a flower).
43. मेल *mēl*, meet, be met by a person.
44. ब्वव *bȍv*, be born, grow.
45. राव *rāv*, be lost.
46. दष *dȍṣ*, trickle.
47. पोष *pōṣ*, be competent, victorious.
48. मष *maṣ*, forget.
49. रोष *rōṣ*, be angry.
50. आस *ās*, be.
51. खस *khas*, mount, ascent.
52. फस *phas*, be entangled, caught.
53. बस *bas*, dwell.
54. लस *las*, live long, live in good health.
55. लोस *lōs*, be weary.
56. वस *was*, come down, descend.
57. ब्यह *byah*, sit.

Of the above, the verb रोट *rōṭ*, be stopped, may optionally be conjugated in the third conjugation (viii. iii. 84). Thus,—

2nd Conjugation.	Past Participle,		रुटु *rüṭ**
	Aorist	„	रोच्योव् *rōcyōv*.
	Pluperfect	„	रोच्याव् *rōcyāv*.
3rd Conjugation.	Aorist	„ in sense of Past	रोट्योव् *rōṭyōv*.
	Pluperfect	„ „ Aorist	रोट्याव् *rōṭyāv*.
	True Pluperfect	„	रोटियाव् *rōṭiyāv*.

The verbs वुप *wup*, burn inside, and ग्रप *grap*, be digested, optionally form their Pluperfect after the manner of the third conjugation (viii. iii. 89). Thus,—

2nd Conjugation.	Pluperfect Participle	वुप्याव् *wupyāv*,
		ग्रप्याव् *grapyāv*.
3rd Conjugation.	True Pluperfect Participle	वुपियाव् *wupiyāv*,
		ग्रपियाव् *grapiyāv*.

The above 57 verbs are those given by Īçvara-kaula in the *Bhūta-pāda* of the *Ākhyāta-prakriyā* of his Grammar (viii. iii. 77–97), but the following are added to the second conjugation by my Paṇḍit.

58. पलस *palas*, be useful.

59. पलट *palaṭ*, melt, deliquesce.

60. पुन *pun*, come true (of a curse).

61. प्रार *prār*, wait.

62. फोर *phōr*, quiver.

63. नश *naç*, disappear.

64. तोष *tōṣ*, be satisfied.

65. बास *bās*, become clear, evident.

66. ववस *wŏbas*, increase.

The third conjugation includes all other neuter verbs, except those used impersonally.

I shall now describe each of the Past tenses separately.

4 (*a*). The Verbal Past Participle.

This Participle, from which, as will be seen, the Past Tense is derived, is formed by adding ु *u-mātrā* to the root. Thus, कर *kar*, do; Past Participle कॖरु *kạr*^{u}. Its feminine singular is formed by changing *u-mātrā* to *ū-mātrā*. Thus, कॖरू *kạr*^{ū}. The masculine plural by changing the *u-mātrā* to *i-mātrā*. Thus, कॖरि *kar*^{i}, and the feminine plural by changing the *ū-mātrā* to य *y*^{a} (*ĕ*), thus, करे *karĕ*. Before the *mātrā*-vowels, the root-vowel of the verb is liable to modifications. But (this is important) before the य *y*^{a} (*ĕ*) of the feminine plural, there is no modification. The modifications caused by *mātrā*-vowels are as follows,—

If the root-vowel is *a*, before *u-mātrā*, it becomes *ạ* (*o*). Thus, कर *kar*, make, कॖरु *kạr*^{u}, pronounced *kor*, he (was) made (viii. iii. 19).

If the root-vowel is *a*, before *ū-mātrā*, it becomes *ạ* (*ü*). Thus, कॖरू *kạr*^{ū}, pronounced *kür*, she (was) made (viii. iii. 19).

If the root-vowel is *a*, before *i-mātrā*, it becomes *ạ* (*a*^{i}). Thus, कॖरि *kạr*^{i}, pronounced *ka*^{i}*r*^{i}, they (masc.) (were) made (viii. iii. 19).

If the root-vowel is *ā*, before *u-mātrā*, it becomes *ō*. Thus, मार *mār*, kill, मोरु *mōr*^{u}, he (was) killed (viii. iii. 20).

If the root-vowel is *ā*, before *ū-mātrā*, it becomes *ạ̄* (*ŏ*). Thus, माॖरू *mạ̄r*^{ū}, pronounced *mör*, she (was) killed (viii. iii. 19).

If the root-vowel is *ā*, before *i-mātra* it becomes *ạ̄* (*ŏ*^{i}). Thus, माॖरि *mạr*^{i}, pronounced *mö*^{i}*r*^{i}, they (masc.) (were) killed (viii. iii. 19).

If the root-vowel is *i*, before *u-mātrā* it becomes *yu*. Thus, लिव *lir*, plaster, ल्युवु *lyuv*^{u}, he (was) plastered.

If the root-vowel is *i*, before *ū-mātrā* it becomes *i* (pronounced *yü*). Thus, लिवू *liv*^{ū}, pronounced *lyüv*, she (was) plastered.

If the root-vowel is *i*, before *i-mātrā*, it is unchanged. Thus, लिवि *livⁱ*, they (masc.) (were) plastered.

If the root-vowel is *ī*, before *u-mātrā*, it becomes *yū*. Thus, चीर *cīr*, squeeze out, च्यूरु *cyūrᵘ*, he (was) squeezed out.

If the root-vowel is *ī*, before *ū-mātrā* it is unchanged. Thus, चीरू *cīrᵘ*, she (was) squeezed out.

If the root-vowel is *ī*, before *i-mātrā* it is unchanged. Thus, चीरि *cīrⁱ*, they (masc.) (were) squeezed out.

If the root-vowel *u* or *ū*, it always remains unchanged. Thus, from बुस *bus*, parch, बुसु *busᵘ*, बुसू *busᵘ*, बुसि *busⁱ*. From लूट *lūṭ*, rob, लूटु *lūṭᵘ*, लूटू *lūṭᵘ*, लूटि *lūṭⁱ*.

If the root-vowel is *ē*, before *u-mātrā*, it becomes *yū*. Thus, फेर *phēr*, be turned, फ्यूरु *phyūrᵘ*, he (was) turned (viii. iii. 21, 22).

If the root-vowel is *ē*, before *ū-mātrā*, it becomes *ī*. Thus, फीरू *phīrᵘ*, she (was) turned (viii. iii. 23).

If the root-vowel is *ē*, before *i-mātrā*, it becomes *ī*. Thus, फीरि *phīrⁱ*, they (were) turned (viii. iii. 21, 22).

If the root-vowel is *ō*, before *u-mātrā*, it becomes *ū*. Thus, बोस *bōs*, hear, बूसु *būsᵘ*, he (was) heard (viii. iii. 24).

If the root-vowel is *ō*, before *ū-mātrā*, it becomes *ū*. Thus, बूसू *būsᵘ*, she (was) heard (viii. iii. 25).

If the root-vowel is *ō*, before *i-mātrā*, it becomes *ū*. Thus, बूसि *būsⁱ*, they (masc.) (were) heard (viii. iii. 24).

Before ए *ĕ* or अ *a* of the feminine plural, the root-vowel is always unchanged. Thus, करे *karĕ*, मारे *mārĕ*, लिवे *livĕ*, चीरे *cīrĕ*, बुस *busᵃ*, फेरे *phērĕ*, बोस *bōsᵃ*.

When any pronominal suffix except व *wᵃ* is added to a form ending in a *mātrā*-vowel, that *mātrā*-vowel becomes fully pronounced, but the modification of the root-vowel remains unchanged. Thus, कॊरु *kọrᵘ* (pronounced *kor*) + न *n*, becomes कॊरुन *kọrun*, pronounced *korun*, and not *karun* or *korn*. So मोरु *mōrᵘ* + न becomes मोरुन *mōrun*, and so on. In such a case, *ū-mātrā* is pronounced as a short German *ü*. Thus, कॊरू *kọrᵘ* (pronounced *kür*) + न *n*, becomes *kọrᵘn*, pronounced *kürün*. If the suffix is

व w^a, the *mātrā*-vowel remains unchanged. Thus, करु + व *kạr*^{u} + *w*^{a}, he (was) made by you, becomes करुव *kạr*^{u}*w*^{a}, and is pronounced *korw*^{a}, and not *koruw*^{a}. So करू *kạr*^{ū} + व *w*^{a} made (fem.) by you, becomes करूव *kạr*^{ū}-*w*^{a}, and is pronounced *kürw*^{a}. Similarly, when a *mātrā*-vowel is followed by any other vocalised syllable, it remains a *mātrā*-vowel. Thus, करुनस् *kạr*^{u}-*n-as*, not करुनस् *kạrunas*, (was) made-by-him-I. Even in such cases, Īçvara-kaula (as in viii. iii. 3 and 4) writes करुव *kạruw*^{a}, लीखिव *likhiw*^{a}, &c., with the *mātrā*-vowel apparently fully pronounced, but in this he is, according to my Paṇḍit, incorrect, and it is a mere slip of the pen.

When, in the feminine plural, य y^a (*ĕ*) follows one of the letters च़् *ts*, छ़् *tsh*, स् *s*, or ञ् *ñ*, the y^a becomes अ ^{a} (viii. iii. 47). Thus, दिच़् *dits* + य y^a becomes दिच़अ *dits*^{a}, they (fem.) (were) given. So ह्योच़् *hĕts* + य y^a, becomes ह्योच़अ *hĕts*^{a}, they (fem.) (were) taken. So वाच़् *wāts* + य y^a becomes वाच़अ *wāts*^{a}, they (fem.) arrived, दज़् *daz* + य y^a becomes दज़अ *daz*^{a}, they (fem.) were burnt (viii. iii. 7, 12).

So also य् *y* is often elided after स् *s* (viii. iii. 13). Thus, आस् *ās* + य y^a, becomes आसअ *ās*^{a}, they (fem.) were. बस् *bas* + य y^a, बसअ *bas*^{a}, they (fem.) dwelt. Īçvara-kaula restricts this to verbs of the 2nd conjugation, but, according to my Paṇḍit, य् *y* is also elided after all verbs of the 1st conjugation, except in the case of च़स *tsas*, laugh loudly (impersonal). Thus, from कस *kas*, fry, feminine plural कसअ *kas*^{a}, but, from च़स *tsas*, च़स्य *tsasĕ*.

In the case of the following verbs of the 1st conjugation, the य् *y* may, according to my Paṇḍit, be optionally retained. थास *thās* bury; दस *das*, beat; मुस *mus*, eat improperly; सुस *s*^{u}*s*, break wind. Thus, थासअ *thās*^{a}, or थास्य *thāsĕ*.

It will be seen that the feminine of this participle ends in *ū-mātrā*, in y^a (*ĕ*), or in ^{a}. Before these terminations, the final consonant of the Past Participle undergoes certain changes. These changes only occur in the first and second conjugations. They are as follows :—

Final क् *k*, ख् *kh*, and ग् *g*, become च् *c*, छ् *ch*, and ज् *j* respectively, before both ू *ū-mātrā* and य *ya* (*ĕ*) (viii. iii. 7). Thus,—

From Root थक *thak*, be weary; *thạk^{u}*, he (was) weary; but *thạc^{ü}*, she (was) weary; *thacĕ*, they (fem.) (were) weary.

" " लेख *lekh*, write; *lyūkh^{u}*, he (was) written; but *lîch^{ü}*, she (was) written; *lechĕ*, they (fem.) (were) written.

" " दग *dag*, pound; *dạg^{u}*, he (was) pounded; but *dạj^{ü}*, she (was) pounded; *dajĕ*, they (fem.) (were) pounded.

ट् *ṭ*, ठ् *ṭh*, and ड् *ḍ*, become च् *c*, छ् *ch*, and ज् *j* respectively, before *y^{e}* (*ĕ*), but not before *ü-mātrā* (viii. iii. 70). Thus,—

From Root फट *phaṭ*, be split; *phaṭ^{u}*, he (was) split; *phạṭ^{ü}*, she (was) split; but *phacĕ*, they (fem.) (were) split.

" " मठ *maṭ*, forget; *mạṭh^{u}*, he (was) forgotten; *mạṭh^{ü}*, she (was) forgotten; but *machĕ*, they (fem.) (were) forgotten.

" " गंड *gaṇḍ*, bind; *gaṇḍ^{u}*, he (was) bound; *gaṇḍ^{ü}*, she (was) bound; but *ganjĕ*, they (fem.) (were) bound.

त् *t*, थ् *th*, द् *d*, and न् *n*, become *ts*, *tsh*, *z*, and *ñ* respectively, before both *ü-mātrā*, and before *y^{e}* (*ĕ*), which latter then becomes *a* by the rule given on the last page (viii. iii. 72, 73). Thus,—

From Root कत *kat*, spin; *kạt^{u}*, he (was) spun; but *kạts^{ü}*, she (was) spun; *kats^{a}*, they (fem.) (were) spun.

" " वोथ *wŏth*, arise; *wọ̆th^{u}*, he arose; but *wọ̆tsh^{ü}*, she arose, and *wŏtsh^{a}*, they (fem.) arose.

" " लद *lad*, build; *lạd^{u}*, he (was) built; but *lạz^{ü}*, she (was) built, and *laz^{a}*, they (fem.) (were) built.

" " रन *ran*, cook; *rạn^{u}*, he (was) cooked; but *rạñ^{ü}*, she (was) cooked, and *rañ^{a}*, they (fem.) (were) cooked.

ल् *l* becomes ज् *j* before both *ü-mātrā* and *y^{e}* (*ĕ*) (viii. iii. 74). Thus,—

From Root त्सल *tsal*, flee; *tsạl^{u}*, he fled; but *tsạj^{ü}*, she fled, and *tsajĕ*, they (fem.) fled.

The verbs पिह *pih*, grind; मुह *muh*, deceive; सह *sah*, bear; गह् *g*^{a}*h*, grind; and च़ह *ts*^{a}*h*, suck, under similar circumstances change their final ह् *h* to श् *ç* (viii. iii. 75). Thus,—

प्युहु *pyuh*^{u}, he (was) ground; but पिशु *piç*^{u}, she (was) ground; and पिशॆ *piçĕ*, they (fem.) were ground.

Combining what is said here, together with what has been said above (pp. 40 and ff.) regarding vowel changes, we come to the three following general rules, all of which apply only to the first and second conjugations, and do not apply to the third.

1. *In the Past Participle masculine, both singular and plural, only the root vowel, and not the final consonant, is liable to change.*

2. *In the Past Participle feminine singular, both the root vowel and the final consonant are liable to change.*

3. *In the Past Participle feminine plural, only the final consonant, and not the root vowel, is liable to change.*

These three rules are most important, as the whole scheme of conjugating the Past Tense depends upon them.

Irregular Past Participles.

The following verbs have irregular Past Participles. The irregularities are, of course, carried through the Past tense.

Verb.	PAST PARTICIPLE.			
	Singular.		Plural.	
	Masculine.	Feminine.	Masculine.	Feminine.
खस *khas*, mount (viii. iii. 66).	खॊठु *khǫth*^{u} [or खॊतु *khǫt*^{u}].	खॊछु *khǫtsh*^{u}, [or खॊचु *khǫts*^{u}].	खॊठि *khǫth*^{i} [or खॊति *khǫt*^{i}].	खछ *khatsh*^{a} [or खच *khats*^{a}].
वस *vas*, descend (66).	वॊठु *wǫth*^{u}.	वॊछु *wǫtsh*^{u}.	वॊठि *wǫth*^{i}.	वछ *watsh*^{a}.

Verb.	PAST PARTICIPLE.			
	SINGULAR.		PLURAL.	
	Masculine.	Feminine.	Masculine.	Feminine.
लस *las*, live long (27, 28, 33, 67, 96).	लूस्तु *lūst*^{u}.*	लूछु *lūṭsh*^{u}.*	लुंस्ति *lust*^{i}.*	लोंछ *lǫ̈ṭsh*^{a}.*
लोस *lōs*, be weary (67, 96).	लूसु *lūs*^{u}.	लूस *lūs*^{a} or लूछु *lūṭsh*^{u}.	लूसि *lūs*^{i}.	लोस *lōs*^{a} लोछ *lōṭsh*^{a}.
मर *mar*, die (26, 31, 59). मर *mar*, unite, is regular.	मूदु *mūd*^{u}.	म्वय *mŏy*^{a}.	मूदि *mūd*^{i}.	म्वय *mŏy*^{a}.
हि *hi*, take (32).	ह्युतु *hyat*^{u}.	हेंछु *hĕṭs*^{a}.	हेंति *hĕt*^{i}.	ह्यछ *hĕṭs*^{a}.
दि *di*, give (32).	द्युतु *dyut*^{u}.	दिछु *diṭs*^{a}.	दिति *dit*^{i}.	दिछ *diṭs*^{a}.
खि *khi*, eat (viii. iii. 6, ix. i. 37).	ख्यौव् *khyauv*.	ख्वय *khŏy*^{a}.	ख्येय् *khyēy*.	ख्वय *khŏy*^{a}.
चि *ci*, drink (viii. iii. 6, ix. i. 37).	च्यौव् *cyauv*.	च्वय *cŏy*^{a}.	च्येय् *cyēy*.	च्वय *cŏy*^{a}.
नि *ni*, take (viii. iii. 6, 34, ix. i. 38).	न्यूव् *nyūv*.	निय *niy*^{a}.	नीय् *nīy*.	निय *niy*^{a}.

* लस *las*, is sometimes used regularly by the vulgar, thus, लंसु *las*^{u}, &c. (viii. iii. 96). In the fem. sing. Içvara-kaula sometimes writes लूंछु *lǫ̈ṭsh*^{u}, and sometimes लूछु *lūṭsh*^{u}. According to my Paṇḍit, the latter is the correct form.

Verb.	PAST PARTICIPLE.			
	SINGULAR.		PLURAL.	
	Masculine.	Feminine.	Masculine.	Feminine.
डेष *ḍēṣ*, see (viii. iii. 62).	द्यूठु *dyūṭh*^{u}.	डीठ *ḍīṭh*^{a}.	डीठि *ḍīṭh*^{i}.	डेछ *ḍēchĕ*.
रोष *rōṣ*, be angry (24, 62).	रूठु *rūṭh*^{u}.	रूठ *rūṭh*^{a}.	रूठि *rūṭh*^{i}.	रोछ *rōchĕ*.
मष *maṣ*, forget (62).	मंठु *mạṭh*^{u}.	मंठ *mạṭh*^{a}.	मंठि *mạṭh*^{i}.	मछ *machĕ*.
ब्यह् *byah*, sit (22, 62).	ब्यूठु *byūṭh*^{u}.	बीठ *bīṭh*^{a}.	बीठि *bīṭh*^{i}.	बेछ *bēchĕ*.
कॖच *k*^{a}*ts*, be wet (63).	कतु *k*^{a}*t*^{u}.	कॖच *k*^{a}*ts*^{a}.	कति *k*^{a}*t*^{i}.	कॖच *k*^{a}*ts*^{e}.
हॊच *hŏts*, decay (63).	हंतु *họt*^{u}.	हंच *họts*^{a}.	हंति *họt*^{i}.	हॊच *hŏts*^{e}.
दज़ *daz*, be burnt (64).	दंदु *dạd*^{u}.	दंज़ *dạz*^{a}.	दंदि *dạd*^{i}.	दज़ *daz*^{e}.
रोज़ *rōz*, stop (64).	रूदु *rūd*^{u}.	रूज़ *rūz*^{a}.	रूदि *rūd*^{i}.	रोज़ *rōz*^{e}.
ऑपज़ *wŏpaz*, be born (64).	ऑपंदु *wŏpạd*^{u}.	ऑपंज़ *wŏpạz*^{a}.	ऑपंदि *wŏpạd*^{i}.	ऑपज़ *wŏpaz*^{e}.
हहर *hahar*, to marry off (a girl) (76).	हहंरु *hahạr*^{u} (rare).	हहंर *hahạr*^{a} or हरंच *harạç*^{a}.	हहंरि *hahạr*^{i} (rare).	हहरे *harhară*, or हरछ *haraçŏ*.

4 (*b*). The Past Tense.

This tense is peculiar to the first and second conjugations. It does not occur in the third conjugation. It describes something which has happened lately, *e.g.*, करुन् *karun*, he has (just) made.

It is formed from the Past Participle in ु ^{u}. This Participle is Passive in the case of verbs of the first conjugation. Thus, करु *kar*^{u}, done, असु *as*^{u} (impersonal verb), laughed. It is Neuter in the case of verbs of the second conjugation. Thus, बूवु *bǒv*^{u}, become. Verbs of the first conjugation are therefore passive in construction. Instead of saying 'I made this,' we must say 'this was made by me,' यिह् मै करु *yih mĕ kar*^{u}, this (*yih*) by me (*mĕ*) made (*kar*^{u}). Here the original object of the sentence has become the grammatical subject, and the logical subject has been put into the case of the agent. If the object (grammatical subject) is feminine, the participle must be feminine. If it is plural, the participle must be plural. Thus,—

> करु मै करु *kar*^{u} *mĕ kar*^{u}, the bracelet (masc.) was made by me.
>
> पटू मै करू *paṭ*^{ü} *mĕ kar*^{ü}, the tablet (fem.) was made by me.
>
> करि मै करि *kar*^{i} *mĕ kar*^{i}, the bracelets were made by me.
>
> पचे मै करे *pacĕ mĕ karĕ*, the tablets were made by me.

As regards the original subject, it is put in the agent case, and may also be added to the verb in the form of a pronominal suffix of the agent case. This *must* always be done in the second person singular and plural. These suffixes are given on pp. 15 and ff. For the sake of ready reference, they are here repeated.

	Singular.	Plural.
1st Person.	अम् *am*.	———
2nd „	अथ् *ath*.	अव *aw*^{a}.
3rd „	अन् *an*.	अख् *akh*.

The initial अ *a* is elided when following a vowel.

When the pronominal suffix is added to a verb (it is *always* added in the case of the second person), the original subject (now agent), if a pronoun, may be omitted. Thus, for 'he made,' we may say,—

47

(*a*) तमि करु *tạm*^{i} *kạr*^{u}, by him made,

or (*b*) तमि करुन *tạm*^{i} *kạru-n*, by him made-by-him,

or (*c*) करुन *kạru-n*, made-by-him.

In the second person we cannot use the first or (*a*) form. We can only say,—

(*b*) च करुथ *tsĕ kạru-th*, by thee made-by-thee,

or (*c*) करुथ *karu-th*, made-by-thee.

So in the plural.

(*b*) तुह्य करुव *tŏhĕ kạr*^{u}*-w*^{a}, by you made-by-you,

or (*c*) करुव *kạr*^{u}*-w*^{a}, made-by-you.

We cannot say च करु *tsĕ kạr*^{u} or तुह्य करु *tŏhĕ kạr*^{u}.

This Passive construction is called in Sanskrit Grammar the *karmaṇi prayōga*, and is described in Īçvara-kaula's Grammar under that name (viii. iii. 3).

The Impersonal Construction.

Impersonal verbs are used passively with all persons. The terminations are the same as in the case of active verbs. An example is,—

(*a*) तमि असु *tạm*^{i} *ạs*^{u}, by him it was laughed,

or (*b*) तमि असुन *tạm*^{i} *ạsu-n*, by him it was laughed-by-him,

or (*c*) असुन *ạsu-n*, it was laughed-by-him,

all three of which mean 'he laughed' (viii. iii. 3). So असुम *ạsu-m*, I laughed.

The two verbs ज़ुव *tsuv*, quarrel, and मोरव *mōrav*, bear pain, may be used impersonally, and are then put in the feminine (viii. iii. 9).

Thus, ज़ुवुन *tsuv*^{ü}*n*, quarrelling was done-by-him, he quarrelled, the verb agreeing with the nominative हर् *har*, a quarrel, which is feminine. So मोरवुन *mōrạv*^{ü}*n*, pain was suffered-by-him, he suffered pain, the true nominative being some feminine word like पीड् *pīḍ*, pain, understood.

In these cases we may use all the three forms, except, as before, in the second person. Thus,—

(*a*) तमि ज़ुवु *tạm*^{i} *tsuv*^{ü},

or (*b*) तमि ज़ुवुन *tạm*^{i} *tsuv*^{ü}*n*,

or (*c*) ज़ुवुन *tsuv*^{ü}*n*.

These two words can even be used in the fem. plur. Thus, दुवव्, he quarrelled (many times); मोरवव् *mŏravyan*, he suffered pains.

The following verbs (repeated from pp. 16 and 22) are also impersonal but have this peculiarity that they are conjugated with suffixes of the dative instead of suffixes of the agent, and are also in the feminine.

चर *tsar*, be inwardly wrathful.

फच *phŏç*, ditto.

फुह *phuh*, ditto.

मर्छ *marts*, ditto.

वुछ *wuts*, be burnt.

फिछ *phits*, forget.

त्यंब *tyamb*, look eagerly (conjugated in the third conjugation).

Thus, चॖरुस् *tsar*[a]*-s*, not चॖरुन् *tsar*[a]*-n*, there was inward anger to him, he was angry.

चॖरुय् *tsar*[a]*-y*, not चॖरुथ् *tsar*[a]*-th*, thou wast angry.

चॖरुम् *tsar*[a]*-m*, I was angry.

So वुछुय् *wuts*[a]*y*, thou wast burnt. These verbs are given here, because the first six are used in the Past Tense. त्यंब *tyamb*, look eagerly, belongs to the third conjugation, and does not use the Past Tense.

This impersonal construction, whether with the Dative or with the Agent, is called in Sanskrit, the *bhāvĕ-prayŏga*.

NEUTER VERBS.

Neuter verbs of the second conjugation, having their Past Participle neuter, are conjugated, in the Past tenses actively. They thus take the pronominal suffixes of the nominative, and agree with the subject of the sentence in number and person. The addition of the pronominal suffixes is obligatory.

They are here quoted for ready reference.

	SINGULAR.	PLURAL.
1.	अस् *as*.	———
2.	अख् *akh*.	अव *aw*[a].
3.	———	———

There are no nominative suffixes of the first person plural or of the third person.

Taking, therefore, the verb बुव् *bŏv*, become, for 'I became' we may say,—

(*b*) बुह् बुवुस् *bŏh bǫvu-s*,

or (*c*) बुवुस् *bǫvu-s*.

We cannot say बुह् बुव् *bŏh bǫv*^{u}, any more than we can say तोह् कंर् *tŏhĕ kąr*^{u}.

These preliminaries being understood, I shall, in the paradigms, only give the (*c*) forms of the past tenses. From these the (*b*) forms and (when they exist) the (*a*) forms can easily be deduced.

A. First Conjugation.

(*a*) **Transitive Verb** (viii. iii. 2–9) (*c*. forms only) 'I made,' *Lit.* 'he, she, it, &c., was (were) made by me, you, him, us, &c.'

	Singular.		Plural.	
	Masculine.[1] कंर् *kąr*^{u}, made.	Feminine.[1] कंर् *kąr*^{ü}.	Masculine.[1] कंरि *kąr*^{i}.	Feminine.[1] करे *karĕ*.
Sing.				
1	कंरुम् *kąru-m*.	कंरूम् *kąr*^{ü}*-m*.	कंरिम् *kąri-m*.	कर्येम् *karya-m*.[2]
2	कंरुथ् *kąru-th*.	कंरूथ् *kąr*^{ü}*-th*.	कंरिथ् *kąri-th*.	कर्येथ् *karya-th*.
3	कंरुन् *kąru-n*.	कंरून् *kąr*^{ü}*-n*.	कंरिन् *kąri-n*.	कर्येन् *karya-n*.
Plur.				
1	कंर् *kąr*^{u}.	कंर् *kąr*^{ü}.	कंरि *kąr*^{i}.	करे *karĕ*.
2	कंरुव *kąr*^{u}*-w*^{a}.	कंरूव *kąr*^{ü}*-w*^{a}.	कंरिव *kąr*^{i}*-w*^{a}.	करेव *karĕ-w*^{a}.
3	कंरुख् *kąru-kh*.	कंरूख् *kąr*^{ü}*-kh*.	कंरिख् *kąri-kh*.	कर्येख् *karya-kh*.

Verbs ending in vowels are slightly irregular in the masculine singular and plural, and in the feminine singular, which latter is the

[1] *E.g.* The object of the sentence, which has now become the grammatical subject, as explained above.

[2] Or *karĕ-m*, and so throughout.

same as the feminine plural (viii. iii. 6). None of these verbs belong to the second conjugation.

As usual there are two groups of these verbs, *viz.*, those which change their final vowel, *i*, to *ya*, such as खि *eat*, and others (*vide* p. 1) and those which do not, which are three in number, नि *ni*, take, दि *di*, give, and यि *yi*, come, of which the last belongs to the third conjugation. Taking the verb खि *khi*, eat, we get.

	SINGULAR.		PLURAL.	
	Masculine. ख्यौव् *khyauv*.	Feminine. ख्यव *khĕyᵃ*.	Masculine. ख्येव् *khyēy*.	Feminine. ख्यव *khĕyᵃ*.
Sing.				Same as singular.
1	ख्योम् *khyō-m* or ख्यौम् *khyau-m* (ix. i. 37).	ख्यवम् *khĕya-m*.	ख्येम् *khyē-m*.	
2	ख्योथ् *khyō-th* or ख्यौथ् *khyau-th*.	ख्यवथ् *khĕya-th*.	ख्येथ् *khyē-th*.	
3	ख्योन् *khyōn* or ख्यौन् *khyau-n*.	ख्यवन् *khĕya-n*.	ख्येन् *khyē-n*.	
Plur.				
1	ख्यौव् *khyauv*.	ख्यव *khĕyᵃ*.	ख्येव् *khyēy*.	
2	ख्योव *khyō-wᵃ* or ख्यौव *khyau-wᵃ*.	ख्यवव *khĕyᵃ-wᵃ*.	ख्येव *khyē-wᵃ*.	
3	ख्योख् *khyō-kh* or ख्यौख् *khyau-kh*.	ख्यवख् *khĕya-kh*.	ख्येख् *khyē-kh*.	

Similarly is conjugated, चि *ci*, drink.

The verb नि take, is further irregular (viii. iii. 6, 34; ix. i. 38).

	Singular.		**Plural.**	
	Masculine.	**Feminine.**	**Masculine.**	**Feminine.**
Sing.				
1	न्यूम् *nyū-m.*	नियम् *niya-m.*	नीम् *nī-m.*	Same as singular.
2	न्यूथ् *nyū-th.*	नियथ् *niya-th.*	नीथ् *nī-th.*	
3	न्यून् *nyū-n.*	नियन् *niya-n.*	नीन् *nī-n.*	
Plur.				
1	न्यूव् *nyūv.*	निय *niyᵃ.*	नीय् *nīy.*	
2	न्यूव *nyū-wᵃ.*	नियव *niyᵃ-wᵃ.*	नीव *nī-wᵃ.*	
3	न्यूख् *nyū-kh.*	नियख् *niya-kh.*	नीख् *nī-kh.*	

The verbs हि *hi*, take, and दि *di*, give, are still further irregular (viii. iii. 7, 32). Thus,—

	Singular.		**Plural.**	
	Masculine.	**Feminine.**	**Masculine.**	**Feminine.**
Sing.				
1	ह्यतुम् *hyatu-m.*	ह्यचूम् *hĕtsᵃ-m.*	ह्यतिम् *hĕti-m.*	हचम् *hĕtsa-m.*
2	ह्यतुथ् *hyatu-th.*	ह्यचूथ् *hĕtsᵃ-th.*	ह्यतिथ् *hĕti-th.*	हचथ् *hĕtsa-th.*
3	ह्यतुन् *hyatu-n.*	ह्यचून् *hĕtsᵃ-n.*	ह्यतिन् *hĕti-n.*	हचन् *hĕtsa-n.*

	Singular.		Plural.	
	Masculine.	Feminine.	Masculine.	Feminine.
Plur.				
1	ह्यांतु *hyạt*^{u}.	ह्यांचॖ *hĕ̮ts*^{a}.	ह्यांति *hĕ̮t*^{i}.	ह्यच *hĕts*^{a}.
2	ह्यांतुव *hyạt*^{u}*-w*^{a}.	ह्यांचॖव *hĕ̮ts*^{a}*-w*^{a}.	ह्यांतिव *hĕ̮t*^{i}*-w*^{a}.	ह्यचव *hĕts*^{a}*-w*^{a}.
3	ह्यांतुख् *hyạtu-kh*.	ह्यांचॖख् *hĕ̮ts*^{a}*-kh*.	ह्यांतिख् *hĕ̮ti-kh*.	ह्यचख् *hĕtsa-kh*.

दि *di*, give, is similarly declined, but its first person is दितुम् or द्युतुम् *dyutu-m*, दिचॖम् *dits*^{a}*-m*, दितिम् *diti-m*, दिचम् *ditsa-m*, and so throughout.

The verb हहर *hahar*, to get a girl married, is of necessity, conjugated in the past tenses only in the feminine. Moreover it forms its feminine Past Participle, optionally, in an irregular fashion (viii. iii. 76), Thus, हहंरॖन् *hahạr*^{a}*-n* or हरंचॖन् *haraç*^{a}*-n*, he got her married.

Notes. (1) Once for all. By the first person singular, is meant, 'I made him, her, them (masc.), or them (fem.),' literally, 'he, she, they (masc.), or they (fem.) were made by me.' So the second person singular means 'thou madest him, her, them (masc.), or them (fem.),' and so on, through the other persons.

(2) There is no suffix for the first person plural. Hence this form is always the same as the past participle.

(b) **Impersonal Verb** (viii. iii. 3–9) (*c.* forms only), 'I laughed,' literally, 'it was laughed by me,' &c.

Singular 1 अंसुम् *ạsu-m*, I laughed.
2 अंसुथ् *ạsu-th*, thou laughedst.
3 अंसुन् *ạsu-n*, he laughed.
Plural 1 अंसु *ạs*^{u}, we laughed.
2 अंसुव *ạs*^{u}*-w*^{a}, you laughed.
3 अंसुख् *ạsu-kh*, they laughed.

When an Impersonal Verb is conjugated in the feminine (see pp. 22 and 48), we get forms such as the following, (चुव *tsuv*, quarrel) (viii. iii. 9),—

Singular 1 चुवम् *tsuv^{u}-m*, I quarrelled.
2 चुवथ् *tsuv^{u}-th*, thou didst quarrel.
3 चुवन् *tsuv^{u}-n*, he quarrelled.
Plural 1 चुव *tsuv^{u}*, we quarrelled.
2 चुवव *tsuv^{u}-w^{a}*, you quarrelled.
3 चुवख् *tsuv^{u}-kh*, they quarrelled.

If such an Impersonal Verb is conjugated in the plural, we get—

Singular 1 चुव्यम् *tsuvya-m*, I quarrelled many times, and so on.
2 चुव्यथ् *tsuvya-th*.
3 चुव्यन् *tsuvya-n*.
Plural 1 चुवे *tsuvĕ*.
2 चुव्यव *tsuvya-w^{a}*.
3 चुव्यख् *tsuvya-kh*.

So मोरव *mōrav*, bear pain.

चर *tsar* and the others are thus conjugated (see pp. 16, 22, and 49).

Singular 1 चरुम् *tsar^{a}-m*, I was inwardly angry, and so on.
2 चरुय् *tsar^{a}-y*.
3 चरुस् *tsar^{a}-s*.
Plural 1 चरु *tsar^{a}*.
2 चरुव *tsar^{a}-w^{a}*.
3 चरुख् *tsar^{a}-kh*.

In the case of Transitive verbs, when the grammatical subject (*i.e.*, the logical object) is a pronoun, it may be added to the verb in the shape of an additional pronominal suffix in the Nominative case. The following are the masculine forms which occur. The feminine ones can easily be made on the same principle.

From करुम् *karu-m*, made by me, I made.

करुमख् *kar^{a}-m-akh*, thou wast made by me, I made thee.

So करुमख् *kar^{a}-m-akh*, thou (fem.) wast made by me, I made thee (fem.).

[कॅरमन् *kǫr*^{u}*-m-an*, I made him, is not used. We always say सुह् कॅरुम् *suh kǫru-m.* कॅरमस् *kar*^{u}*-m-as* means 'I made for him.']

कॅरिमव *kǫr*^{i}*-m-aw*^{a}, I made you.

[कॅरिमख् *kǫr*^{i}*-m-akh*, I made them, is not used. We always say तिम् कॅरिम् *tim kǫri-m.* कॅरिमख् *kǫr*^{i}*-m-akh* means 'I made them for them.']

From कॅरुथ् *kǫru-th*, made by thee, thou madest.

कॅरथस् *kǫr*^{u}*-th-as*, thou madest me (or thou madest for him).

कॅरथन् *kǫr*^{u}*-th-an*, thou madest him.

कॅरिथख् *kǫr*^{i}*-th-akh*, thou madest them (or for them).

From कॅरुन् *kǫru-n*, made by him, he made.

कॅरनस् *kǫr*^{u}*-n-as*, he made me (or he made for him).

कॅरनख् *kǫr*^{u}*-n-akh*, he made thee (or he made for them).

[कॅरनन् *kǫr*^{u}*-n-an*, he made him, is not used. We say सुह् कॅरुन् *suh kǫrun.*]

कॅरिनव *kǫr*^{i}*-n-aw*^{a}, he made you (or for you).

[कॅरिनख् *kǫr*^{i}*-n-akh*, he made them, is not used. We say तिम् कॅरिन् *tim kǫri-n.* कॅरिनख् *kǫr*^{i}*-n-akh*, means 'he made them for them.']

From कॅर् *kǫr*^{u}, made by us, we made.

कॅरुख् *kǫru-kh*, we made thee.

[कॅरुन् *kǫru-n*, we made him, is not used. We say सुह कॅर् *suh kǫr*^{u}].

कॅरिव *kǫr*^{i}*-w*^{a}, we made you.

[कॅरिख् *kǫri-kh*, we made them, is not used. We say तिम् कॅरि *tim kǫr*^{i}].

From कॅरव *kǫr*^{u}*-w*^{a}, made by you, you made.

कॅरवस् *kǫr*^{u}*-wa-s*, you made me (or for him)

कॅरवन् *kǫr*^{u}*-wa-n*, you made him.

कॅरिवख् *kǫr*^{i}*-wa-kh*, you made them.

From करुख् *kạru-kh*, made by them, they made.

करुहस् *kạr^{u}-h-as*, they made me (or they made for him).

करुहख् *kạr^{u}-h-akh*, they made thee (or for them).

[करुहन् *kạr^{u}-h-an*, they made him, is not used. We say, सुह् करुख् *suh kạru-kh*].

करिहव *kạr^{i}-h-aw^{a}*, they made you.

[करिहख् *kạr^{i}-h-akh*, they made them, is not used. We say, तिम् करिख् *tim kạri-kh*. करिहख् *kạr^{i}-h-akh*, means 'he made them for them'].

There being no suffix for the first person plural, there are no special forms for thou, he, you, or they made us.

With regard to all these forms, the full forms of the pronouns may also be used, with, or without the suffixes. Thus,—

We may say either

(*a*) म्य करुमख् च़ह् *mĕ kạr^{u}-m-akh ts^{a}h*, by me was-made-by-me-thou thou, or

(*b*) करुमख् च़ह् *kạr^{u}-m-akh ts^{a}h*, was-made-by-me-thou thou, or

(*c*) म्य करुमख् *mĕ kạr^{u}-m-akh*, by me was-made-by-me-thou, or

(*d*) करुमख् *kạr^{u}makh*, was-made-by-me-thou, or

(*e*) म्य करुख् च़ह् *mĕ kạru-kh ts^{a}h*, by me was-made-thou thou, or

(*f*) म्य करुख् *mĕ kạru-kh*, by me was-made-thou.

We cannot, however, use the two following forms.

(*g*) म्य करु च़ह् *mĕ kạr^{u} ts^{a}h*, by-me was-made thou or

(*h*) करुम् च़ह् *kạru-m ts^{a}h*, was-made-by-me thou.

In other words when the full form of the pronoun in the nominative is used, the corresponding suffix must always accompany it.

Other pronominal suffixes can similarly be used. Thus, करुमय् *kạr^{u}-m-ay*, I made for thee.

B. Second Conjugation.

Neuter Verb (viii. iii. 77–97). (*c.* Forms only).

I became, &c.

	Singular.		Plural.	
	Masculine.	Feminine.	Masculine.	Feminine.
1	बॊवुस् *bŏvu-s.*	बॊवॖस् *bŏv^{a}-s.*	बॊवि *bŏv^{i}.*	बॊवॖ *bŏvĕ.*
2	बॊवुख् *bŏvu-kh.*	बॊवॖख् *bŏv^{a}-kh.*	बॊविव *bŏv^{i}-w^{a}.*	बॊवॖव *bŏvĕ-w^{a}.*
3	बॊवु *bŏv^{u}.*	बॊवॖ *bŏv^{a}.*	बॊवि *bŏv^{i}.*	बॊवॖ *bŏvĕ.*

The verb मर *mar*, die, has its past tense irregular. It is thus conjugated (viii. iii. 26, 31, 59, 65, 92).

	Singular.		Plural.	
	Masculine.	Feminine.	Masculine.	Feminine.
1	मूडुस् *mūdu-s.*	म्ययस् *mŏya-s.*	मूडि *mūd^{i}.*	म्यय *mŏy^{e}.*
2	मूडुख् *mūdu-kh.*	म्ययख् *mŏya-kh.*	मूडिव *mūd^{i}-w^{a}.*	म्ययव *mŏy^{e}-w^{a}.*
3	मूडु *mūd^{u}.*	म्यय *mŏy^{e}.*	मूडि *mūd^{i}.*	म्यय *mŏy^{e}.*

When मर *mar* means to unite, it is regular. Thus, मरुन् *marun*, he united him.

5 (*a.*) The Verbal Aorist Participle.

This participle occurs in all three conjugations. In the first and second (viii. iii. 78) conjugations it is a true aorist. It expresses past time indefinitely, with no reference to proximity or distance. *E.g.*, करेयॊव् *karyŏv*, he (was) made (by us), we made; बॊव्यॊव् *bŏvyŏv*, he became. It is therefore the participle, and the aorist is the tense, of narration in these two conjugations.

In the third conjugation, it is used instead of the past participle; and describes something which has happened lately. Thus, वुफ्योव् *wuphyōv*, he flew (a short time ago).

This participle is formed in the first and second conjugations by changing the final य् *y*ᵉ (*ĕ*) of the feminine plural of the past participle to योव् *yōv*. Thus, कर् *kar*, do; past participle कॖर् *kạr*ᵉ, fem. plur. करे *karĕ*; aorist participle कर्योव् *karyōv*.

In those cases, in which the feminine plural ends in अ *a*, instead of in य् *y*ᵉ (*ĕ*), (see p. 42) the aorist participle ends in ओव् *ōv*, not in योव् *yōv*. Thus, दज़ *das*, burn; past participle दॖद् *dạd*ᵉ, fem. plur. दज़ *daz*ᵉ; aorist participle दज़ोव् *dazōv*. There are four exceptions (viii. iii. 49, 81). The aorist participle of कॖच *k*ᵉ*ts*, be moist, is कॖच्योव् *k*ᵉ*tsyōv*; that of व्यच *vyats*, pervade, is व्यच्योव् *vyatsyōv*; that of रोच *rōts*, be preferred, रोच्योव् *rōtsyōv*; [and that of वुच *wuts*, be burnt, वुच्योव् *wutsyōv*]. Note that in the fem. pl. Past, in these verbs, the य *y* is elided. Thus कॖच *k*ᵉ*ts*ᵉ, not कॖच्य् *k*ᵉ*tsĕ*; व्यच *vyats*ᵉ, not व्यच्य् *vyatsĕ*; रोच *rōts*ᵉ not रोच्य् *rōtsĕ* (viii. iii. 49, 81).

In the third conjugation, the aorist participle is formed by adding योव् *yōv* to the root direct. Thus, वुफ *wuph*, fly, aorist participle वुफ्योव् *wuphyōv*, but there are exceptions which will be dealt with later on.

Īçvara-kaula spells this participle indifferently with योव् *yōv* or with यौव् *yauv*. Both are pronounced the same, like योव् *yōv* (viii. iii. 39).

[The true termination of this participle is *yō*, the *v*, as well as the *y* of the plural to be noted later, are only added for the sake of euphony].

Special Rules for the First and Second Conjugations.

The base of the aorist participle of the first and second conjugations being the same as the feminine plural of the past participle, the final consonant of the verbal root undergoes certain changes (viii. iii. 69, 70, 71, 72, 73, 74, 75). For the same reason, in the aorist participle, the vowel of the verbal root remains unchanged (see page 41). The following are examples of the changes. The reader is referred to pp. 42 and ff. for details.

1	Root	थक *thak*, be tired,	aorist participle	थच्योव् *thacyōv*.
2	„	लेख *lĕkh*, write	„	लेछ्योव् *lĕchyōv*.
3	„	दग *dag*, pound	„	दज्योव् *dajyōv*.

4 Root फट *phaṭ*, be split aorist participle फच्योव् *phacyōv*.
5 „ मठ *maṭh*, forget „ मछ्योव् *machyōv*.
6 „ गंड *gaṇḍ*, bind „ गंज्योव् *ganjyōv*.
7 „ कत *kat*, spin „ कच़ोव् *kaṭsōv*.
8 „ व्वथ *wŏth*, arise „ व्वछ़ोव् *wŏṭshōv*.
9 „ लड़ *lad*, build „ लज़ोव् *lazōv*.
10 „ रन *ran*, cook „ रञोव् *rañōv*.
11 „ च़ल *ṭsal*, flee „ च़ज्योव् *ṭsajyōv*.
12 „ पिह *pih*, grind „ पिश्योव् *piçyōv*.
13 „ मुह *muh*, deceive „ मुश्योव् *muçyōv*.*
14 „ सह *sah*, bear „ सश्योव् *saçyōv*.
15 „ गृह *g*^{a}*h*, grind „ गृश्योव् *g*^{a}*çyōv*.
16 „ च़ृह *ṭs*^{a}*h*, suck „ च़ृश्योव् *ṭs*^{a}*çyōv*.

Nos. 7–10 are also examples of the elision of य *y*. The following are further examples, see p. 42 for details.

1 Root दि *di*, give aorist participle दिच़ोव् *diṭsōv*.
2 „ हि *hi*, take „ हेच़ोव् *hēṭsōv*.

The past participles of these two verbs are irregular, *vide* p. 45.

3 Root दज़ *daz*, burn, aorist participle दज़ोव् *dazōv*.
4 „ बस *bas*, dwell „ बसोव् *basōv*.
5 „ कस *kas*, fry „ कसोव् *kasōv*.

But from,—

6 Root थास *thās*, bury „ थासोव् *thāsōv*, or थास्योव् *thāsyōv*.
7 „ दस *das*, beat „ दसोव् *dasōv*, or दस्योव् *dasyōv*.

And from—

8 Root क्च़ *k*^{a}*ṭs*, be wet „ only क्च़्योव् *k*^{a}*ṭsyōv* (p. 58).
9 „ च़स *ṭsas*, laugh loudly „ only च़स्योव् *ṭsasyōv* (p. 42).

Remember that all these changes occur only in the first and second conjugations. The rules for the third conjugation are quite different.

* My Paṇḍit prefers मुह्योव् *muhyōv*.

Special Rules for the Third Conjugation.

In this conjugation, the participle (and consequently, the tense formed from it) is not used as an aorist, but as a past; with the same meaning as the past participle of the first and second conjugations. It is *not* the tense of narration.

The aorist participle is formed by adding योव् *yōv* to the root. Thus, वुफ *wuph*, fly, वुफ्योव् *wuphyōv*. Before this the final consonant of a root is *not* liable to change, as it is in the case of verbs of the first and second conjugations. Thus, from सेठ *sěth*, be long, a verb of the 3rd conjugation, the aorist participle is सेठ्योव् *sōthyōv*, and not सेच्योव् *sächyōv*, as it would be, if the verb belonged to the 2nd conjugation.

Note also that in this conjugation, य् *y* is not elided after च् *ts*, छ् *tsh*, स् *s*, or ज़् *z* (viii. iii. 49). Içvara-kaula in this *sūtra* gives the following list of verbs, which do not elide य् *y*. It includes many of the verbs ending in these letters which belong to the third conjugation.

ग्रच *grǒts*, be splashed out; चच *tsǒts*, have insufficient means of livelihood; छुच *tshǒts*, be empty; तेज़ *těz*, be sharp; पज़ *pas*, be fit; ब्रज़ *bras*, shine; बावज़ *bāwas*, be preferred; लच *lǒts*, be weak; ग्रोच *grǒts*, be pure. Thus, ग्रुच्योव् *grǒtsyōv*, not ग्रुचोव् *grǒtsōv*.

The other verbs belonging to the third conjugation, which end in these letters, and which are not mentioned by Içvara-kaula in the above *sūtra* are the following:—

अच *ats*, enter; त्रच *trats*, fear; म्यच *mǒts*, remain over and above; अछ *atsh*, be weak; गछ *gatsh*, go; पलज़ *palas*, be useful; रञ्ज़ *rans*, be pleased; लज़ *laz*, be suitable; वुज़ *wus*, be wide awake, appear. सपज़ *sapas*, become, is considered the same as सपन *sapan*, or सपद् *sapad*, and belongs to the second conjugation. According to my Paṇḍit पलज़ *palas*, above recorded, belongs to the second conjugation.

According to my Paṇḍit, of these, त्रच *trats* and अछ *atsh*, always retain य् *y*. The others retain it optionally except अच *ats* and गछ *gatsh*, which are irregular. See below, pp. 64 and 65.

Moreover, य् *y* is not, in this conjugation, elided after स् *s*. All the examples of the elision of य् *y* after this letter given by Içvara-kaula belong either to the first or second conjugation.

The Aorist Participle Generally.

The masculine plural of this participle is formed by changing the final योव् *yōv* to येय् *yěy*. Thus, कर्योव् *karyōv*, plural कर्येय् *karyěy* (viii. iii. 15). The feminine is formed योव् *yōv* to येय *yěy*ᵉ (viii. iii. 16). The feminine singular and the feminine plural are the same. Thus, कर्योव् *karyōv*, fem. sing. and plur. कर्येय *karyěy*ᵉ.

When the base of the participle ends च् *ts*, छ् *tsh*, स् *s*, or ञ् *ñ*, and elides the य् *y* in योव् *yōv* of the masculine singular, the येय् *yěy* of the masculine plural becomes ड्य् *ḍy* (viii. iii. 18), and the येय *yěy*ᵉ of the feminine, becomes ड्य *ḍy*ᵉ (viii. iii. 17). Thus,—

Root कत *kat*, spin. Aorist part. कचोव् *katsōv*; masc. pl. कच्ड्य् *katsḍy*; fem. कच्ड्य *katsḍy*ᵉ.

„ वथ *wŏth*, arise. Aorist part. वछोव् *wŏtshōv*; masc. pl. वछ्ड्य् *watsḍy*; fem. वछ्ड्य *wŏtshḍy*ᵉ.

„ दज *das*, burn. Aorist part. दसोव् *dasōv*; masc. pl. दस्ड्य् *dasḍy*; fem. दस्ड्य *dasḍy*ᵉ.

„ रन *ran*, cook. Aorist part. रञोव् *rañōv*; masc. pl. रञ्ड्य् *rañḍy*; fem. रञ्ड्य *rañḍy*ᵉ.

Most verbs of the third conjugation ending in these letters do not elide the य् *y* (see page 60). So also the verbs क्च *kᵉts*, व्यच *vyats*, रोच *rōts*, वुच *wuts* (see p. 58) of the second conjugation. These verbs form the masculine plural either in ड्य् *ḍy* or एय् *ěy*, and the feminine in ड्य *ḍy*ᵉ or एय *ěy*ᵉ (viii. iii. 17). Thus,—

Root क्च *kᵉts*, (second conjugation) be wet; masc. sing. क्च्योव् *kᵉtsyōv*; masc. plural क्च्ड्य् *kᵉtsḍy* or क्चेय् *kᵉtsěy*.

„ प्रोच *prōts*, (third conjugation) be pure; masc. sing. प्रोच्योव् *prōtsyōv*; masc. plural प्रोच्ड्य् *prōtsḍy* or प्रोचेय् *prōtsěy*.

„ तेज *tĕs*, (third conjugation), be sharp; masc. sing. तेस्योव् *tĕsyōv*; masc. plural तेस्ड्य् *tĕsḍy* or तेसेय् *tĕsěy*. ¶

The following verbs have irregular aorist participles. The irregularities are, of course, carried through the aorist tense.

VERB.	AORIST PARTICIPLE.			
	Singular.		**Plural.**	
	Masculine.	Feminine.	Masculine.	Feminine.
हि *hi*, take (17, 32).	ह्यॆछोव् *hĕt̲s̲ōv*.	ह्यॆछाय *hĕt̲s̲ạ̄y*ᵉ.	ह्यॆछाय् *hĕt̲s̲ạ̄y*.	Same as singular.
दि *di*, give (17, 32).	दिछोव् *dit̲s̲ōv*.	दिछाय *dit̲s̲ạ̄y*ᵉ.	दिछाय् *dit̲s̲ạ̄y*.	
खस *khas*, mount (12, 66).	खछोव् *khat̲s̲ōv* or खछ़ोव् *khat̲s̲hōv*.	खछाय *khat̲s̲ạ̄y*ᵉ or खछ़ाय *khat̲s̲ạ̄y*ᵉ.	खछाय् *khat̲s̲ạ̄y* or खछ़ाय् *khat̲s̲hạ̄y*.	
वस *was*, descend (12, 66).	वछ़ोव् *wat̲s̲hōv*.	वछ़ाय *wat̲s̲hạ̄y*ᵉ.	वछ़ाय् *wat̲s̲hạ̄y*.	
लस *las*,* live long (18, 29, 67).	लाछ़ोव् *lạ̄t̲s̲hōv*.	लाछ़ाय *lạ̄t̲s̲hạ̄y*ᵉ.	लाछ़ाय् *lạ̄t̲s̲hạ̄y*.	
लोस *lōs*, be weary (67).	लोसोव् *lōsōv*, or लोछ़ोव् *lōt̲s̲hōv*.	लोसाय *lōsạ̄y*ᵉ or लोछ़ाय *lōt̲s̲hạ̄y*ᵉ.	लोसाय् *lōsạ̄y* or लोछ़ाय् *lōt̲s̲hạ̄y*.	
मर *mar*, die (30).	म्यॊयोव् *mŏyōv*.	म्यॊयेय *mŏyēy*ᵉ.	म्यॊयेय् *mŏyēy*.	

यि *yi*, come (53).				
Past.	आव् *āv*.	आय *āy**.	आय् *āy*.	Same as singular.
Aorist.	आयोव् *āyōv*.	आयेय *āyēy**.	आयेय् *āyēy*.	
Plup.	आयाव् *āyāv*.	आयेय *āyēy**.	आयाय् *āyāy*.	
ज़्यि *zi*, be born (54).				
Past.	ज़ाव् *zāv*.	ज़ाय *zāy**.	ज़ाय् *zāy*.	
Aorist.	ज़ायोव् *zāyōv*.	ज़ायेय *zāyēy**.	ज़ायेय् *zāyēy*.	
Plup.	ज़ायाव् *zāyāv*.	ज़ायेय *zāyēy**.	ज़ायाय् *zāyāy*.	
नेर *nēr*, go forth (56).				
Past.	द्राव् *drāv*.	द्राय *drāy**.	द्राय् *drāy*.	
Aorist.	द्रायोव् *drāyōv*.	द्रायेय *drāyēy**.	द्रायेय् *drāyēy*.	
Plup.	द्रायाव् *drāyāv*.	द्रायेय *drāyēy**.	द्रायाय् *drāyāy*.	

* लस *las* is sometimes used regularly by the vulgar. Thus, लसोव् *lasōv* (viii. iii. 96).

VERB.	AORIST PARTICIPLE.			
	SINGULAR.		PLURAL.	
	Masculine.	Feminine.	Masculine.	Feminine.
अच़ *ats*, enter (52, 57).				
Past.	च़ाव् *tsāv*.	च़ाय *tsāy*^{e}.	च़ाय् *tsāy*.	Same as singular.
Aorist.	च़ायोव् *tsāyōv*.	च़ायेय *tsāyĕy*^{e}.	च़ायेय् *tsāyĕy*.	
Plup.	च़ायाव् *tsāyāv*.	च़ायेय *tsāyĕy*^{e}.	च़ायाय् *tsāyāy*.	
प्रस *pras*, be born (52, 55).				
Past.	प्याव् *pyāv*.	प्याय *pyāy*^{e}.	प्याय् *pyāy*.	
Aorist.	प्यायोव् *pyāyōv*.	प्यायेय *pyāyĕy*^{e}.	प्यायेय् *pyāyĕy*.	
Plup.	प्यायाव् *pyāyāv*.	प्यायेय *pyāyĕy*^{e}.	प्यायाय् *pyāyāy*.	

पि *pi*, fall (48, 60).				
Past.	प्यौव् *pyauv.*	पय *pĕy*^{e}.	पय् *pĕy.*	
Aorist.	पयोव् *pĕyŏv.*	पयेय *pĕyĕy*^{e}.	पयेय् *pĕyĕy.*	
Plup.	पयाव् *pĕyāv.*	पयेय *pĕyĕy*^{e}.	पयाय् *pĕyāy.*	
गछ *gatsh*, go (48, 58, 60).				
Past.	गौव् *gauv.*	गय *gay*^{e}.	गय् *gay.*	
Aorist.	गयोव् *gayŏv.*	गयेय *gayĕy*^{e}.	गयेय् *gayĕy.*	Same as singular.
Plup.	गयाव् *gayāv.*	गयेय *gayĕy*^{e}.	गयाय् *gayāy.*	
देष *dēs*, see (62).	देछ्योव् *dĕchyŏv.*	देछ्येय *dĕchyĕy*^{e}.	देछ्येय् *dĕchyĕy.*	
रोष *rōs*, be angry (62).	रोछ्योव् *rŏchyŏv.*	रोछ्येय *rŏchyĕy*^{e}.	रोछ्येय् *rŏchyĕy.*	
मष *mas*, forget (62).	मछ्योव् *machyŏv.*	मछ्येय *machyĕy*^{e}.	मछ्येय् *machyĕy.*	
ब्यह *byah*, sit (62).	बेछ्योव् *bĕchyŏv.*	बेछ्येय *bĕchyĕy*^{e}.	बेछ्येय् *bĕchyĕy.*	
हहर *kahar*, to get a girl married (76).	Not used.	हहर्येय *haharyĕy*^{e} or हरछ्येय *haraçyĕy*^{e}.	Not used.	

5 (*b*). The Aorist Tense.

This is formed from the Aorist Participle, exactly as the Past tense is formed from the Past Participle, except that a final व् *v* or a final य् *y* is always elided before a pronominal suffix (viii. iii. 41). Thus, कर्योव् *karyōv* + अम् *am*, made-by-me = कर्योम् *karyō-m*, not कर्योवम् *karyōv-am*. The अ *a* of अम् *am*, is elided under the general rules for pronominal suffixes (*vide* p. 15). So also forms like कुमल्योस् *kumalyō-s* (*kumalyōv* + *as*), he was tender for him; कुमल्येस् *kumalyē-s*, they were tender for him.

We thus get the following forms,—

A. First Conjugation.

(*a*). Transitive verb (viii. iii. 14). (*c.* forms only).

'I made,' *lit.* 'he, she, it, &c., was (were) made by me, you, him, us, &c.'

	Singular.		Plural.	
	Masculine. कर्योव् *karyōv*.	Feminine. कर्येय *karyēy*[a].	Masculine. कर्येय् *karyēy*.	Feminine. कर्येय *karyēy*[a].
Sing.				
1	कर्योम् *karyō-m*.	कर्येयम् *karyēya-m*.	कर्येम् *karyē-m*.	कर्येयम् *karyēya-m*.
2	कर्योथ् *karyō-th*.	कर्येयथ् *karyēya-th*.	कर्येथ् *karyē-th*.	कर्येयथ् *karyēya-th*.
3	कर्योन् *karyō-n*.	कर्येयन् *karyēya-n*.	कर्येन् *karyē-n*.	कर्येयन् *karyēya-n*.
Plur.				
1	कर्योव् *karyōv*.	कर्येय *karyēy*[a].	कर्येय् *karyēy*.	कर्येय *karyēy*[a].
2	कर्योव *karyō-w*[a].	कर्येयव *karyēy*[a]*-w*[a].	कर्येव *karyē-w*[a].	कर्येयव *karyēy*[a]*-w*[a].
3	कर्योख् *karyō-kh*.	कर्येयख् *karyēya-kh*.	कर्येख् *karyē-kh*.	कर्येयख् *karyēya-kh*.

As regards verbs ending in vowels, the usual rule is followed Thus, from खि *khi*, eat, the aorist participle is ख्योव् *khĕyōv*; and from चि *ci*, drink, च्योव् *cĕyov*.

From नि *ni*, take, we get, as usual नियोव् *niyōv*, not न्योव् *nĕyōv*. दि *di*, give and हि *hi*, take, are, as in the Past, irregular. Of दि *di*, the Aorist Participle is दित्सोव् *ditsōv* (pl. दित्साय् *ditsạ̄y*; fem. दित्साय *ditsạ̄y°*), and of हि *hi*, ह्यत्सोव् *hĕtsōv* (pl. ह्यत्साय् *hĕtsạ̄y*; fem. ह्यत्साय *hĕtsạ̄y°*) (viii. iii. 32). See p. 61.

Double pronominal suffixes can be added, as in the case of the Past. Thus, कर्योथस् *karyō-th-as*, thou madest me; कर्योमय् *karyō-m-ay*, I made for thee; कर्योमस् *karyō-m-as*, I made for him. Other examples are unnecessary. The rules are exactly the same as in the case of the past tense. *Vide*, however, special cases mentioned after the Paradigm of the third conjugation (p. 70).

(*b*). Impersonal verb (viii. iii. 14). (*c.* forms only).

'I laughed,' *lit.* 'it was laughed by me,' &c.

Singular 1 असोम् *asō-m*, I laughed.
2 असोथ् *asō-th*, thou laughedst.
3 असोन् *asō-n*, he laughed.

Plural 1 असोव् *asōv*, we laughed.
2 असोव *asō-w°*, you laughed.
3 असोख् *asō-kh*, they laughed.

When an impersonal verb is conjugated in the feminine (see pp. 22 and 48) we get

SINGULAR AND PLURAL.

Singular 1 च़ुव्येयम् *tsuvyēya-m*, I quarrelled.
2 च़ुव्येयथ् *tsuvyēya-th*, thou didst quarrel.
3 च़ुव्येयन् *tsuvyēya-n*, he quarrelled.

Plural 1 च़ुव्येय *tsuvyēy°*, we quarrelled.
2 च़ुव्येयव *tsuvyēy°-w°*, you quarrelled.
3 च़ुव्येयख् *tsuvyēya-kh*, they quarrelled.

The feminine impersonal verbs चर *tsar*, &c., (see pp. 16, 22 and 49) have the following forms,—

चर्येयम् *tsaryĕya-m*, I was inwardly wrathful.

चर्येयिय् *tsaryĕyi-y* (with inserted *i*; see p. 70 *post*), thou wast inwardly angry.

चर्येयस् *tsaryĕya-s*, he was inwardly angry.

And so on.

So also (viii. iii. 45) त्यंब्येयस् *tyambyĕya-s* (3rd conj.), he glanced eagerly.

B. Second Conjugation.

Neuter verb (viii. iii. 39). (*c.* forms only).

'I became, &c.'

	Singular.		Plural.	
	Masculine.	Feminine.	Masculine.	Feminine.
1	बुव्योस् *bŏvyō-s*.	बुव्येयस् *bŏvyĕya-s*.	बुव्येय् *bŏvyĕy*.	बुव्येय *bŏvyĕy^{a}*.
2	बुव्योख् *bŏvyō-kh*.	बुव्येयख् *bŏvyĕya-kh*.	बुव्येव *bŏvyĕ-w^{a}*.	बुव्येयव *bŏvyĕy^{a}-w^{a}*.[1]
3	बुव्योव् *bŏvyōv*.	बुव्येय *bŏvyĕy^{a}*.	बुव्येय् *bŏvyĕy*.	बुव्येय *bŏvyĕy^{a}*.

C. Third Conjugation.

Neuter verb उफ *wuph*, fly (viii. iii. 39). (*c.* forms only).

'I flew (just now),' used in the sense of the Past, and not as the tense of the Aorist.

1st Sing. Masc. उफ्योस् *wuphyō-s*, &c., exactly as in the second conjugation.

In this tense, the difference between the second and third conjugations consists in the formation of the Aorist Participle, as already explained, and not in the conjugation.

[1] Içvara-kaula (viii. iii. 44) gives बुव्येव *bŏvyĕw^{a}*, but my Paṇḍit says this is a mistake. The form given above is the correct one.

The Aorist of पि *pi*, fall, used in the sense of the Past, is (viii. iii. 48, 60, 61),—

'I fell, &c.'

	Singular.		**Plural.**	
	Masculine.	**Feminine.**	**Masculine.**	**Feminine.**
1	प्यौस् *pyau-s* (not प्योस् *pyō-s*).	पयस् *pĕya-s*.	पय् *pĕy*.	पय *pĕy*^{e}.
2	प्यौख् *pyau-kh*.	पयख् *pĕya-kh*.	प्येव *pyē-w*^{e}.	पयव *pĕy*^{e}*-w*^{e}.
3	प्यौव् *pyauv*.	पय *pĕy*^{e}.	पय् *pĕy*.	पय *pĕy*^{e}.

Note the specially irregular 2nd person plur. masc.

The Aorist of verb गछ् *gatsh*, go, used in the sense of the past, is (viii. iii. 48, 58, 60, 61).

'I went, &c.'

	Singular.		**Plural.**	
	Masculine.	**Feminine.**	**Masculine.**	**Feminine.**
1	गौस् *gau-s*.	गयस् *gaya-s*.	गय् *gay*.	गय *gay*^{e}.
2	गौख् *gau-kh*.	गयख् *gaya-kh*.	गाव *gā-w*^{e}.	गयव *gay*^{e}*-w*^{e}.
3	गौव् *gauv*.	गय *gay*^{e}.	गय् *gay*.	गय *gay*^{e}.

When this verb is used in the meaning of 'be proper,' it is regular, and belongs to the 2nd conjugation. Thus, गछु *gatsh*^{u}, it was proper (viii. iii. 58). In this sense it is only used in the Past. The Aorist and Pluperfect do not occur (82).

There are also other irregular Aorists of this conjugation. There are those of the roots यि *yi*, come; सि *si*, be born; नेर् *nĕr*, go forth; अच़ *ats*, enter; प्रव *pras*, be born. The Aorist Participles, in the sense of the Past will be found in the list of irregular Aorist Participles, and no difficulty will be found in conjugating them. They are here given for ready reference.

	AORIST PARTICIPLES.
यि *yi*, come.	आव् *āv*.
सि *si*, be born.	ज़ाव् *zāv*.
नेर् *nĕr*, issue.	द्राव् *drāv*.
अच़ *ats*, enter.	च़ाव् *tsāv*.
प्रव *pras*, be born.	प्याव् *pyāv*.

The feminine and masculine plurals are given in the list of Aorist Participles. It will be seen that they must be conjugated as if they were Pluperfects. Vide p. 74.

When the suffix of the dative of the second person singular is added to a form ending in ओव् *ōv*, ओ *ō* becomes ॖ *wa* (*ŏ*) (viii. iii. 43). Thus, करेव् *karyōv* + अय् *ay*, करुय् *karyŏy*,[1] we made for thee. वुफुय् *wuphyŏy*,[1] he flew for thee. गौव् *gauv* (root गछ *gatsh*), he went; गुय् *gŏy*, he went for thee. प्यौव् *pyauv*, he fell; प्युय् *pyŏy*, he fell for thee. The plural of गौव् *gauv*, is गय् *gay*, and 'they went for thee' is गय् *gay*. So, 'they fell for thee' is पय् *pyay*.

[When the same form अय् *ay* is added to a form in य *y*ᵉ, इ *i* is inserted. Thus, करेंय *karyĕy*ᵉ, she was made by us; करेंयिय् *karyĕyi-y*, she was made by us for thee. Compare च़रेंयिय् *tsaryĕyi-y* on p. 68 *ante*].

[1] These are the forms according to the *Sūtra*. But my Paṇḍit maintains that the true forms are करेयि *karyō-y*, and वुफ्योय् *wuphyō-y*. The exceptional forms, he says, only occur in the case of the verbs गछ *gatsh*, go, and पि *pi*, fall. The *Sūtra* while making the rule absolutely general, only gives the two last-named verbs as examples.

6 (*a*). The Pluperfect Participle.

This participle occurs in all three conjugations. In the first two conjugations (viii. iii. 78), it expresses remote time. Thus, कर्यान् *karyā-n*, he made (a long time ago); बूव्याव् *bŏvyāv*, he became (a long time ago).

In the third conjugation it is used in the sense of an Aorist Participle, and expresses past time indefinitely, with no reference to proximity or distance. It is hence the participle, and the Pluperfect is the tense, of narration in this conjugation. Thus, वुफ्याव् *wuphyāv*, he flew. In order to supply the place of Pluperfect, a new tense is formed in this conjugation, which may be called the True Pluperfect. Thus, वुफियाव् *wuphiyāv*, he flew a long time ago.

The Pluperfect Participle is formed by changing the termination ओव् *ōv* of the aorist participle to आव् *āv* (viii. iii. 35). Thus Aorist Participle, कर्योव् *karyōv*; Pluperfect Participle, कर्याव् *karyāv*. In the first conjugation, the masculine plural is formed by inserting ए *ĕ*, before the termination of the masculine plural of the Aorist Participle. Thus, कर्योव् *karyōv*; masc. plur. कर्यैय् *karyĕy*; Pluperfect part. masc. plur. करेयेय् *karĕyĕy* (viii. iii. 36). When the Aorist masc. plural ends in आय् *āy* (*vide*, p. 61) this is changed to आयेय् *āyĕy*. Thus; Aorist Participle ह्यचोव् *hĕtsōv*, taken; masc. plur. ह्यचाय् *hĕtsāy*; Pluperfect Part. masc. plur. ह्यचायेय् *hĕtsāyĕy* (viii. iii. 37). The feminine singular and plural are the same as those of the Aorist Participle (viii. iii. 38).

In the second and third conjugations, the masculine plural is formed by changing आव् *āv* of the singular to आय् *āy* (viii, iii, 40). See, however, p. 74. Thus वुफ्याव् *wuphyāv*, flown; masc. pl., वुफ्याय् *wuphyāy*. The feminine (singular and plural) is formed by changing आव् *āv* to एव *ĕy*°. Thus वुफ्येव *wuphyĕy*° (viii, iii. 44).

6 (*b*). The Pluperfect Tense.

This is formed from the Pluperfect Participle, exactly as the Aorist Tense is formed from the Aorist Participle.

We thus get the following forms.

A. First Conjugation.

Transitive verb (viii. iii. 35). (*c.* forms only).

'I made,' *lit.*, 'he, she, it, etc., was (were) made by me, you, him, us, &c.'

	Singular.		Plural.	
	Masculine. कर्यांव् *karyāv*, made.	Feminine. कर्येंय *karyĕy*^{e}.	Masculine. करेयेव् *karĕyĕy*, made.	Feminine. कर्येंय *karyĕy*^{e}.
Sing.				
1	कर्यांम् *karyā-m.*	कर्येंयम् *karyĕya-m.*	करेयेम् *karĕyĕ-m.*	कर्येंयम् *karyĕya-m.*
2	कर्यांथ् *karyā-th.*	कर्येंयथ् *karyĕya-th.*	करेयेथ् *karĕyĕ-th.*	कर्येंयथ् *karyĕya-th.*
3	कर्यांन् *karyā-n.*	कर्येंयन् *karyĕya-n.*	करेयेन् *karĕyĕ-n.*	कर्येंयन् *karyĕya-n.*
Plur.				
1	कर्यांव् *karyāv.*	कर्येंय *karyĕy*^{e}.	करेयेव् *karĕyĕy.*	कर्येंय *karyĕy*^{e}.
2	कर्यांव *karyā-w*^{e}.	कर्येंयव *karyĕy*^{e}*-w*^{e}.	करेयेव *karĕyĕ-w*^{e}.	कर्येंयव *karyĕy*^{e}*-w*^{e}.
3	कर्यांख् *karyā-kh.*	कर्येंयख *karyĕya-kh.*	करेयेख् *karĕyĕ-kh.*	कर्येंयख् *karyĕya-kh.*

From खि *khi*, eat, we have खेयाम् *khĕyā-m*; plur. खेयेयेम् *khĕyĕyĕ-m.* So from चि *ci*, drink.

From नि *ni*, take, नियाम् *niyā-m* and नियेयेम् *niyĕyĕ-m.*

Similarly, from, हि *hi*, take, हॆत्साम् *hĕtsā-m*; plur. हॆत्सांयेम् *hĕtsạyĕ-m*; and from दि *di*, give, दित्साम् *ditsām*, and दित्सांयेम् *ditsạyĕ-m* (see p. 71).

Impersonal verbs are similarly conjugated. Thus, असाम् *asā-m*, I laughed. Those that are conjugated in the feminine (see pp. 16, 22, 49 and 68), are, of course, the same as the Aorist.

Double pronominal suffixes may be added, as in the case of the Past and the Aorist. Thus, कर्याथिस् *karyā-th-as*, thou madest me; कर्यामय् *karyā-m-ay*, I made for thee; कर्यामस् *karyā-m-as*, I made for him. Further examples are unnecessary. See, however, the special cases mentioned after the paradigm of the third conjugation (p. 75).

B. Second Conjugation.

Neuter verb (viii. iii. 40). (*c.* forms only).

'I became a long time ago.'

	Singular.		Plural.	
	Masculine.	Feminine.	Masculine.	Feminine.
1	बुव्यास् *bŏvyā-s.*	बुव्येयस् *bŏvyĕya-s.*	बुव्याय् *bŏvyāy.*	बुव्येय *bŏvyĕy^{e}.*
2	बुव्याख् *bŏvyā-kh.*	बुव्येयख् *bŏvyĕya-kh.*	बुव्याव *bŏvyā-w^{e}.*	बुव्येयव *bŏvyĕy^{e}-w^{e}.*
3	बुव्याव् *bŏvyāv.*	बुव्येय *bŏvyĕy^{e}.*	बुव्याय् *bŏvyāy.*	बुव्येय *bŏvyĕy^{e}.*

C. Third Conjugation.

In this conjugation, the tense has merely the meaning of an Aorist, not of a Pluperfect, and is the tense used in narration. It is conjugated as follows.

Neuter verb (viii. iii. 40, 44). (*c.* forms only).

'I flew, &c.'

	Singular.		Plural.	
	Masculine.	Feminine.	Masculine.	Feminine.
1	वुफ्यास् *wuphya-s.*	वुफ्येयस् *wuphyeya-s.*	वुफ्याय् *wuphyāy.*	वुफ्येय *wuphyey^{e}.*
2	वुफ्याख् *wuphyā-kh.*	वुफ्येयख् *wuphyĕya-kh.*	वुफ्याव *wuphyā-w^{e}.*	वुफ्येयव *wuphyĕy^{e}-w^{e}.*[1]
3	वुफ्याव् *wuphyāv.*	वुफ्येय *wuphyĕy^{e}.*	वुफ्याय् *wuphyāy.*	वुफ्येय *wuphyey^{e}.*

[1] Içvara-kaula gives वुफ्येव *wuphyē-w^{e}*, which my Paṇḍit says is wrong.

In the plural masculine Īçvara-kaula gives वुफ्येय् *wuphyēy*, but this is directly contrary to the rule (viii. iii. 40) of which the word is given as an example.

If it is desired to give the force of the pluperfect to a verb of the 3rd conjugation, we must insert an इ *i* before the याव् *yāv* of the participle. We thus get what I call the True-Pluperfect tense, which is as follows (viii. iii. 50).

True Pluperfect (3rd conjugation only) (*c.* forms only).
'I flew (a long time ago), &c.'

	Singular.		Plural.	
	Masculine.	Feminine.	Masculine.	Feminine.
Sing. 1	वुफियास् *wuphiyā-s.*	वुफियेयस् *wuphiyēya-s.*	वुफियाय् *wuphiyāy.*	वुफियेव *wuphiyēy^{e}.*
2	वुफियाख् *wuphiyā-kh.*	वुफियेयख् *wuphiyēya-kh.*	वुफियाव *wuphiyā-w^{e}.*	वुफियेवव *wuphiyēy^{e}-w^{e}.*
3	वुफियाव् *wuphiyāv.*	वुफियेय *wuphiyēy^{e}.*	वुफियाय् *wuphiyāy.*	वुफियेय *wuphiyēy^{e}.*

For the plural masculine Īçvara-kaula gives (viii. iii. 40) as examples both मुकलियेय् *mŏkaliyēy* and मुकलियाय् *mŏkaliyāy*, we or they were released. According to his own rule, of which these are examples, the latter is the correct form. For the second person plural feminine he gives (44) नवियेव *naviyēw^{e}*, you became new, which, according to my Paṇḍit is incorrect for नवियेवव *naviyēy^{e}-w^{e}*.

This form cannot be used after cases ending in च् *ts*, छ *tsh*, स् *s*, or श् *ś*. Thus, plup. तेस्याव् *tēsyāv*, not तेसियाव् *tēsiyāv* (viii. iii. 51).

As an example of the True Pluperfect of the feminine impersonal verbs (see pp. 16, 22, 49, 54, 67, and 68), we may give (viii. iii. 45)

त्यंबियेयम् *tyambiyēya-m*, I glanced eagerly.

त्यंबियेयिय् *tyambiyēyi-y* (see p. 70), thou didst glance eagerly.

त्यंबियेयस *tyambiyēya-s*, he glanced eagerly.

The formation of the Pluperfect and True Pluperfect participles of the following verbs is irregular :—

	PLUPERFECT PARTICIPLE.	TRUE PLUPERFECT PARTICIPLE.
यि *yi*, come.	आयोव् *āyōv*.	आयाव् *āyāv*.
ज़ि *zi*, be born.	ज़ायोव् *zāyōv*.	ज़ायाव् *zāyāv*.
नेर *nēr*, go forth.	द्रायोव् *drāyōv*.	द्रायाव् *drāyāv*.
अच़ *ats*, enter.	च़ायोव् *tsāyōv*.	च़ायाव् *tsāyāv*.
प्रस *pras*, be born.	प्यायोव् *pyāyōv*.	प्यायाव् *pyāyāv*.
पि *pi*, fall.	प्ययोव् *pĕyōv*.	प्ययाव् *pĕyāv*.
गछ् *gatsh*, go.	गयोव् *gayōv*.	गयाव् *gayāv*.

It will be seen that these Pluperfect Participles (in the sense of the Aorist) are really Aorist Participles of the second conjugation. The feminine, and masculine plural forms, will be found in the list of irregular Aorist Participles (pp. 62 and ff.).

When pronominal suffixes are added to this tense, a final व् *v* or य् *y* is elided, as in the case of the aorist (p. 66). Thus, आयाव् *āyāv* + अस् *as*, आयास् *āyā-s*, he came to him. आयाय् *āyāy* + अस् *as*, आयास् *āyā-s*, they came to him. Other examples of these suffixes are आयाम् *āyā-m* + अस् *as*, आयामस् *āyā-m-as*, I came to him; आयाख् *āyā-kh* + अस् *as*, आयाहस् *āyā-h-as*, thou camest to him; आयाव *āyā-wa* + अस् *as*, आयावस् *āyā-wa-s*, you came to him (viii. iii. 41).

When अय् *ay*, the suffix of the dative of the second person singular is added; आव् *āv* becomes ओ *ō*, and आय् *āy*, ऐ *ạ̄* (42). Thus, ओय् *ōy* (आव् *āv* + अय् *ay*), he came for thee; ऐय् *ạ̄y*, they came for thee; द्रोय् *drōy*, he came out for thee; द्रैय् *drạ̄y*, they came out for thee; च़ोय् *tsōy*, he entered for thee; च़ैय् *tsạ̄y*, they entered for thee. So वुफियोय् *wuphiyōy*, he flew for thee (वुफियाव् *wuphiyāv* + अय् *ay*).

7. Perfect Tense.

This tense is not described by Içvara-kaula. It is formed by conjugating the Adjectival Past Participle with the Present tense of the Auxiliary Verb. As in the case of the other past tenses, the construction is passive in verbs of the first conjugation, and active in verbs of the second and third. The pronominal suffixes are added as in the past tenses. They are added to the Auxiliary Verb, and not to the Participle. In the first conjugation they are suffixes of the agent case, and in the other two of the nominative case. As in the case of the Past tense, there are *a*, *b*, and *c* forms,—*i.e.*, we may omit the suffixes at pleasure, except in the second person. Thus,—

(*a*). तॅमि कॅर्॒मॅतु छुह् *tạm*^{i} *kạr*^{u}*mạt*^{u} *chuh*, by him has been made,—

(*b*). तॅमि कॅर्॒मॅतु छुन् *tạm*^{i} *kạr*^{u}*mạt*^{u} *chu-n*, by him has been made-by-him,—

(*c*). कॅर्॒मॅतु छुन् *kạr*^{u}*mạt*^{u} *chu-n*, has been made-by-him,—

all meaning 'he has made.'

In the second person, only the *b* and *c* forms are used. Thus,—

(*b*). तोह्य कॅर्॒मॅतु छुव् *tŏhĕ kạr*^{u}*mạt*^{u} *chu-w*^{u}, by you has been made-by-you.

(*c*). कॅर्॒मॅतु छुव् *kạr*^{u}*mạt*^{u} *chu-w*^{u}, has been made by you, both meaning 'you made.' We cannot say तोह्य कॅर्॒मॅतु छुह् *tŏhĕ kạr*^{u}*mạt*^{u} *chuh*. In the paradigms, I shall only give the *c.* forms.

The Auxiliary Verb may either precede or follow the Participle. Thus, कॅर्॒मॅतु छुम् *kạr*^{u}*mạt*^{u} *chu-m* or छुम् कॅर्॒मॅतु *chu-m kạr*^{u}*mạt*^{u}, but it is considered more elegant for it to precede, when in a sentence, and not standing by itself. Thus, म्य छुम् गर कॅर्॒मॅतु *mĕ chu-m gar*^{u} *kạr*^{u}*mạt*^{u}, I have built a house. When standing by itself, the Auxiliary Verb usually follows.

The following is the conjugation of this tense. Regarding the formation of the Adjective Past Participle, and its declension, see p. 29.

A. First Conjugation.

(a). Transitive verb, (*c.* Forms only).

'I have made,' *Lit.* 'he, she, it, etc., has (have) been made by me.'

	Singular.		Plural.	
	Masculine. कंरुमंतु *kạr*^{u}*mạt*^{u}.	Feminine. कंरमंचु *kạr*^{ü}*mạts*^{ü}.	Masculine. कंरिमंति *kạr*^{i}*mạt*^{i}.	Feminine. करॆमच *karĕmats*^{a}.
Sing. 1	कंरुमंतु छुम् *kạr*^{u}*mạt*^{u} *chu-m*,	कंरमंचु छम् *kạr*^{ü}*mạts*^{ü} *chĕ-m*	कंरिमंति छिम् *kạr*^{i}*mạt*^{i} *chi-m.*	करॆमच छम् *karĕmats*^{a} *chĕ-m.*
2	कंरुमंतु छुथ् *kạr*^{u}*mạt*^{u} *chu-th.*	कंरमंचु छथ् *kạr*^{ü}*mạts*^{ü} *chĕ-th.*	कंरिमंति छिथ् *kạr*^{i}*mạt*^{i} *chi-th.*	करॆमच छथ् *karĕmats*^{a} *chĕ-th.*
3	कंरुमंतु छुन् *kạr*^{u}*mạt*^{u} *chu-n.*	कंरमंचु छन् *kạr*^{ü}*mạts*^{ü} *chĕ-n.*	कंरिमंति छिन् *kạr*^{i}*mạt*^{i} *chi-n.*	करॆमच छन् *karĕmats*^{a} *chĕ-n.*
Plur. 1	कंरुमंतु छुह् *kạr*^{u}*mạt*^{u} *chuh.*	कंरमंचु छह् *kạr*^{ü}*mạts*^{ü} *chĕh.*	कंरिमंति छिह् *kạr*^{i}*mạt*^{i} *chih.*	करॆमच छह् *karĕmats*^{a} *chĕh.*
2	कंरुमंतु छुव *kạr*^{u}*mạt*^{u} *chu-w*^{a}.	कंरमंचु छव *kạr*^{ü}*mạts*^{ü} *chĕ-w*^{a}.	कंरिमंति छिव *kạr*^{i}*mạt*^{i} *chi-w*^{a}.	करॆमच छव *karĕmats*^{a} *chĕ-w*^{a}.
3	कंरुमंतु छुख् *kạr*^{u}*mạt*^{u} *chu-kh.*	कंरमंचु छख् *kạr*^{ü}*mạts*^{ü} *chĕ-kh.*	कंरिमंति छिख् *kạr*^{i}*mạt*^{i} *chi-kh.*	करॆमच छख् *karĕmats*^{a} *chĕ-kh.*

(*b*). Impersonal verb, (*c.* Forms only).

'I have laughed,' *lit.*, 'it has been laughed by me.'

Sing. 1. असमतु छुम् *as^{u}mat^u chu-m*, I have laughed.

2. असमतु छुथ् *as^{u}mat^u chu-th*, thou hast laughed.

3. असमतु छुन् *as^{u}mat^u chu-n*, he has laughed.

Plur. 1. असमतु छुह् *as^{u}mat^u chuh*, we have laughed.

2. असमतु छुव *as^{u}mat^u chu-w^u*, you have laughed.

3. असमतु छुख् *as^{u}mat^u chu-kh*, they have laughed.

Pronominal Suffixes.

When the grammatical subject (*i.e.*, the logical object) is a pronoun, it is frequently added in the shape of another pronominal suffix (nominative form). The following are the masculine forms used. Feminine forms can be easily made on the same principle :—

करमतु छुथस् *kar^{u}mat^u chu-th-as*, have been made-by thee-I, thou hast made me.

So करमच़ छोथस् *kar^{u}matsa^u chŏ-th-as*, thou hast made me (fem.).

करिमति छिथ् *kar^{i}mat^i chi-th*, thou hast made us (masc.). There is no suffix for the first person plural.

करमतु छुनस् *kar^{u}mat^u chu-n-as*, he has made me.

करमतु छुवस् *kar^{u}mat^u chu-w-as*, you have made me.

करमतु छुहस् *kar^{u}mat^u chu-h-as*, they have made me.

करमतु *kar^{u}mat^u* {
छुमख् *chu-m-akh*, I have made thee.
छुनख् *chu-n-akh*, he has made thee.
छुख् *chu-kh*, we have made thee.
छुहख् *chu-h-akh*, they have made thee.
}

When the logical object is the third person, the forms of the first and third persons are not used in this way. This applies also to the plural. We thus have only the two following forms:—

करमतु *kar^{u}mat^u*, {
छुथन् *chu-th-an*, thou hast made him.
छुवन् *chu-w-an*, you have made him.
}

For 'I have made him,' we must use the full pronoun ; thus, सुह् छुम् करमतु *suh chu-m kar^{u}mat^u*, and so for the others.

कॊरिमॊति } kạr^{i}mạt^{i}, { छिमव chi-m-aw^{e}, I have made you.
{ छिनव chi-n-aw^{e}, he has made you.
{ छिहव chi-h-aw^{e}, they have made you.

कॊरिमॊति } kạr^{i}mạt^{i}, { छिथख chi-th-akh, thou hast made them.
{ छिवख chi-w-akh, you have made them.

B. Second Conjugation.

Neuter verb. (c. forms only).

I have become, &c.

	Singular.		Plural.	
	Masculine.	Feminine.	Masculine.	Feminine.
1	बॊवमॊतु छुस bộv^{u}mạt^{u} chu-s.	बॊवमॊचु छस bộv^{ü}mạts^{ü} chĕ-s.	बॊविमॊति छिह् bộv^{i}mạt^{i} chih.	बॊवमच छह् bŏvŏmats^{e} chĕh.
2	बॊवमॊतु छुख bộv^{u}mạt^{u} chu-kh.	बॊवमॊचु छख bộv^{ü}mạts^{ü} chĕ-kh.	बॊविमॊति छिव bộv^{i}mạt^{i} chi-w^{e}.	बॊवमच छव bŏvŏmats^{e} chĕ-w^{e}.
3	बॊवमॊतु छुह् bộv^{u}mạt^{u} chuh.	बॊवमॊचु छह् bộv^{ü}mạts^{ü} chĕh.	बॊविमॊति छिह् bộv^{i}mạt^{i} chih.	बॊवमच छह् bŏvŏmats^{e} chĕh.

C. Third Conjugation.

Neuter verb. (c. forms only).

I have flown, &c.

	Singular.		Plural.	
	Masculine.	Feminine.	Masculine.	Feminine.
1	वुफ्योमॊतु छुस wuphyōmạt^{u} chu-s.	वुफ्येमॊचु छस wuphyĕmạts^{ü} chĕ-s.	वुफ्येमॊति छिह् wuphyĕmạt^{i} chih.	वुफ्येमच छह् wuphyĕmats^{e} chĕh.
2	वुफ्योमॊतु छुख wuphyōmạt^{u} chu-kh.	वुफ्येमॊचु छख wuphyĕmạts^{ü} chĕ-kh.	वुफ्येमॊति छिव wuphyĕmạt^{i} chi-w^{e}.	वुफ्येमच छव wuphyĕmats^{e} chĕ-w^{e}.
3	वुफ्योमॊतु छुह् wuphyōmạt^{u} chuh.	वुफ्येमॊचु छह् wuphyĕmạts^{ü} chĕh.	वुफ्येमॊति छिह् wuphyĕmạt^{i} chih.	वुफ्येमच छह् wuphyĕmạts^{e} chĕh.

8. The Periphrastic Pluperfect Tense.

This tense, also, is not mentioned by Īçvara-kaula. It is formed exactly like the perfect, except that the past tense of the auxiliary verb is used instead of the present. It is unnecessary to give full paradigms, the following examples will suffice.

कंर्मंतु ओसुम् *kạrᵘmạtᵘ ōsu-m*, I had made (him).

कंर्मंतू आसूम् *kạrᵘmạtsᵘ ạsᵘ-m*, I had made (her).

कंरिमंति आसिम् *kạrⁱmạtⁱ ạsi-m*, I had made (them, masc.).

करेमच आसम् *karĕmatsᵘ āsa-m*, I had made (them, fem.).

बूंवमंतु ओसुस् *bŏvᵘmạtᵘ ōsu-s*, I had become.

वुफ्योमंतु ओसुस् *wuphyōmạtᵘ ōsu-s*, I had flown.

Or, with double pronominal suffix.

कंर्मंतु ओसुथस् *kạrᵘmạtᵘ ōsᵘ-th-as*, thou hadst made me.

B. Imperative Mood.

1 (*a*). The Present Tense.

The terminations are (viii. ii. 5).

Singular.		Plural.	
2	ह् *h*.	2	इव् *iv*.
3	इन् *in*.	3	इन् *in*.

If the root ends in a consonant, the ह् *h* of the 2nd singular is elided (6). Thus,—

कर् *kar*, make thou. करिव् *kariv*, make ye.

करिन् *karin*, let him make. करिन् *karin*, let them make.

From दि *di*, give, which does not end in a consonant, we get for 2nd singular दिह् *dih*, not दि *di*.

If the root of the verb contains the letter ओ *ō*, that ओ *ō* becomes ऊ *ū*, in the Imperative (7). Thus,—

रोस् *rōs*, stand, 3rd Sing. Imperat. रूसिन् *rūsin*.

तोल् *tōl*, weigh, „ „ तूलिन् *tūlin*.

पोठ् *poṭh*, be fat, „ „ पूठिन् *pūṭhin*.

So also, if the root contains ए *ē*, it becomes ई *ī* (7). Thus,—

नेर् *nēr*, go forth, नीरिन् *nīrin*.

शेंक *çēk*, fear, शींकिन् *çīkin*.

पेड् *pēḍ*, exude, पीडिन् *pīḍin*.

These changes, however, do not occur in the second person singular (8). Thus, we have, रोज़् *rōs*, तोल् *tōl*, पोठ् *pōṭh*, नेर् *nēr*, पक् *pök*, पोड् *pōḍ*.

We thus find the Present Imperative of रोज़् *rōs*, remain, to be conjugated as follows.

	Singular.	Plural.
1	रोज़् *rōs*.	रूज़िव् *rūsiv*.
2	रूज़िन् *rūsin*.	रूज़िन् *rūsin*.

Every root ending in a vowel, takes the letter य *y* before all terminations, except that of the second person singular (10). Moreover a final इ *i* of the root is changed to य *ya*(ĕ), except in the case of the verbs नि *ni*, take, दि *di*, give, and यि *yi*, come (11). We thus get the following conjugation of a verb whose root ends in a vowel.

(*a*) खि *khi*, eat.

	Singular.	Plural.
2	ख्यह् *khĕh*.	ख्यियिव् *khĕyiv*.
3	ख्यियिन् *khĕyin*.	ख्यियिन् *khĕyin*.

(*b*) दि *di*, give.

	Singular.	Plural.
2	दिह् *dih*.	दियिव् *diyiv*.
3	दियिन् *diyin*.	दियिन् *diyin*.

The root यि *yi*, come, is further irregular, in that, besides being conjugated like दि *di*, it also optionally takes the following form (viii. ii. 12).

	Singular.	Plural.
2	वोल *wŏl*[a] (not वोल् *wŏl*).	वोलिव् *wŏliv*.
3	वोलिन् *wŏlin*.	वोलिन् *wŏlin*.

The root बव *bŏv*, become, has the following forms (14).

	Singular.	Plural.
2	बव् *bŏv*.	बविव् *bŏviv*.
3	बविन् *bŏvin*, बयिन् *bŏyin*.	बविन् *bŏvin* or बयिन् *bŏyin*.

The verbs (see pp. 16, 22, 37 and 49).

त्सर *tsar*, be inwardly wrathful.

फश *phŏç*, be inwardly wrathful.

फुह *phuh*, be inwardly wrathful.

मर्त्स *marts*, be inwardly wrathful.

वुत्स *wuts*, be burnt.

फित्स *phits*, forget.

त्यंब *tyamb*, look eagerly.

All of which are impersonal, and are only used in the third person singular, to which the appropriate pronominal suffixes of the dative are added. (viii. ii. 9).

Thus,—

त्सॊरिनय् *tsǫr*ⁱ*n-ay*, let there be inward anger to thee, *i.e.*, be thou angry.

त्सॊरिनव *tsǫr*ⁱ*n-aw*ᵉ, be ye angry.

त्सॊरिनस् *tsǫr*ⁱ*n-as*, let him be angry.

त्सॊरिनख् *tsǫr*ⁱ*n-akh*, let them be angry.

Regarding the vowel changes, see the following rule.

When a pronominal suffix is added to the Imperative third person singular or plural, the इ *i* of the imperative becomes *i-mātrā*, and the preceding vowel is modified. Thus,

करिन् *karin*, let him make.

कॊरिनम् *kǫr*ⁱ*n-am*, let him make for me.

The second person is,—

Sing. करुम् *karu-m*, make thou for me.

Plur. कर्यूम् *karyū-m*, make ye for me.

When a pronominal suffix is added to the second person singular of the imperative of a root ending in a consonant, the letter उ *u* is inserted (16). Thus, करुन् *karu-n*, make him or it (a very common form); करुम् *karu-m*, make for me; करुस् *karu-s*, make for him; करुख् *karu-kh*, make for them.

As regards roots ending in a vowel, from खि *khi*, eat, we have खॆम् *khĕ-m*, &c. From नि *ni*, take, दि *di*, give, and यि *yi*, come, we have दिम् *di-m*, give thou to me, &c.

When a pronominal suffix is added to the second plural imperative of any verb, इव् *iv*, becomes यू *yū* (17). Thus, करयूम् *karyū-m*, make ye for me; करयूस् *karyū-s*, make ye for him; करयूख् *karyū-kh*, make ye for them. So from खि *khi*, eat, खययूम् *khyayū-m*, &c., and from नि *ni*, दि *di*, and यि *yi*, दियूम् *diyū-m*, &c.

1 (*b*). The Modified Present Imperative.

This, though not a respectful imperative, is more polite than the simple tense. It is formed by inserting the particle त *ta*. It expresses encouragement, like the Hindī करो तो *karō tō!* It also expresses permission; thus, 'very well, if you wish to do it, do it.' The terminations are as follows (viii. ii. 14).

	Singular.	Plural.
2	त *tᵃ*.	इतव् *ⁱtav*.
3	इतन् *ⁱtan*.	इतन् *ⁱtan*.

The terminations are all added to the root direct (15). The ⁱ being *i-mātrā*, a preceding vowel is modified in the 2nd plural, and 3rd sing. and plur. Thus,

	Singular.	Plural.
2	कर्त *kartᵃ*.	करितव् *kąrⁱtav*.
3	करितन् *kąrⁱtan*.	करितन् *kąrⁱtan*.

So also from खार् *khār*, mount, खारितन् *khą̄rⁱtan*; from वाल् *wāl*, bring down, वालितन् *wą̄lⁱtan*; from रोज़ *rōz*, remain, 2nd sing. रोज़्त *rōztᵃ*, 3rd sing. रूज़ितन् *rūzⁱtan*; from नेर् *nēr*, go forth, नेर्त *nērtᵃ*, नीरितन् *nīrⁱtan*; and from ज़र् *tsar*, be inwardly wrathful, &c., ज़रितनय् *tsąrⁱtanay*, &c., (see p. 82).

Regarding roots ending in vowels we have from खि *khi*, eat.

	Singular.	Plural.
2	खेत *khētᵃ*.	खेयितव् *khę̄yⁱtav*.
3	खेयितन् *khę̄yⁱtan*.	खेयितन् *khę̄yⁱtan*.

For नि *ni*, take, दि *di*, give, and यि *yi*, come, we have, however, the following forms.

	SINGULAR.	PLURAL.
2	दित *dit°.*	दिर्यितव् *diy^{i}tav.*
3	दिर्यितन् *diy^{i}tan.*	दिर्यितन् *diy^{i}tan.*

The pronominal suffixes are added regularly, except that in the second plural, अव् *av* becomes ओ *ō* (18). Thus, करितोम् *kạr^{i}tō-m*, make ye for me; करितोन् *kạr^{i}tō-n*, make ye him; करितोस् *kạr^{i}tō-s*, make ye for him; करितोख् *kạr^{i}tō-kh*, make ye for them.

2. THE FUTURE IMPERATIVE.

This is formed by adding इज़ि *'zi* if the root ends in a consonant, and ज़ि *zi* if it ends in a vowel. Before इज़ि *'zi*, a preceding vowel is modified (viii. ii. 22, 24). This tense does not change for number or person. It means 'you, or he, should do a thing at some future time,' or 'make a practice of doing it.' Thus

चह् करिज़ि *ts°h kạr^{i}zi*, thou shouldest do.
तॊहि करिज़ि *tọh^{i} kạr^{i}zi*, you should do.
सुह् करिज़ि *suh kạr^{i}zi*, he should do.
तिम् करिज़ि *tim kạr^{i}zi*, they should do.

So also from खार् *khār*, mount, खारिज़ि *khār^{i}zi;* from वाल *wāl*, bring down, वालिज़ि *wạl^{i}zi;* from रोस् *rōs*, stand, रूसिज़ि *rūs^{i}zi;* and from नेर् *nēr*, go forth, नीरिज़ि *nīr^{i}zi.* I cannot find that this form is used with impersonal verbs like ज़ार् *tsạr* etc., mentioned when dealing with the Simple Imperative.

As regards verbs ending in a vowel, we have from खि *khi*, eat, खेज़ि *khēzi;* so also in other cases, but from नि *ni*, take, दि *di*, give, and यि *yi*, come, we have दिज़ि *dizi*, etc.

When the pronominal suffixes अम् *am* and अस् *as* are used with this form, ज़ि *zi* becomes ज्य *zya.* (viii. ii. 25).

Thus करिज़्यम् *kạr^{i}zy-am*, you should make me, or for me.
So करिज़्यस् *kạr^{i}zy-as*, you should make for him.

In other cases, the शि *si*, is unchanged.

Thus कॅरिशिय् *kạr'si-y*, he should make for thee.

[Note. My Pandit also says कॅरिस्यन् *kạr'sy-an*, not कॅरिशिन् *kạr'sin*; so also he says कॅरिस्यव *kạr'sy-aw*, and कॅरिस्यख् *kạr'sy-akh*].

3. The Past Imperative.

This is formed by adding हे *hē* for all persons and numbers to the Future Imperative (viii. ii. 23). It means 'you should have made so and so,' implying that he had not done it.

Thus कॅरिशिहे *kạr'sihē*, thou shouldst, you, he, or they, should have made.

Pronominal suffixes are added regularly (25). Thus कॅरिशिहेम् *kạr'sihē-m*, you should have made for me.

C. Benedictive Mood.

1. Future Tense.

This tense expresses a wish. It is formed from the Pluperfect Indicative, by substituting the following terminations (viii. ii. 26).

	Singular.	Plural.
2	यख् *yakh*.	इव् *iv*.
3	यन् *yan*.	यन् *yan*.

The tense expresses a wish. Thus, लछ्यन् *laçyan*, may he live long. The following is a specimen of the conjugation of the tense of the verb कर् *kar*, make; Pluperfect कर्यान् *karyā-n* he made.

'Mayst thou make, &c.'

	Singular.	Plural.
2	कर्यख् *karyakh*.	करिव *kariv*.
3	कर्यन् *karyan*.	कर्यन् *karyan*.

So from रन् *ran*, cook; 3rd sing. Plup. रञान् *rañā-n*; 3rd sing. Bened. रञ्यन् *rañyan*. Similarly ज़ेञ्यन् *zēñyan*, may he conquer.

Roots ending in स *s* change the final स *s* to छ *ç*. Thus, from लस् *las*, live long; 3rd sing. plup. ल्यूस्हाव *lyūshāv*, but 3rd sing. Bened. लछ्यन् *laçyan*. So also, from आस *ās*, be, आछ्यन् *āçyan*.

The verb चाव *chāv*, use, has for its second singular Bened. either चाव्यख् *chāvyakh* or चाय्यख् *chāyyakh*. The latter form is peculiar to the second person singular (27).

The verb बोव *bŏv*, be, become, changes its final व *v* to य *y* throughout. Thus, बुय्यन् *bŏyyan* (not बुव्यन् *bŏvyan*), may it be; म बुय्यन् *m*^{e} *bŏyyan*, may it not be, God forbid! (26).

Pronominal suffixes are added in the usual way. Thus, लस्यनय् *laçyan-ay*, may he live for thee! पोष्यनय् *pōṣyan-ay*, may he be victorious for thee!

This tense only occurs in the above verbs (26).

D. Conditional Mood.

1. Present Future Tense.

This is the same as Future Indicative. An example of its use is बुय गछ सुह् वुछन् *bŏ-y gatsh*^{e}, *suh wucha-n*. If I go, I shall see him. बुय् *bŏy* is contracted from बुह् *bŏh*, I, and अय् *ay*, if. The object is mentioned twice. First fully in सुह् *suh*, and again as a pronominal suffix (न् *n*).

2. The Past Conditional Tense.

This tense is used if things are spoken of that might have, but have not, happened. Thus, रूद् अय् प्यिये स्वछ् सपज़िहे *rūd ay pĕyihē*, *sŏch sapazihē*, if there had been rain, there would have been plenty. It is conjugated as follows (viii. ii. 32).

	Singular.	Plural.
1	करहा *karahạ̄*, (if) I had made.	करहाव् *karahạ̄v*.
2	करहाख् *karahạ̄kh*,	करिहीव् *kạr*^{i}*hīv*.
3	करिहे *karihē*,	करहान् *karahạ̄n*.

Notes. (1) When the last syllable contains the vowel आ *ā*, that vowel is always modified. This is not mentioned by Īçvara-kaula, but is a fact.

(2) The short *i* in the second person plural is *i-mātrā*, and modifies the preceding root vowel when possible.

Verbs ending in vowels are declined as follows, inserting म् *m* in the first person, as in the Future Indicative.

	Singular.	Plural.
1	ख्यमहा *khyamahạ̄*, (if) I had eaten.	ख्यमहाव् *khyamahạ̄v*.
2	ख्यहाख् *khyahạ̄kh*.	खँयिहीव् *khö̃y'hīv*.
3	खियिहे *khö̆yihē*.	ख्यहान् *khyahạ̄n*.

From मि *mi*, take, दि *di*, give, and यि *yi*, come, we have as follows.

	Singular.	Plural.
1	दिमहा *dimahạ̄*.	दिमहाव् *dimahạ̄v*.
2	दिहाख् *dihạ̄kh*.	दियिहीव् *diy'hīv*.
3	दियिहे *diyihē*.	दिहान् *dihạ̄n*.

Pronominal suffixes are added as follows:—

Added to 1st person.	करहाम् *karahạ̄-m*, (if) I or we had made	myself or for myself.
	करहाय् *karahạ̄-y*, „	thee, or for thee.
	करहाव *karahạ̄-w*ᵃ, „	you, or for you.
	करहान् *karahạ̄-n*, „	him.
	करहास् *karahạ̄-s*, „	for him.
	करहाख् *karahạ̄-kh*, „	them, or for them.
Added to 2nd person singular.	करहाम् *karahạ̄-m*, (if) thou hadst made	me, or for me.
	करहान् *karahạ̄-n*, „	him.
	करहास् *karahạ̄-s*, „	for him.
	करहाख् *karahạ̄-kh*, „	them, or for them.
Added to 2nd person plural.	करिह्यूम् *kạr'hyū-m*, (if) you had made	me or for me.
	करिह्यून् *kạr'hyū-n*, „	him.
	करिह्यूस् *kạr'hyū-s*, „	for him.
	करिह्यूख् *kạr'hyū-kh*, „	them, or for them.
Added to 3rd person singular.	करिहेम् *karihē-m*, (if) he had made	me or for me.
	करिहीय् *karihī-y*, „	thee, or for thee.
	करिहेव *karihē-w*ᵃ, „	you, or for you.
	करिहेस् *karihē-s*, „	him, or for him.
	करिहेख् *karihē-kh* „	them, or for them.

Added to 3rd person plural.

करहानम् *karahạ̄n-am*, if they had made		me or for me.	
करहानय् *karahạ̄n-ay*,	„	thee or for thee.	
करहानव *karahạ̄n-awᵃ*,	„	you or for you.	
करहानस् *karahạ̄n-as*,	„	him or for him.	
करहानख् *karahạ̄n-akh*,	„	them or for them.	

Note.—All the forms added to the second person are irregular; and also the suffix of the second person singular, when added to the verb in the third person singular.

The feminine impersonal verbs a च़र *tsar*, be inwardly angry, etc. (see pp. 16, 22, 37, 49, 54, 68 and 82) are conjugated as follows:—

च़रिहेम् *tsarihē-m*, (if) there had been inward anger to me; (if) I had been inwardly angry.

असि च़रिहे *asĕ tsarihē*, (if) we had been inwardly angry.

च़रिहीय् *tsarihī-y*, if thou hadst been „ „

च़रिहेव *tsarihē-wᵃ*, if you had been „ „

च़रिहेस् *tsarihē-s*, if he had been „ „

च़रिहेख् *tsarihē-kh*, if they had been „ „

This tense may also be used in expressions like the following:—

सुय् करिहे *su-y karihē*, even he did it. That is to say, 'why did you do it? It was his business, and he has done it already.' (35).

From the Journal, Asiatic Society of Bengal, Vol. LXVII. Part I, No. 1,
1899.

On Indeclinable Particles in Kāçmīrī.—*By* G. A. Grierson,
C.I.E., Ph.D., I.C.S.

[Read January, 1899.]

Içvara-kaula does not formally deal with particles in his grammar, but here and there he refers to them, and the following is a collection of his scattered rules. It in no way pretends to be a complete account of Indeclinables.

Emphatic and indefinite particles have been described by me in Vol. LXVII, Part I, pp. 88, and following.

The following two conjunctions are also there mentioned. They are repeated here for the sake of completeness.

त *t^e*, and (iv. 178). *E.g.*, सुह् त त्सॖह् *suh t^e ts^eh*, he and thou.

ति *ti*, also (iv. 179). It is also used instead of त *t^e* with plurals. Thus, सुह् ति त्सॖह् ति *suh ti, ts^eh ti*, he also, you also. मह्निवि ति गुपन् ति आय् *$mahanio^i$ ti gupan ti āy*, both the men and the cattle came. In the last sentence we cannot use त *t^e*.

The negative particle is न *n^e*, not (viii. ii. 19); but ordinarily negative forms of the verb are used, as described under the head of adverbial verbal suffixes. In other words, the न *n^e* is usually compounded with the verb as a suffix. Thus, छुस्न *chu-s-n^e*, I am not.

The prohibitive particle म *m^e* is only used with the Simple Imperative (viii. ii. 19).

म करिन् *m^e karin*, let him not make.

म कर् *m^e kar*, make thou not.

म करिव् *m^e kariv*, make not ye.

With the Modified Imperative मत *mat^e* is used (20). Thus, मत करितन् *mat^e kar^itan*, let him not make.

Instead of म *m°* and मत *mat°*, we may use मा *mā* and मता *matā* respectively (20). Thus, मा कर *mā kar*, मता करे *matā kart°*.

Other vocative particles may also be added. Thus, मबा कर् *mabā kar*, मशा कर *masạ̄ kar*, मतबा करे *matabā kart°*, मतशा करे *matasạ̄ kart°*, and so on (20). See forms of address given in Vol. LXVII, Part I, pp. 92 and ff.

With other tenses of the imperative न *n°* is used (19). Thus, करिजि न *kạr'si n°*, you should not make. करिजिहे न *kạr'sihē n°*, you should not have made.

मा *mā* is used before or after a verb, to indicate a question in hesitation (viii. i. 29). Thus,—

> करान् मा छुह् *karān mā chuh*, or मा छुह् करान् *mā chuh karān*, or मा करान् छुह् *mā karān chuh*, is he making? (*I.e.*, see if he is not making it, or if he is making it or not, or perhaps he is not making it?)
>
> कर्योन् मा *karyōn mā*, did he make?
>
> सुह् मा करि *suh mā kari*, will he make?
>
> ब्वह् मा कर *bŏh mā kar°*, shall I make?

The particle ताञ् *tāñ*, or ताञत् *tāñat*, is used in asking a question, when the speaker is really in doubt as to whether there is anything to ask (viii. i. 26). Thus,—

> क्याह् ताञ् वनुन् *kyāh tāñ wạnun*, did he say anything? Here the speaker did not notice at the time what the man said, and afterwards recalls the fact, and, being in doubt, asks the question?
>
> कर् ताञ् आव् *kar tāñ āv*, did he come at any time? If so, when?
>
> कूत ताञ् द्युतुन् *kūt° tāñ dyutun*, did he give anything? If so, how much?
>
> ताम् *tām*, or तामत् *tāmat*, may be used instead of ताञ् *tāñ*, or ताञत् *tāñat*. Thus, क्याह् ताम् वनुन् *kyāh tām wạnun*.

द्यठ *dyath°*. This added to an interrogative word converts it into an intensive one (viii. i. 27). Thus,—

> कर् *kar*, or कन *kan°*, when?

दठ कर आव् *ḍyath*^{a} *kur āv*, or दठ कन आव् *ḍyath*^{a} *kan*^{a} *āv*, he he came a long time ago.

क्याह् *kyāh*, what? दठ क्याह् *ḍyath*^{a} *kyāh*, a great deal.

कुति *kŭt*^{i}, how many? दठ कुति *ḍyath*^{a} *kŭt*^{i}, a great many, So दठ कनि *dyath*^{a} *kan*^{i}, for a long time.

The usual word for 'if' is अय् *ay*, but, with the Past Conditional (viii. ii. 33), हय् *hay* may be used instead of अय् *ay*, after the verb. Thus,—

करिहे हय् *karihē hay*, if he had made.

करहान् हय् *karahăn hay*, if they had made;

करिहेस् हय् *karihē-s hay*, if he had made it.

With the same tense 'if not' is represented by नय् *nay* (34). Thus, करिहे नय् *karihē nay*, if he had made it; रूद् नय् पियिहे *rūd nay pĕyihē*, if rain had not fallen.

These particles can also be attached to the subject of the verb (35). Thus, सुहय् करिहे *suh-ay karihē*, if he had made; तिमहय् करहान् *tim-hay karahăn*, if they had made: सुनय् करिहे *su-nay karihē*, if he had not made, बुय् ख्यमहा *bŏ-y khyamahă*, if I had eaten.

From the Journal, Asiatic Society of Bengal, Vol. LXV, Part I, No. 4,
1896, p. 306.

A List of Kāçmīrī Verbs.—*By* George A. Grierson, C. I. E., I. C. S.

[Read December, 1896.]

The following list of Kāçmīrī Verbs, is founded on the *dhātu-pāṭha* of *Īçvara-kaula's* Kāçmīrī Grammar, entitled the *Kaçmīra-çabdāmṛta.* The verbs are quoted under their root forms. In the *dhātu-pāṭha* they are all given as ending in *a* or rather in ॰, and I have followed this in the Dēva-nāgarī list. In the transcription in the Roman character, I have followed the usual custom of European scholars in dealing with modern Indo-Aryan roots, and have omitted the final vowel.

There are two conjugations of Kāçmīrī verbs, which differ only in the tenses formed from the Past Participle. The First Conjugation consists of Active and Impersonal Verbs, and its terminations (in these tenses) are formed by the addition of pronominal suffixes of the Instrumental Case. Examples are; (Transitive Verb); *kạru-n* he made (him), literally, he was-made-by-him; (Impersonal Verb); *ạsu-n*, he laughed, lit. it-was-laughed-by-him. Impersonal Verbs only appear in the third person masc. singular.

Active Verbs occur in all genders, numbers and persons. Thus *kạr*ᵉ*-n*, he made (her) (lit. she was-made-by-him); *kạri-n*, he made (them) (lit. they [masc.] were-made-by-him); *karĕ-n* he made them (fem.), (lit. they [fem.] were-made-by-him).

The Second Conjugation consists of Neuter Verbs, and its terminations (in these tenses) are formed by the addition of pronominal suffixes of the Nominative Case (which, however, are omitted in the third person singular and plural, and in the first person plural). Thus *pạku-s*, I went, lit. gone-I. The verb agrees with the subject in gender and number. Thus *pạc*ᵉ*-s*, I (fem.) went. In the accompanying list, Active Verbs are marked (in the first column) with the letter क, *i.e.*, *karmaṇi prayōga*, or passive construction. Impersonal Verbs are marked भा, *i.e.*, *bhāvē prayōga*, or impersonal construction. Neuter Verbs are left unmarked. This information is taken from the *Kaçmīra-çabdāmṛta.*

Three simple tenses are derived from the Past Participle; the Past, the Aorist, and the Pluperfect. In the masculine, the characteristic letter of the Past is *u*, of the Aorist is *yau* or *yō*, and of the Pluperfect *yă*.

The **Past** tense describes something which has happened lately, *e.g.*, *kọru-n*, he has (just) made. It is formed directly from the Past Participle.

Only a small number of verbs of the second conjugation possess this tense. As a rule, Neuter Verbs employ the Aorist to express the idea conveyed, in the case of verbs of the first conjugation, by the Past Tense.

The following verbs (according to the *Kaçmīra-çabdāmṛta*) are the only ones of the second conjugation which have the Past proper.

Thak, pak, samakh, hŏkh, tag, lag, çŏṅg, kᵘts, khŏts, pats, rŏts, vyats, hŏts, gatsh (be proper), *wŏpas, das, rōs, phaṭ, phuṭ, rŏṭ, bŏḍ, wŏl, wŏth, tshyann, sapan, wup, çrap, pray, lay, way, khar, tar, phar, phŏr, mar, sŏr, gal, tsal, ḍal, ḍŏl, phal, phŏll, mŏl, bŏv, rŏv, dŏṣ, pŏṣ, maṣ, rŏṣ, ās, khas, phas, bas, las, lōs, was, byah.*

These verbs, which I shall in future "Listed Verbs' form a class by themselves, and, in the treatment of the final consonant follow the example of verbs of the first conjugation.

Before *ŭ-mātrā* (*i.e.*, in the fem. sg., Past), and before *y* (*i.e.*, in the fem. plur., Past, and in the Aorist and Pluperfect), in the case of verbs of the first conjugation, and of the abovementioned listed Neuter Verbs, certain final consonants of the past participle become palatalized: as follows:—

k, kh and *g*, become *c, ch* and *j*, respectively.

Thus—

3 Masc. sg. Past.	3 Fem. sg. Past.	3 Masc. Aorist.
thọkᵘ, he was weary	*thọcᵘ*	*thacyōv*
lyūkhun (√ *lĕkh*), he wrote	*lichᵘn*	*lĕchyōn*
dọgun, he pounded	*dọjᵘn*	*dajyōn*

ṭ, ṭh and *ḍ*, become *c, ch*, and *j* respectively, but not before *ŭ-mātrā*, only before *y*.

Thus—

phọṭᵘ, he was split	*phọṭᵘ*	*phacyōn*
mọṭhᵘ [√ *maṭ*] he was forgotten	*mọṭhᵘ*	*machyōv*
gọṇḍun, he bound	*gọṇḍᵘn*	*gañjyōn*

t, th, d and *n* become *ts, tsh, z*, and *ñ* respectively, in both cases,

Thus—

kọtun, he spun	*kọtsᵘn*	*katsōn*
wŏthᵘ, he arose	*wŏtshᵘ*	*wotshōv*
lọdun, he built	*lọzᵘn*	*lazōn*
rọnun, he cooked	*rọñᵘn*	*rañōn*

Verbs in *l* change it to *j*.

Thus—

pōlun (√ *pāl*), he protected	*pāj*ᵃ*n*	*pājyōn*
tsalᵘ, he fled	*tsajᵃ*	*tsajyōv*

These changes do *not* occur in the case of verbs of the second conjugation which are not mentioned in the above list. Thus, from the √ *tsēṭh*, be long, we have the Aorist *zēṭhyauv*, not *sēchyauv*.

Note that *y* is elided after *ts*, *tsh*, *s* and *ṡ*, and *z*. It is also elided in the case of the verbs *pi*, 'fall' (*pyauv* not *pi-y-auv*), and *gatsh*, 'go' (*gauv* not *gyauv*).

It is, however, retained in the case of the following Neuter Verbs. *K*ᵃ*ts*, be wet, *grōts*, be splashed out, *tsōts*, be without employment, *tshōts*, be empty, *tēz*, be sharp, *paz*, be fit, *rōts*, be pleasant, *vyats*, be contained, *braz*, shine, *bāwaz*, be pleasant, *lyats*, be weak, *çrōts*, be pure.

Thus, *grōtsyōv*, not *grotsōv*, he was splashed out.

[It is also retained in the following verbs ending in *s*, *ūvas*, *ḍōs*, *tsas*, *tras*, *ras*, *r*ᵃ*s*, *lis*, *vis*, *wōlas*, *wōs*, and optionally in *thās*, *das*, *bās*, *mus*, and *s*ᵃ*s*].

The vowel changes in these verbs are caused by the presence of *mātrā* vowels in the final syllable of the masc. and fem. sg. and masc. plural of the past. There are no vowel changes in the fem. plural, as it never ends in a *mātrā*-vowel, or in the Aorist or Pluperfect. These changes have been explained in my previous paper on Kāçmīrī pronunciation.[1] They are given briefly in the following table, which applies to all verbs of both conjugations.

[1] Vide supra, pp. 280 and ff.

Radical.	As in	Becomes							
		before u-mātrā (masc. sg. past.)	As in	before ū-mātrā (fem. sg. past.)	As in	before i-mātrā, (masc. pl. past.)	As in	before ya (ĕ), (fem. pl. past, & throughout aorist.)	As in
a ...	*karun*, to do,	*ạ*	*kạrun*, (pr. *korun*) he made him,	*ạ*	*kạr*^{ă}*n*, (pr. *kürăn*) he made her,	*ạ*	*kạrin*, (pr. *ka*^{i}*rin*) he made them,	Remains unchanged.	*karĕn, karyŏn.*
ā ...	*mārun*, to kill,	*ō*	*mōrun*,	*ạ̄*	*mạ̄r*^{ă}*n*, (pr. *mōrŭn*)	*ạ̄*	*mạ̄rin*, (pr. *mō*^{i}*rin*)		*mārĕn, māryŏn.*
i ...	*livun*, to plaster,	*yu*	*lyuvun*,	*i* (pr. *yü*)	*liv*^{ă}*n*, (pr. *lyŭvŭn*)	*i*	*livin*,		*livyĕn, livyŏn.*
ī ...	*cīrun*, to squeeze out,	*yū*	*cyūrun*,	*ī*	*cīr*^{ă}*n*,	*ī*	*cīrin*,		*cīrĕn, cīryŏn.*
u ...	*busun*, to parch,	un-changed	*busun*,	un-changed	*bus*^{ă}*n*,	un-changed	*busin*, (pr. *bu*^{i}*sin*)		*busan, busŏn.*
ū ...	*lūṭun*, to rob,	un-changed	*lūṭun*,	un-changed	*lūṭ*^{ă}*n*,	un-changed	*lūṭin*, (pr. *lū*^{i}*ṭin*,		*lūcĕn, lūcyŏn.*
ē ...	*phērun*, to be turned,	*yū*	*phyūr*^{u},	*ī*	*phīr*^{ă},	*ī*	*phīr*^{i},		*phērĕ, phēryŏv.*
ō ...	*bōzun*, to hear,	*ū*	*būzun*,	*ū*	*būz*^{ă}*n*,	*ū*	*bụ̄zin*, (pr. *bū*^{i}*zin*,		*bōzĕn, bōzŏn.*

The **Aorist**, expresses past time indefinitely, with no reference to proximity or distance, *e.g.*, *karyō-n*, he made. In the second conjugation in most cases it is, however, used instead of the Past Tense, and then the Pluperfect is used for the Aorist. It is formed in the masculine singular by adding *yau* or *yō* to the root of the verb, and then affixing the pronominal suffixes. The termination is generally written यौ *yau*, but is always pronounced यो *yō*. A Kāçmīrī Paṇḍit makes no distinction in pronunciation between *au* and *ō*.

In those verbs which have a Past Tense, the base of the Fem. Plur. Past, is the same as that of the Aorist. Thus *pąkᵘ*, he went, Fem. pl. *pacya* or *pacĕ*, Aorist *pacyōv*.

The **Pluperfect** expresses remote time, and is formed in the masculine by changing the *yō* of the Aorist to *yā*. Thus, *karyā-n*, he did (a long time ago), he had done. It is the tense of narrative. Thus *sakhariyāv*, (in telling a story), he went. Those Neuter Verbs of the second conjugation, which use the Aorist for the Past Tense, also use the Pluperfect in the Indefinite sense of the Aorist. If they end in a consonant, they form a new Pluperfect by inserting *i* before the *yā*. Thus *zĕṭhiyāv*, he had been long, but *zĕṭhyāv*, he was long (not *zĕchyāv*, as the √ *zĕṭh* is not one of the listed verbs).

The above rules are those given in the *Kaçmīra-çabdāmṛta*. As the Past Tenses form one of the chief difficulties of the Kāçmīrī Verb, and, moreover, present irregularities which are not referred to in the above abstract (especially those which occur in the formation of the Past Participle), I have given in the fourth column of the accompanying list, the third person singular masculine, of the Past and of the Aorist of every verb mentioned. These have been carefully tested in each instance by my Paṇḍit, and by myself, independently, with the *Çabdāmṛta*, and may be, I believe, taken as correct according to the teaching of its author. Here and there my Paṇḍit has given me a form not sanctioned by the *Çabdāmṛta*. In any such case I have inserted it in square brackets.

Dr. Elmslie's Vocabulary contains about four-hundred verbs, while this list contains about double that number. It may, therefore, be considered a somewhat important contribution to Kāçmīrī lexicography.

I have compared Dr. Elmslie's Vocabulary with this throughout. I have found in it (after excluding a number of perfectly regular causals) about a dozen verbs which were not in the *Dhātu-pāṭha*. Most of these my Paṇḍit condemns as Panjābī and as not Kāçmīrī, but two or three have passed his test, and have been inserted between square brackets. An asterisk is inserted in the fifth column in the case of each verb occurring in the *Vocabulary*.

The fifth column in the list contains the meaning of the roots in English. These meanings are not translations of the Sanskrit meanings given in the third column, but are based upon them. Each meaning inserted has the express sanction of my Paṇḍit who is a Kāçmīrī born and bred.

To conclude, the following are the full conjugational forms of the three Past Tenses of the Kāçmīrī Verb, according to the *Kaçmīra-çabdāmṛta*.

First Conjugation. *Transitive and Impersonal Verbs.*

(भूतकाल) *Past Tense,* I made.

	He was made	She was made	They (masc.) were made	They (fem.) were made
by me	कंरुम् *kạrum*	कंरूम् *kạr^{u}m*	कंरिम् *kạrim*	करेम् *karĕm*[1]
by thee	कंरुथ् *kạruth*	कंरूथ् *kạr^{u}th*	कंरिथ् *kạrith*	करेथ् *karĕth*
by him	कंरुन् *kạrun*	कंरून् *kạr^{u}n*	कंरिन् *kạrin*	करेन् *karĕn*
by us	कंरु *kạr^{u}*	कंरू *kạr^{u}*	कंरि *kạr^{i}*	करे *karĕ*
by you	कंरुव *kạruw^{a}*	कंरूव *kạr^{u}w^{a}*	कंरिव *kạr^{i}w^{a}*	करेव *karĕw^{a}*
by them	कंरुख् *kạrukh*	कंरूख् *kạr^{u}kh*	कंरिख् *kạrikh*	करेख् *karĕkh*

(सामान्यभूतकाल) *Aorist,* I made.

	He was made	She was made	They (masc.) were made	They (fem.) were made
by me	{ कर्योम् *karyōm*[2] { कर्यौम् *karyaum*	कर्येयम् *karyĕyam*	कर्येम् *karyĕm*	कर्येयम् *karyĕ-yam*
by thee	{ कर्योथ् *karyōth* { कर्यौथ् *karyauth*	कर्येयथ् *karyĕyath*	कर्येथ् *karyĕth*	and so on, same as singular.
by him	{ कर्योन् *karyōn* { कर्यौन् *karyaun*	कर्येयन् *karyĕyan*	कर्येन् *karyĕn*	
by us	{ कर्योव् *karyōv* { कर्यौव् *karyauv*	कर्येय *karyĕya*	कर्येय् *karyĕy*	
by you	{ कर्योव *karyōw^{a}* { कर्यौव *karyauw^{a}*	कर्येयव *karyĕyaw^{a}*	कर्येव *karyĕw^{a}*	
by them	{ कर्योख् *karyōkh* { कर्यौख् *karyaukh*	कर्येयख् *karyĕyakh*	कर्येख् *karyĕkh*	

[1] Pronounced *karyĕm.*

[2] *Pronounced* कर्योम् and so throughout.

(पूर्वभूतकाल) *Pluperfect*, I had made.

	He had been made	She had been made	They (masc.) had been made	They (fem.) had been made
by me	कर्यांम् *karyām*	same as in Aorist	करॆयॆम् *karĕyĕm*	same as in Aorist
by thee	कर्यांथ् *karyāth*		करॆयॆथ् *karĕyĕth*	
by him	कर्यांन् *karyān*		करॆयॆन् *karĕyĕn*	
by us	कर्यांव् *karyāv*		करॆयॆव् *karĕyĕy*	
by you	कर्यांव *karyāw*^{a}		करॆयॆव *karĕyĕw*^{a}	
by them	कर्यांख् *karyākh*		करॆयॆख् *karĕyĕkh*	

Second Conjugation. ***Neuter Verbs.***

Neuter Verbs. Except in verbs specially listed above, the Past does not occur. One of these listed verbs is पक, *pak*, 'go.'

(भूतकाल) *Past*, I went.

	Masculine.	Feminine.
I went	पंकुस् *pąkus*	पंचुस् *pąc*^{u}*s*
They wentest	पंकुख् *pąkukh*	पंचुख् *pąc*^{u}*kh*
He went	पंकु *pąk*^{u}	पंचु *pąc*^{u}
We went	पंकि *pąk*^{i}	पच *pacĕ*[1]
You went	पंकिव *pąk*^{i}*w*^{a}	पचव *pacĕw*^{a}
They went	पंकि *pąk*^{i}	पच *pacĕ*

[1] Pronounced *pacyĕ*.

Aorist (सामान्यभूतकाल) in the case of listed verbs. *Past* (भूतकाल) in the case of non-listed verbs.

वुफ् *wuph*, fly, is a non-listed verb.

	Masculine.	Feminine.
I flew	वुफ्योस् *wuphyōs*	वुफ्येयस् *wuphyēyas*
Thou flewest	वुफ्योख् *wuphyōkh*	वुफ्येयख् *wuphyēyakh*
He flew	वुफ्योव् or वुफ्यौव् *wuphyōv* or *wuphyauv*	वुफ्येय *wuphyēy*^{a}
We flew	वुफ्येय् *wuphyēy*	वुफ्येय *wuphyēy*^{a}
You flew	वुफ्येव *wuphyēw*^{a}	वुफ्येव *wuphyēw*^{a}
They flew	वुफ्येय् *wuphyēy*	वुफ्येय *wuphyēy*^{a}

Pluperfect (पूर्णभूतकाल) in the case of listed verbs, and in the case of non-listed verbs ending in vowels. *Aorist* (सामान्यभूतकाल) in the case of non-listed verbs ending in consonants.

I flew.

		Masculine.	Feminine.
Singular ...	1	वुफ्यास् *wuphyās*	वुफ्येयस् *wuphyēyas*, &c., as in the Past.
	2	वुफ्याख् *wuphyākh*	
	3	वुफ्याव् *wuphyāv*	
Plural ...	1	वुफ्याय् *wuphyāy*	
	2	वुफ्याव *wuphyāw*^{a}	
	3	वुफ्याय् *wuphyāy*	

Pluperfect (पूर्णभूतकाल) in the case of non-listed verbs only, which end in consonants.

I had flown.

		Masculine.	Feminine.
Singular ...	1	वुफियास् *wuphiyās*	वुफियेयस् *wuphiyēyas*
	2	वुफियाख् *wuphiyākh*	वुफियेयख् *wuphiyēyakh*
	3	वुफियाव् *wuphiyāv*	वुफियेय *wuphiyēy*^{a}
Plural ...	1	वुफियाय् *wuphiyāy*	वुफियेय *wuphiyēy*^{a}
	2	वुफियाव *wuphiyāw*^{a}	वुफियेव *wuphiyēw*^{a}
	3	वुफियाय् *wuphiyāy*	वुफियेय *wuphiyēy*^{a}

	Root.	Sanskrit Meaning.	Past and Aorist.	English Meaning.
	अच् *ats*	प्रवेशे	च़ाव् *tsāv*	*enter.
	अछ् *atsh*	दौर्बल्ये	अछ़ोव् *atshauv*	be weak.
	अड् *aḍ*	नैर्बल्ये ऽभिनिवेशे च	अड्योव् *aḍyauv*	be powerless, persevere.
	ॳदुर् *ọd*^{e}*r*	आर्द्रीभवने	ॳद्र्योव् *ọd*^{e}*ryauv*	be moist.
क	ॳदुराव *ọd*^{e}*rāv*	आर्द्रीकरणे	ॳदुरोवुन् *ọd*^{e}*rōvun*, ॳदुराव्योन् *ọd*^{e}*rāvyaun*	*make moist.
क	अन *an*, आन *ān* इति केचित्	आनयने	ॳनुन् *ọnun*, अञोन् *añaun*	*bring.
क	ॳंसुर् *ọns*^{e}*r*	समापने	ॳंसरुन् *ọnsᵉrun*, ॳंसुर्योन् *ọns*^{e}*ryaun*	finish.
क	ॳंसुराव *ọns*^{e}*rāv*	च	ॳंसुरोवुन् *ọns*^{e}*rōvun*, ॳंसुराव्योन् *ọns*^{e}*rāvyaun*	ditto.
	अन्द् *and*	अवसाने	अन्द्योव् *andyauv*	be finished.
क	अबस, अबसाव च, *abas*, *abasāv*	वेष्टने	अबॳसुन् *abọsun*, अबस्योन् *abasyaun*	wrap up, enfold.
क	ॳबुर् *ọb*^{e}*r*	मेघाविर्भावे	ॳबरुन् *ọb*^{e}*run*, ॳबुर्योन् *ọb*^{e}*ryaun*	cloud up.
क	ॳबुराव *ọb*^{e}*rāv*	च	ॳबुरोवुन् *ọb*^{e}*rōvun*, ॳबुराव्योन् *abarāvyaun*	ditto.

क	अर्जे ars	अर्जने	अर्जुन् arzun, अर्ज्यौंन् arzaun	earn.
क	अर्पाव arpāv	पातने	अर्पोवुन् arpōvun, अर्पाव्यौन् arpāvyaun	fell.
	अल al	अभुवीभावे	अल्यौव् alyauv	be insecure, shake.
क	अलर alar	चेष्टादाने कम्पने च	अलरुन् alarun, अलर्यौंन् alaryaun	move, tremble.
क	अलराव alarāv	च	अलरोवुन् alarovun, अलराव्यौन् alarāvyaun	ditto.
क	अस as	हसने	असुन् asun, असौन् asaun	*laugh.
क	अहल ahal	मानने	अहलुन् ahalun, अहलौन् ahalaun	honour.
क	आछन ātshan	परिचयने	आछनुन् ātshanun, आछञौन् ātshañaun	practice.
क	आंसूर ās*r	तत्परताचाम्	आंसूरुन् ās*run, आंसूर्यौंन् ās*ryaun	be devoted to.
क	आंडूर ād*r	मिश्रणे पिण्डीकरणे च	आंडूरुन् ād*run, आंडूर्यौंन् ād*ryaun	*mix, heap up.
क	आंडूराव ād*rāv	च	आंडूरोवुन् ād*rōvun, आंडूराव्यौन् ād*rāvyaun	*ditto.
क	आंटूर āt*r	कोपाद्विचारणे	आंटूरुन् āt*run, आंटूर्यौंन् āt*ryaun	meditate in wrath against a person.
क	आपर āpar	स्वहस्तेन परभुजापने	आपरुन् āparun, आपर्यौंन् āparyaun	feed another with one's own hand.
क	आपराव āparāv	च	आपरोवुन् āparōvun, आपराव्यौन् āparāvyaun	ditto.

* Found in Dr. Elmslie's Vocabulary.

	Root.	Sanskrit Meaning.	Past and Aorist.	English Meaning.
	आमन *āman*	वैवर्ण्ये	आमन्यौव् *āmanyauv*	change for the bad.
क	आरद् *ārad*	आराधने	आरदुन् *ārạdun*, आरज़ौन् *ārasaun*	conciliate.
क	आरव *ārav*	परुषीकरणे	आरवुन् *ārạvun*, आरव्यौन् *āravyaun*	make rough.
क	आयव *āyuv*	संमुखलक्षीकरणे	आयवुन् *āyạvun*, आयव्यौन् *āyavyaun*	aim straight at.
क	आलव *ālav*	ऊर्ध्वभ्रामणे नौपरिवर्तने च	आलवुन् *ālạvun*, आलव्यौन् *ālavyaun*	*whirl aloft, bring a boat near the shore.
क	आवर *āvar*	आपणे आवरणे च	आवरुन् *āvạrun*, आवर्यौन् *āvaryaun*	cover.
क	आवराव *āvarāv*	च	आवरावुन् *āvarāvun*, आवराव्यौन् *āvarāvyaun*	ditto
	आस *ās*	सत्तायाम्	ओसु *ōsu* [आस्यौव् *āsyauv* not used]	*be.
	आवस *āvas*	विशरणे	आवस्यौव् *āvasyauv*	crumble to pieces.
क	इछ् *yitsh*	इच्छायाम्	इछुन् *yitshun*, इछौन् *yitshaun*	* wish.
	ईर *yīr*	ऊर्ध्वभ्रमणे	ईर्यौव् *yīryauv*	be whirled aloft.
क	कड *kaḍ*	निष्कासने	कडुन् *kạḍun*, कज्यौन् *kajyaun*	*bring out, drag out.
क	कत *kat*	सूत्रवेष्टने	कतुन् *kạtun*, कच़ौन् *katsaun*	*spin.

क	कतर *katar*	कल्पने	कतंरुन् *katạrun*, कतर्यौन् *kataryaun*	cut in slices.
क	कंस *kans*	पक्षिभर्जने	कंसुन् *kạnsun*, कंसौन् *kansaun*	singe (as a plucked fowl).
भा	कंसूर *kạnzᵊr*	निःस्वीभवने	कंसूरुन् *kạnzᵊrun*, कंसूर्यौन् *kạnzᵊryaun*	be impoverished.
भा	कंसूराव *kạnzᵊrāv*	च	कंसूरोवुन् *kạnzᵊrōvun*, कंसूराव्योन् *kạnzᵊrāvyaun*	ditto.
क	कपट *kapaṭ*	छेदने	कपंटुन् *kapạṭun*	cut (clothes, etc.).
क	कपटाव *kapaṭāv*	च	कपटोवुन् *kapaṭōvun*	ditto.
क	कमाव *kamāv*	अर्जने	कमंवुन् *kamạvun*, कमव्योन् *kamavyaun*	earn.
क	कमनाव *kamanāv*	च	कमनोवुन् *kamanōvun*, कमनाव्योन् *kamanāvyaun*	*ditto.
क	कर *kar*	करणे	कंरुन् *kạrun*, कर्यौन् *karyaun*	*do, make.
	कल *kal*	मूकीभावे	कल्योन् *kalyauv*	be dumb.
भा	कश *kaç*	कण्डूयने	कंशुन् *kạçun*, कश्योन् *kaçyaun*	*itch.
क	कस *kas*	तैलादिपचने	कंसुन् *kạsun*, कसौन् *kasaun*	fry.
	कहर *kahar*	पारुष्ये	कहर्यौन् *kaharyauv*	be rough.

* Found in Dr. Elmslie's Vocabulary.

	Root.	Sanskrit Meaning.	Past and Aorist.	English Meaning.
	काचर् *kāṭsar*	पिङ्गलीभवने	काचर्यौव् *kāṭsaryauv*	be tawny.
क	कांछ *kā̃ch*	काङ्क्षायाम्	कोछुन् *kŏchun* कांछ्यौन् *kā̃chyaun*	wish.
क	कांट *kā̃ṭ*	अप्रत्यक्षहरणे	कोटुन् *kŏṭun*, कांट्यौन् *kā̃ṭyaun*	to pilfer secretly.
	काठ *kāṭh*	कर्कशीभावे	काठ्यौव् *kāṭhyauv*	be hard.
	काण *kāṇ*	काणीभवने पराभवे च	काण्यौव् *kāṇyauv*	be one-eyed, be conquered.
	कांप *kā̃mp*	कम्पने	कांप्यौव् *kā̃mpyauv*	tremble.
क	काय *kāy*	आलस्ये	कोयुन् *kŏyun*, काय्यौन् *kāyyaun*	be lazy *lit.* make (oneself) lazy.
	कायर *kāyar*	निःसारीभावे	कायर्यौव् *kāyaryauv*	be powerless.
क	कार *kār*	क्वथने	कोरुन् *kŏrun*, कार्यौन् *kāryaun*	boil.
	काव्र *kāv°r*	श्यामीभवने	काव्र्यौव् *kāv°ryauv*	be black.
क	काश *kāś*	मुण्डनापनयनयोः	कोशुन् *kŏśun*, काश्यौन् *kāśyaun*	*shave, put a stop to (*e.g.*, a quarrel).
	क्यन्न *kyann*	क्लेदने	क्यन्न्यौव् *kĕnnyauv*	be moist.

	कुठ kuth	दुःखितंभावे	कुठ्योव् kuthyauv	* be in distress.
	कुप kup	कोपे	कुप्योव् kupyauv	be angry.
	[कुब kŏb	कुब्जीभवने	कुब्योव् kŏbyauv	be hunch backed.]
	कुमल kumal	कोमलीभवने	कुमल्योव् kumalyauv	* be tender.
क	कुह kuh	निष्कर्षे	कुङ्कुन् kuhun, कुह्योन् kuhyaun	pull out.
क	कूर kūr	निष्कर्षे मूलशिथिली-करणयोः	कूरुन् kūrun, कूर्योन् kūryaun	pull out, loosen from the foundation.
	कूर kūr	क्रूरत्वे	कूर्योव् kūryauv	be fierce.
	कृट krṭ, क्रट kraṭ	कार्श्ये	कृट्योव् krṭyauv, क्रट्योव् kraṭyauv	be thin.
क	कृप krp	कर्तने	कृपुन् krpun, कृप्योन् krpyaun	* cut (with scissors).
	कृहन krhan	कृष्णीभवने	कृहन्योव् krhanyauv	become black.
क	कोकव kŏkav	गुणप्रशंसायाम्	कोकवुन् kŏkavun, कोकव्योन् kŏkavyaun	recommeud (a person).
	कोल kŏl	लौहित्ये	कोल्योव् kŏlyauv	be red.
	क्युछ kets	आर्द्रीभवने	क्युछु ketsu, क्युछ्योव् ketsyauv	be wet.
क	क्युछव ketsav	आर्द्रीकरणे	क्युछवुन् ketsavun, क्युछव्योन् ketsavyaun	make wet.

* Found in Dr. Elmslie's Vocabulary.

	ROOT.	SANSKRIT MEANING.	PAST AND AORIST.	ENGLISH MEANING.
क	कुन् *k*^{a}*n*	विक्रीयते	कुनुन् *k*^{a}*nun*, कुञौव् *k*^{a}*ñaun*	* sell.
क	क्राव *krāv*	करवे	क्रोवुन् *krövun*, क्राव्यौव् *krāvyaun*	do, make.
	क्रेठ *krēṭh*	कार्कश्ये	क्रेठ्यौव् *krēṭhyauv*	be hard.
क	क्रेप *krēp*	अनुतापाय	क्र्यूपुन् *kryūpun*, क्रेप्यौव् *krēpyaun*	long for.
क	खट *khaṭ*	गोपने	खटुन् *khaṭun*, खच्यौव् *khacyaun*	* conceal.
क	खंडर् *khaṇḍ*^{a}*r*	विभाजने	खंडरुन् *khaṇḍ*^{a}*rnn*, खंडर्यौव् *khaṇḍ*^{a}*ryaun*	divide into shares.
क	खंडराव *khaṇḍ*^{a}*rāv*	च	खंडरोवुन् *khaṇḍ*^{a}*rövun*, खंडराव्यौव् *khaṇḍ*^{a}*rāvyaun*	ditto.
क	खन *khan*	अवदारणे	खनुन् *khanun* खञौव् *khañaun*	* dig.
आ	खप *khap*	व्यभिचारे	खपुन् *khapun*, खप्यौव् *khapyaun*	act badly.
आ	खम *kham*	उच्छ्वासनिःश्वासे	खमुन् *khamun*, खम्यौव् *khamyaun*	* breathe hard.
	खर *khar*	अप्रीतौ	खर् *khar*^{a}, खर्यौव् *kharyauv*	dislike.
	खल *khal*	शिथिले	खल्यौव् *khalyauv*	be loose.
	[खरच *khar*^{a}*c*	व्ययीकरणे	खरचुन् *khar*^{a}*cun*, खरच्यौव् *khar*^{a}*cyaun*	spend, only used in past tenses].

	खस *khas*	खारोहे	ख॑ठ् *khạthᵘ*, [ख॑ट् *khạtᵘ*], खछ्योव् *khatshauv* [खछ्योव् *khatsauv*]	* mount, ascend.
क	खह *khah*	चित्रीकरणे	ख॑हुन् *khạhun*, खह्योव् *khahyaun*	ornament (with a pattern).
क	खार *khār*	खारोपणे	खोरुन् *khōrun*, खार्योव् *khāryaun*	*cause to mount, raise.
क	खि *khi*	खादने	ख्योन् *khyōn* खियोव् *khiyaun*	* eat.
अ	खिस्क *khisk*	दृप्यतो	ख्युस्कुन् *khyuskun*, खिस्च्योव् *khiscyaun*	walk arrogantly.
	खोखर *khŏkhar*	निःसारतायाम्	खोखर्योव् *khŏkharyauv*	be hollow (of a tree).
क	खोखलाव *khŏkhalāv*	मध्ये जलक्षालने	खोखलोवुन् *khŏkhalōvun*, खोखलाव्योव् *khŏkhalāvyaun*	wash anything in water.
क	खुट *khut*	अधः खनने	खुटुन् *khutun*, खुछ्योव् *khutsaun*	dig from below.
क	खूल *khūl*	उद्घाटने	खूलुन् *khūlun*, खूज्योव् *khūjyaun*	open (act.).
क	खूंस *khūns*	तनूरुहकर्षणे	खूंसुन् *khūnsun*, खूंज्योव् *khūnzaun*	pluck (hair, feathers).
	खोछ् *khōts*	भये	खूछ् *khūtsᵘ*, खोछ्योव् *khōtsauv*	* fear.
	खोर *khōr*	भये	खोर्योव् *khōryauv*	fear.
	खुस *khᵘs*	तनूरुहकर्षणे	खुसुन् *khᵘsun*, खुस्योव् *khᵘsaun*	pluck (more specially. hair).

* Found in Dr. Elmslie's Vocabulary.

	Root.	Sanskrit Meaning.	Past and Aorist.	English Meaning.
	गछ् gatsh	गतौ युक्तीभवने च	गौव् gauv; (युक्तीभवने) गंछु gatshᵘ; गयौव् gayauv	* go, be proper.
क	गण्ड gaṇḍ	बन्धे	गंण्डुन् gaṇḍun गञ्ज्यौव् gañjyaun	* tie, bind.
	[गन gan	घनीभवने	गन्यौव् ganyauv	* become thick (of liquids), be strong].
क	गंझूर ganzᵊr	संख्याने	गंझूरुन् ganzᵊrun, गंझूर्यौन् ganzᵊryaun	* count.
क	गंझूराव ganzᵊrāv	च	गंझूरोवुन् ganzᵊrövun गंझूराव्यौन् ganzᵊrāvyaun	* ditto.
क	गर gar	घटने	गंरुन् garun गर्यौन् garyaun	* work metal.
	गर्म garm	घर्मीभवने	गर्म्यौव् garmyauv	be hot.
	गल gal	गाले	गंलु galᵘ गज्यौव् gajyauv	* melt (neut.)
	गँगल gãgal	परिबाधने	गँगल्यौव् gãgalyauv	be disturbed in one's work by others.
	ग्रँगल grãgal	च	ग्रँगल्यौव् grãgalyauv	ditto.
क	गार gār	स्मरणे [अन्वेषणे च]	गोरुन् görun, गार्यौन् gāryaun	* remember affectionately, search eagerly for.

क	गाल *gāl*	गालने	गोलुन् *gōlun*, गाल्योन् *gājyaun*	*melt (active).
क	गिन्द *gind*	क्रीडायां	ग्युन्दुन् *gyundun*, गिन्झोन् *ginzaun*	* play.
	ग्यमट *gyamaț*	कृशीभवने	ग्यमट्योव् *gyamațyauv*	be thin.
क	गिलव *gilav*	अपहरणे भ्रमणे च	गिलवुन् *gilạvun*, गिलव्योन् *gilavyaun*	steal, whirl about.
क	ग्यव *gyav*	गीतौ	ग्यवुन् *gyạvun*, ग्यव्योन् *gĕvyaun*	*sing.
	गीर *gīr*	भ्रमणे	गीर्योव् *gīryauv*	totter, reel.
अ	गुज़राव *guzarāv*	क्षपीकायाम्	गुज़रोवुन् *guzarōwun*, गुज़राव्योन् *guzarāvyaun*	pass time.
अ	गुन्द *gund*	उपालम्भे	गुन्दुन् *gundun*, गुन्झोन् *gunzaun*	censure.
क	गुप *gup*	गोपने	गुपुन् *gupun*, गुप्योन् *gupyaun*	hide.
	ग्वब *gŏb*	गौरवे	ग्वब्योव् *gŏbyauv*	*be too heavy.
	गुमन *guman*	धूसरे [धूसरतायाम्]	गुमन्योव् *gumanyauv*	be grey.
	गुरट *gurаț*	गौरे [गौरतायाम्]	गुरट्योव् *gurațyauv*	be fair coloured.
क	गुलव *gulav*	गुडकाकने	गुलवुन् *gulạvun*, गुलव्योन् *gulavyaun*	roll in the mouth.
	ग्वह *gŏh*	दीप्तौ	ग्वह्योव् *gŏhyauv*	shine.
क	गेर *gēr*	आवरणे	ग्यूरुन् *gyūrun*, गेर्योन् *gēryaun*	surround.

* Found in Dr. Elmslie's Vocabulary.

	Root.	Sanskrit Meaning.	Past and Aorist.	English Meaning.
	गेल gōl	विप्रोषे [उपहासे च]	गेल्योव् gōlyauv, [उपहासे ग्यूलुन् gyūlun]	be far away, [joke].
क	गोर gōr	विलापे	गूरुन् gūrun, गोर्यौन् gōryaun	lament.
	गोवर gōvar	निद्रावसने	गोवर्यौव् gōvaryauv	be suddenly wakened (before one is thoroughly awake).
	ग्रक grak	पात्रस्थपाकातिशयचलनेः	ग्रक्यौव् grakyauv	*splash about (of liquids), boil over.
आ	ग्रस् gras	गर्जने	ग्रसुन् grạsun, ग्रस्यौन् grasaun	*roar.
आ	ग्रांग्र grāçᵉr	ग्रहणे वृष्टिपन्ने च	ग्रांग्रुन् grāçᵉrun, ग्रांग्र्यौन् grāçᵉryaun	take, stop raining.
क	ग्रांग्राव grāçᵉrāv	च	ग्रांग्रोवुन् grāçᵉrōvun, ग्रांग्राव्यौन् grāçᵉrāvyaun	ditto.
	ग्रुच grŏts	पात्रस्थजलादिचेष्टायाम्	ग्रुच्यौव् grŏtsyauv	*shake liquid in a vessel.
क	गुह gᵉh	घर्षणे	गुहुन् gᵉhun, गुह्यौन् gᵉçaun	*grind.
क	चताव catāv	स्तुतौ	चतोवुन् catōvun, चताव्यौन् catāvyaun	praise.
	चमक camak	दीप्तौ	चमक्यौव् camakyauv	shine.

क	चार् *cār*	[illegible]	चोरुन् *cōrun*, चार्योन् *cāryaun*.	tie tightly.
क	चाव् *cāv*	पायने	चोवुन् *cōvun*, चाव्योन् *cāvyaun*	*give to drink.
क	चि *ci*	पाने	च्योन् *cyaun*	*drink.
क	चीर् *cīr*	निचोड्ने	च्यूरुन् *cyūrun*, चीर्योन् *cīryaun*	*squeeze or wring (cloth).
क	चुकाव् *cukāv*	मूल्यनिश्चयीकरणे	चुकोवुन् *cukōvun*, चुकाव्योन् *cukāvyaun*	fix a price.
क	चुम् *cum*	दीनतामाप्	चुमुन् *cumun*, चुम्योन् *cumyaun*	be humble before, show humility to.
	चौँखर् *caũkhar*	संकोचने	चौँखर्योव् *caũkharyauv*	contract.
क	छक् *chạk*	कीर्णने	छकुन् *chạkun*, छच्योन् *chacyaun*	scatter.
क	छकᵊर् *chạkᵊr*	अवकीर्णने	छकᵊरुन् *chạkᵊrun*, छकᵊर्योन् *chạkᵊryaun*	*scatter.
क	छकᵊराव् *chạkᵊrāv*	च	छकᵊरोवुन् *chạkᵊrōvun*, छकᵊराव्योन् *chạkᵊrāvyaun*	ditto
क	छचᵊराव् *chạtsᵊrāv*	श्वेतीकरणे	छचᵊरोवुन् *chạtsᵊrōvun*, छचᵊराव्योन् *chạtsᵊrāvyaun*	make white.
	छत् *chat*	श्वेते	छत्योव् *chatyauv*	be white.
	छन् *chan*	पाते	छन्योव् *chanyauv*	fall from a mass (*e.g.*, grain falling from a basket.)

* Found in Dr. Elmslie's Vocabulary.

	Root.	Sanskrit Meaning.	Past and Aorist.	English Meaning.
क	छप *chap*	वृष्टिकालक्षयोः क्षेपे	छंपुन् *chạpun*, छप्योव् *chapyaun*	*wait for rain to pass over, pass time.
भा	छर *char*	पुरीषोत्सर्गे	छंरुन् *chạrun*, छर्यौव् *charyaun*	*evacuate, go to stool.
क	छल *chal*	क्षालने	छंलुन् *chạlun*, छज्योव् *chajyaun*	*wash, clean.
क	छान *chān*	उत्पवने गालने च	छोनुन् *chōnun*, छाञोव् *chāñaun*	*strain, sift, trim.
क	छाँट *chā̃ṭ*	क्रोधाद्गुह्याविष्कारे	छोंटुन् *chõṭun*, छाँच्योव् *chā̃cyaun*	disclose a secret in anger
क	छाव *chāv*	उपभोगे क्षेपणे च	छोवुन् *chọ̄vun*, छाव्योव् *chāvyaun*	use, throw at.
भा	छिक *chik*	सेचने प्रस्रवणे च	छ्युकुन् *chyukun*, छिच्योव् *chicyaun*	*sprinkle, urinate.
क	छिन्दर् *chindᵃr*	मोहने	छ्युन्दरुन् *chyundᵘrun*, छिन्दर्यौव् *chindᵃryaun*	be stupified.
	छिव *chiv*	मदे	छिव्योव् *chivyauv*	be proud.
क	छिवराव *chivᵃrāv*	मादने	छिवरोवुन् *chivᵃrōvun*, छिवराव्योव् *chivᵃrā-vyaun*	make proud.
	छ़कल *chŏkal*	संघट्टाभावे	छ़कल्योव् *chŏkalyauv*	be scattered.
क	छ़कव *chŏkav*	प्रक्षालने	छ़कंवुन् *chŏkạvun*, छ़कव्योव् *chŏkavyaun*	wash (active).

प	छ्वँन्‌र् *chŏñ^er*	तनूकरणे	छ्वँन्‌रुन् *chŏñ^erun*, छ्वँन्‌र्यौव् *chŏñ^eryaun*	reduce (active).
प	छ्वँन्‌राव *chŏñ^erāv*	च	छ्वँन्‌रोवुन् *chŏñ^erōvun*, छ्वँन्‌राव्योव् *chŏñ^erā-vyaun*	ditto
	छ्वन *chŏnn*	अपचये	छ्वन्यौव् *chŏnnyauv*	be reduced.
प	छ्वँपर् *chŏp^er*	व्ययीकरणे	छ्वँपरुन् *chŏp^erun*, छ्वँपर्यौव् *chŏp^eryaun*	spend.
प	छ्वँपराव *chŏp^erāv*	च	छ्वँपरोवुन् *chŏp^erōvun*, छ्वँपराव्योव् *chŏp^erā-vyaun*	ditto
प	छ्वम्ब *chŏmb*	कणमर्दने	छ्वम्बुन् *chombun*, छ्वम्ब्योव् *chŏmbyaun*	thresh grain (by beating the stalks).
प	छेर *chēr*	अभिक्षेपे	छ्यूरुन् *chyūrun*, छेर्यौव् *chēryaun*	irritate.
प	छोर *chōr*	त्यागे	छूरुन् *chūrun*, छोर्यौव् *chōryaun*	*give up, dismiss.
आ	जख *jakh*	सेवायाम्	जखुन् *jakhun*, जछ्योव् *jachyaun*	serve or work (in one's own house).
प	जर *jar*	जड़ने	जरुन् *jarun*, जर्यौव् *jaryaun*	inlay, set with jewels.
आ	जूर *jūr*	उपसेवायाम्	जूरुन् *jūrun*, जूर्यौव् *jūryaun*	serve or work (in one's own house).
प	चुट *tsat*	छेदने	चुटुन् *tsatun*, चच्योव् *tsacyaun*	*cut.

* Found in Dr. Elmslie's Vocabulary.

	Root.	Sanskrit Meaning.	Past and Aorist.	English Meaning.
	चम tsam	अल्पीभवने संभवे च	चम्योव् tsamyauv	(1) decrease in size (2) attend to, pay heed to (active).
	चमठ tsamath	पर्युषिते	चमथ्योव् tsamathyauv	* be stale.
	चर tsar	उपचये	चर्योव् tsaryauv	increase.
	चर tsar	अन्तःकोपे [स्त्री भा]	चॖर् tsọr[a] (fem.)	be inwardly wrathful (of a woman). Only used in Past Part. fem.
क	चर्छ tsarts	चारक्रियायाम्	चॖर्छुन् tsọrtsun, चर्छौन् tsartsaun	spy.
	चल tsal	चलने	चॖलु tsọl[u], चज्योव् tsajyauv	* go away, escape.
आ	चस tsas	अतिहासे	चॖसुन् tsọsun, चस्योन् tsasyaun	laugh loudly.
क	चान tsān	प्रवेशने	चोनुन् tsōnun, चाञौन् tsāñaun	* bring in.
क	चाप tsāp	भक्षणे	चोपुन् tsōpun, चाप्यौन् tsāpyaun	* eat, gnaw
क	चार tsār	चयने	चोरुन् tsōrun, चार्यौन् tsāryaun	* collect.
क	चाल tsāl	सहने	चोलुन् tsōlun, चाज्यौन् tsājyaun	bear, endure

आ	चखल *tsyakhal*	सोत्प्रासे	चखलुन् *tsyakhalun*, चखज्यौन् *tsyakhajyaun*	laugh loudly.
आ	चङ्ग *tsyang*	हर्षे	चङ्गुन् *tsyangun*, चञ्ज्यौन् *tsăñjyaun*	*rejoice.
आ	च्यतर *tsyat^{e}r*	उपेक्षयेव प्रेक्षणे	चतरुन् *tsyat^{e}run*, चतर्यौन् *tsăt^{e}ryaun*	look at with some scorn.
प	चल *tsyall*	बलात्प्रवेशने [बलात्प्रवेशे-नान्यस्य पीडने]	चल्लुन् *tsyallun*, चज्ज्यौन् *tsăjjyaun*	enter violently, hurt by entering violently.
प	चीञर *tsiñ^{e}r*	संज्ञापने	चूञरुन् *tsyūñ^{e}run*, चीञर्यौन् *tsiñ^{e}ryaun*	make a sign.
प	चीञराव *tsiñ^{e}rāv*	च	चीञरोवुन् *tsiñ^{e}rōvun*, चीञराव्यौन् *tsiñ^{e}rāvyaun*	ditto.
	चोक *tsŏk*	क्रोधेऽम्लीभवने च	चोक्यौव् *tsŏkyauv*	*be angry, be sour.
प	चोकर *tsŏk^{e}r*	कोपने	चोकरुन् *tsŏk^{e}run*, चोकर्यौन् *tsŏk^{e}ryaun*	make angry.
प	चोकराव *tsŏk^{e}rāv*	च	चोकरोवुन् *tsŏkarōvun*, चोकराव्यौन् *tsŏk^{e}rāvyaun*	ditto.
प	चोगनाव *tsŏg^{e}nāv*	चतुर्गुणीकरणे	चोगनोवुन् *tsŏg^{e}nōvun*, चोगनाव्यौन् *tsŏg^{e}nāvyaun*	make fourfold.
	चोच *tsŏts*	[illegible]	चोच्यौव् *tsŏtsyauv*	have insufficient means of livelihood.

* Found in Dr. Elmslie's Vocabulary.

	ROOT.	SANSKRIT MEANING.	PAST AND AORIST.	ENGLISH MEANING.
क	चम्ब tsŏmb	वेधने	चम्बुन् tsombun, चम्ब्यौन् tsŏmbyaun	*pierce, bore.
क	चम्रराव tsŏmᵊrāv	अल्पीकरणे युंक्तीकरणे च	चम्ररोवुन् tsŏmᵊrŏvun, चम्रराव्यौन् tsŏmᵊrā-vyaun	make less, cause to decrease, cause to attend to.
क	चुव tsuv	कलहे	चुवन् tsuvᵘn, चुवेयन् tsuvyŏyan	quarrel (only used in fem.).
क	चूँट tsūṭ	अधःशब्दे [अपानशब्दे]	चूँटुन् tsūṭun, चूँट्यौन् tsūṭyaun	break wind with noise.
क	चूर tsūr	योन्याघाते	चूरुन् tsūrun, चूर्यौन् tsūryaun	have sexual inter-course with.
क	चेट tsĕṭ	कुट्टने	च्यूटुन् tsyūṭun, चेट्यौन tsĕṭyaun	*pound to powder.
क	चेन tsĕn	चेतने	च्यूनुन् tsyūnun, चेन्यौन् tsĕnyaun	know by a sign.
क	चूष tsᵃh	चूषे	चूषुन् tsᵊhun, चूष्यौन् tsᵃṣaun	*suck.
क	छट tshaṭ	उत्क्षेपणे	छटुन् tshaṭun, छट्यौन् tshaṭyaun	winnow.
	छर tshar	रिक्तीभवने	छर्यौव् tsharyauv	be empty.
[क]	छल tshal	छलने	छलुन् tshalun, छल्यौन् tshajyaun	deceive.
क	छांड tshāḍ	अन्वेषणे	छोंडुन् tshŏḍun, छांड्यौन् tsājyaun	*search.

क	[illegible] *tshā̃ḍ*	च	[illegible] *tshō̃ḍun*, [illegible] *tshā̃jyaun*	* search.
क	[illegible] *tshaṇḍ*	च	[illegible] *tshaṇḍun*, [illegible] *tshañjyaun*	ditto.
	[illegible] *tshātshan*	लघूभवने	[illegible] *tshā̃tshanyauv*	be light.
	[illegible] *tshyaṭ*	[illegible]	[illegible] *tshĕṭyauv*	be impure.
क	[illegible] *tshyaṭᵊr*	[illegible]	[illegible] *tshyaṭᵊrun*, [illegible] *tshĕṭᵊryaun*	make impure.
क	[illegible] *tshyaṭᵊrāv*	च	[illegible] *tshyaṭᵊrōvun*, [illegible] *tshyaṭᵊrāvyaun*.	ditto.
	[illegible] *tshyann*	छेदे	[illegible] *tshyannᵘ*, [illegible] *tshĕññauv*	* be bored, be torn, be split.
	[illegible] *tshyav*	शमे	[illegible] *tshĕvyauv*	be quieted.
क	[illegible] *tshyavᵊr*	शमने	[illegible] *tshyavᵊrun*, [illegible] *tshĕvᵊryaun*	make quiet.
क	[illegible] *tshyavᵊrāv*	च	[illegible] *tshyavᵊrōvun*, [illegible] *tshyavᵊrāvyaun*	ditto.
क	[illegible] *tshŏts*	निःसारीभवने	[illegible] *tshokun*, [illegible] *tshŏtsyauv*	be empty (though apparently full).
	[illegible] *tshŏṭ*	ह्रस्वीभवने	[illegible] *tshŏṭyauv*	* be short.
क	[illegible] *tshŏṭᵊr*	ह्रस्वीकरणे	[illegible] *tshŏṭᵊrun*, [illegible] *tshŏṭᵊryaun*	make short.

* Found in Dr. Elmslie's Vocabulary.

	Root.	Sanskrit Meaning.	Past and Aorist.	English Meaning.
प	छ्होट्राव tshöṭᵉrāv	च	छ्होट्रोवुन् tshöṭᵉrövun, छ्होट्राव्यौन् tshöṭᵉrāvyaun	make short.
प	छुन tshun	पातने	छुनुन् tshunun, छुञौन् tshuñaun	* pour, clothe.
प	ज़्जर zᵊjar	तक्षणे	ज़्जरुन् zᵊjarun, ज़्जर्यौन् zᵊjaryaun	pare.
प	ज़प zap	जपने	ज़पुन् zapun, ज़प्यौन् zapyaun	pray.
प	ज़र zar	क्षरणे	ज़रुन् zarun, ज़र्यौन् zaryaun	* bear.
	ज़ल zal	जलवत्स्वादास्वादने	ज़ल्यौव् zalyauv	* taste like water.
आ	ज़ाग zāg	प्रतिजागरे	ज़ोगुन् zögun, ज़ाज्यौन् zājyaun	be watchful.
प	ज़ान zān	अवबोधने	ज़ोनुन् zönun, ज़ाञौन् zāñaun	* know.
प	ज़ाल zāl	दाहे	ज़ोलुन् zölun, ज़ाज्यौन् zājyaun	burn.
	ज़ि zi	जनने	ज़ाव् zāv, ज़ायौव् zāyauv.	* be born.
	ज़िङ्गर ziŋgar	विकशीभवने	ज़िङ्गर्यौव् ziŋgaryauv	be thin.
	ज़्यङ्गर zöŋgar	तैक्ष्ण्ये	ज़्यङ्गर्यौव् zöŋgaryauv	ditto.
	ज़्यसर zösar	जर्जरे	ज़्यसर्यौव् zösaryauv	be dried up, ready to wither.

	जुव् *zuv*	जीवने	जुवीव् *zuvyauv*	live.
क	जुवर् *zuv^{e}r*	सञ्जीवीकरणे	जुवरुन् *zuv^{e}run*, जुवर्यौन् *zuv^{e}ryaun*	cause to live.
क	जुवराव *zuv^{e}rāv*	„	जुवरोवुन् *zuv^{e}rōvun*, जुवराव्यौन् *zuvarāvyaun*	ditto.
भा	जस् *zōs*	कासे	जसुन् *zosun*, जस्यौन् *zōsyaun*	cough.
क	जीठर् *zīṭh^{e}r*	दीर्घीकरणे	ज्यूठरुन् *zyūṭh^{e}run*, जीठर्यौन् *zīṭh^{e}ryaun*	make long.
क	जीठराव *zīṭh^{e}rāv*	„	जीठरोवुन् *zīṭh^{e}rōvun*, जीठराव्यौन् *zīṭh^{e}rā-vyaun*	ditto.
	ज़ेठ *zēṭh*	आयतीभवने	ज़ेठ्यौव् *zēṭhyauv*	be long.
क	ज़ेन *zēn*	जये	ज्यूनुन् *zyūnun*, ज़ेन्यौन् *zēñaun*	* conquer.
	ज़ोत *zōt*	दीप्तौ	ज़ोत्यौव् *zōtyauv*	* shine.
क	ज़ोवर् *zōv^{e}r*	उत्पादने	ज़ूवरुन् *zūv^{e}run*, ज़ोवर्यौन् *zōv^{e}ryaun*	bring forth.
क	ज़ोवराव *zōv^{e}rāv*	„	ज़ोवरोवुन् *zōv^{e}rōvun*, ज़ोवराव्यौन् *zōv^{e}rāvyaun*	ditto.
क	ज़रव *z^{e}rav*	सवने	ज़रवुन् *z^{e}ravun*, ज़रव्यौन् *z^{e}ravyaun*	bear.
क	ज़ल *z^{e}l*	तक्षणे	ज़लुन् *z^{e}lun*, ज़ल्यौन् *z^{e}lyaun*	* pare.
क	टक *ṭak*	सशब्ददन्तैश्छेदने	टकुन् *ṭakun*, टच्यौन् *ṭacyaun*	bite in two with a noise.

* Found in Dr. Elmslie's Vocabulary.

	Root.	Sanskrit Meaning.	Past and Aorist.	English Meaning.
क	ठप ṭap	परोक्षपरिभाषणे	ठपुन् ṭapun, ठप्योव् ṭapyaun	blame behind one's back.
	ठल ṭal	परिवर्ते	ठल्योव् ṭalyauv	be exchanged.
आ	ठाँग ṭą̈g	चीत्काशब्दे	ठोंगुन् ṭŏgun, ठाँज्योव् ṭą̈jyaun	emit a loud cry or roar.
आ	ठाल ṭāl	उपेक्षागमने	ठोलुन् ṭŏlun, ठाज्योव् ṭājyaun	go away with indifference.
	ठ्यठ ṭyaṭh	तिक्तीभवने	ठ्यठ्योव् ṭĕṭhyauv	* be bitter.
क	ठ्यप ṭyap	संबद्धे	ठ्यपुन् ṭyąpun, ठ्यप्योव् ṭĕpyaun	squeeze something in.
	ठ्यम्ब ṭyamb	कोपे	ठ्यम्ब्योव् ṭĕmbyauv	hammer.
क	ठुकव ṭŏkav	लुडापने	ठुकवुन् ṭŏkąvun, ठुकव्योव् ṭŏkavyaun	cause to disappear.
क	ठुक ṭuk	खातुकच्छेदने	ठुकुन् ṭukun, ठुच्योव् ṭucyaun	bore like a rat.
	ठुट ṭŏṭ	हमिसंकोचे	ठुट्योव् ṭŏṭyauv	have insufficient means of livelihood.
क	ठुव ṭuv	संकोचने	ठुवुन् ṭuvun, ठुव्योव् ṭuvyaun	close (eyes, a flower, &c.)
	ठोठ ṭŏṭh	प्रसादे	ठोठ्योव् ṭŏṭhyauv	be pleased.

	ट्‌क *ṭᵊk*	धावने	ट्‌क्योव् *ṭᵊkyāuv*	* run.
क	ट्‌स *ṭᵊs*	बलात्प्रवेशयने	ट्‌सुन् *ṭᵊsun*, ट्‌स्योन् *ṭᵊsaun*	cause to forcibly enter.
क	ट्‌सन *ṭᵊsan*	च	ट्‌सनुन् *ṭᵊsanun*, ट्‌सन्योन् *ṭᵊsañaun*	ditto.
	ठग *ṭhag*	वञ्चने	ठग्योव् *ṭhagyauv*	be deceived.
क	ठगाव *ṭhagāv*	[illegible]	ठगोवुन् *ṭhagōvun*, ठगाव्योन् *ṭhagāvyaun*	deceive.
	ठहर *ṭhahar*	संस्थाने	ठहर्योव् *ṭhaharyauv*	stop.
क	ठाक *ṭhāk*	उत्खनने	ठोकुन् *ṭhōkun*, ठाच्योन् *ṭhācyaun*	bury.
क	ठास *ṭhās*	च	ठोसुन् *ṭhōsun*, ठास्योन् *ṭhāsyaun* or ठासोन् *ṭhāsaun*	ditto.
	ठीक *ṭhīk*	स्थितौ	ठीक्योव् *ṭhīkyauv*	stand firmly.
क	ठुक *ṭhuk*	उत्खनने	ठुकुन् *ṭhukun*, ठुच्योन् *ṭhucyaun*	bury.
क	डक *ḍak*	सशब्दपाने	डकुन् *ḍakun*, डच्योन् *ḍacyaun*	drink with a noise.
क	डखर *ḍakhᵊr*	आधारीकरणे	डखरुन् *ḍakhᵊrun*, डखर्योन् *ḍakhᵊryaun*	depend upon.
क	डखराव *ḍakhᵊrāv*	च	डखरोवुन् *ḍakhᵊrōvun*, डखराव्योन् *ḍakhᵊrāvyaun*	ditto.
क	डखव *ḍakhav*	दण्डवदाधारीकरणे	डखवुन् *ḍakhavun*, डखव्योन् *ḍakhavyaun*	lean upon a support, such as a stick.

* Found in Dr. Elmslie's Vocabulary.

	Root.	Sanskrit Meaning.	Past and Aorist.	English Meaning.
	डर ḍar	भये	डर्यौव् ḍaryauv	*fear.
	डल ḍal	उल्लङ्घने	डंलु ḍạlᵘ, डज्यौव् ḍajyauv	*pass over.
क	डाँट ḍą̄ṭ	विद्वेषे	डूँटुन् ḍūṭun, डाँच्यौन् ḍą̄cyaun	hate.
क	डाल ḍāl	परिवर्तने	डोलुन् ḍōlun, डाज्यौन् ḍājyaun	exchange.
	ड्यल ḍyal	शैथिल्ये	ड्यल्यौव् ḍĕlyauv	be slack.
	डॊक ḍŏk	देहानार्जवे	डॊक्यौव् ḍŏkyauv	be bent (of the body).
	डुब ḍub	मज्जने	डुब्यौव् ḍubyauv	dive.
क	डुलव ḍulav	लोठनक्रामणे	डुलंवुन् ḍulạvun, डुलव्यौन् ḍulavyaun	*roll (act).
क	डुलनाव ḍulanāv	च	डुलनोवुन् ḍulanōvun, डुलनाव्यौन् ḍulanāvyaun	ditto.
क	डुव ḍuv	संमार्जने	डुवुन् ḍuvun, डुव्यौन् ḍuvyaun	*sweep.
	डॊष ḍŏṣ	देहानार्जवे	डॊष्यौव् ḍŏsyauv	be bent (of the body).
क	डेष ḍēṣ	प्रेक्षणे	ड्यूठुन् dyūṭhun, डेछ्यौन् ḍēchyaun	*look, see.
	डोल ḍōl	अपरिचयने	डूलु ḍūlᵘ, डोज्यौव् ḍōjyauv	be unused.

	तग tag	तज्ज्ञातायाम्	तगु tạgᵘ, तज्यौव् tajyauv	be possible, be known how to be done.
	तङ्ग tang	संकोचे	तङ्ग्याव् tangyauv	be tight.
क	तचुर tạtsᵃr	तापने	तचुरुन् tạtsᵃrun, तचुर्यौन् tạtsᵃryaun	make hot.
क	तचुराव tạtsᵃrāv	"	तचुरोवुन् tạtsᵃrōvun, तचुराव्यौन् tạtsᵃrāvyaun	* ditto.
क	तछ tach	तक्षणे	तछुन् tạchun, तछ्यौन् tachyaun	* pare.
क	तञुर tạñᵃr	विरलीकरणे	तञुरुन् tạñᵃrun, तञुर्यौन् tạñᵃryaun	make thin.
क	तञुराव tạñᵃrāv	"	तञुरोवुन् tạñᵃrōvun, तञुराव्यौन् tañᵃrāvyaun	ditto.
	तत tat	तप्तीभवने	तत्यौव् tatyauv	* be hot.
	तन tan	विरलीभवने	तन्यौव् tanyauv	* be thin.
क	तप tap	औष्ण्योपादाने	तपुन् tạpun, तप्यौन् tapyaun	take for the sake of warmth.
	तम्बल tambal	चापल्ये	तम्बल्यौव् tambalyauv	* change one's mind (from sudden grief or joy).
	तर tar	तरणे	तरु tạrᵘ, तर्यौव् taryauv	* cross.
क	तल tal	स्नेहपाके	तलुन् tạlun, तल्यौन् tajyaun	fry.

* Found in Dr. Elmslie's Vocabulary.

	Root.	Sanskrit Meaning.	Past and Aorist.	English Meaning.
क	तव *tav*	भर्जने	तवुन् *tavun*, तव्यौन् *tavyaun*	roast.
क	ताड *tāḍ*	कोपाद्विचारणे	तोडुन् *tōḍun*, ताज्यौन् *tājyaun* [ताड्यौन् *tāḍyaun*]	be angry with, reproach angrily.
क	तार *tār*	तारणे	तोरुन् *torun*, तार्यौन् *tāryaun*	* pass over (act.)
क	ताल *tāl*	उत्थापने	तोलुन् *tolun*, ताज्यौन् *tajyaun*	set up.
क	ताव *tāv*	तापने	तोवुन् *tovun*, ताव्यौन् *tāryaun*	* heat, make red hot.
	त्यम्ब *tyamb*	दृक्पाशने	त्यम्ब्यौव् *tŏmbyauv*	look eagerly.
क	तीज़र *tīz^{a}r*	निशाने	त्यूज़रुन् *tyūz^{a}run*, तीज़र्यौन् *tīz^{a}ryaun*	sharpen, whet.
क	तीज़राव *tīz^{a}rāv*	च	तीज़रोवुन *tīz^{a}rōvun*, तीज़राव्यौन् *tīz^{a}rāvyaun*	ditto.
	तीलन *tīlan*	त्रिलपूतीभावे	तीलन्यौव् *tīlanyauv*	have a bad taste of oil.
	तुन्द *tund*	तीक्ष्णीभवने	तुन्द्यौव् *tundyauv*	be hot tempered.
क	त्वम्ब *tŏmb*	तूलवद्विवरणे	तंबुन् *tombun* त्वम्ब्यौन् *tŏmbyaun*	expand a thing (like cotton).
क	तुल *tul*	उत्थापने	तुलुन् *tulun*, तुज्यौन् *tujyaun*	* set up, left.
	तुर *tųr*	शीतीभवने	तुर्गौव् *tųrgauv*	be cold.

	तुरव *tụraṣ*	च	तुरंवीव् *tụraṇyauv*	be cold.
	वेज् *tēz*	तीक्ष्णीभवने	वेज्यौव् *tezyauv*	be sharp (of a man, a knife, &c).
	वेल *tēl*	विस्फोटादिदंशे	वेल्यौव् *tēlyauv*	to smart, of pimples, &c.
क	तोल *tōl*	तुलने	तुलुन् *tūlun*, तोज्यौन् *tōjyaun*	* weigh.
क	तोवर *tōvar*	क्रूरदृष्टौ	तोवरुन् *tōvạrun*, तोवर्यौन् *tōvaryaun*	* look in a fierce way.
क	तोवराव *tōvarāv*	च	तोवरोवुन् *tōvarōvun*, तोवराव्यौन् *tōvarāvyaun*	ditto.
	तोष *tōṣ*	तोषे	[तुठ् *tūṭhᵉ*], तोठ्यौव् *tōṭhyauv*, [तोछ्यौव् *tōchyauv*]	be satisfied.
	त्रकर *trakar*	कर्कशीभवने	त्रकर्यौव् *trakaryauv*	be hard.
क	त्रकराव *trakarāv*	कर्कशीकरणे	त्रकरोवुन् *trakarōvun*, त्रकराव्यौन् *trakarāvyaun*	make hard.
क	त्रगनाव *tragᵉnāv*	त्रिगुणीकरणे	त्रगनोवुन् *tragᵉnōvun*, त्रगनाव्यौन् *tragᵉnāvyaun*	make three-fold.
	त्रछ् *tratṣ*	भये	त्रछ्यौव् *tratṣyauv*	fear.
क	त्रछराव *trạtṣᵉrāv*	त्रासने	त्रछरोवुन् *trạtṣᵉrōvun*, त्रछराव्यौन् *tratṣᵉrāvyaun*	cause to fear.

* Found in Dr. Elmslie's Vocabulary.

	Root.	Sanskrit Meaning.	Past and Aorist.	English Meaning.
क	त्रप *trap*	आच्छादने	त्रंपुन् *trapun*, त्रप्यौन् *trapyaun*	cover up, close.
क	त्रुपुर *trupur*	च	त्रुपुरुन् *trupurun*, त्रुपुर्यौन् *trupuryaun*	ditto.
	त्रस *tras*	भये	त्रस्यौव् *trasyauv*	fear.
क	त्रंसराव *trasᵊrāv*	त्रासने	त्रंसरोवुन् *trasᵊrövun*, त्रंसराव्यौन् *trasᵊrāvyaun*	cause to fear.
क	त्राव *trāv*	त्यागे	त्रोवुन् *trövun*, त्राव्यौन् *trāvyaun*	* let go.
क	त्रुक *truk*	कवलच्छेदने भक्षणे च	त्रुकुन् *trukun*, त्रुच्यौन् *trucyaun*	cut to pieces, eat.
क	त्रम्ब *trŏmb*	व्यधीभावे	त्रंम्बुन् *trombun*, त्रम्ब्यौन् *trŏmbyaun*	prick.
क	त्रम्बव *trŏmbav*	च	त्रम्बवुन् *trŏmbavun*, त्रम्बव्यौन् *trŏmbavyaun*	ditto.
	त्रञ *trŏç*	कठिनीभवने	त्रञ्यौव् *trŏçyauv*	be hard.
क	त्रञराव *trŏçᵊrāv*	कठिनीकरणे	त्रञरोवुन् *trŏçᵊrövun*, त्रञराव्यौन् *trŏçᵊrāvyaun*	make hard.
	त्रोर *trŏr*	पिटकादिविकारकोमे	त्रोर्यौव् *troryauv*	be hardened (of an opened boil, &c.)
	थक *thak*	श्रमे	थंकु, थच्यौव्	* be weary.
क	थंजर *thasᵊr*	उच्चीकरणे	थंजरुन् *thasᵊrun*, थंजर्यौन् *thasᵊryaun*	make high.

क	थ॑ज़रव *thąsᵉrāv*	”	थ॑ज़रोवुन् *thąsᵉrōvun*, थ॑ज़राव्योन् *thąsᵉrā-vyaun*	make high.
	थद् *thad*	उन्नतीभवने	थद्योव् *thadyauv*	*be high.
	थम *tham*	व्यवहृते	थम्योव् *thamyauv*	be at rest.
	थर *thar*	कम्पने	थर्योव् *tharyauv*	tremble.
क	थल *thal*	शाखाच्छेदने	थ॑लुन् *thąlun*, थज्योन् *thajyaun*	trim branches.
क	थव *thav*	स्थापने	थ॑वुन् *thąvun*, थव्योन् *thavyaun*	set up.
	थाव *thāv* इति केचित्	”	थोवुन् *thōvun*, थाव्योन् *thāvyaun*	*ditto.
	थ॑थर *thąthar*	त्वरायाम्	थ॑थर्योव् *thąthryauv*	be in a hurry.
	थार *thār*	त्वरायाम्	थार्योव् *thāryauv*	ditto.
क	थ्यक *thyak*	श्लाघायाम्	थ्य॑कुन् *thyąkun*, थ्योच्योन् *thŏcyaun*	*praise oneself falsely, boast.
क	थिप *thip*	ताडने	थ्युपुन् *thyupun*, थिप्योन् *thipyaun*	beat, slap.
क	थोक *thŏk*	निष्ठीवने	थ॑कुन् *thokun*, थ॑च्योन् *thŏcyaun*	spit.
क	थुर *thur*	घटने	थुरुन् *thurun*, थुर्योन् *thuryaun*	*form (a pot, used of potters).

* Found in Dr. Elmslie's Vocabulary.

	ROOT.	SANSKRIT MEANING.	PAST AND AORIST.	ENGLISH MEANING.
क	दग *dag*	ताडने	दॊगुन् *dạgun*, दज्यौन् *dajyaun*	*beat, pound.
	दज़् *das*	भस्मीभवने	दॖद् *dạd°*, दज़ौव् *dasauv*	*be burnt.
क	दॖदुराव *dạd°rāv*	क्षीणीकरणे	दॖदुरोवुन् *dạd°rövun*, दॖदुराव्यौन् *dạd°rāvyaun*	make wasted, make weak.
क	दप *dap*	आज्ञायां कथने च	दॊपुन् *dạpun*, दप्यौन् *dapyaun*	*say, order.
क	दबव *dabav*	भूमिक्षेपे	दबॊवुन् *dabạvun*, दबव्यौन् *dabavyaun*	press down to the ground.
भा	दम *dam*	वाताग्निशब्दयोः	दॊमुन् *dạmun*, दम्यौन् *damyaun*	roar (of wind on fire).
	दर *dar*	धैर्यविस्मृतिवर्षनिरोधेषु	दर्यौव् *daryauv*	be steady, (2) remember, (3) stop raining.
क	दर्र *darr*	स्थिरीकरणे	दॊर्रुन् *dạrrun*, दर्र्यौन् *darryaun*	make steady.
क	दल *dal*	विदारणे	दॊलुन् *dạlun*, दज्यौन् *dajyaun*	tear in pieces.
भा	दव *dav*	शीघ्रगतौ	दॊवुन् *dạvun*, दव्यौन् *davyaun*	*run.
क	दस *das*	ताडने	दॊसुन् *dạsun*, दस्यौन् *dasyaun* or दसौन् *dasaun*	beat.
क	दाँदुर *dạ̄ñ°r*	ध्याने	दाँदुरुन् *dạ̄ñ°run*, दाँदुर्यौन् *dạ̄ñ°ryaun*	consider, reflect.

क	दांञ़राव dą̄ñᵉrāv	च	दांञ़रोवुन् dą̄ñᵉrōvun, दांञ़राव्यौन् dą̄ñᵉrāvyaun	consider, reflect.
क	दार dār	धारणोद्धारयोः	दोरुन् dōrun, दार्यौन् dāryaun.	* place, lend money.
क	दाव dāv	दापने	दोवुन् dōvun, दाव्यौन् dāvyaun	cause to give.
क	दि di	दाने	दियुतुन् dyutun, दित्सौन् ditsaun	* give.
क	दगव dŏgav	[illegible]	दगोवुन् dŏgovun, दगव्यौन् dŏgavyaun	husk (grain).
क	दग़नाव dŏgᵉnāv	द्विगुणीकरणे	दग़नोवुन् dŏgᵉnōvun, दग़नाव्यौन् dŏgᵉnāvyaun	double.
	ददर dŏdar	जीर्णीभवने	ददर्यौव् dŏdaryauv	* rot.
क	ददराव dŏdarāv	जीर्णीकरणे	ददरोवुन् dŏdarōvun, ददराव्यौन् dŏdarāvyaun	cause to rot.
क	दंबर dŏbᵉr	भूनिक्षेपे	दंबरुन् dŏbᵉrun, दंबर्यौन् dŏbᵉryaun	* bury, hide in the ground.
क	दंबराव dŏbᵉrāv	च	दंबरोवुन् dŏbᵉrōvun, दंबराव्यौन dŏbᵉrāvyaun	ditto.
क	दय dŏy	दोहने	दोयुन् doyun, दय्यौन् dŏyyaun	* milk.
	दष dŏṣ	[illegible]	दोषु doṣᵘ, दष्यौव् dŏṣyauv	trickle.
क	दूञ्छर dūntshᵉr	पृथक्करणे	दूञ्छरुन् dūntshᵉrun, दूञ्छर्यौन् dūntshᵉryaun	separate.
क	दूञ्छराव dūntshᵉrāv	च	दूञ्छरोवुन् dūntshᵉrōvun, दूञ्छराव्यौन् dūntshᵉrāvyaun	ditto.

* Found in Dr. Elmslie's Vocabulary.

	Root.	Sanskrit Meaning.	Past and Aorist.	English Meaning.
	दूर *dūr*	दूरीभवने	दूर्यौव् *dūryauv*	be distant.
क	दोन *dōn*	पिचविकरणे	दूनुन् *dūnun*, दोञ्यौन् *dōñaun*	* card cotton.
	दोर *dōr*	गतिचातुर्ये	दोर्यौव् *dōryauv*	* run.
क	दुन *dᵃn*	रजआदिरजोपकरणे	दुनुन् *dᵊnun*, दुञ्यौन् *dᵃñaun*	* shake out dust, disperse.
क	दुनव *dᵃnav*	च	दुनोवुन् *dᵃnạvun*, दुनव्यौन् *dᵃnavyaun*	ditto.
क	दुय *dᵃy*	वैमनस्ये	दुयुन् *dᵊyun*, दुय्यौन् *dᵃyyaun*	regret.
क	द्रुक *druk*	क्रीडायाम्	द्रुकुन् *drukun*, द्रुच्यौन् *drucyaun*	play.
	द्रुग *drug*	मूल्यातिशये	द्रुग्यौव् *drugyauv*	be dear, expensive.
क	द्रुगराव *drūgᵃrāv*	दुर्मूल्यीकरणे	द्रुगरोवुन् *drugᵃrōvun*, द्रुगराव्यौन् *drugᵃrāvyaun*	make dear, expensive.
क	दुप्राव *dᵃṣrāv*	दोषदाने	दुप्रोवुन् *dᵃṣrōvun*, दुप्राव्यौन् *dᵃṣrāvyaun*	blame.
	द्रेँठ *drĕṭh*	काठिन्ये	द्रेँठ्यौव् *drĕṭhyauv*	be hard.
भा	नच् *nats*	नर्तने	नचुन् *nạtsun*, नच्यौन् *natsaun*	* dance.
क	नङ्गर *nạñᵉr*	नग्नीकरणे	नङ्गुरुन् *nạñᵉrun*, नङ्गुर्यौन् *nạñᵉryaun*	make naked.

क	नंञ्राव nąñ^{a}rāv	च	नंञ्रोवुन् nąñ^{a}rōvun, नंञ्राव्यौन् nąñ^{a}rāvyaun	make naked.
	नट naṭ	कम्पे	नंट्यौव् nąṭyauv	* tremble.
क	नंट्राव nąṭ^{a}rāv	कम्पने	नंट्रोवुन् nąṭ^{a}rōvun, नंट्राव्यौन् nąṭ^{a}rāvyaun	cause to shake, wave.
	नन nan	नग्नीभवने	नन्यौव् nanyauv	be naked.
आ	नप nap	उत्कोचदाने	नंपुन् nąpun, नप्यौन् napyaun	bribe.
	नम nam	नम्रीभवने	नम्यौव् namyauv	* bend, bow.
	नव nav	अतिशयीभवने नूतनतायां च	नव्यौव् navyauv	be excessive, be new.
	नश naç	अदर्शने	[नूठ् nūṭh^{u}], नश्यौव् naçyauv	* disappear.
क	नहाव nahāv	क्रियाघाते	नहोवुन् nahōvun, नहाव्यौन् nahāvyaun	* obliterate (writing) put a stop to.
	नाँठ nā̃ṭh	निष्फलीभवने	नाँठ्यौव् nā̃ṭhyauv	be fruitless.
	नाँप nā̃p	दीप्तौ	नाँप्यौव् nā̃pyauv	shine.
क	नाव nāv	शोधने	नोवुन् nōvun, नाव्यौन् nāvyaun	clean, polish.
क	नाश़र nāç^{a}r	नाशने	नाश़रुन् nāç^{a}run, नाश़र्यौन् nāçaryaun	destroy.
क	नाश़राव nāç^{a}rāv	च	नाश़रोवुन् nāç^{a}rōvun, नाश़राव्यौन् nāç^{a}rāvyaun	ditto.

* Found in Dr. Elmslie's Vocabulary.

346	Root.	Sanskrit Meaning.	Past and Aorist.	English Meaning.
क	नि *ni*	हरणे	न्यून् *nyūn*, नियौन् *niyaun*	* take.
	निक *nik*	अल्पीभवने	निक्यौव् *nikyauv*	* become small.
क	निकर् *nikᵊr*	खण्डशः करणे	न्युक्रुन् *nyukᵊrun*, निक्र्यौन् *nikᵊryaun*	break to pieces.
	निकराव *nikᵊrāv*	च	निकरोवुन् *nikᵊrōvun*, निकराव्यौन् *nikᵊrāvyaun*	* ditto.
क	न्यङ्गल *nyaŋgal*	निगरणे	न्यङ्गलुन् *nyaŋgạlun*, न्यङ्[illegible]्यौन् *nyaŋgajyaun*	swallow.
क	न्यत *nyat*	पशुरोमकृन्तने	न्यतुन् *nyạtun*, न्यच्यौन् *nyatsaun*	* shear (animals).
क	न्यवास *nyawās*	निवेदने	न्यवोसुन् *nyawōsun*, न्यवास्यौन् *nyawāsaun*	address.
	नील *nil*	हरितीभवने	नील्यौव् *nīlyauv*	become blue.
क	न्यमर् *nŏmᵊr*	नम्रीकरणे	न्यमरुन् *nŏmᵊrun*, न्यम्र्यौन् *nŏmᵊryaun*	* cause to bow.
क	न्यमराव *nŏmᵊrāv*	च	न्यमरोवुन् *nŏmᵊrōvun*, न्यमराव्यौन् *nŏmᵊrāvyaun*	ditto.
क	न्यवर् *nŏvᵊr*	अतिशयीकरणे	न्यवरुन् *nŏvᵊrun*, न्यव्र्यौन् *nŏvᵊryaun*	make excessive.
क	न्यवराव *nŏvᵊrāv*	च	न्यवरोवुन् *nŏvᵊrōvun*, न्यवराव्यौन् *nŏvᵊrāvyaun*	ditto.

क	नेचव nĕchav	ख्यातीकरणे	नेचुवुन् nĕchavun, नेचव्योन् nĕchavyaun	proclaim.
	नेर nĕr	निर्गमने	द्राव् drāv, द्राय्योव् drāyauv	*go forth.
क	नोमुर nōmᵊr	संक्षेपीकरणे	नूमुरुन् nūmᵊrun, नोमुर्योन् nōmᵊryaun	abstract, abridge.
क	नोमुराव nōmᵊrāv	च	नोमुरोवुन् nōmᵊrōvun, नोमुराव्योन् nōmᵊrāvyaun	ditto.
क	न्याव nyāv	धारणे	न्योवुन् nyōvun, न्याव्योन् nyāvyaun	cause to take.
	पक pak	गतौ	पकु pakᵘ, पच्योव् pacyauv	*go.
क	पछताव pachatāv	पश्चात्तापे	पछतोवुन् pachatōvun, पछताव्योन् pachatāvyaun	regret.
क	पछान pachān	उपलक्षणे	पछोनुन् pachōnun, पछाञ्योन् pachāñaun	recognize.
	पच pats	ऋणविश्वासे	पचु patsᵘ, पच्योव् patsauv	trust with a loan.
क	पंजुर pajᵊr	धारेवस्त्र सीवने	पंजुरुन् pajᵊrun, पंजुर्योन् pajᵊryaun	fell a hem (in sewing).
क	पंजुराव pajᵊrāv	च	पंजुरोवुन् pajᵊrōvun, पंजुराव्योन् pajᵊrāvyaun	ditto.
	पज pas	युक्तीभवने सत्याविर्भावे च	पज्योव् pasyauv	be fit, turn out to be true.
क	पंजुर pasᵊr	सत्याविष्करणे	पंजुरुन् pasᵊrun, पंजुर्योन् pasᵊryaun	show to be true.

* Found in Dr. Elmslie's Vocabulary.

	ROOT.	SANSKRIT MEANING.	PAST AND AORIST.	ENGLISH MEANING.
क	पंज़राव *pạsᵊrāv*	च	पंज़रोवुन् *pạsᵊrōvun*, पंज़राव्योन् *pạsᵊrāvyaun*	show to be true.
	पट *paṭ*	प्राप्तौ	पट्यौव् *paṭyauv*	obtain.
क	पटाव *paṭāv*	गतौ	पटोवुन् *paṭōvun*, पटाव्योन् *paṭāvyaun*	go.
	पठ *paṭh*	सिद्धात्	पठ्यौव् *paṭhyauv*	be successfully complete.
क	पंठर *pạṭhᵊr*	संस्कारे मीनादिशोधने च	पंठरुन् *pạṭhᵊrun*, पंठर्योन् *pạṭhᵊryaun*	clean, gut fishes.
क	पंठराव *pạṭhᵊrāv*	संस्कारवे शोधने च	पंठरोवुन् *pạṭhᵊrōvun*, पंठराव्योन् *pạṭhᵊrāvyaun*	ditto.
क	पद *pad*	कुत्सिते शब्दे	पंदुन् *pạdun*, पज्योन् *pajyaun*	break wind.
	पप *pap*	परिपाके	पप्यौव् *papyauv*	ripen.
क	पय *pay*	धात्वादिपाके	पंयुन् *pạyun*, पय्योन् *payyaun*	roast (metals, &c.), burn (bricks).
क	पर *par*	पठने	पंरुन् *pạrun*, पर्योन् *paryaun*	*read.
क	परखाव *parkhāv*	परीक्षायाम्	परखोवुन् *parkhōvun*, परखाव्योन् *parkhāvyaun*	test.
क	परज़न *parzan*	उपलक्षणे	परज़ोनुन् *parzọnun*, परज़न्योन् *parzañaun*	*recognize.

क	पर्ज़ंनाव् *parzanāv*	च	पर्ज़ंनोवुन् *parzanōvun*, पर्ज़ंनाव्यौन् *parzanāvyaun*	*recognize.
क	प्रज़न *prazan*	च	प्रज़ंनुन् *prazạnun*, प्रज़ञ्यौन् *prazañaun*	ditto.
क	पल *pal*	गुप्तदाने	पंलुन् *pạlun*, पल्यौन् *paĵyaun*	give privately.
	पलज़् *palaz*	उपयोगाधाम्	[पलंज़ु *palạz**], पलज़्यौव् *palazyauv*	be useful.
	पलट *palat*	द्रवीभवने	[पलंटु *palạt**], पलट्यौव् *palaṭyauv*	melt, deliquesce.
क	पश *paç*	विषादे	पंशुन् *paçun*, पश्यौन् *paçyaun*	make sorrowful.
	पस्प *paṣp*	क्षरणे	पस्प्यौव् *paṣpyauv*	*drip.
	पाकन *pākan*	विस्फोटादिपाके	पाकन्यौव् *pākanyauv*	roast grain (pop-corn.)
क	पाकव *pākav*	पचने	पाकंवुन् *pākạvun*, पाकव्यौन् *pākavyaun*	*cook.
क	पाज़् *pāz*	निःसारणे	पोज़ुन् *pōzun*, पाज़्यौन् *pāzyaun*	bring out from.
	पाथ *pāth*	भवने	पाथ्यौव् *pāthyauv*	be, become.
क	पार *pār*	केशवेणीकरणे प्रचयापने च	पोरुन् *pōrun*, पार्यौन् *pāryaun*	*tie the hair, toss for an innings, &c.
क	पाल *pāl*	रक्षणे	पोलुन् *pōlun*, पाल्यौन् *pāĵyaun*	protect.
क	पाव *pāv*	पातने	पोवुन् *pōvun*, पाव्यौन् *pāvyaun*	*cause to fall, fell.

* Found in Dr. Elmslie's Vocabulary.

350

	Root.	Sanskrit Meaning.	Past and Aorist.	English Meaning.
आ	पासॣर् *pās°r*	धिक्करणे	पासॣरुन् *pās°run*, पासॣरीयौन् *pās°ryaun*	blame.
क	पासॣराव् *pās°rāv*	च	पासॣरोवुन् *pās°rövun*, पासॣराव्यौन् *pās°rāvyaun*	ditto.
	पि *pi*	पतने	प्यौव् *pyauv*	* fall.
आ	पिठ *piṭ*	परिदेवने	प्युठुन् *pyuṭun*, पिच्यौन् *picyaun*	lament.
क	पिठॣराव् *piṭ°rāv*	दीनीकरणे	पिठॣरोवुन् *piṭ°rövun*, पिठॣराव्यौन् *piṭ°rāvyaun*	cause to lament.
क	प्यतर् *pyatar*	पालने	प्यतॖरुन् *pyatạrun*, प्यतर्यौन् *pyataryaun*	protect.
	प्यद् *pyad*	इज्ञतायाम्	प्यद्यौव् *pĕdyauv*	be cognisant of.
	पिल *pil*	प्राप्तौ	पिल्यौव् *pilyauv*	be possible, arrive at.
क	पिलन *pilan*	प्रापणे	पिलॖनुन् *pilạnun*, पिलञ्यौन् *pilañaun*	cause to arrive, convey.
क	प्यव *pyav*	पाकार्थमग्न्यारम्भे	प्यॖवुन् *pyạvun*, प्यव्यौन् *pĕvyaun*	light fire for cooking.
	पिशल *piçal*	पेशलीभवने	पिशल्यौव् *piçalyauv*	be soft.
	पिस *pis*	पाकेन बहिर्निःसरणे	पिस्यौव् *pisyauv*	boil over.
क	पिह *pih*	संचूर्णने	प्युहुन् *pyuhun*, पिश्यौन् *piçyaun*	* grind.
	पीर *pīr*	मेदुरतायाम्	पीर्यौव् *pīryauv*	be smooth, slippery.

	पीठ् *pīṭ*	खेदात्प्रतीक्षणे	पीठ्यौव् *pīṭyauv*	wait wearily.
क	पीठर् *pīṭhᵊr*	सशिक्षं प्रतिक्षेपणे	प्यूठरुन् *pyūṭhᵊrun*, पीठर्यौन् *pīṭhᵊryaun*	blame and instruct at once.
क	पीठराव *pīṭhᵊrāv*	च	पीठरोवुन् *pīṭhᵊrōvun*, पीठराव्यौन् *pīṭhᵊrāvyaun*	ditto.
क	पीनव *pīnav*	प्रसवने	पीनवुन् *pīnavun*, पीनव्यौन् *pīnavyaun*	bear (young).
क	पुछन *puṭsan*	पुष्पादिखण्डशः करणे	पुछनुन् *puṭsanun*, पुछञौन् *puṭsañaun*	pluck flowers, &c., to pieces.
	पुन *pun*	शापसाफल्ये	[पुनु *pun**], पुन्यौव् *punyauv*	come true (of a curse).
क	पंद *pŏnd*	क्षुते	पंदुन् *pondun*, पंज्यौन् *pŏñjyaun*	sneeze.
	पल *pŏl*	मैदके	पल्यौव् *pŏlyauv*	be weak.
क	पुछर *puçᵊr*	अर्पणे	पुछरुन् *puçᵊrun*, पुछर्यौन् *puçᵊryaun*	* make over (to any one).
क	पुछराव *puçᵊrāv*	च	पुछरोवुन् *puçᵊrōvun*, पुछराव्यौन् *puçᵊrāvyaun*	* ditto.
क	पूज *pūz*	पूजायाम्	पूजुन् *pūzun*, पूज्यौन् *pūzaun*	worship.
क	पूठर *pūṭhᵊr*	स्थूलीकरणे	पूठरुन् *pūṭhᵊrun*, पूठर्यौन् *pūṭhᵊryaun*	make fat.

* Found in Dr. Elmslie's Vocabulary.

	Root.	Sanskrit Meaning.	Past and Aorist.	English Meaning.
क	पूठ्राव *pūṭhᵃrav*	च	पूठ्रोवुन् *pūṭhᵃrōvun*, पूठ्राव्यौन् *pūṭhᵃrā-vyaun*	make fat.
क	पूर् *pūr*	पूरणे	पूरुन् *pūrun*, पूर्यौन् *pūryaun*	fill.
	पेड *pēd*	निर्यासे	पेड्यौव् *pēḍyauv*	* exude.
क	पैर् *pair*	अलंकरणे	पैरुन् *pairun*, पैर्यौन् *pairyaun*	* adorn.
	पोठ *pōṭh*	स्थूलीभवने	पोठ्यौव् *pōṭhyauv*	be fat.
	पोर् *pōr*	पर्याप्तशोषणयोः	पोर्यौव् *pōryauv*	be competent, be dry.
क	पोरव *pōrav*	बाधने	पोर्वुन् *pōrąvun*, पोरव्यौन् *pōravyaun*	oppress.
	पोष *pōṣ*	पर्याप्ततायाम्	पूषु *pūṣᵘ*, पोष्यौव् *pōṣyauv*	* be competent, victo-rious.
	प्रंखट *prakhᵃṭ*	प्रकटने	प्रंखट्यौव् *prąkᵃṭyauv*	be manifest.
क	प्रजन *prazan*	उपलक्षणे	प्रज्नुन् *praząnun*, प्रजञ्यौन् *prazañaun*	recognize.
क	प्रजनाव *prazanāv*	च	प्रजनोवुन् *prazanōvun*, प्रजनाव्यौन् *prazanā-vyaun*	ditto.
	[प्रजल *prazal*	प्रज्वलने	प्रजल्यौव् *prazalyauv*	shine.]

	प्रन् *pran*	[illegible]	प्रन्यौव् *pranyauv*	* be clean and white.
	प्रय् *pray*	प्रीयते	प्रयु *pray**, प्रय्यौव् *prayyauv*.	be pleased.
	प्रस् *pras*	प्रसवे	प्याव् *pyāv*	* be born.
क	प्राट् *prāṭ*	खनने	प्रोटुन् *prōṭun*, प्राच्यौन् *prācyaun*	dig.
	प्राण् *prāṇ*	पुरातनीभवने	प्राण्यौव् *prāṇyauv*	be old.
	प्रार् *prār*	समीक्षणे	[प्रोर् *prōr**], प्रार्यौव् *prāryauv*	* wait.
क	प्राव् *prāv*	प्राप्तौ	प्रोवुन् *prōvun*, प्राव्यौन् *prāvyaun*	* obtain.
क	प्रिण् *priṇ*	उपालम्भे	प्र्युणुन् *pryuṇun*, प्रिञौन् *priñaun*	reproach.
क	प्रिछ् *pritsh*	[illegible]	प्र्युछुन् *pryutshun*, प्रिछौन् *pritshaun*	* ask.
क	प्रिंज् *prins*	प्रेरणे	प्र्युंजुन् *pryunzun*, प्रिंजौन् *prinzaun*	send.
क	फक् *phak*	सक्त्वादिभक्षणे	फकुन् *phạkun*	(?) eat *sattū*; (usually) spit out after chewing.
	फट् *phaṭ*	काष्ठभेदाङ्कुरोद्भेदयोर्जलनिमज्जनादिषु च	फटु *phạṭ**, फच्यौव् *phacyauv*	split (of wood) (neut.) sprout (of a plant), sink into water.
	फब् *phab*	प्रशस्तीभवने	फब्यौव् *phabyauv*	be excellent.

* Found in Dr. Elmslie's Vocabulary.

	Root.	Sanskrit Meaning.	Past and Aorist.	English Meaning.
	फर phar	चौर्ये	फंर् phạr°, फर्यौव् pharyauv	be stolen, be a cause of loss to.
क	फर्काव pharkāv	पर्यालोचने	फर्कोवुन् pharkövun, फर्काव्यौन् pharkāvyaun	enquire into the meaning, enquire.
	फल phal	फलजीर्णे शाकलविभागेषु	फंलु phạl°, फज्यौव् phajyauv	*become old (of clothes), bear fruit, be divided.
	फस phas	बद्धीभवने	फंसु phạs°, फसौव् phasauv	be entangled, caught.
क	फंस्र phạs°r	बद्धीकरणे	फंस्रुन् phạs°run, फंस्र्यौन् phạs°ryaun	entangle, catch in anything.
क	फास्र phạ̄s°r	च	फास्रुन् phạ̄s°run, फास्र्यौन् phạ̄s°ryaun	ditto.
क	फास्राव phạ̄s°rāv	च	फास्रोवुन् phạ̄s°rövun, फास्राव्यौन् phạ̄s°rāvyaun	ditto.
	फहर phahar	पारुष्ये	फहर्यौव् phaharyauv	be hard.
भा	फाँग phā̃g	शिशुमार्जाररोदने	फोंगुन् phõgun, फांज्यौन् phā̃jyaun	cry (of children), mew.
क	फान phān	निःशेषीकरणे	फोनुन् phōnun, फाञौन् phāñaun	carry away totally.

	फाँफल् *phãphal*	क्रियायोग्यीभवने	फाँफल्यौव् *phãphalyauv*	be fit for any work.
क	फालव *phālav*	काष्ठभेदने	फालंवुन् *phālạvun*, फालव्यौन् *phālavyaun*	split (wood) (act.)
	फिच़् *phits*	विस्मरणे	फिच़्यौव् *phitsauv* [फिच़्यौव् *phitsyauv*]	forget.
क	फ्यच़व *phyatsav*	अप्रत्यक्षहरणे	फ्यच़ंवुन् *phyatsạvun*, फ्यच़व्यौन् *phyatsavyaun*	take secretly.
क	फिर *phir*	पुस्तककथाभाण्डानां परिवर्तने	फ्युरुन् *phyurun*, फिर्यौन् *phiryaun*	*turn over (pages), call to memory, pour from one vessel to another.
क	फिरव *phirav*	भ्रामणे	फिरंवुन् *phirạvun*, फिरव्यौन् *phiravyaun*	cause to go round.
क	फ्यश *phyaç*	ओष्ठादिलेहने	फ्यंशुन् *phyạçun*, फ्यश्यौन् *phĕçyaun*	lick the lips or the like.
	फेश *phēç*	च	फ्यूशुन् *phyūçun*, फेश्यौन् *phēçyaun*	lick the lips or the like.
क	फुक *phuk*	ज्वालाप्रदीपने	फुकुन् *phukun*, फुच्यौन् *phucyaun*	*blow a fire (with the mouth to make it burn).
क	फुकार *phukār*	कोपालापे	फुकोरुन् *phukōrun*, फुकार्यौन् *phukāryaun*	speak in anger.
	फुट *phuṭ*	भङ्गे	फुटु *phuṭ°*, फुच्यौव् *phucyauv*	*be broken.
क	फुटर *phuṭ°r*	भञ्जने	फुटरुन् *phuṭ°run*, फुटर्यौन् *phuṭ°ryaun*	*break.

* Found in Dr. Elmslie's Vocabulary.

	Root.	Sanskrit Meaning.	Past and Aorist.	English Meaning.
	फुट्राव phuṭ°rāv	च	फुट्रोवुन् phuṭ°rōvun फुट्राव्यौन् phuṭ°rāvyaun	*break.
	फ्रञ्ज phŏll	विकसने	फॊल्ल pholl° फ्रज्यौव् phŏjjyauv	*expand (of a flower).
भा	फुष phuç	चण्डःकोपे	फुष्यौव् phuçyauv	be inwardly angry.
	फुह phuh	च	फुह्यौव् phuhyauv	ditto.
क	फूँक phūk	आघ्राणे	फूँकुन् phūkun, फूँच्यौन् phūcyaun	smell.
	फेर phēr	भ्रमणविलोभवनपश्चात्ताप-वैपरीत्येषु	फ्यूर् phyūr°, फेर्यौव् phēryauv	*go round, rot, regret, be inverted.
	फोर phōr	स्फुरणे	[फूर् phūr°], फोर्यौव् phōryauv	quiver.
क	फ्यार phyār	रसनिष्क्रासने	फ्योरुन् phyōrun, फ्यार्यौन् phyāryaun	strain.
भा	फ्रक ph°rak	उच्छ्वासनिःश्वासयोः	फ्रकुन् ph°rakun, फ्रच्यौन् ph°racyaun.	breath violently, be out of breath.
क	बक bak	भषणे	बकुन् bakun, बच्यौन् bacyaun	bark, growl, speak angrily.
क	बगार bagār	भर्जने	बगोरुन् bagōrun, बगार्यौन् bagāryaun	fry in oil, &c.

	बच् baç	अगाधजलतायाम्	बच्यौव् baçyauv	*escape.
क	बंचुराव् bąçᵉrāv	भयाद्रिरक्षणे	बंचुरोवुन् bąçᵉrōvun, बंचुराव्यौन् bąçᵉrāvyaun	protect.
क	बस् bas	सेवायां क्षेपणे च	बंसुन् bąsun, बसौन् basaun	*serve, fry in oil, &c.
	बड् baḍ	गतिवृद्ध्योः	बड्यौव् baḍyauv	*go, be great.
क	बडाव् baḍāv	गतिशमनयोः	बडोवुन् baḍōvun, बडाव्यौन् baḍāvyaun	*go, (neut.) quell, (act.) extinguish.
क	बंडुर् bąḍᵉr	वर्धने	बंडुरुन् bąḍᵉrun, बंडुर्यौन् bąḍᵉryaun	cause to be great, increase.
क	बंडुराव् bąḍᵉrāv	च	बंडुरोवुन् bąḍᵉrōvun, बंडुराव्यौन् bąḍᵉrāvyaun	* ditto.
क	बंडुराव् bąḍᵉrāv	पूपाख्यपाके	बंडुरोवुन् bąḍᵉrōvun, बंडुराव्यौन् bąḍᵉrāvyaun	bake bread.
	बन् ban	भवने	बन्यौव् banyauv	*be.
क	बंसुर् bąnsᵉr	विभाजने	बंसुरुन् bąnsᵉrun, बंसुर्यौन् bąnsᵉryaun	*divide, [sell cheaply.]
क	बंसुराव् bąnsᵉrāv	च	बंसुरोवुन् bąnsᵉrōvun, बंसुराव्यौन् bąnsᵉrāvyaun	ditto.
क	बर् bar	पूरणे वियोगदैन्ये च	बंरुन् bąrun, बर्यौन् baryaun	* fill, pine in absence.

* Found in Dr. Elmslie's Vocabulary.

	ROOT.	SANSCRIT MEANING.	PAST AND AORIST.	ENGLISH MEANING.
क	बंकाव *bạrkāv*	पातने	बंकोवुन् *bạrkövun*, बंकाव्योन् *bạrkāvyaun*	cause to fall.
	बल *bal*	आरोग्ये प्राणने च	बल्योव् *balyauv*	*be convalescent, live.
क	बंलर *bạl*^{e}*r*	आरोग्यीकरणे	बंलरुन् *bạl*^{e}*run*, बंलर्योन् *bạl*^{e}*ryaun*	cure.
क	बंलराव *bạl*^{e}*rāv*	च	बंलरोवुन् *bạl*^{e}*rövun*, बंलराव्योन् *bạl*^{e}*rāvyaun*	ditto.
	बस *bas*	निवासे	बंसु *bạs*^{e}, बसोव् *basauv*	* dwell.
	बसन *basan*	पीतीभवने	बसन्योव् *basanyauv*	be yellow.
	बहर *bahar*	शूरतायाम्	बहर्योव् *baharyauv*	be brave.
	बाखन *bākhan*	बुद्धिभ्रंशे	बाखन्योव् *bākhanyauv*	be mistaken.
क	बांगर *bāg*^{e}*r*	विभाजने	बांगरुन् *bāg*^{e}*run*, बांगर्योन् *bāg*^{e}*ryaun*	* divide.
क	बांजर *bāj*^{e}*r*	च	बांजरुन् *bāj*^{e}*run*, बांजर्योन् *bāj*^{e}*ryaun*	ditto.
क	बांगराव *bāg*^{e}*rāv*	च	बांगरोवुन् *bāg*^{e}*rövun*, बांगराव्योन् *bāg*^{e}*rāvyaun*	ditto.
क	बांजराव *bāj*^{e}*rāv*	च	बांजरोवुन् *bāj*^{e}*rövun*, बांजराव्योन् *bāj*^{e}*rāvyaun*	ditto.

	बाद् bād [ब्राद् brād]	प्रबलीभवने	बाद्यौव् bādyauv, [ब्राद्यौव् brādyauv]	be powerful.
	बाँबर् bā̃bar	त्वरायाम्	बाँबर्यौव् bā̃baryauv	be quick.
क	बाव bāv	अभिप्रायाविष्करणे ईश्वरार्पणे च	बोवुन् bōvun, बाव्यौन् bāvyaun	* shew, declare one's intentions, devote to God.
	बावस् bāwas	रोचने	बावज्यौव् bāwazyauv	be preferred (usually food).
क	बाष bāṣ	उच्चारणे	बोषुन् bōṣun, बाष्यौन् bāṣyaun	speak.
	बास bās	भासने	[बोसु bōs^{u}], बास्यौव् bāsyauv, बासौव् bāsauv	become clear, evident.
	बिगर् bigar	विकारे	बिगर्यौव् bigaryauv	be spoiled.
क	ब्यँनर् bĕñ^{a}r	विवरणे भिन्नीकरणे च	ब्यँनरुन् bĕñ^{a}run, ब्यँनर्यौन् bĕñ^{a}ryaun	open, separate (act.)
क	ब्यँनराव bĕñ^{a}rāv	च	ब्यँनरोवुन् bĕñ^{a}rōvun, ब्यँनराव्यौन् bĕñ^{a}rā-vyaun	ditto.
	ब्यन्न byann	भिन्नीभवने	ब्यन्न्यौव् bĕnnyauv	be separate.
	बिय biy	पर्युषिते	बिय्यौव् biyyauv	be stale.
	ब्यह byah	उपवेशने	ब्यूठ byūṭh^{u}, बेछ्यौव् bĕchyauv (sic)	* sit.
क	बुछ buch	दंशक्रियायाम्	बुछुन् buchun, बुछ्यौन् buchyaun	* bite.

* Found in Dr. Elmslie's Vocabulary.

	ROOT.	SANSCRIT MEANING.	PAST AND AORIST.	ENGLISH MEANING.
क	बुस् *bus*	भर्जने	बुसुन् *busun*, बुस्यौन् *busaun*	* parch (grain).
	ब्वड *bŏḍ*	निमज्जने	ब्वड् *boḍ*ᵘ, ब्वज्यौव् *bŏjyauv*	* dive, sink.
	बुड *buḍ*	स्थविरीभवने	बुड्यौव् *buḍyauv*	* be old.
	ब्वव *bŏv*	उत्पत्तौ	ब्वव् *bov*ᵘ, ब्वव्यौव् *bŏvyauv*	* be born, grow.
क	बूग *būg*	भोगे	बूगुन् *būgun*, बूज्यौन् *būjyaun*	enjoy.
क	बेछ *bēch*	भिक्षायाम्	ब्यूछुन् *byūchun*, बेछ्यौन् *bēchyaun*	beg.
	बोज़् *bōz*	निशामने	बूज़ुन् *būzun*, बोज़्यौन् *bōzaun*	* hear.
क	बोल *bōl*	पक्षिशब्दे	बूलुन् *būlun*, बोज्यौन् *bōjyaun*	sing, speak (of birds).
क	ब्रक *brak*	दंष्ट्राघातकोपयोः	ब्रंकुन् *brąkun*, ब्रच्यौन् *bracyaun*	clench with the teeth, be angry.
	ब्रज़् *braz*	दीप्तौ	ब्रज़्यौव् *brazyauv*	shine.
	ब्रम *bram*	भ्रान्तौ	ब्रम्यौव् *bramyauv*	go round in circles.
क	ब्रंमुर *brąm*ᵊ*r*	मुविवरत्वे	ब्रंमुरुन् *brąm*ᵊ*run*, ब्रंमुर्यौन् *brąm*ᵊ*ryaun*	mislead.
क	ब्रंमुराव *brąm*ᵊ*rāv*	च	ब्रंमुरोवुन् *brąm*ᵊ*rōvun*, ब्रंमुराव्यौन् *brąm*ᵊ*rā-vyaun*	*mislead.

क	ब्रंश् brạç	च	ब्रंशुन् brạçun, ब्रंशोन् brạçyaun	clench with the teeth, (*not* to be angry).
क	ब्रिछ् britsh	परिदेवने	ब्रुछुन् bryutshun, ब्रिछोन् britshaun	lament.
	ब्रेठ b̆rēṭh	मूर्खीभवने	ब्रेठ्योव् brēṭhyauv	be a fool.
क	मंग् mạŋg	याचने	मंगुन् mạŋgun, मञ्ज्योन् mañjyaun	*ask.
क	मंचूराव् mạtsᵊrāv	वञ्चने	मंचूरोवुन् mạtsᵊrōvun, मंचूराव्योन् mạtsᵊrā-vyaun	*delude.
क	मठार mathār	समीकरणे सान्त्वने च	मठोरुन् mathōrun, मठार्योन् mathāryaun	make level, calm, console.
क	मंड mạṇḍ	वस्त्रमार्दवीकरणाय...	मंडुन् mạṇḍun, मञ्ज्योन् mañjyaun	*knead clothes in water to soften and clean them, adorn.
	मत mat	उन्मादे	मत्योव् matyauv	*be mad, foolish.
क	मंथ math	मर्दने	मंथुन् mạthun, मछोन् matshaun	*pound, beat, churn.
क	मनव manav	कोपापनयने	मनवुन् manạvun, मनव्योन् manavyaun	calm an angry person.
क	मंझूर mạnzᵊr	विकलीकरणे	मंझरुन् mạnzᵊrun, मंझूर्योन् mạnzᵊryaun	make imperfect, diminish.
क	मंझूराव mạñzᵊrāv	च	मंझूरोवुन् mạnzᵊrōvun, मंझूराव्योन् mạnzᵊrā-vyaun	ditto.

* Found in Dr. Elmslie's Vocabulary.

362	ROOT.	SANSKRIT MEANING.	PAST AND AORIST.	ENGLISH MEANING.
क	मन्द *mand*	मन्थने	मंन्दुन् *mạndun*, मन्सौन् *mansaun*	churn.
	मन्दछ *mandach*	मन्दाचे	मन्दछ्यौव् *mandachyauv*	* be ashamed.
	ममल *mamal*	निर्चेतन्ये	ममल्यौव् *mamalyauv*	* be asleep (of a limb).
क	मर *mar*	मरणसंधापनयोः	मूद् (संधापने मंरुन्) *mūd*ᵘ, die, (*mạrun*, unite), म्वयौव् *mŏyauv*	die, unite, join together.
	मर्च़ *marts*	अन्तःकोपे	मर्च़ौव् *martsauv*	be inwardly wrathful.
क	मर्दाव *mardāv*	विस्फोटादिमर्दने	मर्दोवुन् *mardōvun*, मर्दाव्यौन् *mardāvyaun*	rub a boil or pimple.
क	मल *mal*	मर्दने	मंलुन् *mạlun*, मज्यौन् *majyaun*	*rub, shampoo.
	मष *maṣ*	विस्मृतौ	मंठ् *mạth*ᵘ, मछ्यौव् *machyauv*	*forget.
क	मंषर *mạṣ*ᵉ*r*	विस्मारणे	मंषरुन् *mạṣ*ᵉ*run*, मंषर्यौन् *mạṣ*ᵉ*ryaun*	cause to forget.
क	मंषराव *mạṣ*ᵉ*rāv*	च	मंषरोवुन् *mạṣ*ᵉ*rōvun*, मंषराव्यौन् *mạṣ*ᵉ*rāvyaun*	ditto.
क	महार *mahār*	खण्डशः करणे	महोरुन् *mahōrun*, महार्यौन् *mahāryaun*	crumble (act.)
क	मास *mās*	तत्परतायां शोधने च	मोसुन् *mōsun*, मासौन् *māsaun*	be intent upon, make clean.

क	मांञ्राव *mạ̄ñ°rāv*	स्वीकारकारवे	मांञ्रोवुन् *mạ̄ñ°rōvun*, मांञ्राव्योन् *mạ̄ñ°rā-vyaun*	cause to confess.
क	मांज *mā̃j*	धातुनिर्मलीकरवे	मोंजुन् *mŏ̃jun*, मांज्योन् *mā̃jyaun*	clean metals, &c.
क	मांड *mā̃ḍ*	मिश्रीकरवे	मोंडुन् *mŏ̃ḍun*, मांज्योन् *mā̃jyaun*	*mingle (act.), knead.
क	मान *mān*	स्वीकरवे	मोनुन् *mōnun*, मान्योन् *māñaun*	*admit, confess.
क	मार *mār*	मारवे	मोरुन् *mōrun*, मार्योन् *māryaun*	*kill.
क	मिलव *milav*	संयोजने	मिलवुन् *milạvun*, मिलव्योन् *milavyaun*	*mix, unite.
क	मिलनाव *milanāv*	च	मिलनोवुन् *milanōvun*, मिलनाव्योन् *milanā-vyaun*	*ditto.
	मुकल *mŏkal*	मुक्तौ	मुकल्योव् *mŏkalyauv*	*be released.
	मुच *mŏts*	अवशेषे	मोंचु *mots**, [मोंतु *mot**], मुच्योव् *mŏtsauv*	remain over and above.
क	मुचर *mutsar*	उद्घाटने	मुचरुन् *mutsạrun*, मुचर्योन् *mutsaryaun*	*open (act.), disclose.
क	मुचराव *mutsarāv*	च	मुचरोवुन् *mutsarōvun*, मुचराव्योन् *mutsarā-vyaun*	*ditto.
क	मुच *much*	व्रतादित्यागे	मुचुन् *muchun*, मुच्योन् *muchyaun*	complete a vow.
	मोट *mŏṭ*	स्थूलीभवने	मोट्योव् *mŏṭyauv*	be fat.

* Found in Dr. Elmslie's Vocabulary.

364	Root.	Sanskrit Meaning.	Past and Aorist.	English Meaning.
क	म्वटर् mŏṭᵊr	स्थूलीकरणे	मोटरुन् moṭᵊrun, म्वटर्योव् mŏṭᵊryaun	make fat, make thick (by boiling).
	म्वटराव mŏṭᵊrāv	च	म्वटरोवुन् mŏṭᵊrōvun, म्वटराव्योव् mŏṭᵊrāvyaun	ditto.
	म्वण्ड mŏṇḍ	कुण्ठीभवने	म्वण्ड्योव् mŏṇḍyauv	be blunt, dulled, weak.
क	म्वण्डर् mŏṇḍᵊr	कुण्ठीकरणे	म्वण्डरुन् mŏṇḍᵊrun, म्वण्डर्योव् mŏṇḍᵊryaun	causal of preceding.
	म्वण्डराव mŏṇḍᵊrāv	च	म्वण्डरोवुन् mŏṇḍᵊrōvun, म्वण्डराव्योव् mŏṇḍᵊrāvyaun	ditto.
	म्वदुर् mŏdᵊr	मधुरीभवने	म्वदुर्योव् mŏdᵊryauv	* be sweet.
क	म्वदुराव mŏdᵊrāv	मधुरीकरणे	म्वदुरोवुन् mŏdᵊrōvun, म्वदुराव्योव् mŏdᵊrāvyaun	* make sweet.
क	मुन mun	धान्यखण्डने	मुनुन् munun, मुञ्योव् muñaun	pound (rice).
क	म्वलव mŏlav	मूल्यनिश्चयीकरणे	म्वलवुन् mŏlavun, म्वलव्योव् mŏlavyaun	settle a price of a thing.
क	मुष mus̱	मोषणे	मुषुन् mus̱un, मुष्योव् mus̱yaun	steal.
क	मुस mus	भक्ष्याभक्षणे	मुसुन् musun, मुस्योव् musyaun or मुसोव् musaun	eat improperly.

क	मुसर *musar*	उद्घाटने	मुसॅरुन् *musarun*, मुसर्योन् *musaryaun*	open.
क	मुसराव *musarāv*	च	मुसरोवुन् *musarōvun*, मुसराव्योन् *musarā-vyaun*	ditto.
क	मुह *muh*	मोहने	मुहुन् *muhun*, मुग्योन् *mugyaun*, [मुह्योन् *muhyaun*]	deceive.
आ	मूञ्छर *mŭntshar*	प्रतीक्षणे	मूञ्छॅरुन् *mŭntsharun*, मूञ्छर्योन् *mŭntsha-ryaun*	wait.
आ	मूञ्छराव *mŭntsharāv*	च	मूञ्छरोवुन् *mŭntsharōvun*, मूञ्छराव्योन् *mŭn-tsharāvyaun*	ditto.
क	मूँत्र *mŭ̃tr*	मन्त्रवशी [वशे] भवने	मूँत्रुन् *mŭ̃trun*, मूँत्र्योन् *mŭ̃tryaun*	be subject to a charm.
क	मूँत्राव *mŭ̃trāv*	मन्त्रवशीकरणे	मूँत्रोवुन् *mŭ̃trōvun*, मूँत्राव्योन् *mŭ̃trāvyaun*	make subject to a charm.
क	मूर *mūr*	शमी शिम्बूषँ भक्षणे च	मूरुन् *mūrun*, मूर्योन् *mūryaun*	shell (peas, &c.), eat.
	मेठ *meṭh*	मधुरीभवने	मेठ्योव् *meṭhyauv*	* be sweet.
क	मेन *mĕn*	मापने	म्यूनुन् *myūnun*, मेन्योन् *mĕnaun*	* measure.
क	मेळ *mel*	संगमे	म्यूळु *myūlu*, मेळ्योव् *mejyauv*	* meet.
	मोर *mōr*	शमे	मोर्योव् *mōryauv*	be calmed.

* Found in Dr. Elmslie's Vocabulary.

	Root.	Sanskrit Meaning.	Past and Aorist.	English Meaning.
क	मोरव *mōrav*	पीडासहने	मोरॅवुन् *mōrạvun*, मोरव्यौन् *mōravyaun*	bear pain (only used in fem.).
क	यॅतॖर *yạtᵊr*	शक्तौ	यॅतॖरुन् *yạtᵊrun*, यतॖर्यौन् *yạtᵊryaun*	be able.
क	यॅतॖराव *yạtᵊrāv*	च	यॅतॖरोवुन् *yạtᵊrōvun*, यॅतॖराव्यौन् *yạtᵊrāvyaun*	ditto.
	याप *yāp*	व्याप्तौ	याप्यौव् *yāyyauv*	pẹrvade.
क	यार *yār*	संख्याने	योरुन् *yōrun*, यार्यौन् *yāryaun*	calculate.
	यि *yi*	आगमे	आव् *āv*	* come.
क	येर *yēr*	तन्तुसंताने	य्यूरुन् *yyūrun*, येर्यौन् *yēryaun*	* arrange thread for weaving.
क	रङ्ग *raṅg*	रञ्जने	रॅङ्गुन् *rạṅgun*, रञ्ज्यौन् *rañjyaun*	* colour (act.), dye.
क	रछ *rach*	रक्षायाम्	रॅछुन् *rạchun*, रछ्यौन् *rachyaun*	* protect.
क	रॅछॖर *rạtshᵊr*	सम्यक्संस्कारे	रॅछॖरुन् *rạtshᵊrun*, रॅछॖर्यौन् *rạtshᵊryaun*	put in complete order.
क	रछॖराव *ratshᵊrāv*	च	रॅछॖरोवुन् *rạtshᵊrōvun*, रॅछॖराव्यौन् *rạtshᵊrā-vyaun*	ditto.
क	रट *raṭ*	ग्रहणे	रॅटुन् *rạṭun*, रट्यौन् *racyaun*	* take.

क	रन् *ran*	पाके	रंनुन् *ranun*, रञौन् *rañaun*	* cook.
	रंस् *rans*	प्रीतौ रागे च	रंस्यौव् *ransyauv*	be pleased, show love to.
क	रंसव *ransav*	प्रीणने	रंसवुन् *ransavun*, रंसव्यौन् *ransavyaun*	gratify.
क	रंसनाव *ransanāv*	च	रंसनोवुन् *ransanōvun*, रंसनाव्यौन् *ransanāvyaun*	ditto.
	रम्ब *ramb*	शोभायाम्	रम्ब्यौव् *rambyauv*	be beautiful.
	रस *ras*	सरसीभवने	रस्यौव् *rasyauv*	be full of juice.
	राव *rāv*	नष्टीभवने	रोवु *rōv**, राव्यौव् *rāvyauv*	* be lost.
क	रावर *rāvar*	नष्टीकरणे	रावरुन् *rāvarun*, रावर्यौन् *rāvaryaun*	* lose.
क	रावराव *rāvarāv*	च	रावरोवुन् *rāvarōvun*, रावराव्यौन् *rāvarāvyaun*	ditto.
क	रिंसव *rinsav*	प्रच्छन्नतो	रिंसवुन् *rinsavun*, रिंसव्यौन् *rinsavyaun*	escape secretly.
क	रिव *riv*	अलंकरणतत्परतायाम्	र्युवुन् *ryuvun*, रिव्यौन् *rivyaun*	be intent on adorning oneself [lament].
क	रुव *ruv*	रोपणे	रुवुन् *ruvun*, रुव्यौन् *ruvyaun*	plant (act.).
	रोट् *rōṭ*	रोचने	रूटु *rūṭu**, रोट्यौव् *rōṭyauv*	be preferred.

* Found in Dr. Elmslie's Vocabulary.

	Root.	Sanskrit Meaning.	Past and Aorist.	English Meaning.
	रोज़् *rōz*	स्थितौ	रूदॖ *rūd*^{u}, रोज़ोव् *rōzauv*	* stop, stand.
	रोट *rōṭ*	अवरुद्धे	रूटॖ *rūṭ*^{u}, रोच्योव् *rōcyauv*, [रोट्योव् *roṭyauv*]	be stopped.
	रोष *rōṣ*	रुषौ	रूठॖ *rūṭh*^{u}, रोछ्योव् *rōchyauv*	* be angry.
क	रॖकव *r*^{a}*kav*	भूसंमार्जने	रॖकॊवुन् *r*^{a}*kǫvun*, रॖकव्योन् *r*^{a}*kavyaun*	drag along the ground.
	रॖड *r*^{a}*ḍ*	हठीभवने	रॖड्योव् *r*^{a}*ḍyauv*	persistently follow.
	रॖत *r*^{a}*t*	साध्वीभवने	रॖत्योव् *r*^{a}*tyauv*	be good.
	रॖण *r*^{a}*ṇ*	जीर्णीभवने	रॖण्योव् *r*^{a}*ṇyauv*	be worn out.
भा	रॖस *r*^{a}*s*	गमने	रॖसुन् *r*^{a}*sun*, रॖसोन् *r*^{a}*saun*	go.
क	लख *lakh*	अन्तर्नयने	लॊखुन् *lǫkhun*, लछ्योन् *lachyaun*	bring inside.
क	लग *lag*	सङ्गे पीडायां सामञ्जस्ये च	लॊगॖ *lǫg*^{u}, लज्योव् *lajyauv*	* be with, suffer pain, fit.
भा	लङ्ग *laṅg*	पङ्गूभवने	लॊङ्गुन् *lǫṅgun*, लञ्ज्योन् *lañjyaun*	be lame.
	लज़् *laz*	योग्यतायाम्	लज़्योव् *lazauv*	be suitable.
क	लठाव *laṭāv*	गमने	लठोवुन् *laṭōvun*, लठाव्योन् *laṭāvyaun*	go.

क	लड़ *laḍ*	युद्धे	लंडुन् *lạḍun*, लज्यौन् *lajyaun*	fight.
क	लडाव *laḍāv*	संप्रहारे	लडोवुन् *laḍōvun*, लडाव्यौन् *laḍāvyaun*	use in fight.
क	लतव *latav*	लताघाते	लतंवुन् *latạvun*, लतव्यौन् *latavyaun*	kick.
क	लतार *latār*	अधिक्षेपे	लतोरुन् *latōrun*, लतार्यौन् *latāryaun*	blame.
क	लद *lad*	वस्तुप्रेषणे गृहादिनिर्माणो-र्ध्वीकरणयोः धनुरादि-कर्मणि च	लंदुन् *lạdun*, लज़ौन् *lazaun*	* send, build, raise, load, wind up string.
क	लब *lab*	प्राप्तौ	लंबुन् *lạbun*, लब्यौन् *labyaun*	* find, get.
क	लम *lam*	आकर्षणे	लंमुन् *lạmun*, लम्यौन् *lamyaun*	* drag.
	लय *lay*	अर्घणे	लंयु *lạyᵘ*, लय्यौव् *layyauv*	be worth.
क	ललव *lalav*	वक्षःपालने	ललंवुन् *lalạvun*, ललव्यौन् *lalavyaun*	* take to ones breast, protect.
	लस *las*	दीर्घजीवने	लूस्तु *lūstᵘ*, लाछ्यौव् *lāṭṣhauv*	* live long.
	लहन *lahan*	नाडीशिथिलीभवने	लहन्यौव् *lahanyauv*	have a weak pulse.
क	लाग *lāg*	अनुकरणधारणकृषि-संपर्कनेषु	लोगुन् *lōgun*, लाज्यौन् *lājyaun*	* imitate, place, cultivate, unite.

* Found in Dr. Elmslie's Vocabulary.

	Root.	Sanskrit Meaning.	Past and Aorist.	English Meaning.
क	लाय lăy	आघाते प्रक्षेपे च	लोयुन् lŏyun, लायीान् lăyyaun	* strike, throw to a distance.
क	लार lăr	स्पर्शानुगमनविमलीकरणेषु	लोरुन् lŏrun, लार्यौन् lăryaun	* touch, follow, polish.
क	लिख likh	लेखने	ल्युखुन् lyukhun, लिख्यौन् lichyaun	* write.
	ल्यच़् lyats	निर्बलीभवने	ल्यच़ौव् lyatsauv	be weak.
क	लिथव lithav	मर्दने	लिथवुन् lithavun, लिथव्यौन् lithavyaun	rub or drag about in the dust or in dirt.
	ल्यड lyaḍ	पराजयीभवने	ल्यड्यौव् lĕḍyauv	be conquered.
	ल्यदुर lyadᵊr	पीतीभवने	ल्यदुर्यौव् lĕdᵊryauv	be yellow.
क	ल्यदुराव lyadᵊrāv	पीतीकरणे	ल्यदुरोवुन् lyadᵊrōvun ल्यदुराव्यौन् lyadᵊrā-vyaun	make yellow.
क	लिव liv	लेपने	ल्युवुन् lyuvun, लिव्यौन् livyaun	plaster.
क	ल्यव lyav	लेहने	ल्यवुन् lyovun, ल्यव्यौन् lĕvyaun	* lick.
	लिस lis	प्रसन्नतायाम्	लिस्यौव् lisyauv	be pleased.
	लत lŏt	लाघवे	लत्यौव् lŏtyauv	* be light.

क	लल *lŏl*	उपक्रीडायाम्	ललुन् *lŏlun*, लज्यौन् *lŏjyaun*	play with a customer (*i.e.*, to refuse to sell a thing at first in order to get a better price).
	लूकराव *lūk^{a}rāv*	क्षुद्रीकरणे	लूकरोवुन् *lūk^{a}rōvun*, लूकराव्यौन् *lūk^{a}rāvyaun*	make small.
क	लूट *lūṭ*	लुण्ठने	लूटुन् *lūṭun*, लूच्यौन् *lūcyaun*	*plunder.
	लूब *lūb*	लोभने	लूब्यौव् *lūbyauv*	be desirous.
क	लूर *lūr*	विनष्टीकरणे निपातने च	लूरुन् *lūrun*, लूर्यौन् *lūryaun*	destroy, knock down.
क	लेख *lĕkh*	लेखने	ल्यूखुन् *lyūkhun*, लेछ्यौन् *lĕchyaun*	write.
	लोक *lŏk*	क्षुद्रीभवने	लोक्यौव् *lŏkyauv*	*be small.
क	लोन *lŏn*	लवने	लूनुन् *lūnun*, लोञ्यौन् *loñaun*	*reap.
	लान *lŏ̃n* इति केचित्			
	लोस *lŏs*	श्रमे	लूस *lūs^{a}*, लोसौव् *lŏsauv*	*be weary.
	लोर *lŏr*	वैकल्ये	लोर्यौव् *lŏryauv*	become deficient.
	लय *l^{a}y*	सम्यक्पर्याप्तौ	लय्यौव् *l^{a}yyauv*	be sufficient.
	लह *l^{a}h*	सम्यक्पर्याप्तौ	लह्यौव् *l^{a}hyauv*	ditto.

* Found in Dr. Elmslie's Vocabulary.

	Root.	Sanskrit Meaning.	Past and Aorist.	English Meaning.
	ल्हन *lᵃhan*	पाकविकारे	ल्हन्यौव् *lᵃhanyauv*	delay ripening.
क	वखन *wakhan*	व्याख्याने	वखनुन् *wakhạnun*, वखन्यौन् *wakhañaun*	lecture.
क	वस् *was*	वाद्यशब्दे	वसुन् *wạsun*, वस्यौन् *wasaun*	*sound (of a musical instrument).
क	वसव *wasav*	आर्द्रीकरणे	वसोवुन् *wasọvun*, वसव्यौन् *wasavyaun*	moisten.
क	वट *waṭ*	वेष्टने	वटुन् *wạṭun*, वच्यौन् *wacyaun*	*fold up, shut up.
क	वडर *wạḍᵃr*	निक्षेपे	वडरुन् *wạḍᵃrun*, वड्यौन् *wạḍᵃryaun*	bury.
क	वडराव *wạḍᵃrāv*	च	वडरोवुन् *wạḍᵃrōvun*, वडराव्यौन् *wạḍᵃrāvyaun*	ditto.
क	वथर *wathar*	आस्तरणे	वथरुन् *wathạrun*, वथर्यौन् *watharyaun*	spread out.
क	वथराव *watharāv*	च	वथरोवुन् *watharōvun*, वथराव्यौन् *watharā-vyaun*	* ditto.
क	वद् *wad*	रोदने	वदुन् *wạdun*, वद्यौन् *wasaun*	*weep.
क	वन *wan*	भाषणे	वनुन् *wạnun*, वन्यौन् *wañaun*	*speak, say.
क	वनव *wanav*	स्त्रीणामेकस्वरगाने	वनोवुन् *wanọvun*, वनव्यौन् *wanavyaun*	sing in chorus (of women).

क	वन्द् *wand*	उपचारे	वंन्दुन् *wandun*, वञ्जौन् *wanzaun*	devote.
	वय् *way*	पथ्यीभवने	वय् *way*ᵘ वय्यौव् *wayyauv*	*be fit to eat, agree with, suit.
क	वर् *war*	वरणे	वंरुन् *warun*, वर्यौन् *waryaun*	choose.
क	वल् *wal*	आच्छादने	वंलुन् *walun*, वज्यौन् *wajyaun*	*cover, dress oneself.
क	वव् *wav*	वापने	वंवुन् *wavun*, वव्यौन् *wavyaun*	*sow.
क	वष् *waṣ*	वर्षणे	वंषुन् *waṣun*, वष्यौन् *waṣyaun*	rain.
	वस् *was*	अवरोहणे	वंस् *wath*ᵘ, वछौव् *watshauv*	* come down, descend.
	वहार् *wahār*	विस्तारणे मक्षिकाद्यपसारणे च	वहोरुन् *wahōrun*, वहार्यौन् *wahāryaun*	spread out, drive away (flies, &c.).
क	वहाराव् *wahārāv*	च	वहारोवुन् *wahārōvun*, वहाराव्यौन् *wahārāvyaun*	ditto.
आ	वांछ् *wā̆ts*	वञ्चने	वूंछुन् *wūtsun*, वांछ्यौन् *wā̆tsaun*	cheat.
क	वाठ् *wāṭ*	संधापने	वोठुन् *wōṭun*, वाच्यौन् *wācyaun*	unite.
	वात् *wāt*	प्रापणे	वोत् *wōt*ᵘ, वाच्यौव् *wācauv*	* arrive.
क	वाम् *wām*	मक्षिकाद्यपसारणे	वोमुन् *wōmun*, वाम्यौन् *wāmyaun*	drive away (flies, &c.)

* Found in Dr. Elmslie's Vocabulary.

	Root.	Sanskrit Meaning.	Past and Aorist.	English Meaning.
क	वार *wār*	च	वोरुन् *wōrun*, वार्यौन् *wāryaun*	drive away (flies, &c.).
भा	वाय *wāy*	ध्माने नौकावाहने च	वोयुन् *wōyun*, वाय्यौन् *wāyyaun*	* blow (a musical instrument), row a boat.
क	वाल *wāl*	अवतारणे दृष्टिपाते च	वोलुन् *wōlun*, वाल्यौन् *wājyaun*	cause to descend, fall (of rain).
	विगल *vigal*	विगलने	विगल्यौव् *vigalyauv*	melt.
क	विचार *vitsār*	विचारे	विचोरुन्, *vitsorun*, विचार्यौन् *vitsāryaun*	consider, decide.
	व्यच *vyats*	संभवे	व्यचु *vyatsᵘ*, व्यच्यौव् *vĕtsyauv*	* pervade, fit into.
क	व्यछन *vyatshan*	विवरणे	व्यछनुन् *vyatshanun*, व्यछन्यौन् *vyatshañaun*	separate, tease out (wool, &c.).
क	व्यसर *vyasᵃr*	प्रतीकरणे	व्यसरुन् *vyasᵃrun*, व्यसर्यौन् *vyasᵃryaun*	prove.
क	व्यसराव *vyasᵃrāv*	च	व्यसरोवुन् *vyasᵃrōvun*, व्यसराव्यौन् *vyasᵃrā-vyaun*	ditto.
क	व्यञर *vĕñᵃr*	पृथक्करणे	व्यञरुन् *vĕñᵃrun*, व्यञर्यौन् *vĕñᵃryaun*	separate.
क	व्यञराव *vĕñᵃrāv*	च	व्यञरोवुन् *vĕñᵃrōvun*, व्यञराव्यौन् *vĕñᵃrā-vyaun*	ditto.

	बठ vyath	स्थूलीभवने	बथोव् vĕthyauv	* be fat.
क	बंठर् vyạth^{a}r	स्थूलीकरणे	बंठरुन् vyạth^{a}run, बठ्यौन् vĕth^{a}ryaun	make fat.
क	बंठराव vyạth^{a}rāv	च	बंठरोवुन् vyạth^{a}rōvun, बंठरावोन् vyạth^{a}rā-vyaun	ditto.
	बंडुर vyạd^{a}r	शैथिल्ये	बंडुर्यौव् vĕd^{a}ryauv	be loose, slack.
क	बंडुराव vyạdarāv	शिथिलीकरणे	बंडुरोवुन् vyạd^{a}rōvun, बंडुरावोन् vyad^{a}rā-vyaun	make loose.
क	बन्द vyand	आदरणे	बंन्दुन् vyạndun, बञ्ज़ोन् vyanzaun	* serve, revere.
	बप vyap	संभवे	बंप्योव् vĕpyauv	pervade.
क	बंपर् vyạp^{a}r	संभावने	बंपरुन् vyạp^{a}run, बंप्र्यौन् vyạp^{a}ryaun	cause to pervade.
क	बंपराव vyạp^{a}rāv	च	बंपरोवुन् vyạp^{a}rōvun, बंपरावोन् vyạp^{a}rā-vyaun	ditto.
	बलर vyalar	अव्यवस्थायां	बलर्यौव् vyalaryauv	go out of order.
क	बव vyav	विकीर्णने	बंवुन् vyạvun, बवोन् vĕvyaun	scatter.
क	बंवर् vyạv^{a}r	विकीर्णने	बंवरुन् vyạv^{a}run, बंव्र्यौन् vĕv^{a}ryaun	ditto.
क	बवराव vyav^{a}ryāv	च	बंवरोवुन् vyạv^{a}rōvun, बंवरावोन् vyạv^{a}rā-vyaun	ditto.

* Found in Dr. Elmslie's Vocabulary.

	ROOT.	SANSKRIT MEANING.	PAST AND AORIST.	ENGLISH MEANING.
	व्यसर् *vyasar*	विशीर्णने	व्यसर्यौव् *vyasaryauv*	* be ruined, fade (of a flour.)
	विस् *vis*	प्रसन्नीभवने	विस्यौव् *visyauv*	be pleased.
	वॊक् *wŏk*	रोगादिपीडायाम्	वॊक्यौव् *wŏkyauv*	suffer pain from disease.
	वुकॖर् *wukᵊr*	वक्रीभवने	वुकॖर्यौव् *wukᵊryauv*	be crooked.
क	वुकॖराव *wukᵊrāv*	वक्रीकरणे	वुकॖरोवुन् *wukᵊrŏvun*, वुकॖराव्यौन् *wukᵊrāvyaun*	make crooked.
क	वॊखर् *wŏkhar*	ऊर्ध्वाधरीकरणे	वॊखरुन् *wŏkharun*, वॊखर्यौन् *wŏkharyaun*	turn upside down.
क	वॊखराव *wŏkharāv*	च	वॊखरोवुन् *wŏkharŏvun*, वॊखराव्यौन् *wŏkharāvyaun*	ditto.
	[वॊगन *wogan*	उत्तानीभवने	वॊगन्यौव् *wŏganyauv*	be shallow.]
क	वुगॖराव *wugᵊrāv*	ऋणप्रतिपादने	वुगॖरोवुन् *wugᵊrŏvun*, वुगॖराव्यौन् *wugᵊrāvyaun*	recover a debt.
क	वुङ्ग *wuŋg* .	भषणे	वुङ्गुन् *wuŋgun*, वुञ्ज्यौन् *wuñjyaun*	bark (of a dog).
	वुछ *wuts*	दग्धीभवने	वुछौव् *wutsauv*, [वुछ्यौव् *wutsyauv*]	be burnt.

क	वुछ् *wuch*	प्रेक्षणे	वुछुन् *wuchun*, वुछ्योन् *wuchyaun*	* see
	वुज् *wuz*	जागरणे जलादिप्रकटीभवने च	वुज्योव् *wuzauv*	be wide awake; appear (as water from a spring).
	व्वज़ल *wŏzal*	रक्तीभवने	व्वज़ल्योव् *wŏzalyauv*	be red.
	व्वठ *wŏṭ*	प्लवने	———	leap [not used as an independent verb].
क	वुठ *wuṭh*	वेष्टने	वुठुन् *wuṭhun*, वुछ्योन् *wuchyaun*	* twist (a rope, &c.).
	वुड *wuḍ*	उड्डयने	वुड्योव् *wuḍyauv*	* fly.
क	वुडाव *wuḍāv*	नाशने चालने च	वुडोवुन् *wuḍŏvun*, वुडाव्योन् *wuḍāvyaun*	destroy, cause to move.
	व्वतल *wŏtal*	ऊर्ध्वीभवने	व्वतल्योव् *wŏtalyauv*	rise.
	व्वथ *wŏth*	उत्थाने	व्वथ् *woth**, व्वछ्योव् *wŏtshauv*	* stand up.
क	व्वथर *wŏthar*	प्रमार्जने	व्वथुरुन् *wŏthạrun*, व्वथर्योन् *wŏtharyaun*	wipe clean.
क	व्वथराव *wŏtharāv*	च	व्वथरोवुन् *wŏtharŏvun*, व्वथराव्योन् *wŏtharā-vyaun*	ditto.
	वुद *wud*	जागरणे	[वुदु *wud**], वुद्योव् *wudyauv*	be wide awake.

* Found in Dr. Elmslie's Vocabulary.

	ROOT.	SANSKRIT MEANING.	PAST AND AORIST.	ENGLISH MEANING.
	वुदर *wudar*	वियोगखेदे	वुदर्यौव् *wudaryauv*	sorrow in separation.
	वुन *wun*	दैवाभावे	वुन्यौव् *wunyauv*	have bad luck.
	वोन्नत *wŏnnat*	उन्नतीभावे	वोन्नत्यौव् *wŏnnatyauv*	be high.
	वुप *wup*	अन्तर्दाहे	वुपु *wup**, वुप्यौव् *wupyauv*	burn inside.
	वोपज् *wŏpas*	उत्पत्तौ	वोपद् *wŏpad**, वोपज्यौव् *wŏpasauv*	* be born.
	वुफ *wuph*	विहायसा गतौ	वुफ्यौव् *wuphyauv*	* fly (of birds only).
क	वोफर *wŏphar*	शैथिल्ये	वोफरुन् *wŏpharun*, वोफर्यौन् *wŏpharyaun*	make slack.
	वोबर *wŏbar*	समाप्तौ	[वोबरुन् *wŏbarun*], वोबर्यौन् *wŏbaryaun*	be finished.
	वोबस *wŏbas*	बहुलीभवने	[वोबसु *wŏbas**], वोबस्यौव् *wŏbasyauv*	increase.
	वोम *wŏm*	विश्रामविरहे	वोमु *wom**, वोम्यौव् *wŏmyauv*	go on without stopping.
	वुय *wuy*	पर्याप्तौ	वुय्यौव् *wuyyauv*	arrive.
क	वुर *wur*	ग्रथनपटप्रच्छादननिपातनेषु	वुरुन् *wurun*, वुर्यौन् *wuryaun*	string (a garland, &c.); put on (clothes); let fall into.

क	अलङ्ग *wŏlańg*	उल्लङ्घने	अलंगुन् *wŏlańgun*, अलाञ्ज्यौन् *wŏlañjyaun*	pass over.
क	अलल *wŏlal*	अलंकरणे	अलंलुन् *wŏlalun*, अलल्यौन् *wŏlalyaun*	adorn.
क	अलस *wŏlas*	उल्लसने	अलंसुन् *wŏlasun*, अलस्यौन् *wŏlasyaun*	rejoice.
	अशल *wŏçal*	लौहित्ये	अशल्यौव् *wŏçalyauv*	be red (of the complexion, from anger, &c.).
	वुष्ण *wuṣṇ*	उष्णीभवने	वुष्ण्यौव् *wuṣṇyauv*	*be hot.
	अस *wŏs*	बाहुल्ये	अस्यौव् *wŏsyauv*	be much.
क	वुसर *wusar*	उद्घाटने	वुसंरुन् *wusarun*, वुसर्यौन् *wusaryaun*	open.
क	वुसराव *wusarāv*	च	वुसरोवुन् *wusarōvun*, वुसराव्यौन् *wusarāvyaun*	ditto.
	वुह *wuh*	अनिर्वाणे	वुह्यौव् *wuhyauv*	be not extinguished (of fire).
भा	वुहव *wuhav*	शापे	वुहंवुन् *wuhavun*, वुहव्यौन् *wuhavyaun*	*curse.
क	वोन *wōn*	तन्तुवायकर्मणि	वूनुन् *wūnun*, वोन्यौन् *wōñaun*	*weave.
क	वोर *wōr*	भषणे निद्रालापे च	वूरुन् *wūrun*, वोर्यौन् *wōryaun*	*bark, talk in one's sleep.
	वोल *wōl*	चपलीभवने	वोल्यौव् *wōlyauv*	be fickle.

* Found in Dr. Elmslie's Vocabulary.

	Root.	Sanskrit Meaning.	Past and Aorist.	English Meaning.
क	वोवुर *wöv^er*	धातूनां तक्षणे	वूवुरुन् *wüvtrun*, वोवुर्योन् *wöv^eryaun*	shave metal.
क	वोवुराव *wöv^erāv*	च	वोवुरोवुन् *wöv^erövun*, वोवुराव्योन् *wov^erā-vyaun*	ditto.
क	शेंक *çĕk*	शङ्कायाम्	शूंकुन् *çyŭkun*, शेंक्योन् *çĕoyaun*	doubt.
क	शंगाव *çąg^enāv*	षड्गुणीकरणे	शंगोवुन् *çąg^enövun*, शंगाव्योन् *çąg^enāvyaun*	divide into six, multiply by six.
	शम *çam*	उपशमे	शम्योव् *çamyauv*	be quieted.
क	शष *çaș*	सहने	शंषुन् *çașun*, शष्योन् *çașyaun*	bear.
	शहल *çahal*	शीतीभवने	शहल्योव् *çahalyauv*	be cold.
क	शाश *çāç*	उच्छ्वासनिश्वासे	शोशुन् *çöçun*, शाश्योन् *çāçyaun*	breathe.
	[शिगुनाव *çig^enāv*	परेर्ष्यादाने	शिगन्योव् *çig^enyauv*	be jealous of another.]
	शिठ *çiṭh*	शीतीभवने	शिठ्योव् *çiṭhyauv*	be congealed.
	श्रिठ *çriṭh*	च	श्रिठ्योव् *çriṭhyauv*	ditto.
	शङ *çöṅg*	शयने	शंगु *çoṅg^u*, शङ्ग्योव् *çöñjyauv*	* lie down, go to sleep.
	शुद्ध *çöddh*	शोधने	शुद्ध्योव् *çöddhyauv*	be pure.

	शूब् çūb	शोभायाम्	शूब्यौव् çūbyauv	* be beautiful.
क	शूबर् çūbᵊr	शोभने	शूब्रुन् çubᵊrun, शूबर्यौन् çūbᵊryaun	make beautiful.
क	शूबराव् çūbᵊrāv	„	शूबरोवुन् çūbᵊrōvun, शूबराव्यौन् çūbᵊrā-vyaun	* ditto.
क	चोर् çōr	संस्करणे	च्यूरुन् çyūrun, चोर्यौन् çōrjaun	* repair.
	चप् çrap	शोषणे	चपु çrapᵘ, चप्यौव् çrapyauv	* evaporate, be digest-ed, be soaked up.
आ	चक् çrak	क्रन्दने	चकुन् çrakun, चच्यौन् çracyaun	weep.
क	चुट् çrut	सशब्दपाने	चुटुन् çrutun, चुट्यौन् çrutsaun	drink with a noise.
	चोछ् çrōts	शुद्धौ	चोछ्यौव् çrotsyauv	be pure.
	सखर् sakhar	प्रस्थाने	सखर्यौव् sakharyauv	prepare to set forth.
क	सगव् sagav	जलादिसिञ्चने	सगवुन् sagavun, सगव्यौन् sagavyaun	sprinkle, or water (plants, &c.).
क	सगनाव् sagandv	„	सगनोवुन् saganōvun, सगनाव्यौन् sagandryaun	ditto.
क	संञर् sañᵊr	खननाधोकरणे	संञरुन् sañᵊrun, संञर्यौन् sañᵊryaun	make deep (a well, &c.).
क	संञराव् sañᵊrāv	„	संञरोवुन् sañᵊrōvun, संञराव्यौन् sañᵊrā-vyaun	ditto.

* Found in Dr. Elmslie's Vocabulary.

	Root.	Sanskrit Meaning.	Past and Aorist.	English Meaning.
भा	सताव *satāv*	बाधने	सतोवुन् *satōvun*, सताव्योन् *satāvyaun*	* persecute.
	सन *san*	अगाधीभवने	सन्योव् *sanyauv*	be deep.
क	संस्रुर *sąns^{e}r*	सज्जीकरणे	संस्रुरुन् *sąnsērun*, संस्रुर्योन् *sąns^{e}ryaun*	be ready.
क	सन्दर *sandar*	संधुक्षणे	सन्दरुन् *sandąrun*, सन्दर्योन् *sandaryaun*	kindle.
क	सन्दराव *sandarāv*	„	सन्दरोवुन् *sandarōvun*, सन्दराव्योन् *sandarāvyaun*	ditto.
क	सन्दार *sandār*	प्राणलाभे	सन्दोरुन् *sandōrun*, सन्दार्योन् *sandāryaun*	come to oneself from faint, &c.).
	सपज् *sapas*	सिद्धौ	सपज़् *sapąs^{u}*, सपज्योव् *sapasauv*	be complete.
	सपद् *sapad*	„	सपद् *sapąd^{u}*, सपज्योव् *sapasauv*	* ditto.
	सपन *sapan*	„	सपन् *sapąn^{u}*, सपन्योव् *sapañauv*	ditto.
	सम *sam*	साम्ये	सम्योव् *samyauv*	* be level, [assemble].
	समख *samakh*	समक्षीभवने	समख् *samąkh^{u}*, समछ्योव् *samachyauv*	* become visible, be seen, meet a person.
क	संबाल *sambāl*	संस्करणे	संबोलुन् *sambōlun*, संबाज्योन् *sambājyaun*	* repair.

क	सर् *sar*	स्मरणे	संरुन् *sarun*, सर्यौन् *saryaun*	remember.
क	सह् *sah*	सहने	संहुन् *sahun*, सच्योन् *saçyaun*	bear, endure.
	साँगर् *sãgar*	विस्तरणे	साँगर्योव् *sãgaryauv*	be broken.
क	साद् *sād*	संराधौ	सोदुन् *sodun*, साज़ोन् *sāsaun*	accomplish, make perfect.
क	सार् *sār*	स्वादेकत्रीभवनक्रमानयनेषु	सोरुन् *sōrun*, सार्यौन् *sāryaun*	* feel, be collected, be gradually brought.
क	साव् *sāv*	शायने	सोवुन् *sōvun*, साव्योन् *sāvyaun*	*put to sleep.
क	स्यज़र् *syaz*ᵃ*r*	ऋजूकरणे	स्यज़रुन् *syaz*ᵃ*run*, स्यज़र्यौन् *sĕz*ᵃ*ryaun*	make straight.
क	स्यज़राव् *syaz*ᵃ*rāv*	च	स्यज़रावुन् *syaz*ᵃ*rōvun*, स्यज़राव्योन् *syaz*ᵃ*rāvyaun*	ditto.
क	स्यञराव् *sĕñ*ᵃ*rāv*	मृदूकरणे	स्यञरावुन् *sĕñ*ᵃ*rōvun*, स्यञराव्योन् *sĕñ*ᵃ*rāvyaun*	make soft (as a hard ball of earth with water).
	स्यद् *syad*	सिद्ध्यार्जवीभवनयोः	स्यद्योव् *sĕdyauv*	*be successful, be straight.
	स्यन्दर् *syand*ᵃ*r*	रक्तीभवने	स्यन्दर्यौव् *sĕnd*ᵃ*ryauv*	change to a red colour.
	स्यन्न् *syann*	मृदूभूतीभवने	स्यन्न्योव् *sĕnnyauv*	become soft.

* Found in Dr. Elmslie's Vocabulary.

	Root.	Sanskrit Meaning.	Past and Aorist.	English Meaning.
क	सिव् *siv*	सेवने पाकविशेषे च	स्युवुन् *syuvun*, सिव्यौन् *sivyaun*	* serve, stew.
	सीर् *sir*	भ्रमणे	सीर्यौव् *sīryauv*	circulate.
क	सुक् *suk*	अभिचारे [अन्तरावेशने]	सुकुन् *sukun*, सुच्यौन् *sucyaun*	behave badly [squeeze into].
क	सखव् *sŏkhav*	सुखने	सखवुन् *sŏkhavun*, सखव्यौन् *sŏkhavyaun*	make happy.
क	सखनाव् *sŏkhanāv*	च	सखनोवुन् *sŏkhanōvun*, सखनाव्यौन् *sŏkhanāv-yaun*.	ditto.
	सग् *sŏg*	मूल्याल्पतायाम्	सग्यौव् *sŏgyauv*	be cheap.
	स्रग् *srŏg*	च	स्रग्यौव् *srŏgyauv*	ditto.
क	सगराव् *sŏgᵊrāv*	लघूकरणे	सगरोवुन् *sŏgᵊrōvun*, सगराव्यौन् *sŏgᵊrāvyaun*	fix a fair price, cheapen.
क	स्रगराव् *srŏgᵊrāv*	च	स्रगरोवुन् *srŏgᵊrōvun*, स्रगराव्यौन् *srŏgᵊrā-vyaun*	ditto.
क	सचुराव् *sŏtsᵊrāv*	शामने	सचुरोवुन् *sŏtsᵊrōvun*, सचुराव्यौन् *sŏtsᵊrā-vyaun*	appease, extinguish (a fire, &c.).
	सत् *sŏt*	शमने	सत्यौव् *sŏtyauv*	be appeased, (be extinguished).

क	सम्बर् *sŏmbᵊr*	समीकरणैकत्रीकरणयोः	सम्बरुन् *sŏmbᵊrun*, सम्बर्यौन् *sŏmbᵊryaun*	*make level, collect.
क	सोर् *sŏr*	स्मरणे	सोरुन् *sŏrun*, सोर्यौन् *sŏryaun*	remember.
क	सुव् *suv*	सूचीकर्मणि	सुवुन् *suvun*, सुव्यौन् *suvyaun*	*sew.
क	सुरव् *surav*	भाजनभस्मघर्षे	सुरवुन् *surạvun*, सुरव्यौन् *suravyaun*	clean a vessel with ashes.
क	सोर्च् *sŏrç*	हस्तादिघर्षे	सोर्चुन् *sorçun*, सोर्च्यौन् *sŏrçyaun*	clean the hands, &c.
क	सुलव् *sulav*	अङ्कपालने	सुलवुन् *sulạvun*, सुलव्यौन् *sulavyaun*	take in ones lap.
	सोसर् *sŏsar*	काष्ठादिजीर्णने	सोसर्यौव् *sŏsaryauv*	decay (of wood, &c.)
क	सोज् *sŏz*	प्राणिप्रेषणे	सूज़ुन् *sūzun*, सोज्यौन् *sŏsaun*	*send (a man, &c.)
	सोर् *sŏr*	व्ययगमने	सूर् *sūrᵊ*, सोर्यौव् *sŏryauv*	be spent, exhausted (of things.)
क	सद् *sᵊḍ*	क्षमायाम्	सदुन् *sᵊḍun*, सज्यौन् *sᵊjyaun*	bear, endure.
क	सट् *sᵊt*	संघट्टने	सटुन् *sᵊtun*, सट्यौन् *sᵊ*[illegible]*aun*	crowd in.
	स्रव् *srav*	स्रवणे	स्रव्यौव् *sravyauv*	trickle, drip.
भा	सस् *sᵊs*	अपानवायौ	ससुन् *sᵊsun*, सस्यौन् *sᵊsyaun* or ससौन् *sᵊsaun*	break wind (without noise.)

* Found in Dr. Elmslie's Vocabulary.

386	Root.	Sanskrit Meaning.	Past and Aorist.	English Meaning.
	हकर *hakar*	कार्कश्ये	हकर्यौव् *hakaryauv*	be hard.
क	हग *hag*	पुरीषोत्सर्गे	हगुन् *hagun*, हज्यौन् *hajyaun*	go to stool.
	हट *hat*	क्षीणीभवने	हट्यौव् *hatyauv*	be thin.
क	हटर् *hatᵊr*	क्षीणीकरणे	हटरुन् *hatᵊrun*, हटर्यौन् *hatᵊryaun*	make thin.
क	हटराव *hatᵊrāv*	च	हटरावुन् *hatᵊrövun*, हटराव्यौन् *hatᵊrāvyaun*	ditto.
	हन्दर *handᵊr*	शीतीभवने	हन्दर्यौव् *handᵊryauv*	be cold.
क	हन्दराव *hadᵊrāv*	शीतीकरणे	हन्दरावुन् *handᵊrövun*, हन्दराव्यौन् *handᵊrāvyaun*	make cold.
	हप *hap*	कार्श्ये	हप्यौव् *hapyauv*	be lean.
	हम *ham*	शमने	हम्यौव् *hamyauv*	be appeased.
	हर *har*	क्षरणपतनयोः	हर्यौव् *haryauv*	*drip, fall (as of leaves from a tree).
	हल *hal*	वक्रतायाम्	हल्यौव् *halyauv*	be crooked.
क	हहर *hahar*	विवाहकर्मणि	हहरुन् *hahạrun* (masc.) हहरुन् *hahạrᵃn* or हर्युन् *hạrᵃọᵃn*	marry off, get a girl married.

	हंकल hą̄kal	शीतसंकोचने	हंकल्यौव् hą̄kalyauv	shrink on account of cold.
	हंठ hą̄th	नैष्फल्ये	हंठ्यौव् hą̄thyauv	be fruitless.
क	हंठराव hą̄thᵃrāv	निष्फलीकरणे	हंठ्रोवुन् hą̄thᵃrōvun हंठराव्यौन् hą̄thᵃrāvyaun	make fruitless.
	हान han	शैत्ये	हान्यौव् hānyauv	be cold.
	हामन hą̄man	शीतलापाके [श्यामीभवने]	हामन्यौव् hāmanyauv	have small-pox eruption, [be dark coloured].
क	हार hār	पराजयनिपातयोः	होरुन् hōrun, हार्यौन् hāryaun	*be conquered, throw down.
क	हाव hāv	दर्शने	होवुन् hōvun, हाव्यौन् hāvyaun	*show.
क	ह्यक hyak	शक्तौ	ह्यकुन् hyąkun, ह्यच्यौन् hĕcyaun	be able.
क	हि hi	ग्रहणक्रयधारणेषु	ह्यतुन् hyątun, ह्यत्सौन् hyatsaun	*take, buy, place.
क	ह्यच hyach	शिक्षायाम्	ह्यचुन् hyąchun, ह्यछ्यौन् hĕchyaun	*teach.
क	ह्यड hyaḍ	परिभाषणे	ह्यडुन् hyąḍun, ह्यज्यौन् hĕjyaun	blame, abuse.
	हिल hil	प्रबलीभवने	हिल्यौव् hilyauv	be mighty.

* Found in Dr. Elmslie's Vocabulary.

388

	Root.	Sanskrit Meaning.	Past and Aorist.	English Meaning.
	हॊख *hŏkh*	शोषे	हॊखु *hokh*^{u}, हॊछ्यौव् *hŏchyauv*	* become dry.
क	हॊखर् *hŏkh*^{a}*r*	शोषये	हॊखरुन् *hŏkh*^{a}*run*, हॊखर्यौन् *hŏkharyaun*	make dry.
क	हॊखराव *hŏkh*^{a}*rāv*	च	हॊखरोवुन् *hŏkh*^{a}*rōvun*, हॊखरावौन् *hŏkh*^{a}*rāvyaun*	ditto.
	हॊच *hŏts*	विशीभवने	हॊतु *hot*^{u}, हॊच्यौव् *hŏtsauv*	* go bad, decay.
क	हॊचराव *hŏts*^{a}*rāv*	विशीकरणे	हॊचरोवुन् *hŏts*^{a}*rōvun*, हॊचरावौन् *hŏts*^{a}*rāvyaun*	cause to go bad.
क	हॊबर् *hŏb*^{a}*r*	पराजये	हॊबरुन् *hŏb*^{a}*run*, हॊबर्यौन् *hŏb*^{a}*ryaun*	conquer.
क	हॊबराव *hŏb*^{a}*rāv*	च	हॊबरोवुन् *hŏb*^{a}*rōvun*, हॊबरावौन् *hŏb*^{a}*rāvyaun*	ditto.
क	हुम *humi*	होमे	हुमुन् *humun*, हुम्यौन् *humyaun*	sacrifice.
क	हॊमर् *hŏm*^{a}*r*	मासने	हॊमरुन् *hŏm*^{a}*run*, हॊमर्यौन् *hŏm*^{a}*ryaun*	appease.
क	हॊमराव *hŏm*^{a}*rāv*	च	हॊमरोवुन् *hŏm*^{a}*rōvun*, हॊमरावौन् *hŏm*^{a}*rāvyaun*	ditto.
	होन *hŏn*	उत्कटीभवने	होन्यौव् *hŏnyauv*	be arrogant, intoxicated.

ब	होर hör	प्रतिदाने	ह्रुरुन् hūrun, होर्यौन् horyaun	*return, give back, repay.
	ह्न $h^{a}n$	शोथे	ह्न्यौव् $h^{a}nyauv$	*swell, intumesce.
	ह्र $h^{a}r$	उपचये	ह्र्यौव् $h^{a}ryauv$	*increase.
	ह्ज $h^{a}l$	प्रसवारम्भे	ह्ज्यौव् $h^{a}jyauv$	begin to be in labour (with a child).
ब	ह्सव $h^{e}sav$	श्वादिप्रेरणायाम्	ह्संवुन् h^{e}sąvun, ह्सव्यौन् h^{e}savyaun	urge on, or excite a dog, &c.
ब	ह्सनाव h^{e}sanāv	च	ह्सनोवुन् h^{e}sanövun, ह्सनाव्यौन् h^{e}sanā-vyaun	ditto.

* Found in Dr. Elmslie's Vocabulary.

APPENDIX II.

List of Kāçmīrī Verbs arranged according to Conjugations and Final Letters.

As the forms taken by a Kāçmīrī Verb depend partly on the Conjugation to which it belongs, and partly on the final letter of its root, the following list of Verbal Roots is arranged under Conjugations, and then alphabetically according to the final letter of each root.

For the meaning of these roots, and the form of the Past and Aorist Tenses of each, the reader is referred to the List of Kāçmīrī Verbs given *ante*, Vol. LXV, Pt. I, pp. 314 and ff.

First Conjugation.

khi, ci, di, ni, hi.

khi^{r}k, chak, chik, ṭak, ṭuk, ṭ^{a}k, thăk, ṭhuk, ḍak, truk, thyak, thŏk, drŏk, phak, phuk, phăk, phrak, bak, brak, çŏk, çrŏk, suk, hyak.

jakh, lakh, likh, lĕkh.

tsyaŋg, săg, ṭăg, dag, phăg, bŭg, maŋg, raŋg, laŋg, lăg, wuŋg, wŏlaŋg, hag.

khar^{a}c.

khăch, tach, buch, bĕch, much, rach, wuch, hyachh.

măj.

tsarts, nats, phits, marts, wŏts, wuts.

yitsh, kătsh, pritsh, britsh.

arz, kanz, khŏnz, graz, nyawăz, păz, pûz, prinz, baz, buz, bŏz, măz, waz, sŏz.

kapaṭ, kŏṭ. khaṭ, chăṭ, tsaṭ, tsŭṭ, tsŏṭ, tshaṭ, ḍŏṭ, piṭ, prăṭ, raṭ, lŭṭ, waṭ, wăṭ.

wuṭh.

kaḍ, ganḍ, tshanḍ, tshăḍ, tsăḍ, tăḍ, manḍ, măḍ, laḍ, s^{a}ḍ, hyaḍ.

priṇ.

kat, khut, nyat, çrut, s^{a}t.

math.

ărad, gind, gund, pad, pŏnd, mand, lad, wad, wand, vyand, săd.

an, ătshan, ăn (=an), k^{a}n, khan, chăn, tsăn, tsĕn, tshun, săn, sĕn, ṭ^{a}san, dŏn, d^{a}n, pachăn, parzan, pilan, putsan, prazan, phăn, măn, mun, mĕn, ran, lŏn, lŏn, wakhan, wan, vyatshan, wŏn.

kŏp, khap, gup, chap, tsăp, sap, ṭap, ṭyap, ṭap, ṭrap, thip, dap, nap.

chŏmb, tsŏmb, tŏmb, trŏmb, lab.

kham, cum, dam, lam, wăm, hum.

kăy, dŏy, d^{a}y, pay, lăy, wăy.

alar, ōpar, āwar, katar, kar, kār, kūr, khār, gar, gār, gēr, gōr, cār, cīr, char, chēr, chōr, jar, jūr, tsar (be inwardly wrathful), tsār, tsūr, zar, tār, tōvar, thur, darr, dār, par, pār, pyatar, pūr, pair, phir, phukār, phyār, bagār, bar, maṭhār, mar (unite), mahār, mār, mutsar, musar, mūtr, mūr, yār, yēr, rāwar, latār, lār, lūr, wathar, war, wahār, wār, witsār, wŏkhar, wŏṭhar, wŏphar, wur, wusar, wōr, çēr, sandar, sandār, sar, sār, sōr, hahar, hār, hōr.

ąns^{e}r, ąb^{e}r, ą̄z^{e}r, ą̄ṭ^{e}r, ą̄ḍ^{e}r, kąnz^{e}r, khąṇḍ^{e}r, gąns^{e}r, grą̄ç^{e}r, chąk^{e}r, chind^{e}r, chǫ̆ñ^{e}r, chǫ̆p^{e}r, tsiñ^{e}r, tsǫ̆k^{e}r, tsyąt^{e}r, tshyąṭ^{e}r, tshyąv^{e}r, tshǫ̆ṭ^{e}r, siṭh^{e}r, suv^{e}r, zōv^{e}r, z^{e}jar, ḍąkh^{e}r, tąts^{e}r, ṭąñ^{e}r, tīz^{e}r, trǫ̆p^{e}r, thąs^{e}r, dą̄ñ^{e}r, dǫ̆b^{e}r, dūntsh^{e}r, nąñ^{e}r, ną̄ç^{e}r, nik^{e}r, nǫ̆m^{e}r, nǫ̆w^{e}r, nōm^{e}r, pąj^{e}r, pąs^{e}r, pąṭh^{e}r, pą̄s^{e}r, pīṭh^{e}r, puç^{e}r, pūṭh^{e}r, phąs^{e}r, phą̄s^{e}r, phuṭ^{e}r. bąd^{e}r, bąnz^{e}r, bal^{e}r, bą̄g^{e}r, bą̄j^{e}r, bę̆ñ^{e}r, brąm^{e}r, mąnz^{e}r, mąṣ^{e}r, mǫ̆ṭ^{e}r, mǫ̆ṇḍ^{e}r, mūntsh^{e}r, yąṭ^{e}r, rątsh^{e}r, wąd^{e}r, vę̆z^{e}r, vę̆ñ^{e}r, vyąṭh^{e}r, vyąd^{e}r, vyąp^{e}r, vyąv^{e}r, wōw^{e}r, çūb^{e}r, sąñ^{e}r, sąnz^{e}r, sę̆z^{e}r, sǫ̆mb^{e}r, hąṭ^{e}r, hǫ̆kh^{e}r, hǫ̆b^{e}r, hǫ̆m^{e}r.

ahal, khōl, gāl, chal, tsāl, tsyakhal, tsyall, tshal, zāl, z^{e}l, ṭāl, ḍāl, tal, tāl, tul, tōl, thal, dal, nyaŋgal, pal, pāl, bōl, mal, lōl, wal, wāl, wŏlal, sambāl.

āyav, ārav, ālav, kamav, kŏkav, k^{e}tsav, gilav, gyav, gulav, chŏkav, z^{e}rav, ṭŏkav, ḍakhav, ḍulav, tav, trŏmbav, thav, dabav, dav, dŏgav, d^{e}nav, nĕchav, pākav, pyav, pīnav, pōrav, phālav, phĕtsav, phirav, manav, milav, mŏlav, mōrav, ranzav, rinzav, r^{e}kav, latav, lalav, lithav, lyav, wasav, wanav, wav, vyav, wŏhav, sagav, sŏkhav, surav, sulav, h^{e}sav.

abasāv, arpāv, alarāv, āparāv, āwarāv, kapaṭāv, kamanāv, krāv, khŏkhalāv, guzarāv, catāv, cāv, cukāv, chāv, tsŏg^{e}nāv, ṭhagāv, ḍulanāv, tāv, tōvarāv, trakarāv, trag^{e}nāv, trāv, thāv, dār, dŏg^{e}nāv, dŏdarāv, d^{e}ṣrāv, nahāv, nāv, nyāv pachaṭāv, paṭāv, parkhāv, parzanāv, pāv, pilanāv, prazanāv, prāv, pharkāv, baḍāv, bąr^{e}kāv, bāv, mardār, milanāv, mutsarāv, musarāv, mūtrāv, ranzanāv, rāwarāv, laṭāv, laḍāv, watharāv, wahārāv, wŏkharāv, wuḍāv, wötharāv, wusurāv, çąg^{e}nāv, saganāv, satāv, sandarāv, sāv, sŏkhanāv, hāv, h^{e}sanāv.

ąd^{e}rāv, ąnz^{e}rāv, ąb^{e}rāv, ą̄ḍ^{e}rāv, kąnz^{e}rāv, khąṇḍ^{e}rāv, gąns^{e}rāv, grą̄ç^{e}rāv, chąk^{e}rāv, chąts^{e}rāv, chiv^{e}rāv, chǫ̆ñ^{e}rāv, chǫ̆p^{e}rāv, tsiñ^{e}rāv, tsǫ̆k^{e}rāv, tsǫ̆m^{e}rāv, tshyąṭ^{e}rāv, tshyąv^{e}rāv, tshǫ̆ṭ^{e}rāv, siṭh^{e}rāv, suv^{e}rāv, sōv^{e}rāv, ḍąkh^{e}rāv, tąts^{e}rāv, ṭąñ^{e}rāv, tīz^{e}rāv, trąts^{e}rāv, trąs^{e}rāv, trǫ̆ç^{e}rāv, thąs^{e}rāv, dąd^{e}rāv, dą̄ñ^{e}rāv, dǫ̆b^{e}rāv, dūntsh^{e}rāv, drǫ̆g^{e}rāv, d^{e}ṣrāv, nąñ^{e}rāv, nąṭ^{e}rāv, ną̄ç^{e}rāv nik^{e}rāv, nǫ̆m^{e}rāv, nǫ̆v^{e}rāv, nōm^{e}rāv, pąj^{e}rāv, pąs^{e}rāv, pąṭh^{e}rāv, pą̄s^{e}rāv, piṭ^{e}rāv, pīṭh^{e}rāv, puç^{e}rāv, pūṭh^{e}rāv, phą̄s^{e}rāv, phuṭ^{e}rāv, bąc^{e}rāv, bąḍ^{e}rāv, bąd^{e}rāv, bąnz^{e}rāv, bąl^{e}rāv, bą̄g^{e}rāv, bą̄j^{e}rāv, bę̆ñ^{e}rāv, brąm^{e}rāv, mąts^{e}rāv, mąns^{e}rāv, mąṣ^{e}rāv, mą̄ñ^{e}rāv, mǫ̆ṭ^{e}rāv, mǫ̆ṇḍ^{e}rāv, mōd^{e}rāv, mūntsh^{e}rāv, yąṭ^{e}rāv, rątsh^{e}rāv, lyąd^{e}rāv, lūk^{e}rāv, wąd^{e}rāv, vę̆z^{e}rāv, vę̆ñ^{e}rāv, vyąṭh^{e}rāv, vyąd^{e}rāv, vyąp^{e}rāv, vyąv^{e}rāv, wuk^{e}rāv, wug^{e}rāv, wōw^{e}rāv, *pūbᵃrāv, hąṅᵃrāv, sąsᵃrāv, sǫṅᵃrāv, sǫgᵃrāv, sǫtsᵃrāv, srǫgᵃrāv, hąṭᵃrāv, hąndᵃrāv, kąṭhᵃrāv, hǫkhᵃrāv, hǫtsᵃrāv, hǫbᵃrāv, hǫmᵃrāv.*

tsuv, ṭuv, ḍuv, riv, ruv; liv, siv, suv.

kaç, krēç, paç, phŏç, phuç, phŏç, phāç, braç, pāç, sŏrç.

ḍāṣ, bāṣ, muṣ, waṣ, çaṣ.

abas, as, kas, kās, khᵃs, tsas, sŏs, ṭᵃs, ṭhās, das, mus, rᵃs, sᵃs.

kuh, khah, gᵃh, tsᵃh, pih, phuh, muh, sah.

Second Conjugation.

thak, pak.

samakh, hŏkh.

tag, lag, pŏyg.

kᵃts, khŏts, pats, rŏts, vyats, hŏts.

gatsh, (be proper).

das, [palas], rōs, wŏpas, sapas.

[palaṭ], phaṭ, phuṭ, rōṭ (also 3rd).

bŏḍ.

wāṭ.

wŏth.

sapad.

tshyann, [pun], sapan.

wup, ṛap. (Both these also optionally 3rd Conj. in Plup.).

pray, lay, way.

khar, tar, [prār], phar, phŏr, [phŏr], mar (die), *sŏr.*

gal, tsal, ḍal, ḍŏl (or *ḍŏl*), *phal, phŏll, mŏl.*

bŏv, rāv.

[naç] [tŏṣ], dŏṣ, pŏṣ, maṣ, rŏṣ.

ās, khas, phas, bas, [bās], las, lŏs, was, [wŏbas].

bŏh.

Third Conjugation.

si, pi, yi.

grak, camak, tsŏk, ṭhik, ḍŏk, nik, lŏk, wŏk.

ṭhag, tayg, drŏg, sŏg, srŏg.

bach.

mandach.

ats, grŏts, tsŏts, tshŏts, trats, mŏts, lŏts, grŏts.

atsh, gatsh(go).

tŏs, pas, bŏwas, bras, rans, las, wus.

kṛṭ, kraṭ, gyamaṭ, guraṭ, tshyaṭ, tshŏṭ, ṭŏṭ, naṭ, paṭ, piṭ, prąkhᵃṭ, mŏṭ, rōṭ (also second), *wŏṭ, haṭ.*

kāṭh, kuṭh, krēṭh, tsamaṭh, sŏṭh, ṭyaṭh, ṭŏṭh, drēṭh, nąṭh, paṭh, pŏṭh, brēṭh, mŏṭh, vyaṭh, çiṭh, çriṭh, hąṭh.

aḍ, pēḍ, baḍ, buḍ, mōṇḍ, rᵉḍ, lyaḍ, wuḍ.

tṣraṇ, prāṇ, rᵉṇ, wuṣṇ.

chat, sōt, tat, mat, rᵉt, lōt, wōnnat, sōt.

pāth.

and, tund, thad, pyad, bād, brād, wud, syad, çōd (this is a better spelling than *çōddh*).

āman, kān, kyann, kṛhan, gan, guman, chan, chōnn, tshṭṣhan, tan, tilan, nan, pākan, pran, ban, basan, bākhan, byann, lahan, lᵉhan, wōgan, wun, çigᵉn, san, syann, hān, hāman, hōn, hᵉn.

kạmp, kup, nạp, pap, paṣp, yāp, wup (optionally in Pluperfect), *vyap, çrap* (optionally in Pluperfect), *hap.*

wuph.

kōb, gōb, ṭyamb, ḍub, tyamb, phab, ramb, lūb, çūb.

garm, tsam, tham, nam, bram, wōm, çam, sam, ham.

biy, lᵉy, wuy.

adᵉr, yīr, kahar, kātsar, kāyar, kāwᵉr, kụr, khōkhar, khōr, gīr, gōwar, cōkhar, tsar (increase), *tshar, siŋgar, sōŋgar, sōsar, ṭhahar, ḍar, tụr, trakar, trōr, thar, thạthar, thār, dar, dōdar, dūr, dōr, nēr, pīr, pōr, phahar, bahar, bābar, bigar, mōḍᵉr, mōr, lyadᵉr, lōr, vyạdᵉr, vyalar, vyasar, wukar, wudar, wōbar, sakhar, sāgar, syạndᵉr, sīr, sōsar, hakar, hạndᵉr, har, hᵉr.*

al, kal, kumal, kōl, khal, gāgal, gōl, grāgal, chōkal, zal, tal, ḍyal, tambal, tēl, nīl, pil, piçal, pōl, prasal, phạphal, bal, mamal, mōkal, wigal, wōzal, wōtal, wōçal, wōl, çahal, hal, hạkal, hil, hᵉl.

chiv, tshyav, zuv, nav, srav.

trōç.

āwas, ḍōs, tras, pis, pras, ras, lis, vis, wōlas, wōs.

gōh, lᵉh, wuh.

CORRIGENDA TO THE LIST OF KĀÇMĪRĪ VERBS.

The following alterations in the List of Kāçmīrī verbs have been suggested by further study since its preparation. They are printed on only one side of the paper, so that they can be cut out and inserted in the proper place:—

अछ *atsh*. According to my Paṇḍit, the Aorist is अछ्यौव् *atshyauv*.

For अंच, read अच, and so throughout.

खर *khar*. The meaning is 'be disliked.'

For खूल *khŭl*, read खोल *khŏl*. The Aorist is therefore खोज्यौन् *khŏjyaun*.

खंस. The transliteration should be *khẹns*, and so throughout.

ग्रुछ *grŏts*. The true meaning is 'to be splashed out.'

चौंखर *caṅkhar*. A better spelling is चोंखर *cŏkhar*, and so throughout.

छर *tsar* (be inwardly wrathful). The Past is *tsarᵘs*, and the Aorist छर्यौयस् *tsaryĕyas*, see pp. 220 and 234. Omit the words 'Past Part.' in the 5th column.

छुव *tsuv*. In column 1 alter अ to औ आ or अ. In col. 5 strike out 'only used in fem.', and substitute, 'see p. 214.'

छोंछन. The translation should be *tshŏtshan*.

छूछ *tshŏts*. Omit अ in col. 1, and छुकुन् *tshokun* in col. 4.

छोहर and छोहराव are wrongly placed in alphabetical order.

तर *tar*. The true meaning is 'to be crossed.'

त्यम्ब *tyamb*. The Aorist is *tŏmbyēyas*. See p. 234.

तुल *tul*. In col. 5 for 'left,' read 'lift.'

पंहर *pẹthᵃr*. For पैथनी read पोथनी.

पलस *palas*. The Aorist is पलसौव् *palasauv*.

फिछ *phits*. In col. 1 insert 'औ आ.' The Past is फिछुस् *phitsᵘs*, and the Aorist फिछोयस *phitsẹyas*. See pp. 220, 226, 227, 234.

फुश *phuç*. An alternative form is फ्वश *phöç*. The entry in the first column should be ओ आ. The Past is फुशुस *phuçᵉs*, and the Aorist फुश्योयस् *phuçyöyaç*. See pp. 220, 234.

फुह *phuh*. The entry in the first column should be ओ आ. The Past is फुहुस *phuhᵉs*, and the Aorist फुह्योयस *phuhyöyas*. See pp. 220, 234.

बंकाव *bąrkāv* should be बंर्काव *bąrᵉkāv*.

बुड *böḍ*. The Past is बुडु *bǫḍᵘ*.

बोश *bös*. Insert ब in col. 1.

मर्छ *marts*. In col. 1 insert ओ आ. The Past is मर्छुस *martsᵉs*, and the Aorist *martsāyas*. See pp. 220, 226, 227, 234.

म्यछ *möts*. Strike out the forms for the Past. The Aorist is म्यछोव् *mötsauv* or (according to my Paṇḍit) म्यछ्योव् *mötsyauv*. See p. 226.

मोरव *mörav*. In col. 1 alter ब to ओ आ or ब. The Impersonal Past is मोरंवुन् *mörąvᵉn*, and the Impersonal Aorist मोरव्येयन् *moravyēyan*. See p. 214.

रज़ *rans*. According to my Paṇḍit, the Aorist may optionally be रज़ोव *ranzauv*. See p. 226.

लस *las*. According to my Paṇḍit, the Aorist may also be लस्योव् *lasyauv*. See p. 226.

ल्यछ *lyats*. The Aorist should be ल्यछ्योव् *lötsyauv*. See p. 226.

लोस *lös*. The Aorist may optionally be लोछोव् *lötshauv*. See p. 228.

वंछ *wąts*. The Past is वेंछुन् *wötsun*.

वात *wāt*. The transliteration of the Aorist should be *wātsauv*.

वुछ *wuts*. Insert ओ आ in col. 1. The Past is वुछुस *wutsᵉs*, and the Aorist वुछायस् *wutsāyas* or वुछेयस् *wutsēyas*. See pp. 220, 224, 227, 234.

वुस *wus*. According to my Paṇḍit, the Aorist may optionally be वुस्योव् *wusyauv*. See p. 226.

चद *çöddh*. A more correct spelling is चद् *çod*, with an Aorist चद्योव् *çödyauv*.